A Preface
to Marketing
Management

A Preface to Marketing Management

Thirteenth Edition

J. Paul Peter
University of Wisconsin–Madison

James H. Donnelly, Jr.
Gatton College of Business and Economics University of Kentucky

A PREFACE TO MARKETING MANAGEMENT, THIRTEENTH EDITION

Published by McGraw-Hill, a business unit of The McGraw-Hill Companies, Inc., 1221 Avenue of the Americas, New York, NY 10020. Copyright © 2013 by The McGraw-Hill Companies, Inc. All rights reserved. Printed in the United States of America. Previous editions © 2011, 2008, and 2006. No part of this publication may be reproduced or distributed in any form or by any means, or stored in a database or retrieval system, without the prior written consent of The McGraw-Hill Companies, Inc., including, but not limited to, in any network or other electronic storage or transmission, or broadcast for distance learning.

Some ancillaries, including electronic and print components, may not be available to customers outside the United States.

This book is printed on acid-free paper.

1 2 3 4 5 6 7 8 9 0 QDB/QDB 1 0 9 8 7 6 5 4 3 2

ISBN 978-0-07-131802-0
MHID 0-07-131802-X

About the Authors

J. Paul Peter

has been a faculty member at the University of Wisconsin since 1981. He was a member of the faculty at Indiana State, Ohio State, and Washington University before joining the Wisconsin faculty. While at Ohio State, he was named Outstanding Marketing Professor by the students and has won the John R. Larson Teaching Award at Wisconsin. He has taught a variety of courses including Marketing Management, Marketing Strategy, Consumer Behavior, Marketing Research, and Marketing Theory, among others.

Professor Peter's research has appeared in the *Journal of Marketing,* the *Journal of Marketing Research,* the *Journal of Consumer Research,* the *Journal of Retailing,* and the *Academy of Management Journal,* among others. His article on construct validity won the prestigious William O'Dell Award from the *Journal of Marketing Research,* and he was a finalist for this award on two other occasions. Recently, he was the recipient of the Churchill Award for Lifetime Achievement in Marketing Research, given by the American Marketing Association and the Gaumnitz Distinguished Faculty Award from the School of Business, University of Wisconsin–Madison. He is an author or editor of over 30 books, including *A Preface to Marketing Management* thirteenth edition; *Marketing Management: Knowledge and Skills,* ninth edition; *Consumer Behavior and Marketing Strategy,* ninth edition; *Strategic Management: Concepts and Applications,* third edition; and *Marketing: Creating Value for Customers,* second edition. He is one of the most cited authors in the marketing literature.

Professor Peter has served on the review boards of the *Journal of Marketing, Journal of Marketing Research, Journal of Consumer Research,* and *Journal of Business Research* and was measurement editor for *JMR* and professional publications editor for the American Marketing Association. He has taught in a variety of executive programs and consulted for several corporations as well as the Federal Trade Commission.

James H. Donnelly, Jr.

has spent his academic career in the Gatton College of Business and Economics at the University of Kentucky. In 1990 he received the first Chancellor's Award for Outstanding Teaching given at the university. Previously, he had twice received the UK Alumni Association's Great Teacher Award, an award one can only be eligible to receive every 10 years. He has also received two Outstanding Teacher awards from Beta Gamma Sigma, national business honorary. In 1992 he received an Acorn Award recognizing "those who shape the future" from the Kentucky Advocates for Higher Education. In 2001 and 2002 he was selected as "Best University of Kentucky Professor." In 1995 he became one of six charter members elected to the American Bankers Association's Bank Marketing Hall of Fame. He has also received a "Distinguished Doctoral Graduate Award" from the University of Maryland.

During his career he has published in the *Journal of Marketing Research, Journal of Marketing, Journal of Retailing, Administrative Science Quarterly, Academy of Management Journal, Journal of Applied Psychology, Personnel Psychology, Journal of Business Research,* and *Operations Research* among others. He has served on the editorial review board of the *Journal of Marketing.* He is the author of more than a dozen books, which include widely adopted academic texts as well as professional books.

Professor Donnelly is very active in the banking industry where he has served on the board of directors of the Institute of Certified Bankers and the ABA's Marketing Network. He has also served as academic dean of the ABA's School of Bank Marketing and Management.

Preface

The purpose of this book has always been very clear to us—to deliver a *clear* and *concise* presentation of the basic principles of marketing. While our purpose is clear, implementing it is a continual challenge that forces us to focus on what students really need to know while at the same time covering the core concepts and ideas in sufficient depth to ensure in-depth understanding. It involves emphasizing quality content and avoiding excess verbiage, pictures, and description.

We believe we have achieved our purpose because our book has been used successfully in a wide variety of course settings and is the best selling book of its kind. We introduce the thirteenth edition knowing that our book and its eight foreign translations have been used throughout the world whenever courses require an overview of the critical aspects of marketing management.

Over the years our book has become known simply as the *Preface*. We want to believe a major reason it has endured is because we continually fine tune and update it to ensure that it meets the current and evolving needs of both students and instructors. Since marketing is about figuring out how to do a superior job of satisfying customers, we simply seek to practice what we preach. Welcome to the *Preface*.

TEXT CHAPTERS

Section I of the book consists of 13 chapters that present the essentials of marketing management. Section I presents the "must know" content of the field useful in analyzing marketing problems and cases and developing marketing plans. It is divided into four parts that focus on strategic planning and marketing planning, understanding target markets, the marketing mix variables, and marketing in special fields. The 13 chapters in this section should provide students a clear understanding of the terminology, techniques, tools, and strategies for effective marketing management and marketing strategy development.

We continually revise and update the text chapters based on feedback from students and instructors as well as our own intuition and judgment. Accordingly we have added innovative content and elements to this and previous editions.

We recently altered two elements that have been well received and expanded and updated them in this edition. "Marketing Insights" now replaces our "Marketing Highlights" feature. This was done to more accurately describe the feature's purpose of assisting students as they solve marketing problems, analyze marketing cases, and develop marketing plans. There are over 75 "Insights" included in the book.

We have also added an "Additional Resources" section at the end of each chapter. This change is designed to highlight our focus on current resources that students can utilize in writing assignments and case presentations. The resources have been selected with students in mind. Our goal is to provide resources accessible to students at various stages of marketing education given the wide spectrum of courses in which the book is utilized.

STUDENT SUPPORT

Knowing that the *Preface* is used for a variety of course levels, programs, and students, we have assembled several elements that we believe will support students for whatever purpose they use our book.

Key Terms and Concepts

Brand new to this edition, we have added a section of key terms and concepts at the conclusion of each chapter. We made the choice to place them at the end of the chapter in which they appear where they will be more visible to students and easier to use than an appendix at the end of the book. More than a glossary, it also presents key concepts covered in the chapter. This new feature has been added for students to help them master basic marketing principles, develop more effective marketing plans, and present sophisticated analyses of marketing cases and problems.

Analyzing Marketing Problems and Cases

Section II presents a comprehensive framework for analyzing, preparing, and presenting case analyses. Included are discussions of what a case is, preparing for the class discussion and written analysis, pitfalls to avoid in case analysis and preparing to do an oral presentation.

For courses utilizing marketing problems and cases, we suggest having students read this guide before the discussion of the problem or case. For this reason it could have been placed at the beginning of the book but since it is usually referred to throughout the semester, we have placed it after the text chapters. Also, for those courses that do not utilize cases, the book may be used without reference to this section.

We strongly encourage students to use this guide when encountering what is often their first experience with case analysis. It has been widely praised by students and instructors as the best presentation on the topic. In fact, it has found its way to other areas of many campuses where it is used by students in fields unrelated to marketing but where case analysis is part of the course.

Financial Analysis for Marketing Decisions

Section III enables students to assess a company's financial position. It is absolutely critical for marketing students to appreciate that the ultimate objectives of marketing are usually expressed in financial terms. With this in mind, this section presents important financial calculations that will be useful in evaluating the financial position of a firm and the financial impact of various decisions and strategies. Included are discussions of break-even analysis, net present value analysis, and ratio analysis.

Developing Marketing Plans

In keeping with the purpose of our book and the needs of its users, Section IV enables readers to develop practical planning skills so they are able to construct a quality marketing plan for any product or service. It provides a complete format for structuring and presenting one, including specific questions to ask in competitive analysis, development of well-stated objectives, analyzing customers, and implementation and control. We know that this section has become a valuable take-away resource for many students long after their course was completed.

A Value-Added Web Site

We encourage students to view the student section of the Online Learning Center (OLC) at Web site www.MHHE.com/peterdonnelly13e which contains a number of useful aids for facilitating learning and supporting student achievement. We believe you will find it a useful resource.

INSTRUCTOR SUPPORT

The *Preface* has been used as a resource in college courses and professional development programs that require an overview of the critical "need-to-know" aspects of marketing management and marketing strategy development. It has been used:

- As the primary introductory text at the undergraduate level.
- At both the undergraduate and MBA level, where several AACSB core curriculum courses are team-taught as one multidisciplinary 9-to-12 hour course.
- At the advanced undergraduate and MBA level where it is used as the content foundation in courses that utilize marketing cases.
- In short courses and executive development programs.

The instructor section of www.MHHE.com/peterdonnelly13e includes an instructor's manual and other support material. It includes two expanded supplements. They were developed in response to instructors' requests. We offer a test bank of nearly 1,300 multiple-choice, true-false, and brief essay questions. It is available in both print and EZ Test Online. We also offer Power Point slides that highlight key text material. Your McGraw-Hill representative can also assist in the delivery of any additional instructor support material.

Acknowledgments

Our book is based on the works of many academic researchers and marketing practitioners. We want to thank those individuals who contributed their ideas to develop the field of marketing throughout the years. Indeed, our book would not be possible without their contributions. We would also like to thank our teachers, colleagues, and students for their many contributions to our education. We would also like to publicly acknowledge those individuals who served as reviewers of this and previous editions. We appreciate their advice and counsel and have done our best to reflect their insightful comments.

Roger D. Absmire
Sam Houston State University

Anna Andriasova
University of Maryland University College

Catherine Axinn
Syracuse University

Mike Ballif
University of Utah

Andrew Bergstein
Pennsylvania State University

Edward Bond
Bradley University

Donald Brady
Millersville University

Glenn Chappell
Meridith College

Newell Chiesl
Indiana State University

Reid P. Claxton
East Carolina University

Larry Crowson
University of Central Florida

Mike Dailey
University of Texas, Arlington

Linda M. Delene
Western Michigan University

Gerard DiBartolo
Salisbury University

Casey Donoho
Northern Arizona University

James A. Eckert
Western Michigan University

Matthew Elbeck
Troy University Dothan

R. E. Evans
University of Oklahoma

Lawrence Feick
University of Pittsburgh

Robert Finney
California State University, Hayward

Stephen Goldberg
Fordham University

David Good
Grand Valley State University

David Griffith
University of Oklahoma

Perry Haan
Tiffin University

Lawrence Hamer
DePaul University

Harry Harmon
Central Missouri

Jack Healey
Golden State University

Betty Jean Hebel
Madonna University

Catherine Holderness
University of North Carolina–Greensboro

JoAnne S. Hooper
Western Carolina University

David Horne
Wayne State University

Nicole Howatt
UCF

Fred Hughes
Faulkner University

Anupam Jaju
GMU

Chris Joiner
George Mason University

Benoy Joseph
Cleveland State University

Sol Klein
Northeastern University

Robert Brock Lawes
Chaminade University of Honolulu

Eunkyu Lee
Syracuse University

Tina Lowrey
University of Texas at San Antonio

Franklyn Manu
Morgan State University

Edward J. Mayo
Western Michigan University

Donald J. Messmer
College of William & Mary

Albert Milhomme
Texas State University

Chip Miller
Drake University

David L. Moore
LeMoyne College

Johannah Jones Nolan
University of Alabama, Birmingham

R. Stephen Parker
Southwest Missouri State University

Joan Phillips
University of Notre Dame

Thomas Powers
University of Alabama at Birmingham

Debu Purohit
Duke University

John Rayburn
University of Tennessee

Martha Reeves
Duke

Gary K. Rhoads
Brigham Young University

Lee Richardson
University of Baltimore

Henry Rodkin
DePaul University

Ritesh Saini
George Mason University

Matthew H. Sauber
Eastern Michigan University

Alan Sawyer
University of Florida

Ronald L. Schill
Brigham Young University

Mark Spriggs
University of St. Thomas

Vernon R. Stauble
California State Polytechnic University

Ann Marie Thompson
Northern Illinois University

John R. Thompson
Memphis State University

Gordon Urquhart
Cornell College

Sean Valentine
University of Wyoming

Ana Valenzuela
Baruch College, CUNY

Stacy Vollmers
University of St. Thomas

Kevin Webb
Drexel University

Kathleen R. Whitney
Central Michigan University

J. B. Wilkinson
University of Akron

Dale Wilson
Michigan State University

Teaming with the professionals at McGraw-Hill has always been enjoyable for us. Sankha Basu, publisher, and Jane Mohr, project manager, supported our efforts with this edition and we are very grateful. Thank you Gabriela Gonzalez, development editor, for always being so helpful. We also wish to acknowledge Francois Ortalo-Magné, dean of the School of Business at the University of Wisconsin, and David Blackwell, dean of the Gatton College of Business and Economics at the University of Kentucky, who support what we do.

J. Paul Peter

James H. Donnelly Jr.

Contents

Introduction

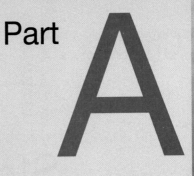

1 Strategic Planning and the Marketing Management Process

Chapter 1

Strategic Planning and the Marketing Management Process

The purpose of this introductory chapter is to present the marketing management process and outline what marketing managers must *manage* if they are to be effective. In doing so, it will also present a framework around which the remaining chapters are organized. Our first task is to review the organizational philosophy known as the marketing concept, since it underlies much of the thinking presented in this book. The remainder of this chapter will focus on the process of strategic planning and its relationship to the process of marketing planning.

THE MARKETING CONCEPT

Simply stated, the marketing concept means that *an organization should seek to make a profit by serving the needs of customer groups*. The concept is very straightforward and has a great deal of commonsense validity. Perhaps this is why it is often misunderstood, forgotten, or overlooked.

The purpose of the marketing concept is to rivet the attention of marketing managers on serving broad classes of customer needs (customer orientation), rather than on the firm's current products (production orientation) or on devising methods to attract customers to current products (selling orientation). Thus, effective marketing starts with the recognition of customer needs and then works backward to devise products and services to satisfy these needs. In this way, marketing managers can satisfy customers more efficiently in the present and anticipate changes in customer needs more accurately in the future. This means that organizations should focus on building long-term customer relationships in which the initial sale is viewed as a beginning step in the process, not as an end goal. As a result, the customer will be more satisfied and the firm will be more profitable.

The principal task of the marketing function operating under the marketing concept is not to manipulate customers to do what suits the interests of the firm, but rather to find effective and efficient means of making the business do what suits the interests of customers. This is not to say that all firms practice marketing in this way. Clearly, many firms still emphasize only production and sales. However, effective marketing, as defined in this text, requires that consumer needs come first in organizational decision making.

1. Create customer focus throughout the business.
2. Listen to the customer.
3. Define and nurture your distinctive competence, that is, what your organization does well, better than competitors.
4. Define marketing as market intelligence.
5. Target customers precisely.
6. Manage for profitability, not sales volume.
7. Make customer value the guiding star.
8. Let customers define quality.
9. Measure and manage customer expectations.
10. Build customer relationships and loyalty.
11. Define the business as a service business.
12. Commit to continuous improvement and innovation.
13. Manage the culture of your organization along with strategy and structure.
14. Grow with strategic partners and alliances.
15. Destroy marketing bureaucracy.

Source: See Frederick E. Webster, Jr., "Defining the New Marketing Concept," *Marketing Management* 2, no. 4 (1994), pp. 22–31. For a classic discussion see Robert L. King, "The Marketing Concept: Fact or Intelligent Platitude," *The Marketing Concept in Action,* Proceedings of the 47th National Conference (Chicago, American Marketing Association, 1964), p. 657. Adapted from William O. Bearden, Thomas N. Ingram, and Raymond W. LaForge, *Marketing: Principles and Perspectives,* 5th ed. (Burr Ridge, IL: McGraw-Hill/Irwin, 2007), p. 9.

One qualification to this statement deals with the question of a conflict between consumer wants and societal needs and wants. For example, if society deems clean air and water as necessary for survival, this need may well take precedence over a consumer's want for goods and services that pollute the environment.

WHAT IS MARKETING?

Everyone reading this book has been a customer for most of his or her life. Last evening you stopped at a local supermarket to graze at the salad bar, pick up some bottled water and a bag of Fritos corn chips. While you were there, you snapped a $1.00 coupon for a new flavor salad dressing out of a dispenser and tasted some new breakfast potatoes being cooked in the back of the store. As you sat down at home to eat your salad, you answered the phone and someone suggested that you need to have your carpets cleaned. Later on in the evening you saw TV commercials for tires, soft drinks, athletic shoes, and the dangers of smoking and drinking during pregnancy. Today when you enrolled in a marketing course, you found that the instructor has decided that you must purchase this book. A friend has already purchased the book on the Internet. All of these activities involve marketing. And each of us knows something about marketing because it has been a part of our life since we had our first dollar to spend.

Since we are all involved in marketing, it may seem strange that one of the persistent problems in the field has been its definition.[1] The American Marketing Association defines marketing as "the activity, set of institutions, and processes for creating, communicating, delivering, and exchanging offerings that have value for customers, clients, partners, and society at large."[2] This definition takes into account all parties involved in the marketing effort: members of the producing organization, resellers of goods and services, and customers or clients. While the broadness of the definition allows the inclusion of nonbusiness

FIGURE 1.1
Major Types of
Marketing

Type	Description	Example
Product	Marketing designed to create exchange for tangible products.	Strategies to sell Gateway computers.
Service	Marketing designed to create exchanges for intangible products.	Strategies by Allstate to sell insurance.
Person	Marketing designed to create favorable actions toward persons.	Strategies to elect a political candidate.
Place	Marketing designed to attract people to places.	Strategies to get people to vacation in national or state parks.
Cause	Marketing designed to create support for ideas, causes, or issues or to get people to change undesirable behaviors.	Strategies to get pregnant women not to drink alcohol.
Organization	Marketing designed to attract donors, members, participants, or volunteers.	Strategies designed to attract blood donors.

exchange processes, the primary emphasis in this text is on marketing in the business environment. However, this emphasis is not meant to imply that marketing concepts, principles, and techniques cannot be fruitfully employed in other areas of exchange as is clearly illustrated in Figure 1.1.

WHAT IS STRATEGIC PLANNING?

Before a production manager, marketing manager, and personnel manager can develop plans for their individual departments, some larger plan or blueprint for the *entire* organization should exist. Otherwise, on what would the individual departmental plans be based?

In other words, there is a larger context for planning activities. Let us assume that we are dealing with a large business organization that has several business divisions and several product lines within each division (e.g., General Electric, Altria). Before individual divisions or departments can implement any marketing planning, a plan has to be developed for the entire organization.[3] This means that senior managers must look toward the future and evaluate their ability to shape their organization's destiny in the years and decades to come. The output of this process is objectives and strategies designed to give the organization a chance to compete effectively in the future. The objectives and strategies established at the top level provide the context for planning in each of the divisions and departments by divisional and departmental managers.

Strategic Planning and Marketing Management

Some of the most successful business organizations are here today because many years ago they offered the right product at the right time to a rapidly growing market. The same can also be said for nonprofit and governmental organizations. Many of the critical decisions of the past were made without the benefit of strategic thinking or planning. Whether these decisions were based on wisdom or were just luck is not important; they worked for these organizations. However, a worse fate befell countless other organizations. Over three-quarters of the 100 largest U.S. corporations of 70 years ago have fallen from the list. These corporations at one time dominated their markets, controlled vast resources, and had the best-trained workers. In the end, they all made the same critical mistake. Their managements failed to recognize that business strategies need to reflect changing environments

1. It costs a great deal more to acquire a new customer than to keep an old one.
2. Loyal customers buy more from your firm over time.
3. The longer you keep a customer, the more profitable they become over time.
4. It costs less to service loyal customers than new customers.
5. Loyal customers are often excellent referrals for new business.
6. Loyal customers are often willing to pay more for the quality and value they desire.

Source: One of the earliest works on the value of the loyal customer was Frederick F. Reichheld, *The Loyalty Effect,* HBS Press, 1996. Also see Roland T. Rust, Katherine N. Lemon, and Valerie A. Zeithamel, "Return on Marketing: Using Customer Equity to Focus Marketing Strategies," *Journal of Marketing,* January 2004, pp. 76–89, William O. Bearden, Thomas N. Ingram, and Raymond W. LaForge, *Marketing: Principles and Perspectives,* 5th ed. (Burr Ridge, IL: McGraw-Hill/Irwin, 2007), p. 8, and W. D. Perreault Jr., J. P. Cannon, and E. Jerome McCarthy. *Basic Marketing: A Marketing Strategy Planning Approach,* 18th ed. (Burr Ridge, IL: McGraw-Hill/Irwin, 2011), pp. 18–20.

and emphasis must be placed on developing business systems that allow for continuous improvement. Instead, they attempted to carry on business as usual.

Present-day managers are increasingly recognizing that wisdom and innovation alone are no longer sufficient to guide the destinies of organizations, both large and small. These same managers also realize that the true mission of the organization is to provide value for three key constituencies: customers, employees, and investors. Without this type of outlook, no one, including shareholders, will profit in the long run.

Strategic planning includes all the activities that lead to the development of a clear organizational mission, organizational objectives, and appropriate strategies to achieve the objectives for the entire organization. The form of the process itself has come under criticism in some quarters for being too structured; however, strategic planning, if performed successfully, plays a key role in achieving an equilibrium between the short and the long term by balancing acceptable financial performance with preparation for inevitable changes in markets, technology, and competition, as well as in economic and political arenas. Managing principally for current cash flows, market share gains, and earnings trends can mortgage the firm's future. An intense focus on the near term can produce an aversion to risk that dooms a business to stagnation. Conversely, an overemphasis on the long run is just as inappropriate. Companies that overextend themselves betting on the future may penalize short-term profitability and other operating results to such an extent that the company is vulnerable to takeover and other threatening actions.

The strategic planning process is depicted in Figure 1.2. In the strategic planning process the organization gathers information about the changing elements of its environment. Managers from all functional areas in the organization assist in this information-gathering process. This information is useful in aiding the organization to adapt better to these changes through the process of strategic planning. The strategic plan(s)[4] and supporting plan are then implemented in the environment. The end results of this implementation are fed back as new information so that continuous adaptation and improvement can take place.

The Strategic Planning Process

The output of the strategic planning process is the development of a strategic plan. Figure 1.2 indicates four components of a strategic plan: mission, objectives, strategies, and portfolio plan. Let us carefully examine each one.

Organizational Mission

The organization's environment provides the resources that sustain the organization, whether it is a business, a college or university, or a government agency. In exchange for

FIGURE 1.2   The Strategic Planning Process

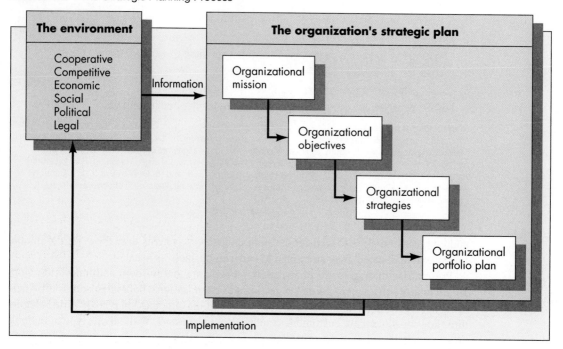

these resources, the organization must supply the environment with quality goods and services at an acceptable price. In other words, every organization exists to accomplish something in the larger environment and that purpose, vision, or mission usually is clear at the organization's inception. As time passes, however, the organization expands, and the environment and managerial personnel change. As a result, one or more things are likely to occur. First, the organization's original purpose may become irrelevant as the organization expands into new products, new markets, and even new industries. For example, Levi Strauss began as a manufacturer of work clothes. Second, the original mission may remain relevant, but managers begin to lose interest in it. Finally, changes in the environment may make the original mission inappropriate, as occurred with the March of Dimes when a cure was found for polio. The result of any or all three of these conditions is a "drifting" organization, without a clear mission, vision, or purpose to guide critical decisions. When this occurs, management must search for a purpose or emphatically restate and reinforce the original purpose.

The mission statement, or purpose, of an organization is the description of its reason for existence. It is the long-run vision of what the organization strives to be, the unique aim that differentiates the organization from similar ones and the means by which this differentiation will take place. In essence, the mission statement defines the direction in which the organization is heading and how it will succeed in reaching its desired goal. While some argue that vision and mission statements differ in their purpose, the perspective we will take is that both reflect the organization's attempt to guide behavior, create a culture, and inspire commitment.[5] However, it is more important that the mission statement comes from the heart and is practical, easy to identify with, and easy to remember so that it will provide direction and significance to all members of the organization regardless of their organizational level.

The basic questions that must be answered when an organization decides to examine and restate its mission are, What is our business? Who is the customer? What do customers

Organization	Mission
Community bank	To help citizens successfully achieve and celebrate important life events with education, information, products, and services.
Skin care products	We will provide luxury skin-care products with therapeutic qualities that make them worth their premium price.
Hotel chain	Grow a worldwide lodging business using total-quality-management (TQM) principles to continuously improve preference and profitability. Our commitment is that *every guest leaves satisfied.*
Mid-size bank	We will become the best bank in the state for medium-size businesses by 2017.

value? and What will our business be?[6] The answers are, in a sense, the assumptions on which the organization is being run and from which future decisions will evolve. While such questions may seem simplistic, they are such difficult and critical ones that the major responsibility for answering them must lie with top management. In fact, the mission statement remains the most widely used management tool in business today. In developing a statement of mission, management must take into account three key elements: the organization's history, its distinctive competencies, and its environment.[7]

1. *The organization's history.* Every organization—large or small, profit or nonprofit—has a history of objectives, accomplishments, mistakes, and policies. In formulating a mission, the critical characteristics and events of the past must be considered.

2. *The organization's distinctive competencies.* While there are many things an organization may be able to do, it should seek to do what it can do best. Distinctive competencies are things that an organization does well—so well in fact that they give it an advantage over similar organizations. For Honeywell, it's their ability to design, manufacture, and distribute a superior line of thermostats.[8] Similarly, Procter & Gamble's distinctive competency is its knowledge of the market for low-priced, repetitively purchased consumer products. No matter how appealing an opportunity may be, to gain advantage over competitors, the organization must formulate strategy based on distinctive competencies.

3. *The organization's environment.* The organization's environment dictates the opportunities, constraints, and threats that must be identified before a mission statement is developed. For example, managers in any industry that is affected by Internet technology breakthroughs should continually be asking, How will the changes in technology affect my customers' behavior and the means by which we need to conduct our business?

However, it is extremely difficult to write a useful and effective mission statement. It is not uncommon for an organization to spend one or two years developing a useful mission statement. When completed, an effective mission statement will be *focused on markets rather than products, achievable, motivating, and specific.*[9]

Focused on Markets Rather than Products   The customers or clients of an organization are critical in determining its mission. Traditionally, many organizations defined their business in terms of what they made ("our business is glass"), and in many cases they named the organization for the product or service (e.g., American Tobacco, Hormel Meats, National Cash Register, Harbor View Savings and Loan Association). Many of these organizations have found that, when products and technologies become obsolete, their mission is no longer relevant and the name of the organization may no longer describe what it does. Thus, a more enduring way of defining the mission is needed. In recent years,

1. Incomplete—not specific as to where the company is headed and what kind of company management is trying to create.
2. Vague—does not provide direction to decision makers when faced with product/market choices.
3. Not motivational—does not provide a sense of purpose or commitment to something bigger than the numbers.
4. Not distinctive—not specific to our company.
5. Too reliant on superlatives—too many superlatives such as *#1, recognized leader, most successful.*
6. Too generic—does not specify the business or industry to which it applies.
7. Too broad—does not rule out any opportunity management might wish to pursue.

Source: Adapted from Arthur A. Thomson, Jr., A. J. Strickland III, and John E. Gamble, *Crafting and Executing Strategy,* 18th ed. (Burr Ridge, IL: McGraw-Hill/Irwin, 2012), p. 24.

Examine the mission statements in Marketing Insight 1–3. Do any of the above shortcomings apply to them?

therefore, a key feature of mission statements has been an *external* rather than *internal* focus. In other words, the mission statement should focus on the broad class of needs that the organization is seeking to satisfy (external focus), not on the physical product or service that the organization is offering at present (internal focus). These market-driven firms stand out in their ability to continuously anticipate market opportunities and respond before their competitors. Peter Drucker has clearly stated this principle:

> A business is not defined by the company's name, statutes, or articles of incorporation. It is defined by the want the customer satisfies when he buys a product or service. To satisfy the customer is the mission and purpose of every business. The question "What is our business?" can, therefore, be answered only by looking at the business from the outside, from the point of view of customer and market.[10]

While Drucker was referring to business organizations, the same necessity exists for both nonprofit and governmental organizations. That necessity is to state the mission in terms of serving a particular group of clients or customers and meeting a particular class of need.

Achievable   While the mission statement should stretch the organization toward more effective performance, it should, at the same time, be realistic and achievable. In other words, it should open a vision of new opportunities but should not lead the organization into unrealistic ventures far beyond its competencies.

Motivational   One of the side (but very important) benefits of a well-defined mission is the guidance it provides employees and managers working in geographically dispersed units and on independent tasks. It provides a shared sense of purpose outside the various activities taking place within the organization. Therefore, such end results as sales, patients cared for, students graduated, and reduction in violent crimes can then be viewed as the result of careful pursuit and accomplishment of the mission and not as the mission itself.

Specific   As we mentioned earlier, public relations should not be the primary purpose of a statement of mission. It must be specific to provide direction and guidelines to management when they are choosing between alternative courses of action. In other words, "to produce the highest-quality products at the lowest possible cost" sounds very good, but it does not provide direction for management.

Functions	What They May Want to Deliver	What Marketers May Want Them to Deliver
Research and development	Basic research projects	Products that deliver customer value
	Product features	Customer benefits
	Few projects	Many new products
Production/operations	Long production runs	Short production runs
	Standardized products	Customized products
	No model changes	Frequent model changes
	Long lead times	Short lead times
	Standard orders	Customer orders
	No new products	Many new products
Finance	Rigid budgets	Flexible budgets
	Budgets based on return on investment	Budgets based on need to increase sales
	Low sales commissions	High sales commissions
Accounting	Standardized billing	Custom billing
	Strict payment terms	Flexible payment terms
	Strict credit standards	Flexible credit standards
Human resources	Trainable employees	Skilled employees
	Low salaries	High salaries

Organizational Objectives

Organizational objectives are the end points of an organization's mission and are what it seeks through the ongoing, long-run operations of the organization. The organizational mission is distilled into a finer set of specific and achievable organizational objectives. These objectives must be *specific, measurable, action commitments* by which the mission of the organization is to be achieved.

As with the statement of mission, organizational objectives are more than good intentions. In fact, if formulated properly, they can accomplish the following:

1. They can be converted into specific action.
2. They will provide direction. That is, they can serve as a starting point for more specific and detailed objectives at lower levels in the organization. Each manager will then know how his or her objectives relate to those at higher levels.
3. They can establish long-run priorities for the organization.
4. They can facilitate management control because they serve as standards against which overall organizational performance can be evaluated.

Organizational objectives are necessary in all areas that may influence the performance and long-run survival of the organization. As shown in Figure 1.3 objectives can be established in and across many areas of the organization. The list provided in Figure 1.3 is by no means exhaustive. For example, some organizations are specifying the primary objective as the attainment of a specific level of quality, either in the marketing of a product or the providing of a service. These organizations believe that objectives should reflect an organization's commitment to the customer rather than its own finances. Obviously, during the strategic planning process conflicts are likely to occur between various functional departments in the organization. The important point is that management must translate the

FIGURE 1.3
Sample
Organizational
Objectives
(manufacturing firm)

Area of Performance	Possible Objective
1. Market standing	To make our brands number one in their field in terms of market share.
2. Innovations	To be a leader in introducing new products by spending no less than 7 percent of sales for research and development.
3. Productivity	To manufacture all products efficiently as measured by the productivity of the workforce.
4. Physical and financial resources	To protect and maintain all resources—equipment, buildings, inventory, and funds.
5. Profitability	To achieve an annual rate of return on investment of at least 15 percent.
6. Manager performance and responsibility	To identify critical areas of management depth and succession.
7. Worker performance and attitude	To maintain levels of employee satisfaction consistent with our own and similar industries.
8. Social responsibility	To respond appropriately whenever possible to societal expectations and environmental needs.

organizational mission into specific objectives that support the realization of the mission. The objectives may flow directly from the mission or be considered subordinate necessities for carrying out the mission. As discussed earlier, the objectives are specific, measurable, action commitments on the part of the organization.

Organizational Strategies

Hopefully, when an organization has formulated its mission and developed its objectives, it knows where it wants to go. The next managerial task is to develop a "grand design" to get there. This grand design constitutes the organizational strategies. Strategy involves the choice of major directions the organization will take in pursuing its objectives. Toward this end, it is critical that strategies are consistent with goals and objectives and that top management ensures strategies are implemented effectively. As many as 60 percent of strategic plans have failed because the strategies in them were not well defined and, thus, could not be implemented effectively.[11] What follows is a discussion of various strategies organizations can pursue. We discuss three approaches: (1) strategies based on products and markets, (2) strategies based on competitive advantage, and (3) strategies based on value.

Organizational Strategies Based on Products and Markets   One means to developing organizational strategies is to focus on the directions the organization can take in order to grow. Figure 1.4, which presents the available strategic choices, is a product–market matrix.[12] It indicates that an organization can grow by better managing what it is

FIGURE 1.4
Organizational
Growth Strategies

Products Markets	Present Products	New Products
Present customers	Market penetration	Product development
New customers	Market development	Diversification

1. *The Fit Test*: How well does the strategy fit the company's situation? A strategy must have good *external fit,* which means it will be well matched to industry and competitive conditions, the company's best market opportunities, and other relevant aspects of its business environment. It also must have a good *internal fit,* which means it is tailored to the company's resources and distinctive competencies and be supported by a complementary set of functional capabilities (sales and marketing, production, etc.).

2. *The Competitive Advantage Test*: Can the strategy help the company achieve a sustainable competitive advantage? Strategies that fail this test are unlikely to produce superior performance for more than a brief period of time. A good strategy should enable the organization to achieve a long-term competitive advantage.

3. *The Performance Test*: Is the strategy producing good company performance? Critical performance indicators are (a) profitability and financial strength and (b) competitive strength and market standing. Above average performance in these two areas is an indicator of a winning strategy.

Source: Adapted from Arthur A. Thompson, Margaret A. Peteraf, John E. Gamble, and A.J. Strickland III, *Crafting and Executing Strategy,* 18th ed. (Burr Ridge IL: McGraw-Hill/Irwin, 2012), pp. 13–14.

presently doing or by finding new things to do. In choosing one or both of these paths, it must also decide whether to concentrate on present customers or to seek new ones. Thus, according to Figure 1.4, there are only four paths an organization can take in order to grow.

Market Penetration Strategies   These strategies focus primarily on increasing the sale of present products to present customers. For example:

- Encouraging present customers to use more of the product: "Orange Juice Isn't Just for Breakfast Anymore."
- Encouraging present customers to purchase more of the product: multiple packages of Pringles, instant winner sweepstakes at a fast-food restaurant.
- Directing programs at current participants: A university directs a fund-raising program at those graduates who already give the most money.

Tactics used to implement a market penetration strategy might include price reductions, advertising that stresses the many benefits of the product (e.g., "Milk Is a Natural"), packaging the product in different-sized packages, or making it available at more locations. Other functional areas of the business could also be involved in implementing the strategy in addition to marketing. A production plan might be developed to produce the product more efficiently. This plan might include increased production runs, the substitution of preassembled components for individual product parts, or the automation of a process that previously was performed manually.

Market Development Strategies   Pursuing growth through market development, an organization would seek to find new customers for its present products. For example:

- Arm & Hammer continues to seek new uses for its baking soda.
- McDonald's continually seeks expansion into overseas markets.
- As the consumption of salt declined, the book *101 Things You Can Do with Salt Besides Eat It* appeared.

Market development strategies involve much, much more than simply getting the product to a new market. Before deciding on marketing techniques such as advertising and packaging, companies often find they must establish a clear position in the market, sometimes spending large sums of money simply to educate consumers as to why they should consider buying the product.

Product Development Strategies   Selecting one of the remaining two strategies means the organization will seek new things to do. With this particular strategy, the new products developed would be directed primarily to present customers. For example:

- Offering a different version of an existing product: mini-Oreos, Ritz with cheese.
- Offering a new and improved version of their product: Gillette's latest improvement in shaving technology.
- Offering a new way to use an existing product: Vaseline's Lip Therapy.

Diversification   This strategy can lead the organization into entirely new and even unrelated businesses. It involves seeking new products (often through acquisitions) for customers not currently being served. For example:

- Altria, originally a manufacturer of cigarettes, is widely diversified in financial services, Post cereals, Sealtest dairy, and Kraft cheese, among others.
- Brown Foreman Distillers acquired Hartmann Luggage, and Sara Lee acquired Coach Leather Products.
- Some universities are establishing corporations to find commercial uses for faculty research.

Organizational Strategies Based on Competitive Advantage   Michael Porter developed a model for formulating organizational strategy that is applicable across a wide variety of industries.[13] The focus of the model is on devising means to gain competitive advantage. Competitive advantage is an ability to outperform competitors in providing something that the market values. Porter suggests that firms should first analyze their industry and then develop either a *cost leadership strategy* or a *strategy based on differentiation*. These general strategies can be used on marketwide bases or in a niche (segment) within the total market.

Using a cost leadership strategy, a firm would focus on being the low-cost company in its industry. They would stress efficiency and offer a standard, no-frills product. They could achieve this through efficiencies in production, product design, manufacturing, distribution, technology, or some other means. The important point is that to succeed, the organization must continually strive to be the cost leader in the industry or market segment it competes in. It must also offer products or services that are acceptable to customers when compared to the competition. Walmart, Southwest Airlines, and Timex Group Ltd. are companies that have succeeded in using a cost leadership strategy.

Using a strategy based on differentiation, a firm seeks to be unique in its industry or market segment along particular dimensions that the customers value. These dimensions might pertain to design, quality, service, variety of offerings, brand name, or some other factor. The important point is that because of uniqueness of the product or service along one or more of these dimensions, the firm can charge a premium price. L. L. Bean, Rolex, Coca-Cola, and Microsoft are companies that have succeeded using a differentiation strategy.

Organizational Strategies Based on Value   As competition increases, the concept of "customer value" has become critical for marketers as well as customers. It can be thought of as an extension of the marketing concept philosophy that focuses on developing and delivering superior value to customers as a way to achieve organizational objectives. Thus, it focuses not only on customer needs, but also on the question, How can we create value for them and still achieve our objectives?

It has become pretty clear that in today's competitive environment it is unlikely that a firm will succeed by trying to be all things to all people.[14] Thus, to succeed firms must seek to build long-term relationships with their customers by offering a unique value that only they can offer. It seems that many firms have succeeded by choosing to deliver superior customer value using one of three value strategies—best price, best product, or best service.

Dell Inc., Costco, and Southwest Airlines are among the success stories in offering customers the best price. Rubbermaid, Nike, Starbucks, and Microsoft believe they offer the best products on the market. Airborne Express, Roadway, Cott Corporation, and Lands' End provide superior customer value by providing outstanding service.

Choosing an Appropriate Strategy

On what basis does an organization choose one (or all) of its strategies? Of extreme importance are the directions set by the mission statement. Management should select those strategies consistent with its mission and capitalize on the organization's distinctive competencies that will lead to a sustainable competitive advantage. A sustainable competitive advantage can be based on either the assets or skills of the organization. Technical superiority, low-cost production, customer service/product support, location, financial resources, continuing product innovation, and overall marketing skills are all examples of distinctive competencies that can lead to a sustainable competitive advantage. For example, Honda is known for providing quality automobiles at a reasonable price. Each succeeding generation of Honda automobiles has shown marked quality improvements over previous generations. Likewise, VF Corporation, manufacturer of Wrangler and Lee jeans, has formed "quick response" partnerships with both discounters and department stores to ensure the efficiency of product flow. The key to sustaining a competitive advantage is to continually focus and build on the assets and skills that will lead to long-term performance gains.

Organizational Portfolio Plan

The final phase of the strategic planning process is the formulation of the organizational portfolio plan. In reality, most organizations at a particular time are a portfolio of businesses, that is, product lines, divisions, and schools. To illustrate, an appliance manufacturer may have several product lines (e.g., televisions, washers and dryers, refrigerators, stereos) as well as two divisions, consumer appliances and industrial appliances. A college or university will have numerous schools (e.g., education, business, law, architecture) and several programs within each school. Some widely diversified organizations such as Altria are in numerous unrelated businesses, such as cigarettes, food products, land development, and industrial paper products.

Managing such groups of businesses is made a little easier if resources are plentiful, cash is plentiful, and each is experiencing growth and profits. Unfortunately, providing larger and larger budgets each year to all businesses is seldom feasible. Many are not experiencing growth, and profits and resources (financial and nonfinancial) are becoming more and more scarce. In such a situation, choices must be made, and some method is necessary to help management make the choices. Management must decide which businesses to build, maintain, or eliminate, or which new businesses to add. Indeed, much of the recent activity in corporate restructuring has centered on decisions relating to which groups of businesses management should focus on.

Obviously, the first step in this approach is to identify the various divisions, product lines, and so on that can be considered a "business." When identified, these are referred to as *strategic business units* (SBUs) and have the following characteristics:

- They have a distinct mission.
- They have their own competitors.

- They are a single business or collection of related businesses.
- They can be planned independently of the other businesses of the total organization.

Thus, depending on the type of organization, an SBU could be a single product, product line, or division; a college of business administration; or a state mental health agency. Once the organization has identified and classified all of its SBUs, some method must be established to determine how resources should be allocated among the various SBUs. These methods are known as *portfolio models*. For those readers interested, the appendix of this chapter presents two of the most popular portfolio models, the Boston Consulting Group model and the General Electric model.

The Complete Strategic Plan

Figure 1.2 indicates that at this point the strategic planning process is complete, and the organization has a time-phased blueprint that outlines its mission, objectives, and strategies. Completion of the strategic plan facilitates the development of marketing plans for each product, product line, or division of the organization. The marketing plan serves as a subset of the strategic plan in that it allows for detailed planning at a target market level. This important relationship between strategic planning and marketing planning is the subject of the final section of this chapter.

THE MARKETING MANAGEMENT PROCESS

Marketing management can be defined as "the process of planning and executing the conception, pricing, promotion, and distribution of goods, services, and ideas to create exchanges with target groups that satisfy customer and organizational objectives."[15] It should be noted that this definition is entirely consistent with the marketing concept, since it emphasizes serving target market needs as the key to achieving organizational objectives. The remainder of this section will be devoted to a discussion of the marketing management process according to the model in Figure 1.5.

Situation Analysis

With a clear understanding of organizational objectives and mission, the marketing manager must then analyze and monitor the position of the firm and, specifically, the marketing department, in terms of its past, present, and future situation. Of course, the future situation is of primary concern. However, analyses of past trends and the current situation are most useful for predicting the future situation.

The situation analysis can be divided into six major areas of concern: (1) the cooperative environment; (2) the competitive environment; (3) the economic environment; (4) the social environment; (5) the political environment; and (6) the legal environment. In analyzing each of these environments, the marketing executive must search both for opportunities and for constraints or threats to achieving objectives. Opportunities for profitable marketing often arise from changes in these environments that bring about new sets of needs to be satisfied. Constraints on marketing activities, such as limited supplies of scarce resources, also arise from these environments.

The Cooperative Environment The cooperative environment includes all firms and individuals who have a vested interest in the firm's accomplishing its objectives. Parties of primary interest to the marketing executive in this environment are (1) suppliers, (2) resellers, (3) other departments in the firm, and (4) subdepartments and employees of the marketing department. Opportunities in this environment are primarily related to methods of increasing efficiency. For example, a company might decide to switch from a competitive bid process of obtaining materials to a single source that is located near the company's plant.

FIGURE 1.5
Strategic Planning
and Marketing
Planning

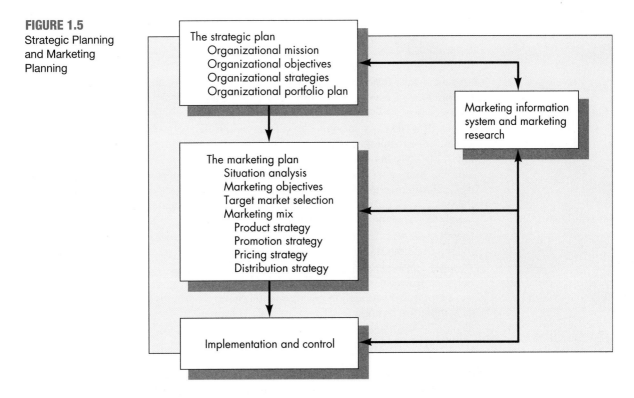

Likewise, members of the marketing, engineering, and manufacturing functions may use a teamwork approach to developing new products versus a sequential approach. Constraints consist of such things as unresolved conflicts and shortages of materials. For example, a company manager may believe that a distributor is doing an insufficient job of promoting and selling the product, or a marketing manager may feel that manufacturing is not taking the steps needed to produce a quality product.

The Competitive Environment   The competitive environment includes primarily other firms in the industry that rival the organization for both resources and sales. Opportunities in this environment include such things as (1) acquiring competing firms; (2) offering demonstrably better value to consumers and attracting them away from competitors; and (3) in some cases, driving competitors out of the industry. For example, one airline purchases another airline, a bank offers depositors a free checking account with no minimum balance requirements, or a grocery chain engages in an everyday low-price strategy that competitors can't meet. The primary constraints in these environments are the demand stimulation activities of competing firms and the number of consumers who cannot be lured away from competition.

The Economic Environment   The state of the macroeconomy and changes in it also bring about marketing opportunities and constraints. For example, such factors as high inflation and unemployment levels can limit the size of the market that can afford to purchase a firm's top-of-the-line product. At the same time, these factors may offer a profitable opportunity to develop rental services for such products or to develop less-expensive models of the product. In addition, changes in technology can provide significant threats and opportunities. For example, in the communications industry, when technology was developed to a level where it was possible to provide cable television using phone lines, such a system posed a severe threat to the cable industry.

Speed of the Process. There is the problem of either being so slow that the process seems to go on forever or so fast that there is an extreme burst of activity to rush out a plan.

Amount of Data Collected. Sufficient data are needed to properly estimate customer needs and competitive trends. However, the law of diminishing returns quickly sets in on the data-collection process.

Responsibility for Developing the Plan. If planning is delegated to professional planners, valuable line management input may be ignored. If the process is left to line managers, planning may be relegated to secondary status.

Structure. Many executives believe the most important part of planning is not the plan itself but the structure of thought about the strategic issues facing the business. However, the structure should not take precedence over the content so that planning becomes merely filling out forms or crunching numbers.

Length of the Plan. The length of a marketing plan must be balanced between being so long that both staff and line managers ignore it and so brief that it ignores key details.

Frequency of Planning. Too frequent reevaluation of strategies can lead to erratic firm behavior. However, when plans are not revised frequently enough, the business may not adapt quickly enough to environmental changes and thus suffer a deterioration in its competitive position.

Number of Alternative Strategies Considered. Discussing too few alternatives raises the likelihood of failure, whereas discussing too many increases the time and cost of the planning effort.

Cross-Functional Acceptance. A common mistake is to view the plan as the proprietary possession of marketing. Successful implementation requires a broad consensus, including other functional areas.

Using the Plan as a Sales Document. A major but often overlooked purpose of a plan and its presentation is to generate funds from either internal or external sources. Therefore, the better the plan, the better the chance of gaining desired funding.

Senior Management Leadership. Commitment from senior management is essential to the success of a marketing planning effort.

Tying Compensation to Successful Planning Efforts. Management compensation should be oriented toward the achievement of objectives stated in the plan.

Source: Donald R. Lehmann and Russell S. Winer, *Analysis for Marketing Planning,* 7th ed. (Burr Ridge, IL: McGraw-Hill//Irwin, 2008), chap. 1.

The Social Environment This environment includes general cultural and social traditions, norms, and attitudes. While these values change slowly, such changes often bring about the need for new products and services. For example, a change in values concerning the desirability of large families brought about an opportunity to market better methods of birth control. On the other hand, cultural and social values also place constraints on marketing activities. As a rule, business practices that are contrary to social values become political issues, which are often resolved by legal constraints. For example, public demand for a cleaner environment has caused the government to require that automobile manufacturers' products meet certain average gas mileage and emission standards.

The Political Environment The political environment includes the attitudes and reactions of the general public, social and business critics, and other organizations, such as the Better Business Bureau. Dissatisfaction with such business and marketing practices as unsafe products, products that waste resources, and unethical sales procedures can have adverse effects on corporation image and customer loyalty. However, adapting business and marketing practices to these attitudes can be an opportunity. For example, these attitudes have brought about markets for such products as unbreakable children's toys, high-efficiency air conditioners, and more economical automobiles.

The Legal Environment This environment includes a host of federal, state, and local legislation directed at protecting both business competition and consumer rights. In past years, legislation reflected social and political attitudes and has been primarily directed at constraining business practices. Such legislation usually acts as a constraint on business behavior, but again can be viewed as providing opportunities for marketing safer and more efficient products. In recent years, there has been less emphasis on creating new laws for constraining business practices. As an example, deregulation has become more common, as evidenced by events in the airlines, financial services, and telecommunications industries.

Marketing Planning

The previous sections emphasized that (1) marketing activities must be aligned with organizational objectives and (2) marketing opportunities are often found by systematically analyzing situational environments. Once an opportunity is recognized, the marketing executive must then plan an appropriate strategy for taking advantage of the opportunity. This process can be viewed in terms of three interrelated tasks: (1) establishing marketing objectives, (2) selecting the target market, and (3) developing the marketing mix.

Establishing Objectives Marketing objectives usually are derived from organizational objectives; in some cases where the firm is totally marketing oriented, the two are identical. In either case, objectives must be specified and performance in achieving them should be measurable. Marketing objectives are usually stated as standards of performance (e.g., a certain percentage of market share or sales volume) or as tasks to be achieved by given dates. While such objectives are useful, the marketing concept emphasizes that profits rather than sales should be the overriding objective of the firm and marketing department. In any case, these objectives provide the framework for the marketing plan.

Selecting the Target Market The success of any marketing plan hinges on how well it can identify customer needs and organize its resources to satisfy them profitably. Thus, a crucial element of the marketing plan is selecting the groups or segments of potential customers the firm is going to serve with each of its products. Four important questions must be answered:

1. What do customers want or need?
2. What must be done to satisfy these wants or needs?
3. What is the size of the market?
4. What is its growth profile?

Present target markets and potential target markets are then ranked according to (1) profitability; (2) present and future sales volume; and (3) the match between what it takes to appeal successfully to the segment and the organization's capabilities. Those that appear to offer the greatest potential are selected. One cautionary note on this process involves the importance of not neglecting present customers when developing market share and sales strategies. A recent study found that for every 10 companies that develop strategies aimed at increasing the number of first-time customers, only four made any serious effort to develop strategies geared toward retaining present customers and increasing their purchases.[16] Chapters 3, 4, and 5 are devoted to discussing consumer behavior, industrial buyers, and market segmentation.

Developing the Marketing Mix The marketing mix is the set of controllable variables that must be managed to satisfy the target market and achieve organizational objectives.

Poorly Stated Objectives	Well-Stated Objectives
Our objective is to be a leader in the industry in terms of new product development.	Our objective is to spend 12 percent of sales revenue between 2011 and 2013 on research and development in an effort to introduce at least five new products in 2014.
Our objective is to maximize profits.	Our objective is to achieve a 10 percent return on investment during 2012, with a payback on new investments of no longer than four years.
Our objective is to better serve customers.	Our objective is to obtain customer satisfaction ratings of at least 90 percent on the 2012 annual customer satisfaction survey, and to retain at least 85 percent of our 2012 customers as repeat purchasers in 2013.
Our objective is to be the best that we can be.	Our objective is to increase market share from 30 percent to 40 percent in 2012 by increasing promotional expenditures by 14 percent.

Source: Adapted from Charles W. Lamb, Jr., Joseph F. Hair, Jr., and Carl McDaniel, *Marketing*, 10th ed. (Mason, OH: Thomson South-Western Publishing Co., 2008), Chapter 2.

These controllable variables are usually classified according to four major decision areas: product, price, promotion, and place (or channels of distribution). The importance of these decision areas cannot be overstated, and in fact, the major portion of this text is devoted to analyzing them. Chapters 6 and 7 are devoted to product and new product strategies, Chapters 8 and 9 to promotion strategies in terms of both nonpersonal and personal selling, Chapter 10 to distribution strategies, and Chapter 11 to pricing strategies. In addition, marketing mix variables are the focus of analysis in two chapters on marketing in special fields, that is, the marketing of services (Chapter 12) and international marketing (Chapter 13). Thus, it should be clear that the marketing mix is the core of the marketing management process.

The output of the foregoing process is the marketing plan. It is a formal statement of decisions that have been made on marketing activities; it is a blueprint of the objectives, strategies, and tasks to be performed.

Implementation and Control of the Marketing Plan

Implementing the marketing plan involves putting the plan into action and performing marketing tasks according to the predefined schedule. Even the most carefully developed plans often cannot be executed with perfect timing. Thus, the marketing executive must closely monitor and coordinate implementation of the plan. In some cases, adjustments may have to be made in the basic plan because of changes in any of the situational environments. For example, competitors may introduce a new product. In this event, it may be desirable to speed up or delay implementation of the plan. In almost all cases, some minor adjustments or fine tuning will be necessary in implementation.

Controlling the marketing plan involves three basic steps. First, the results of the implemented marketing plan are measured. Second, these results are compared with objectives. Third, decisions are made on whether the plan is achieving objectives. If serious deviations exist between actual and planned results, adjustments may have to be made to redirect the plan toward achieving objectives.

Marketing Information Systems and Marketing Research

Throughout the marketing management process, current, reliable, and valid information is needed to make effective marketing decisions. Providing this information is the task of the marketing information system and marketing research. These topics are discussed in detail in Chapter 2.

THE STRATEGIC PLAN, THE MARKETING PLAN, AND OTHER FUNCTIONAL AREA PLANS

Strategic planning is clearly a top-management responsibility. In recent years, however, there has been an increasing shift toward more active participation by marketing managers in strategic analysis and planning. This is because, in reality, nearly all strategic planning questions have marketing implications. In fact, the two major strategic planning questions—What products should we make? and What markets should we serve?—are clearly marketing questions. Thus, marketing executives are involved in the strategic planning process in at least two important ways: (1) They influence the process by providing important inputs in the form of information and suggestions relating to customers, products, and middlemen; and (2) they must always be aware of what the process of stategic planning involves as well as the results because everything they do—the marketing objectives and strategies they develop—must be derived from the strategic plan. In fact, the planning done in all functional areas of the organization should be derived from the strategic plan.

Marketing's Role in Cross-Functional Strategic Planning

More and more organizations are rethinking the traditional role of marketing. Rather than dividing work according to function (e.g., production, finance, technology, human resources), they are bringing managers and employees together to participate in *cross-functional teams*. These teams might have responsibility for a particular product, line of products, or group of customers.

Because team members are responsible for all activities involving their products and/or customers, they are responsible for strategic planning. This means that all personnel working in a cross-functional team will participate in creating a strategic plan to serve customers. Rather than making decisions independently, marketing managers work closely with team members from production, finance, human resources, and other areas to devise plans that address all concerns. Thus, if a team member from production says, "That product will be too difficult to produce," or if a team member from finance says, "We'll never make a profit at that price," the team members from marketing must help resolve the problems. This approach requires a high degree of skill at problem solving and gaining cooperation.

Clearly the greatest advantage of strategic planning with a cross-functional team is the ability of team members to consider a situation from a number of viewpoints. The resulting insights can help the team avoid costly mistakes and poor solutions. Japanese manufacturers are noted for using cross-functional teams to figure out ways to make desirable products at given target costs. In contrast, U.S. manufacturers traditionally have developed products by having one group decide what to make, another calculate production costs, and yet another predict whether enough of the product will sell at a high enough price.

Thus, in well-managed organizations, a direct relationship exists between strategic planning and the planning done by managers at all levels. The focus and time perspectives will, of course, differ. Figure 1.6 illustrates the cross-functional perspective of strategic planning. It indicates very clearly that all functional area plans should be derived from the strategic plan while at the same time contributing to the achievement of it.

FIGURE 1.6   The Cross-Functional Perspective in Planning

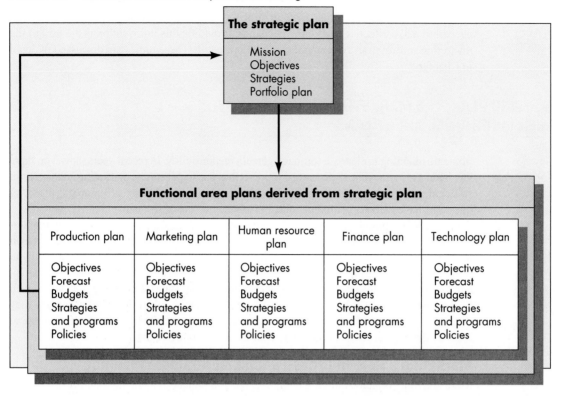

If done properly, strategic planning results in a clearly defined blueprint for management action in all functional areas of the organization. Figure 1.7 clearly illustrates this blueprint using only one organizational objective and two strategies from the strategic plan (above the dotted line) and illustrating how these are translated into elements of the marketing department plan and the production department plan (below the dotted line). Note that in Figure 1.7, all objectives and strategies are related to other objectives and strategies at higher and lower levels in the organization: That is, a hierarchy of objectives and strategies exists. We have illustrated only two possible marketing objectives and two possible production objectives. Obviously, many others could be developed, but our purpose is to illustrate the cross-functional nature of strategic planning and how objectives and strategies from the strategic plan must be translated into objectives and strategies for all functional areas including marketing.

SUMMARY

This chapter has described the marketing management process in the context of the organization's overall strategic plan. Clearly, marketers must understand their cross-functional role in joining the marketing vision for the organization with the financial goals and manufacturing capabilities of the organization. The greater this ability, the better the likelihood is that the organization will be able to achieve and sustain a competitive advantage, the ultimate purpose of the strategic planning process.

At this point it would be useful to review Figures 1.5, 1.6, and 1.7 as well as the book's table of contents. This review will enable you to better relate the content and progression of the material to follow to the marketing management process.

FIGURE 1.7 A Blueprint for Management Action: Relating the Marketing Plan to the Strategic Plan and the Production Plan

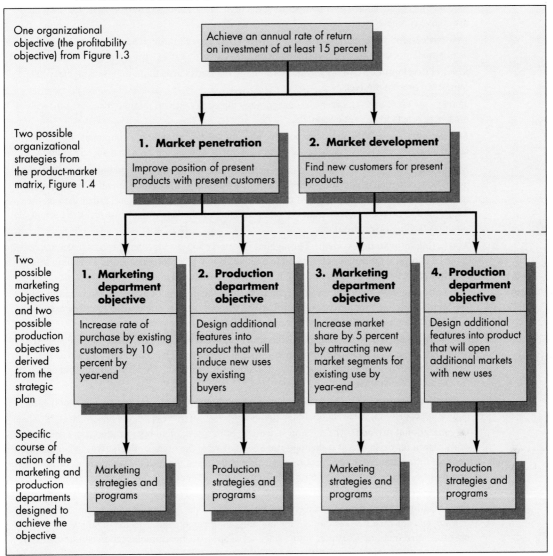

Additional Resources

Charan, Ram. *Leadership in the Era of Economic Uncertainty.* NY: McGraw-Hill, 2009.

Christensen, Clayton, M., Scott Cook, and Tandy Hall. "Marketing Malpractice: The Cause and the Cure." *Harvard Business Review,* December 2005, pp. 74–75.

Dixit, Avinash, K., and Barry J. Noblebuff. *The Art of Strategy.* NY: W.W. Norton and Co., 2009.

Friedman, George. *The Next Decade.* NY: Doubleday, 2011.

Kaplan, Robert S., and David Norton. "How to Implement a New Strategy Without Disrupting Your Organization." *Harvard Business Review,* March 2006, pp. 100–109.

Levitt, Ted. *On Marketing.* Boston: HBS Press, 2006.

London, Ted, and Stuart L. Hart. *Next Generation Business Strategies for the Base of the Pyramid.* Upper Saddle River, NJ: FT Press, 2011.

Markower, Jack. *Strategies for the Green Economy.* NY: McGraw-Hill, 2009.

O'Sullivan, Don, and Andrew W. Abdela. "Marketing Performance Measurement Ability and Performance." *Journal of Marketing,* April 2007, pp. 79–93.

Seiders, Kathleen, and Leonard L. Berry. "Should Business Care about Obesity?" *Sloan Management Review,* Winter 2007, pp. 15–17.

Key Terms and Concepts

Distinctive competencies: Distinctive competencies are things that an organization does so well that they give it an advantage over similar organizations. No matter how appealing an opportunity may be, to gain advantage over competitors, the organization must formulate strategy based on distinctive competencies.

Diversification: An organizational strategy that seeks growth through new products (often through acquisitions) for customers not currently being served.

Market development: An organizational strategy that seeks growth through seeking new customers for present products.

Market penetration: An organizational strategy that seeks growth through increasing the sale of present products to present customers.

Marketing: The activity, set of institutions, and processes for creating, communicating, delivering, and exchanging offerings that have value for customers, clients, partners, and society at large.

Marketing concept: The marketing concept means that an organization should seek to make a profit by serving the needs of customer groups. Its purpose is to rivet the attention of marketing managers on serving broad classes of customer needs (customer orientation), rather than on the firm's products (production orientation) or on devising methods to attract customers to current products (selling orientation).

Marketing information system: Throughout the marketing management process, current, reliable, and valid information is needed to make effective marketing decisions. Providing this information is the task of the marketing information system and marketing research.

Marketing management: Marketing management is the process of planning and executing the conception, pricing, promotion, and distribution of goods, services, and ideas to create exchanges with target groups that satisfy customer and organizational objectives.

Marketing mix: The marketing mix is the set of controllable variables that must be managed to satisfy the target market and achieve organizational objectives. The controllable variables are usually classified according to four major decision areas: product, price, promotion, and place (or channels of distribution).

Marketing planning: The marketing planning process produces three outputs: (1) establishing marketing objectives, (2) selecting the target market, and (3) developing the marketing mix.

Organizational mission: The mission statement, or purpose, of an organization is the description of its reason for existence. It is the long-run vision of what the organization strives to be, the unique aim that differentiates the organization from similar ones and the means by which this differentiation will take place. An effective mission statement will be focused on markets rather than products, achievable, motivating, and specific.

Organizational objectives: Organizational objectives are the end points of an organization's mission and are what it seeks through the ongoing, long-run operation of the organization. The organizational mission is distilled into a finer set of specific, measurable, action commitments by which the mission of the organization is to be achieved.

Organizational portfolio plan: This stage of the strategic plan involves the allocation of resources across the organization's product lines, divisions, or businesses. It involves deciding which ones to build, maintain, or eliminate, or which to add.

Organizational strategies: Organizational strategies are the choice of the major directions the organization will take in pursuing its objectives. There are three major approaches: (1) strategies based on products and markets, (2) strategies based on competitive advantage, and (3) strategies based on value.

Organizational strategies based on competitive advantage: This approach to developing organizational strategy would develop either a cost leadership strategy which focuses on being the lower cost company in the industry or a differentiation strategy which focuses on being unique in the industry or market segment along dimensions that customers value.

Organizational strategies based on products and markets: An approach to developing organizational strategies that focuses on the four paths an organization can grow: market penetration strategies, market development strategies, product development strategies, and diversification strategies.

Organizational strategies based on value: This approach to developing organizational strategy seeks to succeed by choosing to deliver superior customer value using one of three value strategies—best price, best product, or best service.

Product development: An organizational strategy that seeks growth through developing new products primarily for present customers.

Situation analysis: This stage of the marketing planning process involves the analysis of the past, present, and likely future in six major areas of concern: (1) the cooperative environment; (2) the competitive environment; (3) the economic environment; (4) the social environment; (5) the political environment; and (6)) the legal environment. Opportunities for and constraints on marketing activities arise from these environments.

Strategic business units (SBUs): Strategic business units (SBUs) are product lines and divisions that can be considered a "business" for the purpose of the organizational portfolio plan. An SBU must have a distinct mission, have its own competitors, be a single business or collection of related businesses, and be able to be planned independently of the other SBUs.

Strategic planning: Strategic planning provides a blueprint for management actions for the entire organization. It includes all the activities that lead to the development of a clear organizational mission, organizational objectives, and appropriate strategies to achieve the objectives for the entire organization.

Appendix

Portfolio Models

Portfolio models remain a valuable aid to marketing managers in their efforts to develop effective marketing plans. The use of these models can aid managers who face situations that can best be described as "more products, less time, and less money." More specifically, (1) as the number of products a firm produces expands, the time available for developing marketing plans for each product decreases; (2) at a strategic level, management must make resource allocation decisions across lines of products and, in diversified organizations, across different lines of business; and (3) when resources are limited (which they usually are), the process of deciding which strategic business units (SBUs) to emphasize becomes very complex. In such situations, portfolio models can be very useful.

Portfolio analysis is not a new idea. Banks manage loan portfolios seeking to balance risks and yields. Individuals who are serious investors usually have a portfolio of various kinds of investments (common stocks, preferred stocks, bank accounts, and the like), each with different characteristics of risk, growth, and rate of return. The investor seeks to manage the portfolio to maximize whatever objectives he or she might have. Applying this same idea, most organizations have a wide range of products, product lines, and businesses, each with different growth rates and returns. Similar to the investor, managers should seek a desirable balance among alternative SBUs. Specifically, management should seek to develop a business portfolio that will ensure long-run profits and cash flow.

Portfolio models can be used to classify SBUs to determine the future cash contributions that can be expected from each SBU as well as the future resources that each will require. Remember, depending on the organization, an SBU could be a single product, product line, division, or distinct business. While there are many different types of portfolio models, they generally examine the competitive position of the SBU and the chances for improving the SBU's contribution to profitability and cash flow.

There are several portfolio analysis techniques. Two of the most widely used are discussed in this appendix. To truly appreciate the concept of portfolio analysis, however, we must briefly review the development of portfolio theory.

A REVIEW OF PORTFOLIO THEORY

The interest in developing aids for managers in the selection of strategy was spurred by an organization known as the Boston Consulting Group (BCG) over 25 years ago. Its ideas, which will be discussed shortly, and many of those that followed were based on the concept of experience curves.

Experience curves are similar in concept to learning curves. Learning curves were developed to express the idea that the number of labor hours it takes to produce one unit of a particular product declines in a predictable manner as the number of units produced increases. Hence, an accurate estimation of how long it takes to produce the 100th unit is possible if the production times for the 1st and 10th units are known. The concept of experience curves was based on this model.

Experience curves were first widely discussed in the Strategic Planning Institute's ongoing Profit Impact of Marketing Strategies (PIMS) study. The PIMS project studies 150 firms with more than 1,000 individual business units. Its major focus is on determining which environmental and internal firm variables influence the firm's return on investment (ROI) and cash flow. The researchers have concluded that seven categories of variables appear to influence the return on investment: (1) competitive position, (2) industry/market environment, (3) budget allocation, (4) capital structure, (5) production processes, (6) company characteristics, and (7) "change action" factors.[17]

The experience curve includes all costs associated with a product and implies that the per-unit costs of a product should fall, due to cumulative experience, as production volume increases. In a given industry, therefore, the producer with the largest volume and corresponding market share should have the lowest marginal cost. This leader in market share should be able to underprice competitors, discourage entry into the market by potential competitors, and, as a result, achieve an acceptable return on investment. The linkage of experience to cost to price to market share to ROI is exhibited in Figure A.1. The Boston Consulting Group's

FIGURE A.1   **Experience Curve and Resulting Profit**

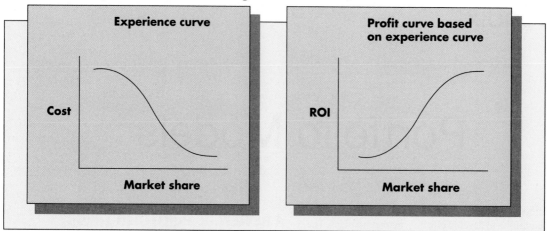

view of the experience curve led the members to develop what has become known as the BCG Portfolio Model.

THE BCG MODEL

The BCG is based on the assumption that profitability and cash flow will be closely related to sales volume. Thus, in this model, SBUs are classified according to their relative market share and the growth rate of the market the SBU is in. Using these dimensions, products are either classified as stars, cash cows, dogs, or question marks. The BCG model is presented in Figure A.2.

• *Stars* are SBUs with a high share of a high-growth market. Because high-growth markets attract competition, such SBUs are usually cash users because they are growing

and because the firm needs to protect their market share position.

• *Cash cows* are often market leaders, but the market they are in is not growing rapidly. Because these SBUs have a high share of a low-growth market, they are cash generators for the firm.

• *Dogs* are SBUs that have a low share of a low-growth market. If the SBU has a very loyal group of customers, it may be a source of profits and cash. Usually, dogs are not large sources of cash.

• *Question marks* are SBUs with a low share of a high-growth market. They have great potential but require great resources if the firm is to successfully build market share.

As you can see, a firm with 10 SBUs will usually have a portfolio that includes some of each of the above. Having

FIGURE A.2
The Boston
Consulting Group
Portfolio Model

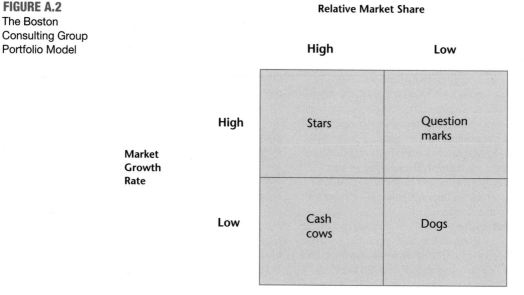

developed this analysis, management must determine what role each SBU should assume. Four basic objectives are possible:

1. *Build share*. This objective sacrifices immediate earnings to improve market share. It is appropriate for promising question marks whose share has to grow if they are ever to become stars.
2. *Hold share*. This objective seeks to preserve the SBU's market share. It is very appropriate for strong cash cows to ensure that they can continue to yield a large cash flow.
3. *Harvest*. Here, the objective seeks to increase the product's short-term cash flow without concern for the long-run impact. It allows market share to decline in order to maximize earnings and cash flow. It is an appropriate objective for weak cash cows, weak question marks, and dogs.
4. *Divest*. This objective involves selling or divesting the SBU because better investment opportunities exist elsewhere. It is very appropriate for dogs and those question marks the firm cannot afford to finance for growth.

There have been several major criticisms of the BCG Portfolio Model, revolving around its focus on market share and market growth as the primary indicators of preference. First, the BCG model assumes market growth is uncontrollable.[18] As a result, managers can become preoccupied with setting market share objectives instead of trying to grow the market. Second, assumptions regarding market share as a critical factor affecting firm performance may not hold true, especially in international markets.[19] Third, the BCG model assumes that the major source of

SBU financing comes from internal means. Fourth, the BCG matrix does not take into account any interdependencies that may exist between SBUs, such as shared distribution.[20] Fifth, the BCG matrix does not take into account any measures of profits and customer satisfaction.[21] Sixth, and perhaps most important, the thrust of the BCG matrix is based on the underlying assumption that corporate strategy begins with an analysis of competitive position. By its very nature, a strategy developed entirely on competitive analysis will always be a reactive one.[22] While the above criticisms are certainly valid ones, managers (especially of large firms) across all industries continue to find the BCG matrix useful in assessing the strategic position of SBUs.[23]

THE GENERAL ELECTRIC MODEL

Although the BCG model can be useful, it does assume that market share is the sole determinant of an SBU's profitability. Also, in projecting market growth rates, a manager should carefully analyze the factors that influence sales and any opportunities for influencing industry sales.

Some firms have developed alternative portfolio models to incorporate more information about market opportunities and competitive positions. The GE model is one of these. The GE model emphasizes all the potential sources of strength, not just market share, and all of the factors that influence the long-term attractiveness of a market, not just its growth rate. As Figure A.3 indicates, all SBUs are classified according to *business strength* and *industry attractiveness*. Figure A.4 presents a list of items that can be used to position SBUs in the matrix.

FIGURE A.3
The General Electric
Portfolio Model

Business Strength

		Strong	Average	Weak
	High	A	A	B
Industry Attractiveness	Medium	A	B	C
	Low	B	C	C

FIGURE A.4
Components
of Industry
Attractiveness
and Business
Strength at GE

Industry Attractiveness	Business Strength
	Market position
Market size	Domestic market share
Market growth	World market share
Profitability	Share growth
Cyclicality	Share compared with leading competitor
Ability to recover from inflation	
World scope	Competitive strengths
	Quality leadership
	Technology
	Marketing
	Relative profitability

Industry attractiveness is a composite index made up of such factors as those listed in Figure A.4. For example: *market size*—the larger the market, the more attractive it will be; *market growth*—high-growth markets are more attractive than low-growth markets; *profitability*—high-profit-margin markets are more attractive than low-profit-margin industries.

Business strength is a composite index made up of such factors as those listed in Figure A.4. Such as *market share*—the higher the SBU's share of market, the greater its business strength; *quality leadership*—the higher the SBU's quality compared to competitors, the greater its business strength; *share compared with leading competitor*—the closer the SBU's share to the market leader, the greater its business strength.

Once the SBUs are classified, they are placed on the grid (Figure A.3). Priority "A" SBUs (often called the *green zone*) are those in the three cells at the upper left, indicating that these are SBUs high in both industry attractiveness and business strength, and that the firm should "build share." Priority "B" SBUs (often called *the yellow zone*) are those medium in both industry attractiveness and business strength. The firm will usually decide to "hold share" on these SBUs. Priority "C" SBUs are those in the three cells at the lower right (often called the *red zone*). These SBUs are low in both industry attractiveness and business strength. The firm will usually decide to harvest or divest these SBUs.

Whether the BCG model, the GE model, or a variation of these models is used, some analyses must be made of the firm's current portfolio of SBUs as part of any strategic planning effort. Marketing must get its direction from the organization's strategic plan.

Marketing Information, Research, and Understanding the Target Market

Part B

Section I Essentials of Marketing Management

2

Marketing Research: Process and Systems for Decision Making

Marketing managers require current, reliable, useful information to make effective decisions. In today's highly competitive global economy, marketers need to exploit opportunities and avoid mistakes if they are to survive and be profitable. Not only is sound marketing research needed, but also a system that gets current, valid information to the marketing decision maker in a timely manner.

This chapter is concerned with the marketing research process and information systems for decision making. It begins by discussing the marketing research process that is used to develop useful information for decision making. Then, marketing information systems are briefly discussed. The chapter is intended to provide a detailed introduction to many of the important topics in the area, but it does not provide a complete explanation of the plethora of marketing research topics.

THE ROLE OF MARKETING RESEARCH

Marketing research is the process by which information about the environment is generated, analyzed, and interpreted for use in marketing decision making.[1] It cannot be overstated that *marketing research is an aid to decision making and not a substitute for it*. In other words, marketing research does not make decisions, but it can substantially increase the chances that good decisions are made. Unfortunately, too many marketing managers view research reports as the final answer to their problems; whatever the research indicates is taken as the appropriate course of action. Instead, marketing managers should recognize that (1) even the most carefully executed research can be fraught with errors; (2) marketing research does not forecast with certainty what will happen in the future; and (3) they should make decisions in light of their own knowledge and experience, since no marketing research study includes all of the factors that could influence the success of a strategy.

Although marketing research does not make decisions, it can reduce the risks associated with managing marketing strategies. For example, it can reduce the risk of introducing new products by evaluating consumer acceptance of them prior to full-scale introduction. Marketing research is also vital for investigating the effects of various marketing strategies after they have been implemented. For example, marketing research can examine the effects of a change in any element of the marketing mix on customer perception and behavior.

At one time, marketing researchers were primarily engaged in the technical aspects of research, but were not heavily involved in the strategic use of research findings. Today, however, many marketing researchers work hand-in-hand with marketing managers throughout the research process and have responsibility for making strategic recommendations based on the research.

THE MARKETING RESEARCH PROCESS

Marketing research can be viewed as systematic processes for obtaining information to aid in decision making. There are many types of marketing research, and the framework illustrated in Figure 2.1 represents a general approach to the process. Each element of this process is discussed next.

Purpose of the Research

The first step in the research process is to determine explicitly why the research is needed and what it is to accomplish. This may be much more difficult than it sounds. Quite often a situation or problem is recognized as needing research, yet the nature of the problem is not clear or well defined nor is the appropriate type of research evident. Thus, managers and researchers need to discuss and clarify the current situation and develop a clear understanding of the problem. At the end of this stage, managers and researchers should agree on (1) the current situation involving the problem to be researched, (2) the nature of the problem, and (3) the specific question or questions the research is designed to investigate. This step is crucial since it influences the type of research to be conducted and the research design.

FIGURE 2.1
The Five Ps of the
Research Process

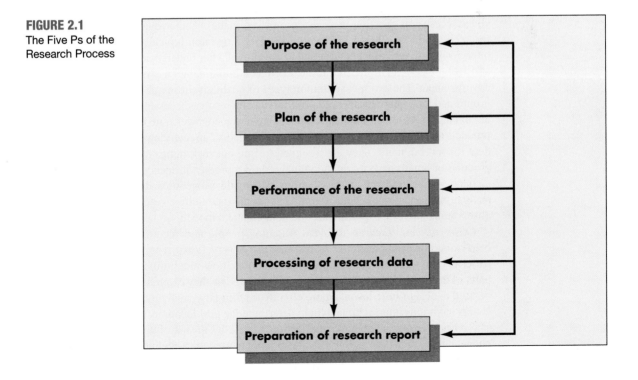

Plan of the Research

Once the specific research question or questions have been agreed on, a research plan can be developed. A research plan spells out the nature of the research to be conducted and includes an explanation of such things as the sample design, measures, and analysis techniques to be used. Three critical issues that influence the research plan are (1) whether primary or secondary data are needed, (2) whether qualitative or quantitative research is needed, and (3) whether the company will do its own research or contract with a marketing research specialist.

Primary versus Secondary Data

Given the information needed and budget constraints, a decision must be made as to whether primary data, secondary data, or some combination of the two is needed. *Primary data* are data collected specifically for the research problem under investigation; *secondary data* are those that have previously been collected for other purposes but can be used for the problem at hand. For example, if a company wanted to know why users of a competitive brand didn't prefer its brand, it may have to collect primary data to find out. On the other hand, if a company wanted to know the population size of key global markets that it might enter, it could find this information from secondary sources. Secondary information has the advantage of usually being cheaper than primary data, although it is not always available for strategy-specific research questions.

There are many sources of secondary data useful for marketing research. Syndicated data providers sell a variety of useful data to companies. Figure 2.2 lists a number of data providers and the type of information they can provide. Government sources, such as the *Statistical Abstracts of the United States* or the *Survey of Current Business,* can provide insights into the economy and industries within it. Trade groups such as the American Medical Association or the National Association of Retail Dealers of America can also be contacted for information relevant to their industries.[2]

Qualitative versus Quantitative Research

Given a research question, a decision must be made whether qualitative or quantitative research would be a better approach. Qualitative research typically involves face-to-face interviews with respondents designed to develop a better understanding of what they think and feel concerning a research topic, such as a brand name, a product, a package, or an advertisement. The two most common types of qualitative research in marketing are focus groups and long interviews. *Focus groups* typically involve discussions among a small number of consumers led by an interviewer and are designed to generate insights and ideas about products and brands. *Long interviews* are conducted by an interviewer with a single respondent for several hours. They are designed to find out such things as the meanings various products or brands have for an individual or how a product influences a person's life.

Quantitative research involves more systematic procedures designed to obtain and analyze numerical data. Four common types of quantitative research in marketing are observation, surveys, experiments, and mathematical modeling.

Observational research involves watching people and recording relevant facts and behaviors. For example, retail stores may use observational research to determine what patterns customers use in walking through stores, how much time they spend in various parts of the store, and how many items of merchandise they examine. This information can be used to design store layouts more effectively. Similarly, many retail marketers do traffic counts at various intersections to help determine the best locations for stores.

Survey research involves the collection of data by means of a questionnaire by mail, phone, online, or in person. Surveys are commonly used in marketing research to investigate

FIGURE 2.2   Some Syndicated Data Providers

Company	Syndicated Service	What it Measures
ACNielsen www.acnielsen.com	Scantrack	Provides sales tracking across grocery, drug, and mass merchandisers.
	Homescan	Provides consumer panel service for tracking retail purchases and motivations.
Yahoo! and ACNielsen www.yahoo.com	Internet Confidence Index	Measures (quarterly) the confidence levels in Internet products and services.
Scarborough Research (a service of Arbitron, Inc., and VNU) www.scarborough.com		Provides a syndicated study to print and electronic media, new media companies, outdoor media, sports teams and leagues, agencies, advertisers, and Yellow Pages on local, regional, and national levels—including local market shopping patterns, demographics, media usage, and lifestyle activities.
Millward Brown www.millwardbrown.com	IntelliQuest www.intelliquest.com	Provides studies enabling clients to understand and improve the position of their technology, brands, products, media, or channels.
Information Resources www.infores.com	BehaviourScan	Collects store tracking data used with consumer panel data to track advertising influence in consumer packaged goods.
Nielsen Media Research www.nielsenmedia.com	National People Meter	Provides audience estimates for all national program sources, including broadcast networks, cable networks, Spanish-language networks, and national syndicators.
NOP World www.nopworld.com	Starch Ad Readership Studies	Provides raw readership scores collected via individual depth interview; records the percent of readers who saw the ad and read the copy. The ad is ranked not only against other ads in the issue but also against other ads in its product category over the last two years.
CSA TMO www.csa-fr.com	OPERBAC	Provides continuous tracking of banking insurance and credit purchases in European markets.
DoubleClick www.doubleclick.com	Diameter	Provides online audience measurement services for Web publishers, advertisers, and agencies.
Nielsen//NetRatings www.nielsen-netratings.com		Measures audience data using actual click-by-click Internet user behavior measured through a comprehensive real-time meter installed on individual computers worldwide (home and work).
Taylor Nelson Sofres Intersearch www.tns-i.com	Global eCommerce	Measures e-commerce activity in 27 countries, providing insights into 37 marketplaces via interviews.
J.D. Power Associates www.jdpower.com	PowerReport, PowerGram, etc.	Publishes in-depth analytical reports on automotive travel, health, and other industries.
MediaMark www.mediamark.com		Supplies multimedia audience research to magazines, television, radio, Internet and other media, leading national advertisers, and over 450 advertising agencies, including 90 of 100 agencies in the U.S.
Simmons (SMRB) www.smrb.com	National	Provides telephone research that covers important markets critical to advertisers—agencies, and media.

Source: Donald R. Cooper and Pamela S. Schindler, *Marketing Research* (Burr Ridge, IL: McGraw-Hill/Irwin, 2006), p. 43.

Qualitative research is commonly used for

- Identifying a business problem or opportunity situation, or establishing information requirements.
- Obtaining preliminary insights into the motivation, emotional, attitudinal, and personality factors that influence marketplace behaviors.
- Building theories and models to explain marketplace behaviors or relationships between two or more marketing variables.
- Developing valid scales for investigating specific market factors, consumer qualities (e.g., attitudes, emotional feelings, preferences, beliefs, perceptions), and behavioral outcomes.
- Determining the preliminary effectiveness of marketing strategies on actual marketplace behaviors.
- Developing new products and services, or repositioning current product or service images.

Quantitative research is commonly used for

- Validating or answering a business problem or information requirements.
- Obtaining detailed descriptions or insights into the motivation, emotional, attitudinal, and personality factors that influence marketplace behaviors.
- Testing theories and models to explain marketplace behaviors or relationships between two or more marketing variables.
- Assessing the reliability and validity of scales for investigating market factors, consumer qualities (e.g., attitudes, emotional feelings, preferences, beliefs, perceptions) and behavioral outcomes.
- Assessing the effectiveness of marketing strategies on marketplace behaviors.
- Examining new-product/service development or repositioning current products or service images.
- Segmenting and/or comparing large or small differences in markets, new products, services, or evaluation and repositioning of current products or service images.

Sources: Joseph F. Hair, Jr., Robert P. Bush, and David J. Ortinau, *Marketing Research.* 4th ed. (Burr Ridge IL: McGraw-Hill/Irwin, 2009), pp.154–155.

customer beliefs, attitudes, satisfaction, and many other issues. Mail surveys are useful for reaching widely dispersed markets but take more time to get responses than telephone surveys; personal surveys involving structured questions are useful but expensive.

Experimental research involves manipulating one variable and examining its impact on other variables. For example, the price of a product could be changed in one test store, while left the same in other stores. Comparing sales in the test store with those in other stores can provide evidence about the likely impact of a price change in the overall market. Experiments are useful for getting a better idea of the causal relationships among variables, but they are often difficult to design and administer effectively in natural settings. Thus, many marketing research experiments are conducted in laboratories or simulated stores to carefully control other variables that could impact results.

Mathematical modeling often involves secondary data, such as scanner data collected and stored in computer files from retail checkout counters. This approach involves the development of equations to model relationships among variables and uses econometric and statistical techniques to investigate the impact of various strategies and tactics on sales and brand choices. Math modeling is useful because it provides an efficient way to study problems with extremely large secondary data sets.

FIGURE 2.3   A Comparison of Data Collection Methods Used in Marketing Research

Method	Advantages	Disadvantages
Focus groups	• Depth of information collected. • Flexibility in use. • Relatively low cost. • Data collected quickly.	• Requires expert moderator. • Questions of group size and acquaintanceships of participants. • Potential for bias from moderator. • Small sample size.
Telephone surveys	• Centralized control of data collection. • More cost-effective than personal interviews. • Data collected quickly.	• Resistance in collecting income, financial data. • Limited depth of response. • Disproportionate coverage of low-income segments. • Abuse of phone by solicitors. • Perceived intrusiveness.
Mail surveys	• Cost-effective per completed response. • Broad geographic dispersion. • Ease of administration. • Data collected quickly.	• Refusal and contact problems with certain segments. • Limited depth of response. • Difficult to estimate nonresponse biases. • Resistance and bias in collecting income, financial data. • Lack of control following mailing.
Personal (in-depth) interviews	• More depth of response than telephone interviews. • Generate substantial number of ideas compared with group methods.	• Easy to transmit biasing cues. • Not-at-homes. • Broad coverage often infeasible. • Cost per contact high. • Data collection time may be excessive.
Mall intercepts	• Flexibility in collecting data, answering questions, probing respondents. • Data collected quickly. • Excellent for concept tests, copy evaluations, other visuals. • Fairly high response rates.	• Limited time. • Sample composition or representativeness is suspect. • Costs depend on incidence rates. • Interviewer supervision difficult.
Internet surveys	• Inexpensive, quickly executed. • Visual stimuli can be evaluated. • Real-time data processing possible. • Can be answered at convenience of respondent.	• Responses must be checked for duplication, bogus responses. • Respondent self-selection bias. • Limited ability to qualify respondents and confirm responses. • Difficulty in generating sample frames for probability sampling.
Projective techniques	• Useful in word association tests of new brand names. • Less threatening to respondents for sensitive topics. • Can identify important motives underlying choices.	• Require trained interviewers. • Cost per interview high.
Observation	• Can collect sensitive data. • Accuracy of measuring overt behaviors. • Different perspective than survey self-reports. • Useful in studies of cross-cultural differences.	• Appropriate only for frequently occurring behaviors. • Unable to assess opinions of attitudes causing behaviors. • May be expensive in data-collection-time costs.

Source: William O. Bearden, Thomas N. Ingram, and Raymond W. LaForge, *Marketing,* 5th ed. (Burr Ridge, IL: McGraw-Hill/Irwin, 2007), p. 134.

Which of these types of research is best for particular research questions requires considerable knowledge of each of them. Often, qualitative research is used in early stages of investigating a topic to get more information and insight about it. Then, quantitative approaches are used to investigate the degree to which the insights hold across a larger sample or population. Figure 2.3 provides a comparison of a variety of qualitative and quantitative data collection methods.

A. Planning

1. Segmentation: What kinds of people buy our products? Where do they live? How much do they earn? How many of them are there?
2. Demand estimation: Are the markets for our products increasing or decreasing? Are there promising markets that we have not yet reached?
3. Environmental assessment: Are the channels of distribution for our products changing? What should our presence on the Internet be?

B. Problem Solving

1. Product
   a. In testing new products and product-line extensions, which product design is likely to be the most successful? What features do consumers value most?
   b. What kind of packaging should we use?
   c. What are the forecasts for the product? How might we reenergize its life cycle?
2. Price
   a. What price should we charge for our products?
   b. How sensitive to price changes are our target segments?
   c. Given the lifetime value assessments of our segments, should we be discounting or charging a premium to our most valued customers?
   d. As production costs decline, should we lower our prices or try to develop higher-quality products?
   e. Do consumers use price as a cue to value or a cue to quality in our industry?
3. Place
   a. Where, and by whom, are our products being sold? Where, and by whom, should our products be sold?
   b. What kinds of incentives should we offer the trade to push our products?
   c. Are our relationships with our suppliers and distributors satisfactory and cooperative?
4. Promotion
   a. How much should we spend on promotion? How should it be allocated to products and to geographic areas?
   b. Which ad copy should we run in our markets? With what frequency and media expenditures?
   c. What combination of media—newspapers, radio, television, magazines, Internet ad banners—should we use?
   d. What is our consumer coupon redemption rate?

C. Control

1. What is our market share overall? In each geographic area? By each customer type?
2. Are customers satisfied with our products? How is our record for service? Are there many returns? Do levels of customer satisfaction vary with market? With segment?
3. Are our employees satisfied? Do they feel well trained and empowered to assist our customers?
4. How does the public perceive our company? What is our reputation with the trade?

Source: Dawn Iacobucci, and Gilbert A. Churchill, Jr. *Marketing Research: Methodological Foundations,* 10th ed. (Mason, OH: Thomson South-Western, 2010), p. 6.

Company versus Contract Research

Most large consumer goods companies have marketing research departments that can perform a variety of types of research. In addition many marketing research firms, advertising agencies, and consulting companies do marketing research on a contract basis. Some marketing research suppliers have special expertise in a particular type of research that makes them a better choice than doing the research internally. A decision about

Traditional marketing research typically involves identifying possible drivers and then collecting data: Increasing couponing (the driver) during spring will increase trial by first-time buyers (the result). Marketing researchers then try to collect information to attempt to verify the truth of the relationship.

In contrast, **data mining** is the extraction of hidden predictive information from large databases. The focus is on finding statistical links about consumer purchasing patterns that suggest marketing actions.

Some of these purchase patterns are common sense: You may not need a computer to suspect that peanut butter and grape jelly purchases are linked and that it might be a good idea sometime to run a joint promotion between Skippy peanut butter and Welch's grape jelly. But would you have expected that men buying diapers in the evening sometimes buy a six-pack of beer as well? This is exactly what supermarkets discovered when they mined checkout data from scanners. So they placed diapers and beer near each other, then placed potato chips between them—and increased sales on all three items! On the near horizon: radio-frequency identification (RFID) technology using a "smart tag" microchip on the diapers and beer to tell whether they wind up in the same shopping bag—at 10 in the evening.

Still, the success in data mining ultimately depends on humans—the judgments of the marketing managers and researchers in how to select, analyze, and interpret the information.

Source: Roger A. Kerin, Steven W. Hartley, and William Rudelius, *Marketing,* 10th ed. (Burr Ridge, IL: McGraw-Hill/Irwin, 2011), pp. 210–211.

whether the marketing research department has the ability to do a particular type of research itself or whether all or part of the research should be contracted with a research supplier must be made. In either case, schedules for task completion, the exact responsibilities of all involved parties, and cost need to be considered.

Performance of the Research

Performance of the research involves preparing for data collection and actually collecting them. The tasks at this stage obviously depend on the type of research that has been selected and the type of data needed. If secondary data are to be used, they must be located, prepared for analysis, and possibly paid for. If primary data are to be collected, then observational forms, questionnaires, or other types of measures must be designed, pretested, and validated. Samples must be drawn and interviews must be scheduled or preparations must be made for mailing or phoning selected individuals.

In terms of actual data collection, a cardinal rule is to obtain and record the maximal amount of useful information, subject to the constraints of time, money, and respondent privacy. Failure to obtain and record data clearly can obviously lead to a poor research study, while failure to consider the rights of respondents raises both practical and ethical problems. Thus, both the objectives and constraints of data collection must be closely monitored.

Processing of Research Data

Processing research data includes the preparation of data for analysis and the actual analysis of them. Preparations include such things as editing and structuring data and coding them for analysis. Data sets should be clearly labeled to ensure they are not misinterpreted or misplaced.

The appropriate analysis techniques for collected data depend on the nature of the research question and the design of the research. Qualitative research data consist of interview records that are content analyzed for ideas or themes. Quantitative research data may be analyzed in a variety of ways depending on the objectives of the research.

A critical part of this stage is interpreting and assessing the research results. Seldom, if ever, do marketing research studies obtain findings that are totally unambiguous. Usually, relationships among variables or differences between groups are small to moderate, and judgment and insight are needed to draw appropriate inferences and conclusions. Marketing researchers should always double-check their analysis and avoid overstating the strength of their findings. The implications for developing or changing a marketing strategy should be carefully thought out and tempered with judgment about the overall quality of the study.

Preparation of the Research Report

The research report is a complete statement of everything done in a research project and includes a write-up of each of the previous stages as well as the strategic recommendations from the research. The limitations of the research should be carefully noted. Figure 2.4 illustrates the types of questions marketing researchers and managers should discuss prior to submitting the final research report.

Research reports should be clear and unambiguous with respect to what was done and what recommendations are made. Often research reports must trade off the apparent precision of scientific jargon for everyday language that managers can understand. Researchers should work closely with managers to ensure that the study and its limitations are fully understood.

Limitations of the Research Process

Although the foregoing discussion presented the research process as a set of simple stages, this does not mean that conducting quality marketing research is a simple task. Many problems and difficulties must be overcome if a research study is to provide valuable information for decision making.[3] For example, consider the difficulties in one type of marketing research, *test marketing.*

The major goal of most test marketing is to measure new product sales on a limited basis where competitive retaliation and other factors are allowed to operate freely. In this way, future sales potential can often be estimated reasonably well. Listed below are a number of problems that could invalidate test marketing study results.

1. Test market areas are not representative of the market in general in terms of population characteristics, competition, and distribution outlets.
2. Sample size and design are incorrectly formulated because of budget constraints.
3. Pretest measurements of competitive brand sales are not made or are inaccurate, limiting the meaningfulness of market share estimates.
4. Test stores do not give complete support to the study such that certain package sizes may not be carried or prices may not be held constant during the test period.

FIGURE 2.4
Eight Criteria for Evaluating Marketing Research Reports

1. Was the type of research appropriate for the research questions?
2. Was the research well designed?
   a. Was the sample studied appropriate for the research questions?
   b. Were measures well developed, pretested, and validated?
   c. Were the data analysis techniques the best ones for the study?
3. Was there adequate supervision of data collection, editing, and coding?
4. Was the analysis conducted according to standards accepted in the field?
5. Do the findings make sense, given the research question and design, and were they considered in light of previous knowledge and experience?
6. Are the limitations of the study recognized and explained in detail?
7. Are the conclusions appropriately drawn or are they over- or understated?
8. Are the recommendations for marketing strategy clear and appropriate?

Marketing researchers have ethical responsibilities to the respondents who provide primary data, clients for whom they work, and subordinates who work under them. Below are a number of ethical responsibilities to these groups.

RESPONSIBILITIES TO RESPONDENTS

1. *Preserving respondent anonymity.* Marketing researchers should ensure that respondents' identities are safe from invasion of privacy.
2. *Avoiding mental stress for respondents.* Marketing researchers should minimize the mental stress placed on respondents.
3. *Avoiding questions detrimental to respondents.* Marketing researchers should avoid asking questions for which the answers conflict with the self-interest of the respondents.
4. *Avoiding the use of dangerous equipment or techniques.* Physical or reputational harm to respondents based on their participation in marketing research should not occur. Respondents should be informed of any other than minimal risks involved in the research and be free to self-determine their participation.
5. *Avoiding deception of respondents.* Respondents should not be deceived about the purpose of the study in most cases. Many consider deception acceptable in research where it is needed to obtain valid results, there is minimal risk to respondents, and respondents are debriefed explaining the real purpose of the study.
6. *Avoiding coercion of respondents.* Marketing researchers should avoid coercing or harassing people to try to get them to agree to be interviewed or fill out questionnaires.

RESPONSIBILITIES TO CLIENTS

1. *Providing confidentiality.* Marketing researchers are obliged not to reveal information about a client to competitors and should carefully consider when a company should be identified as a client.
2. *Providing technical integrity.* Marketing researchers are obliged to design efficient studies without undue expense or complexity and accurately report results.
3. *Providing administrative integrity.* Marketing researchers are obliged to price their work fairly without hidden charges.
4. *Providing guidance on research usage.* Marketing researchers are obliged to promote the correct usage of research and to prevent the misuse of findings.

RESPONSIBILITIES TO SUBORDINATE EMPLOYEES

1. *Creating an ethical work environment.* Marketing research managers are obliged to create an ethical work environment where unethical behavior is not encouraged or overlooked.
2. *Avoiding opportunities for unethical behavior.* Marketing research managers are obliged to avoid placing subordinates in situations where unethical behavior could be concealed but rewarded.

5. Test-market products are advertised or promoted beyond a profitable level for the market in general.
6. The effects of factors that influence sales, such as the sales force, season, weather conditions, competitive retaliation, shelf space, and so forth, are ignored in the research.
7. The test-market period is too short to determine whether the product will be repurchased by customers.

A list of such problems could be developed for any type of marketing research. However, careful research planning, coordination, implementation, and control can help reduce such problems and increase the value of research for decision making.

MARKETING INFORMATION SYSTEMS

Most marketers use computer-based systems to help them gather, sort, store, and distribute information for marketing decisions.[4] A popular form of marketing information system is the marketing decision support system, which is a coordinated collection of data, tools, and techniques involving both computer hardware and software by which marketers gather and interpret relevant information for decision making. These systems require three types of software:

1. Database management software for sorting and retrieving data from internal and external sources.

FIGURE 2.5   Some Information Sources for Marketing Information Systems

Selected Government Sources

American Factfinder	http://factfinder.census.gov/
Economics Statistics Briefing Room	http://www.whitehouse.gov/fsbr/esbr.html
EDGAR Database of Corporate Information (SEC filings)	http://www.sec.gov/edgar.shtml
FedStats	http://www.fedstats.gov/
GPO Access	http://www.gpoaccess.gov/
Stat-USA	http://www.stat-usa.gov/
U.S. Bureau of Labor Statistics	http://www.bls.gov/
U.S. Bureau of the Census	http://www.census.gov/
U.S. Department of Commerce	http://www.commerce.gov/
U.S. Small Business Administration	http://www.sbaonline.sba.gov/
U.S. Patent and Trademark Office	http://www.uspto.gov/
CBDNet (Commerce Business Daily)—government procurement, sales, and contract awards	http://www.cbdnet.access.gpo.gov

Selected Proprietary Sources (with some free information)

Gallup Poll	http://www.gallup.com/poll/
Harris Poll	http://www.harrisinteractive.com/harris_poll/
The Polling Report	http://www.pollingreport.com/
Public Opinion	http://europa.eu.int/comm./public_opinion/
Public Agenda	http://www.publicagenda.org/
Roper Center for Public Opinion Research	http://www.repercenter.uconn.edu
Poll Question Database	http://www.irss.unc.edu/data_archive/pollsearch.html
Forrester Research Reports	http://forrester.com
Roper Reports	http://www.nopworld.com
JD Power Satisfaction Studies	http://www.jdpower.com
Quirk's Marketing Research Review	http://www.quirks.com
Ad Forum	http://www.adforum.com
BizMiner	http://www.bizminer.com

Selected Nonproprietary Sources

Ad* Access	http://scriptorium.lib.duke.edu/adaccess/
Advertising World (ad industry portal)	http://advertising.utexas.edu/world
American Demographics	http://www.demographics.com
Competia Express (industry portal)	http://www.competia.com/express/
Global Edge	http://www.demographics.com
Kerlins.net Qualitative Research Bibliography	http://kerlins.net/bobbi/research/qualresearch/bibliography/
KnowThis.com Marketing Virtual Library	http://knowthis.com
Marketing and Research Library	http://www.mrlibrary.com/
MarketingPower.com	http://ma rketingpower.com

Source: Donald R. Cooper and Pamela S. Schindler, *Marketing Research* (Burr Ridge, IL: McGraw-Hill/Irwin, 2006), pp. 122–123.

2. Model base management software that contains routines for manipulating data in ways that are useful for marketing decision making.

3. A dialog system that permits marketers to explore databases and use models to produce information to address their decision-making needs.

Marketing decision support systems are designed to handle information from both internal and external sources. Internal information includes such things as sales records, which can be divided by territory, package size, brand, price, order size, or salesperson; inventory data that can indicate how rapidly various products are selling; or expenditure data on such things as advertising, personal selling, or packaging. Internal information is particularly important for investigating the efficiency and effectiveness of various marketing strategies.

External information is gathered from outside the organization and concerns changes in the environment that could influence marketing strategies. External information is needed concerning changes in global economies and societies, competitors, customers, and technology. Figure 2.5 lists a sample of sources of external information that could be monitored by a marketing information system to help marketers make better decisions. Of course, information from marketing research studies conducted by an organization is also put into marketing information systems to improve marketing strategy development.

SUMMARY

This chapter emphasized the importance of marketing research for making sound marketing strategy decisions. The chapter discussed marketing research as a process involving several stages, which include determining the purpose of the research, designing the plan for the research, performing the research, processing the research data, and preparing the research report. Then, marketing information systems were discussed and one type, the marketing decision support system, was explained. Such systems should provide decision makers with the right information, at the right time in the right way, to make sound marketing decisions.

Additional Resources

Churchill, Gilbert A., Jr.; Tom J. Brown; and Tracy A. Suter. *Basic Marketing Research*. 7th ed. Mason, OH: Thomson South-Western, 2010.

Cooper, Donald R., and Pamela S. Schindler. *Marketing Research*. Burr Ridge, IL: McGraw-Hill/Irwin, 2006.

Hair, Joseph F., Jr.; Robert P. Bush; and David J. Ortinau. *Marketing Research*. 4th ed. Burr Ridge, IL: McGraw-Hill/Irwin, 2009.

Iacobucci Dawn, and Gilbert A. Churchill, Jr. *Marketing Research: Methodological Foundations*. 10th ed. Mason, OH: Thomson South-Western, 2010.

Molhatra, Naresh K. *Marketing Research*. 6th ed. Upper Saddle River, NJ: Pearson Education, 2010.

Zikmund William G., and Barry J. Babin. *Exploring Marketing Research*. 10th ed. Mason, OH: Thomson South-Western, 2010.

Zikmund William G., and Barry J. Babin. *Essentials of Marketing Research*. 4th ed. Mason, OH: Thomson South-Western, 2010.

Key Terms and Concepts

Experimental research: Experimental research involves manipulating one variable and examining its impact on other variables.

Focus groups: A type of qualitative research that typically involves discussions among a small number of consumers led by an interviewer and designed to generate insights and ideas about products and brands.

Long interviews: A type of qualitative research conducted by an interviewer with a single respondent for several hours and designed to find out such things as the meanings various products and brands have for the person or how a product influences the person's life.

Marketing research: Marketing research is the process by which information about the environment is generated, analyzed, and interpreted for use in marketing decision making. Most often consumers or organizational buyers are the subject of the research.

Mathematical modeling: Mathematical modeling involves developing equations to model relationships among variables to investigate the impact of various strategies and tactics on sales and brand choices.

Observational research: Observational research involves watching people and recording relevant facts and behaviors.

Primary data: Primary data are data collected specifically for the research problem under investigation.

Qualitative research: Qualitative research typically involves face-to-face interviews with respondents designed to develop a better understanding of what they think and feel concerning a research topic, such as a brand name, a product, a package, or an advertisement.

Quantitative research: Quantitative research involves systematic procedures designed to obtain and analyze numerical data.

Secondary data: Secondary data are those that have previously been collected for other purposes but can be used for the problem at hand.

Survey research: Survey research involves the collection of data bv means of a questionnaire either by mail, phone, online, or in person.

Test marketing: The major goal of most test marketing is to measure new product sales on a limited basis where competitive retaliation and other factors are allowed to operate freely. In this way, future sales potential can often be estimated reasonably well.

Chapter 3

Consumer Behavior

The marketing concept emphasizes that profitable marketing begins with the discovery and understanding of consumer needs and then develops a marketing mix to satisfy these needs. Thus, an understanding of consumers and their needs and purchasing behavior is integral to successful marketing. Unfortunately, there is no single theory of consumer behavior that can totally explain why consumers behave as they do. Instead, there are numerous theories, models, and concepts making up the field. In addition, the majority of these notions have been borrowed from a variety of other disciplines, such as sociology, psychology, anthropology, and economics, and must be integrated to understand consumer behavior.

In this chapter, consumer behavior will be examined in terms of the model in Figure 3.1. The chapter begins by reviewing social, marketing, and situational influences on consumer decision making. These provide information that can influence consumers' thoughts and feelings about purchasing various products and brands. The degree to which this information influences consumers' decisions depends on a number of psychological influences. Two of the most important of these are product knowledge and product involvement, which will then be discussed. The chapter concludes by discussing the consumer decision-making process.

FIGURE 3.1 An Overview of the Buying Process

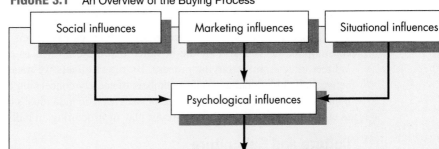

Value	General Features	Relevance to Marketing
Achievement and success activity	Hard work is good; success flows from hard work.	Acts as a justification for acquisition of goods ("You deserve it").
	Keeping busy is healthy and natural.	Stimulates interest in products that are time-savers and enhance leisure time.
Efficiency and practicality	Admiration of things that solve problems (e.g., save time and effort).	Stimulates purchase of products that function well and save time.
	People can improve themselves; tomorrow should be better than today.	Stimulates desire for new products that fulfill unsatisfied needs; ready acceptance of products that claim to be "new" or "improved."
Material comfort	"The good life."	Fosters acceptance of convenience and luxury products that make life more enjoyable.
Individualism	Being oneself (e.g., self-reliance, self-interest, self-esteem).	Stimulates acceptance of customized or unique products that enable a person to "express his or her own personality."
Freedom	Freedom of choice.	Fosters interest in wide product lines and differentiated products.
External conformity	Uniformity of observable behavior; desire for acceptance.	Stimulates interest in products that are used or owned by others in the same social group.
Humanitarianism	Caring for others, particularly the underdog.	Stimulates patronage of firms that compete with market leaders.
Youthfulness	A state of mind that stresses being "young at heart" and having a youthful appearance.	Stimulates acceptance of products that provide the illusion of maintaining or fostering youthfulness.
Fitness and health	Caring about one's body, including the desire to be physically fit and healthy.	Stimulates acceptance of food products, activities, and equipment perceived to maintain or increase physical fitness.

Source: Leon G. Schiffman and Leslie Lazar Kanuck, *Consumer Behavior,* 10th ed., p. 369, 2010. Reprinted by permission of Pearson Prentice Hall, Inc., Upper Saddle River, NJ.

SOCIAL INFLUENCES ON CONSUMER DECISION MAKING

Behavioral scientists have become increasingly aware of the powerful effects of the social environment and personal interactions on human behavior. In terms of consumer behavior, culture, social class, and reference group influences have been related to purchase and consumption decisions. It should be noted that these influences can have both direct and indirect effects on the buying process. By direct effects we mean direct communication between the individual and other members of society concerning a particular decision. By indirect effects we mean the influence of society on an individual's basic values and attitudes as well as the important role that groups play in structuring an individual's personality.

Culture and Subculture

Culture is one of the most basic influences on an individual's needs, wants, and behavior, since all facets of life are carried out against the background of the society in which an individual lives. Cultural antecedents affect everyday behavior, and there is empirical support for the notion that culture is a determinant of certain aspects of consumer behavior.

Cultural values are transmitted through three basic organizations: the family, religious organizations, and educational institutions; and in today's society, educational institutions are playing an increasingly greater role in this regard. Marketing managers should adapt the marketing mix to cultural values and constantly monitor value changes and differences in both domestic and global markets. To illustrate, one of the changing values in America is the increasing emphasis on achievement and career success. This change in values has been recognized by many business firms that have expanded their emphasis on time-saving, convenience-oriented products.

In large nations such as the United States, the population is bound to lose a significant amount of its homogeneity, and thus subcultures arise. In other words, there are subcultures in the American culture where people have more frequent interactions than with the population at large and thus tend to think and act alike in some respects. Subcultures are based on such things as geographic areas, religions, nationalities, ethnic groups, and age. Many subcultural barriers are decreasing because of mass communication, mass transit, and a decline in the influence of religious values. However, age groups, such as the teen market, baby boomers, and the mature market, have become increasingly important for marketing strategy. For example, since baby boomers (those born between 1946 and 1962) make up about a third of the U.S. population and soon will account for about half of discretionary spending, many marketers are repositioning products to serve them. Snickers candy bars, for instance, used to be promoted to children as a treat but are now promoted to adults as a wholesome between-meals snack.

Social Class

While many people like to think of America as a land of equality, a class structure can be observed. Social classes develop on the basis of such things as wealth, skill, and power. The single best indicator of social class is occupation. However, interest at this point is in the influence of social class on the individual's behavior. What is important here is that different social classes tend to have different attitudinal configurations and values that influence the behavior of individual members. For marketing purposes, four different social classes have been identified.[1]

Upper Americans comprise 14 percent of the population and are differentiated mainly by having high incomes. This class remains the group in which quality merchandise is most prized and prestige brands are commonly sought. Spending with good taste is a priority as are products such as theater; books; investments in art; European travel; household help; club memberships for tennis, golf, and swimming; and prestige schooling for children.

The *middle class* comprises 34 percent of the population, and these consumers want to do the right thing and buy what is popular. They are concerned with fashion and buying what experts in the media recommend. Increased earnings have led to spending on more "worthwhile experiences" for children, including winter ski trips, college education, and shopping for better brands of clothes at more expensive stores. Appearance of the home is important. This group emulates the upper Americans, which distinguishes it from the working class.

The *working class* comprises 38 percent of the population, people who are "family folk" who depend heavily on relatives for economic and emotional support. The emphasis on family ties is only one sign of how much more limited and different working-class horizons are socially, psychologically, and geographically compared to those of the middle class. For them, "keeping up with the times" focuses on the mechanical and recreational, and thus, ease of labor and leisure are what they continue to pursue.

Lower Americans comprise 16 percent of the population and are as diverse in values and consumption goals as are other social levels. Some members of this group are homeless and penniless although most work part-time or full-time jobs at low wages. Most receive public housing, food stamps, and Medicaid. The primary demands of this group are food, clothing, and other staples. Given that a number of people in this group have little education or resources, many people feel it is unethical to try to market alcoholic beverages or tobacco products to it.

For the marketing manager, social class offers some insights into consumer behavior and is potentially useful as a market segmentation variable. However, there is considerable controversy as to whether social class is superior to income for the purpose of market segmentation.

Reference Groups and Families

Groups that an individual looks to (uses as a reference) when forming attitudes and opinions are described as *reference groups*.[2] Primary reference groups include family and close friends, while secondary reference groups include fraternal organizations and professional associations. A buyer may also consult a single individual about decisions, and this individual would be considered a reference individual.

A person normally has several reference groups or reference individuals for various subjects or different decisions. For example, a woman may consult one reference group when she is purchasing a car and a different reference group for lingerie. In other words, the nature of the product and the role the individual is playing during the purchasing process influence which reference group will be consulted. Reference group influence is generally considered to be stronger for products that are "public" or conspicuous—that is, products that other people see the individual using, such as clothes or automobiles.

As noted, the family is generally recognized to be an important reference group, and it has been suggested that the household, rather than the individual, is the relevant unit for studying consumer behavior.[3] This is because within a household the purchaser of goods and services is not always the user of these goods and services. Thus, it is important for marketing managers to determine not only who makes the actual purchase but also who makes the decision to purchase. In addition, it has been recognized that the needs, income, assets, debts, and expenditure patterns change over the course of what is called the *family life cycle*. The family life cycle can be divided into a number of stages ranging from single, to married, to married with children of different age groups, to older couples, to solitary survivors. It may also include divorced people, both with and without children. Because the life cycle combines trends in earning power with demands placed on income, it is a useful way of classifying and segmenting individuals and families.[4]

MARKETING INFLUENCES ON CONSUMER DECISION MAKING

Marketing strategies are often designed to influence consumer decision making and lead to profitable exchanges. Each element of the marketing mix (product, price, promotion, place) can affect consumers in various ways.

Product Influences

Many attributes of a company's products, including brand name, quality, newness, and complexity, can affect consumer behavior. The physical appearance of the product, packaging, and labeling information can also influence whether consumers notice a product in-store, examine it, and purchase it. One of the key tasks of marketers is to differentiate their products from those of competitors and create consumer perceptions that the product is worth purchasing.

Price Influences

The price of products and services often influences whether consumers will purchase them at all and, if so, which competitive offering is selected. Stores, such as Walmart, which are perceived to charge the lowest prices, attract many consumers based on this fact alone. For some offerings, higher prices may not deter purchase because consumers believe that the products or services are higher quality or are more prestigious. However,

Marketers know that reference groups can influence both product and brand decisions. They also know that reference group influence varies depending on whether the good is used publicly (a car) or privately (a toothbrush) and whether it is a necessity (a mattress) or a luxury (a sailboat). By examining the nature of products and brands on these two dimensions, the matrix below can be constructed. Marketers could use this matrix to judge how reference group influence should be used in advertising and personal selling efforts. For example, public luxuries could benefit from ads showing owners being admired and complimented for their product and brand selection whereas ads for private necessities might focus more on superior functional performance.

	Necessity	Luxury

Public	**Public necessities**
	Reference group influence
	  Product: Weak
	  Brand: Strong
	Examples: Wristwatch, automobile, man's suit
		Public luxuries
		Reference group influence
		  Product: Strong
		  Brand: Strong
		Examples: Golf clubs, snow skis, sailboat, health club

Private	**Private necessities**
	Reference group influence
	  Product: Weak
	  Brand: Weak
	Examples: Mattress, floor lamp, refrigerator
		Private luxuries
		Reference group influence
		  Product: Strong
		  Brand: Weak
		Examples: Plasma TV, trash compactor, ice maker

Source: Adapted from William O. Bearden and Michael J. Etzel, "Reference Group Influences on Product and Brand Purchase Decisions," *Journal of Consumer Research,* September 1982, p. 185 as reported in J. Paul Peter and Jerry C. Olson, *Consumer Behavior and Marketing Strategy,* 9th ed. (Burr Ridge, IL: McGraw-Hill/Irwin, 2010), pp. 340–341.

many of today's value-conscious consumers may buy products more on the basis of price than other attributes.

Promotion Influences

Advertising, sales promotions, salespeople, and publicity can influence what consumers think about products, what emotions they experience in purchasing and using them, and what behaviors they perform, including shopping in particular stores and purchasing specific brands. Since consumers receive so much information from marketers and screen out a good deal of it, it is important for marketers to devise communications that (1) offer consistent messages about their products and (2) are placed in media that consumers in the target market are likely to use. Marketing communications play a critical role in informing consumers about products and services, including where they can be purchased, and in creating favorable images and perceptions.

Place Influences

The marketer's strategy for distributing products can influence consumers in several ways. First, products that are convenient to buy in a variety of stores increase the chances of consumers finding and buying them. When consumers are seeking low-involvement products, they are unlikely to engage in extensive search, so ready availability is important. Second, products sold in exclusive outlets such as Nordstrom may be perceived by consumers as having higher quality. In fact, one of the ways marketers create brand equity—that is, favorable

The recession starting in 2008 changed the behavior of consumers and marketers. According to a Gallup Poll, 55 percent of consumers said they cut household spending as a result of lower prices in the stock market and fears about the economy. They said they cut back on travel for the holidays (63 percent), eating out at restaurants (81 percent), entertainment such as going to the movies (72 percent), and household services such as housekeeping and lawn service (37 percent).

Consumers also sold old jewelry and ransacked closets to find "stuff" to put on eBay. According to eBay CEO John Donahoe, Americans typically have about $3,200 worth of goods at home they could sell to raise cash. Coupon usage to trim grocery costs also went up for the first time in 15 years. Rather than use credit cards, many consumers started saving money to buy something they wanted, and layaway plans in which consumers pay in advance for items weekly or monthly also made a comeback. eLayaway, a start-up that handles layaway programs for 1,000 retailers, had its customer base jump from 150 to 3,000 in the fall of the year.

The number of consumers who had both a full-time and a part-time job increased 11 percent over the previous year, according to the Bureau of Labor Statistics. Many of these consumers were trying to increase their income so they could save more to help make up some of the losses in their retirement accounts. Also, sales of Blu-ray high definition disks more than tripled during the year as consumers found watching them at home a lot cheaper than a night at the movies. Finally, 29 percent of consumers said they were buying more store and generic brands to save money.

So what did marketers do to try to keep merchandise moving and the economy from stalling? Most retailers put products on sale at deep discounts and many companies tried to promote the idea that their products provided value to consumers. For example, Procter & Gamble promoted its new Total Care versions of Tide detergent and Downy fabric softener as products that preserved the look of new clothes. In other words, the products would keep clothes looking new longer so consumers wouldn't have to buy clothes as often and could save money. Since consumers were eating more meals at home, Campbell and Kraft banded together to promote a low-cost classic meal: tomato soup and a grilled cheese sandwich. "Warm hearts without stretching budgets" read the copy in the ad that shows a package of Kraft Singles cheese slices and a can of Campbell's tomato soup. Kraft's DiGiorno pizza aired ads that stated that a home-delivered pizza cost twice as much as a DiGiorno.

Gillette ran a series of ads to justify the $20 to $25 price for eight Fusion Power razor blades arguing that "In the world of high performance, what machine can you run for as little as a dollar a week?" Kellogg cereals played up the idea that a bowl of cereal with milk was a meal that cost only 50 cents. It also snatched up paid search terms including "cereal," "breakfast," and "value," on portals such as Google.com to drive budget-conscious consumers to its Web site. When they click on the ad, consumers are linked to a site that plays up the "excellent economic value" of Kellogg's cereal and offers a dollar-off coupon to buy some. Velveeta cheese ads tell shoppers to "forget the cheddar, Velveeta is better," and claim that a package of Velveeta is "twice the size of cheddar, for the same price."

In sum, many consumers tried to find new ways to live within their means and still live comfortably during a difficult economic time. Many marketers tried to convince consumers that their products provided good value for the money, but in a way that did not detract from their high-quality image.

Sources: Jarne O'Donnell and Sandra Block, "Consumers Get Frugal, So Retailers Get Creative," *USA Today*, January 28, 2009, p.B1; Mindy Fetterman, "Americans Are Digging Deep to Save Money," *USA Today*, November 17, 2008, p. 1A+; Laura Petrecca, "Marketers Try to Promote Value Without Cheapening Image," *USA Today*, November 17, 2008, p.1B+.

consumer perceptions of brands—is by selling them in prestigious outlets. Third, offering products by nonstore methods, such as on the Internet or in catalogs, can create consumer perceptions that the products are innovative, exclusive, or tailored for specific target markets.

SITUATIONAL INFLUENCES ON CONSUMER DECISION MAKING

Situational influences can be defined as all the factors particular to a time and place that have a demonstrable and systematic effect on current behavior. In terms of purchasing situations, five groups of situational influences have been identified.[5] These influences may be perceived either consciously or subconsciously and may have considerable effect on product and brand choice.

1. *Physical features* are the most readily apparent features of a situation. These features include geographical and institutional location, decor, sounds, aromas, lighting, weather, and visible configurations of merchandise or other materials.

2. *Social features* provide additional depth to a description of a situation. These include other persons present, their characteristics, their apparent roles and interpersonal interactions.

3. *Time* is a dimension of situations that may be specified in units ranging from time of day to season of the year. Time also may be measured relative to some past or future event for the situational participant. This allows such conceptions as time since last purchase, time since or until meals or paydays, and time constraints imposed by prior or standing commitments.

4. *Task features* of a situation include an intent or requirement to select, shop for, or obtain information about a general or specific purchase. In addition, task may reflect different buyer and user roles anticipated by the individual. For instance, a person shopping for a small appliance as a wedding gift for a friend is in a different situation than when shopping for a small appliance for personal use.

5. *Current conditions* make up a final feature that characterizes a situation. These are momentary moods (such as acute anxiety, pleasantness, hostility, and excitation) or momentary conditions (such as cash on hand, fatigue, and illness) rather than chronic individual traits. These conditions are considered to be immediately antecedent to the current situation to distinguish the states the individual brings to the situation from states of the individual resulting from the situation. For instance, people may select a certain motion picture because they feel depressed (an antecedent state and a part of the choice situation), but the fact that the movie causes them to feel happier is a response to the consumption situation. This altered state then may become antecedent for behavior in the next choice situation encountered, such as passing a street vendor on the way out of the theater.

PSYCHOLOGICAL INFLUENCES ON CONSUMER DECISION MAKING

Information from group, marketing, and situational influences affects what consumers think and feel about particular products and brands. However, a number of psychological factors influence how this information is interpreted and used and how it impacts the consumer decision-making process. Two of the most important psychological factors are product knowledge and product involvement.[6]

Product Knowledge

Product knowledge refers to the amount of information a consumer has stored in her or his memory about particular product classes, product forms, brands, models, and ways to purchase them. For example, a consumer may know a lot about coffee (product class), ground versus instant coffee (product form), Folgers versus Maxwell House (brand), and various package sizes (models) and stores that sell it (ways to purchase).

Group, marketing, and situational influences determine the initial level of product knowledge as well as changes in it. For example, a consumer may hear about a new Starbucks opening up from a friend (group influence), see an ad for it in the newspaper (marketing influence), or see the coffee shop on the way to work (situational influence). Any of these increase the amount of product knowledge, in this case, a new source for purchasing the product.

The initial level of product knowledge may influence how much information is sought when deciding to make a purchase. For example, if a consumer already believes that Folgers is the best-tasting coffee, knows where to buy it, and knows how much it costs, little additional information may be sought.

Finally, product knowledge influences how quickly a consumer goes through the decision-making process. For example, when purchasing a new product for which the consumer has little product knowledge, extensive information may be sought and more time may be devoted to the decision.

Product Involvement

Product involvement refers to a consumer's perception of the importance or personal relevance of an item. For example, Harley-Davidson motorcycle owners are generally highly involved in the purchase and use of the product, brand, and accessories. However, a consumer buying a new toothbrush would likely view this as a low-involvement purchase.

Product involvement influences consumer decision making in two ways. First, if the purchase is for a high-involvement product, consumers are likely to develop a high degree of product knowledge so that they can be confident that the item they purchase is just right for them. Second, a high degree of product involvement encourages extensive decision making by consumers, which likely increases the time it takes to go through the decision-making process.

CONSUMER DECISION MAKING

The process by which consumers make decisions to purchase various products and brands is shown in Figure 3.2. In general, consumers recognize a need for a product, search for information about alternatives to meet the need, evaluate the information, make purchases, and evaluate the decision after the purchase. There are three types of decision making, which vary in terms of how complex or expensive a product is and how involved a consumer is in purchasing it.

Extensive decision making requires the most time and effort since the purchase typically involves a highly complex or expensive product that is important to the consumer. For example, the purchase of a car, house, or computer often involves considerable time and effort comparing alternatives and deciding on the right one. In terms of the number of purchases a consumer makes, extensive decision making is relatively rare, but it is critical for marketers of highly complex or expensive products to understand that consumers are willing to process considerable information to make the best choice. Thus, marketers should provide consumers with factual information that highlights competitive advantages for such high-involvement products.

Limited decision making is more moderate but still involves some time and effort searching for and comparing alternatives. For example, when buying shirts or shorts, consumers may shop several stores and compare a number of different brands and styles.

FIGURE 3.2 The Consumer Decision-Making Process

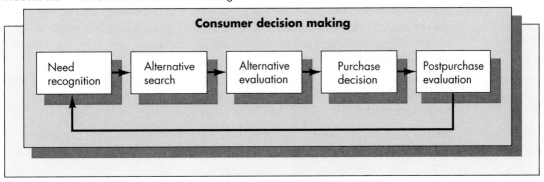

Marketers of products for which consumers usually do limited decision making often use eye-catching advertising and in-store displays to make consumers aware of their products and encourage consumers to consider buying them.

Routine decision making is the most common type and the way consumers purchase most packaged goods. Such products are simple, inexpensive, and familiar; and consumers often have developed favorite brands that they purchase without much deliberation. For example, consumers often make habitual purchases of soft drinks, candy bars, or canned soup without carefully comparing the relative merits of different brands. Marketers of such products need to have them readily available for purchase in a variety of outlets and price them competitively if price is an important criterion to consumers. Marketers of these low-involvement products often use celebrity spokespeople and other non-product-related cues to encourage purchases.

Need Recognition

The starting point in the buying process is the consumer's recognition of an unsatisfied need. Any number of either internal or external stimuli may activate needs or wants and recognition of them. Internal stimuli are such things as feeling hungry and wanting some food, feeling a headache coming on and wanting some Excedrin, or feeling bored and looking for a movie to go to. External stimuli are such things as seeing a McDonald's sign and then feeling hungry or seeing a sale sign for winter parkas and remembering that last year's coat is worn out.

It is the task of marketing managers to find out what needs and wants a particular product can and does satisfy and what unsatisfied needs and wants consumers have for which a new product could be developed. In order to do so, marketing managers should understand what types of needs consumers may have. A well-known classification of needs was developed many years ago by Abraham Maslow and includes five types.[7] Maslow's view is that lower-level needs, starting with physiological and safety needs, must be attended to before higher-level needs can be satisfied. Maslow's hierarchy is described below.

Physiological needs. This category consists of the primary needs of the human body, such as food, water, and sex. Physiological needs will dominate when all needs are unsatisfied. In such a case, none of the other needs will serve as a basis for motivation.

Safety needs. With the physiological needs met, the next higher level assumes importance. Safety needs consist of such things as protection from physical harm, ill health, and economic disaster and avoidance of the unexpected.

Belongingness and love needs. These needs are related to the social and gregarious nature of humans and the need for companionship. This level in the hierarchy is the point of departure from the physical or quasi-physical needs of the two previous levels. Nonsatisfaction of this level of need may affect the mental health of the individual.

Esteem needs. These needs consist of both the need for awareness of importance to others (self-esteem) and actual esteem from others. Satisfaction of these needs leads to feelings of self-confidence and prestige.

Self-actualization needs. These can be defined as the desire to become everything one is capable of becoming. This means that the individual will fully realize her or his talents and capabilities.

Maslow assumed that satisfaction of these needs is only possible after the satisfaction of all the needs lower in the hierarchy. While the hierarchical arrangement of Maslow presents a convenient explanation, it is probably more realistic to assume that the various need categories overlap. Thus, in affluent societies, many products may satisfy more than one of these needs. For example, gourmet foods may satisfy both the basic physiological need of hunger as well as esteem and status needs for those who serve gourmet foods to their guests.

Alternative Search

Once a need is recognized, the individual then searches for alternatives for satisfying the need. The individual can collect information from five basic sources for a particular purchase decision.

1. *Internal sources.* In most cases the individual has had some previous experience in dealing with a particular need. Thus, the individual will usually "search" through whatever stored information and experience is in his or her mind for dealing with the need. If a previously acceptable product for satisfying the need is remembered, the individual may purchase with little or no additional information search or evaluation. This is quite common for routine or habitual purchases.

2. *Group sources.* A common source of information for purchase decisions comes from communication with other people, such as family, friends, neighbors, and acquaintances. Generally, some of these (i.e., relevant others) are selected that the individual views as having particular expertise for the purchase decision. Although it may be quite difficult for the marketing manager to determine the exact nature of this source of information, group sources of information often are considered to be the most powerful influence on purchase decisions.

3. *Marketing sources.* Marketing sources of information include such factors as advertising, salespeople, dealers, packaging, and displays. Generally, this is the primary source of information about a particular product. These sources of information will be discussed in detail in the promotion chapters of this text.

4. *Public sources.* Public sources of information include publicity, such as a newspaper article about the product, and independent ratings of the product, such as *Consumer Reports.* Here product quality is a highly important marketing management consideration, since such articles and reports often discuss such features as dependability and service requirements.

5. *Experiential sources.* Experiential sources refer to handling, examining, and perhaps trying the product while shopping. This usually requires an actual shopping trip by the individual and may be the final source consulted before purchase.

The consumer then processes information collected from these sources.[8] However, the exact nature of how individuals process information to form evaluations of products is not fully understood. In general, information processing is viewed as a four-step process in which the individual is (1) exposed to information, (2) becomes attentive to the information, (3) understands the information, and (4) retains the information.[9]

The marketing profession has long recognized the need to uphold its integrity, honor, and dignity. Below are the ethical norms established by the American Marketing Association to be used by marketers in dealing with consumers and other stakeholders.

As marketers we must:

1. **Do no harm.** This means consciously avoiding harmful actions or omissions by embodying high ethical standards and adhering to all applicable laws and regulations in the choices we make.
2. **Foster trust in the marketing system.** This means striving for good faith and fair dealing so as to contribute toward the efficacy of the exchange process as well as avoiding deception in product design, pricing, communication, and delivery of distribution.
3. **Embrace ethical values.** This means building relationships and enhancing consumer confidence in the integrity of marketing by affirming these core values: honesty, responsibility, fairness, respect, transparency, and citizenship.

Source: marketingpower.com, March 27, 2011.

Alternative Evaluation

During the process of collecting information or, in some cases, after information is acquired, the consumer evaluates alternatives on the basis of what he or she has learned. One approach to describing the evaluation process is as follows:

1. The consumer has information about a number of brands in a product class.
2. The consumer perceives that at least some of the brands in a product class are viable alternatives for satisfying a recognized need.
3. Each of these brands has a set of attributes (color, quality, size, and so forth).
4. A set of these attributes is relevant to the consumer, and the consumer perceives that different brands vary in how much of each attribute they possess.
5. The brand that is perceived as offering the greatest number of desired attributes in the desired amounts and desired order will be the brand the consumer will like best.
6. The brand the consumer likes best is the brand the consumer will intend to purchase.[10]

Purchase Decision

If no other factors intervene after the consumer has decided on the brand that is intended for purchase, the actual purchase is a common result of search and evaluation. Actually, a purchase involves many decisions, which include product type, brand, model, dealer selection, and method of payment, among other factors. In addition, rather than purchasing, the consumer may make a decision to modify, postpone, or avoid purchase based on an inhibitor to purchase or a perceived risk.

Traditional risk theorists believe that consumers tend to make risk-minimizing decisions based on their *perceived* definition of the particular purchase. The perception of risk is based on the possible consequences and uncertainties involved. Consequences may range from economic loss, to embarrassment if a new food product does not turn out well, to actual physical harm. Perceived risk may be either functional (related to financial and performance considerations) or psychosocial (related to whether the product will further one's self- or reference-group image). The amount of risk a consumer perceives in a particular product depends on such things as the price of the product and whether other people will see the individual using it.

The perceived risk literature emphasizes that consumers generally try to reduce risk in their decision making. This can be done by either reducing the possible negative consequences or by reducing the uncertainty. The possible consequences of a purchase might be minimized by purchasing in small quantities or by lowering the individual's aspiration level to expect less in the way of results from the product. However, this cannot always be done. Thus, reducing risk by attempting to increase the certainty of the purchase outcome may be the more widely used strategy. This can be done by seeking additional information regarding the proposed purchase. In general, the more information the consumer collects prior to purchase, the less likely post-purchase dissonance is to occur.

Postpurchase Evaluation

In general, if the individual finds that a certain response achieves a desired goal or satisfies a need, the success of this cue-response pattern will be remembered. The probability of responding in a like manner to the same or similar situation in the future is increased. In other words, the response has a higher probability of being repeated when the need and cue appear together again, and thus it can be said that learning has taken place. Frequent reinforcement increases the habit potential of the particular response. Likewise, if a response does not satisfy the need adequately, the probability that the same response will be repeated is reduced.

For some marketers this means that if an individual finds that a particular product fulfills the need for which it was purchased, the probability is high that the individual will repurchase the product the next time the need arises. The firm's promotional efforts often act as the cue. If an individual repeatedly purchases a product with favorable results, loyalty may develop toward the particular product or brand. This loyalty can result in habitual purchases, and such habits are often extremely difficult for competing firms to alter.

Although many studies in the area of buyer behavior center on the buyer's attitudes, motives, and behavior before and during the purchase decision, behavior after the purchase has also been studied. Specifically, studies have been undertaken to investigate postpurchase dissonance, as well as postpurchase satisfaction.

The occurrence of postdecision dissonance is related to the concept of *cognitive dissonance*. This theory states that there is often a lack of consistency or harmony among an individual's various cognitions, or attitudes and beliefs, after a decision has been made—that is, the individual has doubts and second thoughts about the choice made. Further, it is more likely that the intensity of the anxiety will be greater when any of the following conditions exist:

1. The decision is an important one psychologically or financially, or both.
2. There are a number of forgone alternatives.
3. The forgone alternatives have many favorable features.

These factors can relate to many buying decisions. For example, postpurchase dissonance might be expected to be present among many purchasers of such products as automobiles, major appliances, and homes. In these cases, the decision to purchase is usually an important one both financially and psychologically, and a number of favorable alternatives are usually available.

These findings have much relevance for marketers. In a buying situation, when a purchaser becomes dissonant, it is reasonable to predict such a person would be highly receptive to advertising and sales promotion that support the purchase decision. Such communication presents favorable aspects of the product and can be useful in reinforcing the buyer's wish to believe that a wise purchase decision was made. For example, purchasers of major appliances

Influencing Factor	Increasing the Influencing Factor Causes the Search to:
I. Market characteristics	
A. Number of alternatives	Increase
B. Price range	Increase
C. Store concentration	Increase
D. Information availability	Increase
1. Advertising	
2. Point-of-purchase	
3. Sales personnel	
4. Packaging	
5. Experienced consumers	
6. Independent sources	
II. Product characteristics	
A. Price	Increase
B. Differentiation	Increase
C. Positive products	Increase
III. Consumer characteristics	
A. Learning and experience	Decrease
B. Shopping orientation	Mixed
C. Social status	Increase
D. Age and household life cycle	Mixed
E. Product involvement	Mixed
F. Perceived risk	Increase
IV. Situational characteristics	
A. Time availability	Increase
B. Purchase for self	Decrease
C. Pleasant surroundings	Increase
D. Social surroundings	Mixed
E. Physical/mental energy	Increase

Source: Del I. Hawkins, David L. Mothersbaugh, and Roger Best, *Consumer Behavior: Building Marketing Strategy*, 11th ed. (Burr Ridge, IL: Irwin/McGraw-Hill, 2010), p. 534.

or automobiles might be given a phone call or sent a letter reassuring them that they have made a wise purchase.

As noted, researchers have also studied postpurchase consumer satisfaction. Much of this work has been based on what is called the *disconfirmation paradigm*. Basically, this approach views satisfaction with products and brands as a result of two other variables. The first variable is the expectations a consumer has about a product before purchase. These expectations concern the beliefs the consumer has about the product's performance.

The second variable is the difference between expectations and postpurchase perceptions of how the product actually performed. If the product performed as well as expected or better than expected, the consumer will be satisfied with the product. If the product performed worse than expected, the consumer will be dissatisfied with it.

One implication of this view for marketers is that care must be taken not to raise prepurchase expectations to such a level that the product cannot possibly meet them. Rather, it is important to create positive expectations consistent with the product's likely performance.[11]

SUMMARY

This chapter presented an overview of consumer behavior. Social, marketing, and situational influences on consumer decision making were discussed first, followed by a discussion of two important psychological factors: product knowledge and product involvement. Consumer decision making, which can be extensive, limited, or routine, was viewed as a series of stages: need recognition, alternative search, alternative evaluation, purchase decision, and postpurchase evaluation. Clearly, understanding consumer behavior is a prerequisite for developing successful marketing strategies.

Additional Resources

Hawkins, Del I., and David L. Mothersbaugh. *Consumer Behavior: Building Marketing Strategy.* 11th ed. Burr Ridge, IL: McGraw-Hill/Irwin, 2010.

Hoyer, Wayne D., and Deborah J. MacInnis. *Consumer Behavior.* 5th ed. Mason OH: Southwestern, 2010.

Lindguist, Jay, and M. Joseph Sirgy. *Shopper, Buyer, and Consumer Behavior.* 4th ed. Mason OH: Southwestern, 2009.

Peter, J. Paul, and Jerry C. Olson. *Consumer Behavior and Marketing Strategy.* 9th ed. Burr Ridge, IL: McGraw-Hill/Irwin, 2010.

Schiffman, Leon G., and Leslie Kanuck. *Consumer Behavior.* 10th ed. Upper Saddle River, NJ: Prentice Hall, 2010.

Solomon, Michael R. *Consumer Behavior.* 9th ed. Upper Saddle River NJ: Prentice Hall, 2011.

Key Terms and Concepts

Belongingness and love needs: According to Maslow, the needs related to the social and gregarious nature of humans and the need for companionship.

Cognitive dissonance: A lack of harmony among a person's thoughts after a decision has been made—that is, the individual has doubts and second thoughts about the choice that was made.

Current conditions: Situational influences such as momentary moods and conditions that influence consumer behavior.

Disconfirmation paradigm: Approach that views consumer satisfaction as the degree to which the actual performance of a product is consistent with expectations a consumer had before purchase. If the product is as good as expected, then the consumer will be satisfied; if not, then the consumer's expectations are disconfirmed.

Esteem needs: According to Maslow, the needs that consist of both the need for awareness of importance to others (self-esteem) and actual esteem from others.

Experiential sources of information: The information a consumer gets from handling, examining, and perhaps trying a product while shopping.

Extensive decision making: Level of decision making that requires the most time and effort since the purchase typically involves a highly complex or expensive product that is important to the consumer.

Family life cycle: Framework that divides the development of a family into a number of stages based on the needs, assets, debts, and expenditures that change as a family begins, grows, and matures.

Group sources of information: A common source of information for purchase decisions that comes from communication with other people such as family, friends, neighbors, and acquaintances.

Internal sources of information: Stored information and experience a consumer has in memory for dealing with a particular need.

Limited decision making: Level of decision making that requires a moderate amount of time and effort to search for and compare alternatives.

Lower Americans: Comprise 16 percent of the population and have the lowest education levels and resources; the bottom of the social class hierarchy.

Marketing sources of information: Include such things as advertising, salespeople, dealers, packaging, and displays offered by marketers to influence consumer decision making and behavior.

Middle class: Middle social class; comprises 34 percent of the population and is concerned with doing the right thing and buying what is popular. This class tends to emulate Upper Americans.

Need recognition: The first step in the consumer decision making process; the recognition by the consumer of a felt need or want.

Physical features of a situation: The geographical and institutional decor, sounds, aromas, lighting, weather, and visible configurations of merchandise or other materials.

Physiological needs: According to Maslow, the primary needs of the human body such as food, water, and sex.

Product knowledge: The amount of information a consumer has stored in her or his memory about particular product classes, product forms, brands, and models, and ways to purchase them.

Public sources of information: Publicity, such as newspaper articles about the product, and independent ratings of the product, such as Consumer Reports.

Reference groups: Groups that an individual looks to (uses as a reference) when forming attitudes and opinions.

Routine decision making: The most common type of decision making, involves little in the way of thinking and deliberation. It is often habitual and is the way consumers commonly purchase packaged goods that are inexpensive, simple, and familiar.

Safety needs: According to Maslow, things such as protection from physical harm, ill health, and economic disaster and avoidance of the unexpected.

Self-actualization needs: According to Maslow, the desire to become everything one can become and fully realize talents and capabilities.

Situational influences: All of the factors particular to a time and place that have a demonstrable and systematic effect on current behavior.

Social features of a situation: Include other persons present in a situation, their characteristics, their apparent roles and interpersonal interactions.

Task features of a situation: Include the intent or requirement to select, shop for, or obtain information about a general or specific purchase.

Time dimension of a situation: The temporal dimension of a situation such as the time of day or season of the year. It can also be relative to other life events such as the time since the last purchase or time until payday.

Upper Americans: Social class that comprises 14 percent of the population and is differentiated mainly by having high incomes. This social class remains the group in which quality merchandise is most prized and prestige brands are commonly sought.

Working class: Social class that comprises 38 percent of the population; "family folk" who depend heavily on relatives for economic and emotional support.

Chapter 4

Business, Government, and Institutional Buying

In the previous chapter we discussed consumer behavior and the decision-making process used to purchase products and services. However, final consumers are not the only purchasers of products and services. Rather, businesses, government agencies, and other institutions buy products and services to maintain their organizations and achieve their organizational objectives. These organizations are major customers for many marketers. In this chapter we discuss the nature of these organizations and offer a general model of the buying process for them. The chapter begins by discussing four categories of organizational buyers and then presents an overview of the organizational buying process.

CATEGORIES OF ORGANIZATIONAL BUYERS

Organizational buyers can be classified in many ways. For example, the U.S. government classifies organizations in similar lines of business in the North American Industry Classification System (*NAICS*, pronounced "knacks"). NAICS provides information about the number of establishments, sales volume, and number of employees in each industry broken down by geographic area. Information on NAICS codes is available online at www.naics.com. In addition, a commercial source, Dun's Business Locator, provides information on over 10 million U.S. businesses. Both of these can provide useful information for organizational marketers seeking organizational buyers. However, for the purpose of this text, it is useful to classify organizational buyers into four categories: These include producers, intermediaries, government agencies, and other institutions. Taken collectively, marketing to these organizations is called *business-to-business* or *B2B marketing*. Business-to-business marketing has become a topic of increasing interest because it is the major area where Internet marketing has been done profitably.

Producers

These organizational buyers consist of businesses that buy goods and services in order to produce other goods and services for sale. For example, Dell Inc. buys computer chips from Intel in order to make computers to be sold to consumers and other organizations. Producers are engaged in many different industries, ranging from agriculture to manufacturing, from construction to finance. Together they constitute the largest segment of organizational buyers. Producers of goods tend to be larger and more geographically concentrated than producers of services.

Intermediaries

Marketing intermediaries or resellers purchase products to resell at a profit. This group includes a number of types of resellers such as wholesalers (Grainger) and retailers (Walmart) that buy products from manufacturers and distribute them to consumers and other organizational buyers. Intermediaries also purchase products and services to run their own businesses, such as office supplies and maintenance services. Given their importance to marketing, intermediaries will be discussed in detail in Chapter 10.

Government Agencies

In the United States, government agencies operate at the federal, state, and local levels; there are over 86,000 governmental agencies in this country that purchase machinery, equipment, facilities, supplies, and services. Government agencies account for trillions of dollars worth of buying, and over half of this amount represents purchases by the federal government, making it the world's biggest customer. The governments of other countries also are huge customers for marketers. Marketing to government agencies can be complex since they often have strict purchasing policies and regulations.

Other Institutions

Besides businesses and government agencies, marketers also sell products and services to a variety of other institutions, such as hospitals, museums, universities, nursing homes, and churches. Many of these are nonprofit organizations that purchase products and services to maintain their operations and serve their clientele.

THE ORGANIZATIONAL BUYING PROCESS

Regardless of the type of organization, a buying process is needed to ensure that products and services are purchased and received in a timely and efficient manner. In general, organizations develop a buying process to serve their purchasing needs. Figure 4.1 presents a model of organizational buying that represents some of the common influences and stages in the process.

FIGURE 4.1   A Model of the Organizational Buying Process

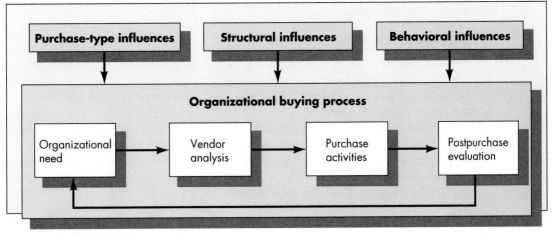

PURCHASE-TYPE INFLUENCES ON ORGANIZATIONAL BUYING

A major consideration that affects the organizational buying process is the complexity of the purchase that is to be made. Three types of organizational purchase based on their degree of complexity include the straight rebuy, modified rebuy, and new task purchase.[1]

Straight Rebuy

The simplest and most common type of purchase is called a *straight rebuy*. This type of purchase involves routinely reordering a product from the same supplier that it had been purchased from in the past. Organizations use a straight rebuy when they are experienced at buying the product, have an ongoing need for it, and have regular suppliers of it. In many cases, organizations have computer systems that automatically reorder certain commonly used products. Organizations use this simple approach to purchasing because it is fast and requires relatively few employees.

Straight rebuys are common among organizations that practice *just-in-time inventory*, which is a system of replenishing parts or goods for resale just before they are needed. Such buyers do not have time to hunt around for potential suppliers and solicit bids. Instead they regularly place their orders with a supplier whose quality and timely delivery can be counted on. If a supplier delivers items that are late or of unacceptable quality, these buyers will not have a reserve in inventory to draw on. Therefore, organizations that use just-in-time inventory tend to favor suppliers with a strong commitment to quality.

To retain customers who use straight rebuys, the marketer needs to maintain high-quality products and reliable service so that the customers will continue to be satisfied with their purchases.

Modified Rebuy

When some aspects of the buying situation are unfamiliar, the organization will use a *modified rebuy*. This type of purchase involves considering a limited number of alternatives before making a selection. Organizational buyers follow this approach rather than a straight rebuy when a routine purchase changes in some way; for example, a supplier discontinues a product or stops satisfying the customer, the price of a usual product rises, or a new product becomes available to meet the same need.

In such situations, the organizational buyer considers the new information and decides what changes to make. If the change proves satisfactory and the product is one needed routinely, the buyer may then make it a straight rebuy. Marketers seek to win new organizational customers by giving them reasons to change from a straight rebuy to a modified rebuy in which the marketer's products are considered.

New Task Purchase

Organizations purchase some products only occasionally, especially in the case of large investments such as machinery, equipment, and real estate. In these cases, the organization may use a *new task purchase*. This type of purchase involves an extensive search for information and a formal decision process.

New task purchases are most often used for big-ticket items, so the cost of a mistake is great. Therefore, a new task purchase is time consuming and involves a relatively large number of decision makers, who may consider many alternatives. This is the type of purchase decision that is most likely to involve joint decision making because many kinds of expertise are required to make the best decision.

A new task purchase is an opportunity for the marketer to learn about the needs of the organizations in its target market and to discuss ways to meet organizational needs, such as

FIGURE 4.2   Marketing Tactics for Reaching Organizational Buyers

Type of Purchase	Marketing Element	Promotional Approach
Straight rebuy	Advertising	Use reminder advertising. Build image for company.
	Promotion	Hospitality events at trade shows.
	Selling	Any personal selling is designed to build relationships. Automate the purchasing process, perhaps through EDI (electronic data exchange).
Modified rebuy	Advertising	Use comparison advertising to show differences between your product and similar products.
	Promotion	Customer site demonstrations, hospitality events at trade shows.
	Selling	Protect relationship with current customers with plant tours, special trade-in pricing, and other offers. Anticipate or respond quickly to changes in customer needs.
New task purchase	Advertising	Detailed, educational ads to try to get users to try product, substitute for old method.
	Promotion	Use demonstrations at trade shows to show how it works. Offer free trials or demonstrations at the customer's site.
	Selling	Heavy emphasis on understanding customers' needs and showing how new product satisfies needs better than old methods.

Source: Based on F. Robert Dwyer and John F. Tanner, Jr., *Business Marketing,* 4th ed. Burr Ridge IL: McGraw-Hill/Irwin, 2009, p. 73.

through the use of new products and technology. Figure 4.2 offers some suggestions for reaching organizational buyers for the three types of purchases.

STRUCTURAL INFLUENCES ON ORGANIZATIONAL BUYING

The term *structural influences* refers to the design of the organizational environment and how it affects the purchasing process. Three important structural influences on organizational buying are purchasing roles, organization-specific factors, and purchasing policies and procedures.

Purchasing Roles

It is common in organizational buying for purchases to be made cross-functionally with representatives from different functional departments playing various roles in the process. Taken collectively, these are called the *buying center* and include the following roles:

1. *Initiators,* who start the purchasing process by recognizing a need or problem in the organization. For example, an executive might see a need for faster computers.
2. *Users,* who are the people in the organization who actually use the product, for example, an assistant who would use a new word processor.

How Marketing to Organizational Buyers Differs	Example
Varying buyer-seller relationships	Relationships can be deep and involve several layers of the industry, BASF partners with Gaskell and GM, for example.
Shorter distribution channels	BASF sells fibers *direct* to DuPont for the manufacture of carpet and through distributors to smaller companies.
Greater emphasis on personal selling	BASF salespeople work directly with fire departments to sell the latest fire-fighting chemicals and ensure that they are used properly.
Greater Web integration	BASF uses its *cc-markets* Web site to create a communication space with special customers.
Unique promotional strategies	BASF exhibits at trade shows like Powder Coatings Europe, a show held every January in Amsterdam.
Consumption	Consumption of business products is by organizations who are then dependent on other markets, so how much carpet protectant BASF can sell to DuPont depends on how much carpet DuPont can sell.
Knowledge of customer's customer	BASF has to understand both consumers (of carpet, for example) and manufacturers like DuPont, not just consumers.
Marketing research	In smaller direct markets (such as carpet manufacturers), marketing research techniques tend toward qualitative.

Source: F. Robert Dwyer and John F. Tanner, *Business Marketing,* 4th ed. (Burr Ridge, IL: McGraw-Hill/Irwin, 2009), p. 9.

3. *Influencers,* who affect the buying decision, usually by helping define the specifications for what is needed. For example, an information systems manager would be a key influencer in the purchase of a new computer system.

4. *Buyers,* who have the formal authority and responsibility to select the supplier and negotiate the terms of the contract. For example, in the purchase of ink cartridges, the *purchasing agent* would likely perform this role.

5. *Deciders,* who have the formal or informal power to select or approve the supplier that receives the contract. For important technical purchases, deciders may come from R&D, engineering, or quality control.

6. *Gatekeepers,* who control the flow of information in the buying center. Purchasing personnel, technical experts, and assistants can all keep marketers and their information from reaching people performing the other four roles.[2]

When several persons are involved in the organizational purchase decision, marketers may need to use a variety of means to reach each individual or group. Fortunately, it is often easy to find which individuals in organizations are involved in a purchase because such information is provided to suppliers. Organizations do this because it makes suppliers more knowledgeable about purchasing practices, thus making the purchasing process more efficient.[3] Also, a number of firms have developed closer channel relationships that facilitate these transactions.

Organization-Specific Factors

Three primary organization-specific factors influence the purchasing process: orientation, size, and degree of centralization. First, in terms of orientation, the dominant function in an organization may control purchasing decisions. For example, if the organization is technology oriented, it is likely to be dominated by engineering personnel, who will make buying decisions. Similarly, if the organization is production oriented, production personnel may dominate buying decisions.

Second, the size of the organization may influence the purchasing process. If the organization is large, it will likely have a high degree of joint decision making for other than straight rebuys. Smaller organizations are likely to have more autonomous decision making.

Finally, the degree of centralization of an organization influences whether decisions are made individually or jointly with others. Organizations that are highly centralized are less likely to have joint decision making. Thus, a privately owned, small company with technology or production orientations will tend toward autonomous decision making, while a large-scale public corporation with considerable decentralization will tend to have greater joint decision making.

Purchasing Policies and Procedures

Organizations typically develop a number of policies and procedures for various types of purchases. These policies and procedures are designed to ensure that the appropriate products and services are purchased efficiently and that responsibility for buying is assigned appropriately. Often a purchasing department will be assigned the task of centralized buying for the whole organization, and individuals within this department will have authority to purchase particular types of products and services in a given price range.

A current trend in many organizations is *sole sourcing,* in which all of a particular type of product is purchased from a single supplier. Sole sourcing has become more popular because organizational buyers have become more concerned with quality and timely delivery and less likely to purchase only on the basis of price. Sole sourcing is advantageous for suppliers because it provides them with predictable and profitable demand and allows them to build long-term relationships with organizational buyers. It is advantageous for organizational buyers because it not only increases timely delivery and quality of supplies but also allows the buyers to work more closely with suppliers to develop superior products that meet their needs and those of their customers. The use of sole sourcing also simplifies the buying process and can make what were formerly modified rebuys into simpler straight rebuys.

Of course, many organizational purchases are more complicated and require policies and procedures to direct the buying process. In many cases, organizations will develop a list of approved vendors from which buyers have authorization to purchase particular products. The buyer's responsibility is to select the vendor that will provide the appropriate levels of quality and service at the lowest cost. These policies and procedures also specify what positions in the purchasing department or buying center have authority to make purchases of different types and dollar amounts.

For large one-time projects, such as the construction of a building, organizations may seek competitive bids for part or all of the project. The development of policies and procedures for handling such purchases is usually complex and involves a number of criteria and committees.

BEHAVIORAL INFLUENCES ON ORGANIZATIONAL BUYING

Organizational buyers are influenced by a variety of psychological and social factors. We will discuss two of these, personal motivations and role perceptions.

Personal Motivations

Organizational buyers are, of course, subject to the same personal motives or motivational forces as other individuals. Although these buyers may emphasize nonpersonal motives in their buying activities, it has been found that organizational buyers often are influenced by such personal factors as friendship, professional pride, fear and uncertainty (risk), trust, and personal ambitions in their buying activities.

1. Is the need or problem pressing enough that it must be acted on now? If not, how long can action be deferred?
2. What types of products or services could conceivably be used to solve our need or problem?
3. Should we make the item ourselves?
4. Must a new product be designed, or has a vendor already developed an acceptable product?
5. Should a value analysis be performed?
6. What is the highest price we can afford to pay?
7. What trade-offs are we prepared to make between price and other product/vendor attributes?
8. Which information sources will we rely on?
9. How many vendors should be considered?
10. Which attributes will be stressed in evaluating vendors?
11. Should bids be solicited?
12. Should the item be leased or purchased outright?
13. How far can a given vendor be pushed in negotiations? On what issues will that vendor bend the most?
14. How much inventory should a vendor be willing to keep on hand?
15. Should we split our order among several vendors?
16. Is a long-term contract in our interest?
17. What contractual guarantees will we require?
18. How shall we establish our order routine?
19. After the purchase, how will vendor performance be evaluated?
20. How will we deal with inadequate product or vendor performance?

Source: Michael H. Morris, Leyland F. Pitt, and Earl D. Honeycutt, Jr., *Business-to-Business Marketing,* 3rd ed. (Thousand Oaks, CA: Sage Publications, 2001), p. 74.

For example, professional pride often expresses itself through efforts to attain status in the firm. One way to achieve this might be to initiate or influence the purchase of goods that will demonstrate a buyer's value to the organization. If new materials, equipment, or components result in cost savings or increased profits, the individuals initiating the changes have demonstrated their value at the same time. Fear and uncertainty are strong motivational forces on organizational buyers, and reduction of risk is often important to them. This can have a strong influence on purchase behavior. Marketers should understand the relative strength of personal gain versus risk-reducing motives and emphasize the more important motives when dealing with buyers.

Thus, in examining buyer motivations, it is necessary to consider both personal and nonpersonal motivational forces and to recognize that the relative importance of each is not a fixed quantity. It will vary with the nature of the product, the climate within the organization, and the relative strength of the two forces in the particular buyer.

Role Perceptions

A final factor that influences organizational buyers is their own perception of their role. The manner in which individuals behave depends on their perception of their role, their commitment to what they believe is expected of their role, the "maturity" of the role type, and the extent to which the institution is committed to the role type.

1. Avoid the intent and appearance of unethical or compromising practice in relationships, actions, and communications.
2. Demonstrate loyalty to the employer by diligently following the lawful instructions of the employer, using reasonable care and only the authority granted.
3. Refrain from any private or professional business activity that would create a conflict between personal interests and the interests of the employer.
4. Refrain from soliciting or accepting money, loans, credits, or prejudicial discounts and the acceptance of gifts, entertainment, favors, or services from past or potential suppliers that might influence or appear to influence purchasing decisions.
5. Handle confidential or proprietary information belonging to employers or suppliers with due care and proper consideration of ethical and legal ramifications and government regulations.
6. Promote positive supplier relationships through courtesy and impartiality throughout all phases of the purchasing cycle.
7. Refrain from reciprocal agreements that restrain competition.
8. Know and obey the letter and spirit of laws governing the purchasing function and remain alert to the legal ramifications of purchasing decisions.
9. Encourage all segments of society to participate by demonstrating support for small, disadvantaged, and minority-owned businesses.
10. Discourage purchasing's involvement in employer-sponsored programs of personal purchases that are not business related.
11. Enhance the proficiency and stature of the purchasing profession by acquiring and maintaining current technical knowledge and the highest standards of ethical behavior.
12. Conduct international purchasing in accordance with the laws, customs, and practices of foreign countries, consistent with U.S. laws, your organization's policies, and these Ethical Standards and Guidelines.

Source: Institute for Supply Management as reported in F. Robert Dwyer and John F. Tanner, *Business Marketing,* 4th ed. (Burr Ridge, IL: McGraw-Hill/Irwin, 2009), p. 86.

Different buyers will have different degrees of commitment to their buying role, which will cause variations in role behavior from one buyer to the next. By *commitment* we mean willingness to perform their job in the manner expected by the organization. For example, some buyers seek to take charge in their role as buyer and have little commitment to company expectations. The implication for marketers is that such buyers expect, even demand, that they be kept constantly advised of all new developments to enable them to more effectively shape their own role. On the other hand, other buyers may have no interest in prescribing their role activities and accept their role as given to them. Such a buyer is most concerned with merely implementing prescribed company activities and buying policies with sanctioned products. Thus, some buyers will be highly committed to play the role the firm dictates (i.e., the formal organization's perception of their role), while others might be extremely innovative and uncommitted to the expected role performance. Obviously, roles may be heavily influenced by the organizational climate existing in the particular organization.[4]

Organizations can be divided into three groups based on differences in degree of employee commitment. These groups include innovative, adaptive, and lethargic firms. In an innovative firms, individuals approach their occupational roles with a weak commitment to expected norms of behavior. In an adaptive organization, there is a moderate commitment. In a lethargic organization, individuals express a strong commitment to traditionally accepted behavior and behave accordingly. Thus, a buyer in a lethargic firm would probably be less innovative in order to maintain acceptance and status within the organization and would keep conflict within the firm to a minimum.

Buyers' perception of their role may differ from the perception of their role held by others in the organization. This difference can result in variance in perception of the actual purchase responsibility held by the buyer. One study involving purchasing agents revealed that, in every firm included in the study, the purchasing agents believed they had more responsibility and control over certain decisions than the other influential purchase decision makers in the firm perceived them as having. The decisions were (1) designing the product, (2) setting a cost for the product, (3) determining performance life, (4) naming a specific supplier, (5) assessing the amount of engineering help available from the supplier, and (6) reducing rejects. This variance in role perception held true regardless of the size of the firm or the significance of the item purchased to the overall success of the firm. It is important, therefore, that the marketer be aware that such perceptual differences may exist and to determine as accurately as possible the amount of control and responsibility over purchasing decisions held by each purchase decision influencer in the firm.

STAGES IN THE ORGANIZATIONAL BUYING PROCESS

As with consumer buying, most organizational purchases are made in response to a particular need or problem. Ideally, the products or services purchased will meet the organizational need and improve the organization's efficiency, effectiveness, and profits. The organizational buying process can be analyzed as a series of four stages: organizational need, vendor analysis, purchase activities, and postpurchase evaluation.

Organizational Need

Organizations have many needs for products and services to help them survive and meet their objectives. For example, a manufacturer may need to purchase new machinery to increase its production capacity and meet demand; a retailer may need to purchase services from a marketing research firm to better understand its market; a government agency may need to purchase faster computers to keep up with growing demand for its services; a hospital may need to purchase more comfortable beds for its patients. Recognizing these needs, and a willingness and ability to meet them, often results in organizational purchases. For straight rebuys, the purchase process may involve little more than a phone call or a few clicks on a computer to order products and arrange payment and delivery. For modified rebuys or new task purchases, the process may be much more complex.

Vendor Analysis

Organizational buyers must search for, locate, and evaluate vendors of products and services to meet their needs. Searching for and locating vendors is often easy since they frequently make sales calls on organizations that might need their products. Vendors also advertise in trade magazines or on the Internet and have displays at industry trade shows to increase their visibility to organizational buyers. For products and services that the organization has previously purchased, the organization may already have developed a list of approved vendors.

Organizational buyers often use a vendor analysis to evaluate possible suppliers. A *vendor analysis* is the process by which organizational buyers rate each potential supplier on various performance measures such as product quality, on-time delivery, price, payment terms, and use of modern technology. Figure 4.3 presents a sample vendor analysis form that lists a number of purchase criteria and the weights one organization used to compare potential suppliers.

A formal vendor analysis can be used for at least three purposes. First, it can be used to develop a list of approved vendors, all of which provide acceptable levels of products and services. Organizational buyers can then select any company on the list, simplifying the

FIGURE 4.3   Sample Vendor Analysis Form

Supplier Name: _____   Type of Product: _____

Shipping Location: _____   Annual Sales Dollars: _____

	5 Excellent	4 Good	3 Satisfactory	2 Fair	1 Poor	0 N/A
Quality (45%)						
Defect rates	―	―	―	―	―	―
Quality of sample	―	―	―	―	―	―
Conformance with quality program	―	―	―	―	―	―
Responsiveness to quality problems	―	―	―	―	―	―
Overall quality	―	―	―	―	―	―
Delivery (25%)						
Avoidance of late shipments	―	―	―	―	―	―
Ability to expand production	―	―	―	―	―	―
Performance in sample delivery	―	―	―	―	―	―
Response to changes in order size	―	―	―	―	―	―
Overall delivery	―	―	―	―	―	―
Price (20%)						
Price competitiveness	―	―	―	―	―	―
Payment terms	―	―	―	―	―	―
Absorption of costs	―	―	―	―	―	―
Submission of cost savings plans	―	―	―	―	―	―
Overall price	―	―	―	―	―	―
Technology (10%)						
State-of-the-art components	―	―	―	―	―	―
Sharing research & development capability	―	―	―	―	―	―
Ability and willingness to help with design	―	―	―	―	―	―
Responsiveness to engineering problems	―	―	―	―	―	―
Overall technology	―	―	―	―	―	―

Buyer: _____   Date: _____

Comments: _____

purchase process. Second, a vendor analysis could be used to compare competing vendors; the buyers then select the best one on the basis of the ratings. This could help the organization pare down vendors to a single supplier for which a long-term, sole-sourcing relationship could be developed. Third, a vendor analysis can be done both before and after purchases to compare performance on evaluation criteria and evaluate the process of vendor selection.

Purchase Activities

Straight rebuys may involve a quick order to an approved vendor or sole-source supplier. However, other types of organizational purchases can involve long time periods with extensive negotiations on price and terms and formal contracts stating quality, delivery, and service criteria. The complexity of the product or service, the number of suppliers available,

FIGURE 4.4
Functional Areas and
Their Key Concerns in
Organizational Buying

Source: Michael H. Morris,
Leyland F. Pitt, and Earl D.
Honeycutt, Jr., *Business-
to-Business Marketing*, 3rd
ed. (Thousand Oaks, CA:
Sage Publications, 2001),
p. 66.

Functional Areas	Key Concerns
Design and development engineering	Name reputation of vendor; ability of vendors to meet design specifications.
Production	Delivery and reliability of purchases such that interruption of production schedules is minimized.
Sales/marketing	Impact of purchased items on marketability of the company's products.
Maintenance	Degree to which purchased items are compatible with existing facilities and equipment; maintenance service offered by vendor; installation arrangements offered by vendor.
Finance/accounting	Effects of purchases on cash flow, balance sheet, and income statement positions; variances in costs of materials over estimates; feasibility of make-or-buy and lease options to purchasing.
Purchasing	Obtaining lowest possible price at acceptable quality levels; maintaining good relations with vendors.
Quality control	Assurance that purchased items meet prescribed specifications and tolerances, governmental regulations, and customer requirements.

the importance of the product to the buying organization, and pricing all influence the number of purchase activities to be performed and their difficulty. For example, an airline buying a fleet of jumbo jets or a car rental agency buying a fleet of cars may take months or years to negotiate and make purchases. While such buyers may have considerable leverage in negotiating, it should be remembered that these organizations need the products just as badly as the sellers need to sell them. Thus, there is often more collaboration among organizational buyers and sellers than in the consumer market.

Postpurchase Evaluation

Organizational buyers must evaluate both the vendors and the products they purchase to determine whether the products are acceptable for future purchases or whether other sources of supply should be found. A comparison of the performance of the vendor and products with the criteria listed on the prior vendor analysis can be useful for this purpose. If the purchase process goes smoothly and products meet price and quality criteria, then the vendor may be put on the approved list or perhaps further negotiations can be made to sole-source with the supplier.

One problem in judging the acceptability of suppliers and products is that different functional areas may have different evaluation criteria. Figure 4.4 presents several functional areas of a manufacturing company and their common concerns in purchasing. Clearly, these concerns should be considered both prior to purchasing from a particular supplier and after purchasing to ensure that every area's needs are being met as well as possible.

SUMMARY

Organizational buyers include individuals involved in purchasing products and services for businesses, government agencies, and other institutions and agencies. The organizational buying process is influenced by whether the purchase is a straight rebuy, modified rebuy, or new task purchase. It is also influenced by people in various purchasing roles, the orientation, size, and degree of centralization of the organization, the organization's purchasing policies and procedures, and individuals' motivations and perceived roles. The organizational buying process can be viewed as a series of four stages ranging from organizational need, to vendor analysis, to purchase activities, to postpurchase evaluation. It is important that companies marketing to organizations understand the influences and process by which organizations buy products and services so their needs can be met fully and profitably.

Additional Resources

Anderson, James C., James A. Narus, and Das Narayandas. *Business Marketing Management.* 3rd ed. Upper Saddle River, NJ: Prentice Hall, 2009.

Brennan, Ross, Louise E. Canning, and Raymond McDowell. *Business-to-Business Marketing.* Thousand Oaks, CA: Sage, 2007.

Dwyer, F. Robert, and John F. Tanner. *Business Marketing.* 4th ed. Burr Ridge, IL: McGraw-Hill/Irwin, 2009.

Hutt, Michael D., and Thomas W. Speh. *Business Marketing Management: B2B.* 10th ed. Mason, OH: Thomson South-Western, 2010.

Vitale Robert, Waldemar Pfoertsch, and Joseph Giglierano. *Business to Business Marketing.* Upper Saddle River NJ: Prentice Hall, 2011.

Key Terms and Concepts

Business-to-business (B2B) marketing: Marketing products and services to producers, intermediaries, government agencies, and other institutions rather than to consumers.

Buyers: In buying centers, the persons who have formal authority and responsibility to select the supplier and negotiate the terms of the contract.

Buying center: An organizational group formed from different departments which has the responsibility to evaluate and select products for purchase. Different members of the group may play different roles in the process.

Deciders: In a buying center, individuals who have the formal and informal power to select or approve the supplier that receives the contract. For routinely purchased products, the decider is likely to be the buyer but for more complex products, the decider could come from R&D, engineering, or quality control.

Gatekeepers: The people who control the flow of information to a buying center.

Influencers: In buying centers, the people who affect the buying decision usually by helping define the specifications for what is needed.

Initiators: In buying centers, the people who start the buying process by recognizing a need or a problem in the organization.

Modified rebuy: A type of organizational purchase that involves the consideration of a limited number of alternatives before making a selection.

NAICS: The North American Industry Classification System which provides information about the number of establishments, sales volume, and number of employees in each industry broken down by geographic area.

New task purchase: A type of organizational purchase that involves an extensive search for information and a formal decision process.

Sole sourcing: Organizational purchasing in which all of a type of product are obtained from a single supplier.

Straight rebuy: A type of organizational purchase that involves routinely reordering a product from the same supplier that it had been purchased from in the past.

Users: In a buying center, the people in the organization that actually use the product to be purchased.

Vendor analysis: The process by which organizational buyers rate each potential supplier on various performance measures such as product quality, on-time delivery, price, payment terms, and use of modern technology.

5

Market Segmentation

Market segmentation is one of the most important concepts in marketing. In fact, a primary reason for studying consumer and organizational buyer behavior is to provide bases for effective segmentation, and a large portion of marketing research is concerned with segmentation. From a marketing management point of view, selection of the appropriate target market is paramount to developing successful marketing programs.

The logic of market segmentation is quite simple and is based on the idea that a single product item can seldom meet the needs and wants of *all* consumers. Typically, consumers vary as to their needs, wants, and preferences for products and services, and successful marketers adapt their marketing programs to fulfill these preference patterns. For example, even a simple product like chewing gum has multiple flavors, package sizes, sugar contents, calories, consistencies (e.g., liquid centers), and colors to meet the preferences of various consumers. While a single product item cannot meet the needs of all consumers, it can almost always serve more than one consumer. Thus, there are usually *groups of consumers* who can be served well by a single item. If a particular group can be served *profitably* by a firm, it is a viable market segment. In other words, the firm should develop a marketing mix to serve the group or market segment.

In this chapter we consider the process of market segmentation. We define *market segmentation* as the process of dividing a market into groups of similar consumers and selecting the most appropriate group(s) for the firm to serve. The group or segment that a company selects to market to is called a *target market*. We break down the process of market segmentation into six steps, as shown in Figure 5.1. While we recognize that the order of these steps may vary, depending on the firm and situation, there are few if any times when market segmentation analysis can be ignored. In fact, even if the final decision is to "mass market" and not segment at all, this decision should be reached only *after* a market segmentation analysis has been conducted. Thus, market segmentation analysis is a cornerstone of sound marketing planning and decision making.

DELINEATE THE FIRM'S CURRENT SITUATION

As emphasized in Chapter 1, a firm must do a complete situational analysis when embarking on a new or modified marketing program. At the marketing planning level, such an analysis aids in determining objectives, opportunities, and constraints to be considered when selecting target markets and developing marketing mixes. In addition, marketing managers must have a clear idea of the amount of financial and other resources that will be available for developing and executing a marketing plan. Thus, the inclusion of this first step in the market segmentation process is intended to be a reminder of tasks to be performed prior to marketing planning.

FIGURE 5.1
A Model of the
Market Segmentation
Process

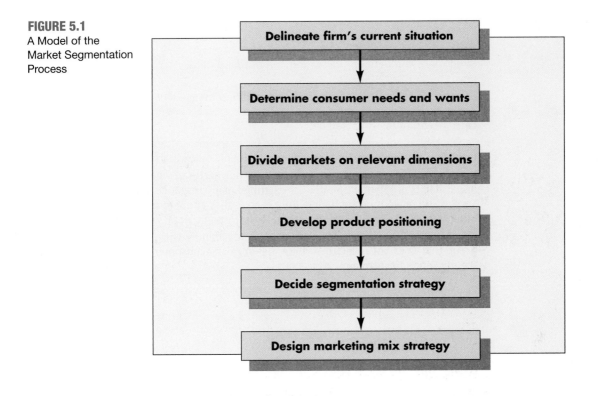

DETERMINE CONSUMER NEEDS AND WANTS

As emphasized throughout this text, successful marketing strategies depend on discovering and satisfying consumer needs and wants. In some cases, this idea is quite operational. To illustrate, suppose a firm has a good deal of venture capital and is seeking to diversify its interest into new markets. A firm in this situation may seek to discover a broad variety of unsatisfied needs. However, in most situations, the industry in which the firm operates specifies the boundaries of a firm's need satisfaction activities. For example, a firm in the communication industry may seek more efficient methods for serving consumers' long-distance telephone needs.

As a practical matter, new technology often brings about an investigation of consumer needs and wants for new or modified products and services. In these situations, the firm is seeking the group of consumers whose needs could best be satisfied by the new or modified product. Further, at a strategic level, consumer needs and wants usually are translated into more operational concepts. For instance, consumer attitudes, preferences, and benefits sought, which are determined through marketing research, are commonly used for segmentation purposes.

DIVIDE MARKETS ON RELEVANT DIMENSIONS

In a narrow sense, this step is often considered to be the whole of market segmentation (i.e., consumers are grouped on the basis of one or more similarities and treated as a homogeneous segment of a heterogeneous total market). Three important questions should be considered here:

1. Should the segmentation be a priori or post hoc?
2. How does one determine the relevant dimensions or bases to use for segmentation?
3. What are some bases for segmenting consumer and organizational buyer markets?

1. Slower rates of market growth, coupled with increased foreign competition, have fostered more competition, increasing the need to identify target markets with unique needs.

2. Social and economic forces, including expanding media, increased educational levels, and general world awareness, have produced customers with more varied and sophisticated needs, tastes, and lifestyles.

3. Technological advances make it possible for marketers to devise marketing programs that focus efficiently on precisely defined segments of the market.

4. Marketers now find that minority buyers do not necessarily adopt the social and economic habits of the mainstream. For example, many Hispanics speak both Spanish and English and retain much of their culture even as they adapt to U.S. lifestyles, while many others remain in Spanish-speaking enclaves in Hispanic states like Texas and California.

5. Roughly 4 in 10 residents in the United States identify with some segment or niche group that does not reflect the white, heterosexual consumer that historically defined the marketing mainstream.

Source: William O. Bearden, Thomas N. Ingram, and Raymond W. LaForge, *Marketing,* Burr Ridge, IL: McGraw-Hill/Irwin, 2007, p. 155.

A Priori versus Post Hoc Segmentation

Real-world segmentation has followed one of two general patterns. An *a priori segmentation* approach is one in which the marketing manager has decided on the appropriate basis for segmentation in advance of doing any research on a market. For example, a manager may decide that a market should be divided on the basis of whether people are nonusers, light users, or heavy users of a particular product. Segmentation research is then conducted to determine the size of each of these groups and their demographic or psychographic profiles.

Post hoc segmentation is an approach in which people are grouped into segments on the basis of research findings. For example, people interviewed concerning their attitudes or benefits sought in a particular product category are grouped according to their responses. The size of each of these groups and their demographic and psychographic profiles are then determined.

Both of these approaches are valuable, and the question of which to use depends in part on how well the firm knows the market for a particular product class. If through previous research and experience a marketing manager has successfully isolated a number of key market dimensions, then an a priori approach based on them may provide more useful information. In the case of segmentation for entirely new products, a post hoc approach may be useful for determining key market dimensions. However, even when using a post hoc approach, some consideration must be given to the variables to be included in the research design. Thus, some consideration must be given to the relevant segmentation dimensions regardless of which approach is used.

Relevance of Segmentation Dimensions

Unfortunately, there is no simple solution for determining the relevant dimensions for segmenting markets. Certainly, managerial expertise and experience are needed for selecting the appropriate dimensions or bases on which to segment particular markets. In most cases, however, at least some initial dimensions can be determined from previous research, purchase trends, and managerial judgment. For instance, suppose we wish to segment the market for all-terrain vehicles. Clearly, several dimensions come to mind for initial consideration, including sex (male), age (18 to 35 years), lifestyle (outdoorsman), and income level (perhaps $30,000 to $80,000). At a minimum, these variables should be included in subsequent segmentation research. Of course, the most market-oriented approach to segmentation is on the basis of what benefits the potential consumer is seeking. Thus, consideration and research of sought benefits are a strongly recommended approach in the marketing literature. This approach will be considered in some detail in the following section.

Bases for Segmentation

A number of useful bases for segmenting consumer and organizational markets are presented in Figure 5.2. This is by no means a complete list of possible segmentation variables but represents some useful bases and categories. Two commonly used approaches for segmenting markets include benefit segmentation and psychographic segmentation. We will discuss these two in some detail. We will also discuss geodemographic segmentation, a recent development with a number of advantages for marketers.

Benefit Segmentation

The belief underlying this segmentation approach is that the benefits people are seeking in consuming a given product are the basic reasons for the existence of true market segments.[1] Thus, this approach attempts to measure consumer value systems and consumer perceptions of various brands in a product class. To illustrate, Russell Haley provided the classic example of a benefit segmentation in terms of the toothpaste market. Haley identified five basic segments, which are presented in Figure 5.3. Haley argued that this segmentation could be very useful for selecting advertising copy, media, commercial length, packaging, and new product design. For example, colorful packages might be appropriate for the sensory segment, perhaps aqua (to indicate fluoride) for the worrier group, and gleaming white for the social segment because of this segment's interest in white teeth.

Calantone and Sawyer also used a benefit segmentation approach to segment the market for bank services.[2] Their research was concerned with the question of whether benefit segments remain stable across time. While they found some stability in segments, there were some differences in attribute importance, size, and demographics at different times. Thus, they argue for ongoing benefit segmentation research to keep track of any changes in a market that might affect marketing strategy.

Benefit segmentation is clearly a market-oriented approach that seeks to identify consumer needs and wants and to satisfy them by providing products and services with the desired benefits. It is clearly very consistent with the approach to marketing suggested by the marketing concept.

Psychographic Segmentation

Whereas benefit segmentation focuses on the benefits sought by the consumer, psychographic segmentation focuses on consumer lifestyles. Consumers are first asked a variety of questions about their lifestyles and then grouped on the basis of the similarity of their responses. Lifestyles are measured by asking consumers about their *activities* (work, hobbies, vacations), *interests* (family, job, community), and *opinions* (about social issues, politics, business). The activity, interest, and opinion (AIO) questions are very general in some studies but in others, at least some of the questions relate to specific products.[3]

FIGURE 5.2 Useful Segmentation Bases for Consumer and Organizational Buyer Markets

Consumer Markets	
Segmentation Base	**Examples of Market Segments**
Geographic:	
Continents	Africa, Asia, Europe, North America, South America
Global regions	Southeast Asia, Mediterranean, Caribbean
Countries	China, Canada, France, United States, Brazil
Country regions	Pacific Northwest, Middle Atlantic, Midwest
City, county, or SMSA size	Under 5,000 people; 5,000–19,999; 20,000–49,999; 50,000–99,999; 100,000–249,999; 250,000–499,999; 500,000–999,999; or over a million
Population density	Urban, suburban, rural
Climate	Tropical, temperate, cold
Demographic:	
Age	Under 6 years old, 6–12, 13–19, 20–29, 30–39, 40–49, 50–59, 60+
Gender	Male, female
Family size	1–2 persons, 3–4 persons, more than 4 persons
Family life cycle	Single, young married, married with children, sole survivor
Income	Under $10,000 per year, $10,000–$19,999, $20,000–$29,999, $30,000–$39,999, $40,000–$49,999, $50,000–59,999, 60,000–69,999, 70,000+
Education	Grade school or less, some high school, graduated from high school, some college, graduated from college, some graduate work, graduate degree
Marital status	Single, married, divorced, widowed
Social:	
Culture	American, Hispanic, African, Asian, European
Subculture	
Religion	Jewish, Catholic, Muslim, Mormon, Buddhist
Race	European American, Asian American, African American, Hispanic American
Nationality	French, Malaysian, Australian, Canadian, Japanese
Social class	Upper class, middle class, working class, lower class
Thoughts and feelings:	
Knowledge	Expert, novice
Involvement	High, medium, low
Attitude	Positive, neutral, negative
Benefits sought	Convenience, economy, prestige
Innovativeness	Innovator, early adopter, early majority, late majority, laggards, nonadopter
Readiness stage	Unaware, aware, interested, desirous, plan to purchase
Perceived risk	High, moderate, low
Behavior:	
Media usage	Newspaper, magazine, TV, Internet
Specific media usage	*Sports Illustrated, Cosmopolitan, Ebony*
Payment method	Cash, Visa, MasterCard, American Express, check
Loyalty status	None, some, total
Usage rate	Light, medium, heavy
User status	Nonuser, ex-user, current user, potential user
Usage situation	Work, home, vacation, commuting
Combined approaches:	
Psychographics	Achievers, strivers, strugglers
Person/situation	College students for lunch, executives for business dinner
Geodemography	Money and Brains, American Dreams, Bohemian Mix

Organizational Buyer Markets	
Segmentation Base	**Examples of Market Segments**
Company size	Small, medium, large relative to industry
Purchase quantity	Small, medium, large account
Product application	Production, maintenance, product component
Organization type	Manufacturer, retailer, government agency, hospital
Location	North, south, east, west sales territory
Purchase status	New customer, occasional purchaser, frequent purchaser, nonpurchaser
Attribute importance	Price, service, reliability of supply

FIGURE 5.3   Toothpaste Market Benefit Segments

	Sensory Segment	Sociable Segment	Worrier Segment	Independent Segment
Principal benefit sought	Flavor and product appearance	Brightness of teeth	Decay prevention	Price
Demographic strengths	Children	Teens, young people	Large families	Men
Special behavioral characteristics	Users of spearmint-flavored toothpaste	Smokers	Heavy users	Heavy users
Brands disproportionately favored	Colgate	Macleans, Ultra Brite	Crest	Cheapest brand
Lifestyle characteristics	Hedonistic	Active	Conservative	Value-oriented

The best-known psychographic segmentation is called VALS™, which stands for "values and lifestyles." Originally developed in the 1970s, it has been redone several times to enhance its ability to explain changing lifestyles and predict consumer behavior. Segmentation research based on VALS™ is a product of SRI Consulting Business Intelligence.

As shown in Figure 5.4, the VALS™ framework has eight psychographic groups arranged in a rectangle based on two dimensions. The vertical dimension segments people

FIGURE 5.4   VALS™ Framework and Segments

Source: **www.strategicbusinessinsights.com/vals/ustypes.shtml,** March 18, 2011.

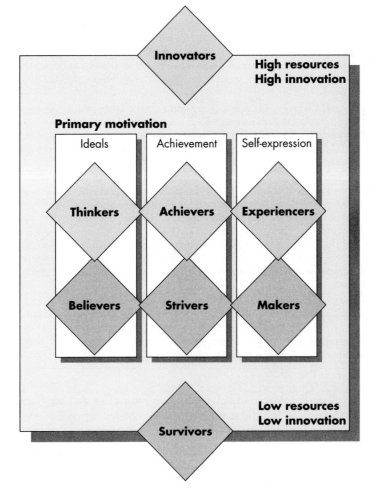

FIGURE 5.4   (continued)

Innovators.   Innovators are successful, sophisticated, take-charge people with high self-esteem. Because they have such abundant resources, they exhibit all three primary motivations in varying degrees. They are change leaders and are the most receptive to new ideas and technologies. Innovators are very active consumers, and their purchases reflect cultivated tastes for upscale, niche products and services. Image is important to Innovators, not as evidence of status or power but as an expression of their taste, independence, and personality. Innovators are among the established and emerging leaders in business and government, yet they continue to seek challenges. Their lives are characterized by variety. Their possessions and recreation reflect a cultivated taste for the finer things in life.

Thinkers.   Thinkers are motivated by ideals. They are mature, satisfied, comfortable, and reflective people who value order, knowledge, and responsibility. They tend to be well educated and actively seek out information in the decision-making process. They are well-informed about world and national events and are alert to opportunities to broaden their knowledge. Thinkers have a moderate respect for the status quo institutions of authority and social decorum, but are open to consider new ideas. Although their incomes allow them many choices, Thinkers are conservative, practical consumers; they look for durability, functionality, and value in the products they buy.

Achievers.   Motivated by the desire for achievement, Achievers have goal-oriented lifestyles and a deep commitment to career and family. Their social lives reflect this focus and are structured around family, their place of worship, and work. Achievers live conventional lives, are politically conservative, and respect authority and the status quo. They value consensus, predictability, and stability over risk, intimacy, and self-discovery. With many wants and needs, Achievers are active in the consumer marketplace. Image is important to Achievers; they favor established, prestige products and services that demonstrate success to their peers. Because of their busy lives, they are often interested in a variety of time-saving devices.

Experiencers.   Experiencers are motivated by self-expression. As young, enthusiastic, and impulsive consumers, Experiencers quickly become enthusiastic about new possibilities but are equally quick to cool. They seek variety and excitement, savoring the new, the offbeat, and the risky. Their energy finds an outlet in exercise, sports, outdoor recreation, and social activities. Experiencers are avid consumers and spend a comparatively high proportion of their income on fashion, entertainment, and socializing. Their purchases reflect the emphasis they place on looking good and having "cool" stuff.

Believers.   Like Thinkers, Believers are motivated by ideals. They are conservative, conventional people with concrete beliefs based on traditional, established codes: family, religion, community, and the nation. Many Believers express moral codes that are deeply rooted and literally interpreted. They follow established routines, organized in large part around home, family, community, and social or religious organizations to which they belong. As consumers, Believers are predictable; they choose familiar products and established brands. They favor American products and are generally loyal customers.

Strivers.   Strivers are trendy and fun loving. Because they are motivated by achievement, Strivers are concerned about the opinions and approval of others. Money defines success for Strivers, who don't have enough of it to meet their desires. They favor stylish products that emulate the purchases of people with greater material wealth. Many see themselves as having a job rather than a career, and a lack of skills and focus often prevents them from moving ahead. Strivers are active consumers because shopping is both a social activity and an opportunity to demonstrate to peers their ability to buy. As consumers, they are as impulsive as their financial circumstance will allow.

Makers.   Like Experiencers, Makers are motivated by self-expression. They express themselves and experience the world by working on it—building a house, raising children, fixing a car, or canning vegetables—and have enough skill and energy to carry out their projects successfully. Makers are practical people who have constructive skills and value self-sufficiency. They live within a traditional context of family, practical work, and physical recreation and have little interest in what lies outside that context. Makers are suspicious of new ideas and large institutions such as big business. They are respectful of government authority and organized labor, but resentful of government intrusion on individual rights. They are unimpressed by material possessions other than those with a practical or functional purpose. Because they prefer value to luxury, they buy basic products.

Survivors.   Survivors live narrowly focused lives. With few resources with which to cope, they often believe that the world is changing too quickly. They are comfortable with the familiar and are primarily concerned with safety and security. Because they must focus on meeting needs rather than fulfilling desires, Survivors do not show a strong primary motivation. Survivors are cautious consumers. They represent a very modest market for most products and services. They are loyal to favorite brands, especially if they can purchase them at a discount.

based on the degree to which they are innovative and have resources such as income, education, self-confidence, intelligence, leadership skills, and energy. The horizontal dimension represents primary motivations for buying and includes three different types. Consumers driven by knowledge and principles are motivated primarily by *ideals*. These consumers include the Thinkers and Believers groups. Consumers driven by a goal of

You can find your VALS classification by filling out a questionnaire on the Internet. The Web address is www.strategicbusinessinsights.com/vals/surveynew.shtml. The questionnaire takes about 10 minutes to complete, and your lifestyle will take about 10 seconds to compute. You will get a report that includes both your primary and secondary VALS type. The VALS Web site has a lot of information describing the program and different types of VALS segments.

demonstrating success to their peers are motivated primarily by *achievement.* These consumers include Achievers and Strivers. Consumers driven by a desire for social or physical activity, variety, and risk taking are motivated primarily by *self-expression.* These consumers include both the Experiencers and Makers. At the top of the rectangle are the Innovators, who have such high resources that they may express any of the three motivations. At the bottom of the rectangle are the Survivors, who live complacently and within their means without a strong primary motivation of the types listed above. Figure 5.4 gives more details about each of the eight groups.[4]

Marketers can purchase research data that show which VALS™ groups are the primary buyers of specific products and services. This information can be used to better focus elements of the marketing mix, such as promotion, on the best target markets.

Geodemographic Segmentation

One problem with many segmentation approaches is that although they identify types or categories of consumers, they do not identify specific individuals or households within a market. Geodemographic segmentation identifies specific households in a market by focusing on local neighborhood geography (such as zip codes) to create classifications of actual, addressable, mappable neighborhoods where consumers live and shop.[5] One geodemographic system, is called Nielsen PRIZM, which stands for consumers "Potential Ranking Index of ZIP Markets." The system classifies every U.S. neighborhood into one of 14 groups. Each of these groups is further divided into 3 to 6 segments, with a total of 66 distinct segments in this system. Each group and segment is based on zip codes, demographic information from the U.S. Census, and information on product use, media use, and lifestyle preferences. Figure 5.5 shows a sample group with five segments. The PRIZM system includes maps of different areas that rank neighborhoods on their potential to purchase specific products and services. The PRIZM segmentation is available on major marketing databases from leading providers.

The PRIZM system is based on the assumptions that consumers in particular neighborhoods are similar in many respects and that the best prospects are those who actually use a product or other consumers like them. Marketers use PRIZM to better understand consumers in various markets, what they are like, where they live, and how to reach them. These data help marketers with target market selection, direct marketing campaigns, site selection, media selection, and analysis of sales potential in various areas.

DEVELOP PRODUCT POSITIONING

By this time, the firm should have a good idea of the basic segments of the market that could potentially be satisfied with its product. The current step is concerned with positioning the product favorably in the minds of customers relative to competitive products. Several different positioning strategies can be used. First, products can be positioned by focusing on their superiority to competitive products based on one or more attributes. For example, a

FIGURE 5.5   PRIZM Social Group U1—Urban Uptown

Source: www.claritas.com/mybestsegments/default.jsp, March 18, 2011.

Group U1 – Urban Uptown

The five segments in Urban Uptown are home to the nation's wealthiest urban consumers. Members of this social group tend to be affluent to middle class, college educated and ethnically diverse, with above-average concentrations of Asian and Hispanic Americans. Although this group is diverse in terms of housing styles and family sizes, residents share an upscale urban perspective that's reflected in their marketplace choices. Urban Uptown consumers tend to frequent the arts, shop at exclusive retailers, drive luxury imports, travel abroad and spend heavily on computer and wireless technology.

The Urban Uptown group consists of the following segments:

- 04. Young Digerati
- 07. Money and Brains
- 16. Bohemian Mix
- 26. The Cosmopolitans
- 29. American Dreams

04. Young Digerati – Young Digerati are the nation's tech–savvy singles and couples living in fashionable neighborhoods on the urban fringe. Affluent, highly educated and ethnically mixed, Young Digerati communities are typically filled with trendy apartments and condos, fitness clubs and clothing boutiques, casual restaurants and all types of bars–from juice to coffee to microbrew.

07. Money and Brains – The residents of Money & Brains seem to have it all: high incomes, advanced degrees and sophisticated tastes to match their credentials. Many of these citydwellers– predominantly white with a high concentration of Asian Americans–are married couples with few children who live in fashionable homes on small, manicured lots.

16. Bohemian Mix – A collection of young, mobile urbanites, Bohemian Mix represents the nation's most liberal lifestyles. Its residents are a progressive mix of young singles and couples, students and professionals, Hispanics, Asians, African– Americans and whites. In their funky rowhouses and apartments, Bohemian Mixers are the early adopters who are quick to check out the latest movie, nightclub, laptop and microbrew.

26. The Cosmopolitans – These immigrants and descendants of multi– cultural backgrounds in multi-racial, multi- lingual neighborhoods typify the American Dream. Married couples, with and without children, as well as single parents are affluent from working hard at multiple trades and public service jobs. They have big families, which is unusual for social group U1.

29. American Dreams – American Dreams is a living example of how ethnically diverse the nation has become: more than half the residents are Hispanic, Asian or African- American. In these multilingual neighborhoods–one in ten speaks a language other than English–middle-aged immigrants and their children live in middle- class comfort.

car could be positioned as less expensive (Hyundai), safer (Volvo), higher quality (Toyota), or more prestigious (Lexus) than other cars. Second, products can be positioned by use or application. For example, Campbell's soup is positioned not only as a lunch item but also for use as a sauce or dip or as an ingredient in main dishes. Third, products can be positioned in terms of particular types of product users. For example, sales for Johnson's Baby Shampoo increased dramatically after the company positioned the product not only for babies but also for active adults who need to wash their hair frequently. Fourth, products can be positioned relative to a product class. For example, Caress soap was positioned by Lever Brothers as a bath oil product rather than as a soap. Finally, products can be positioned directly against particular competitors. For example, Coke and Pepsi and McDonald's and Burger King commonly position directly against each other on various criteria, such as taste. The classic example of positioning is of this last type: Seven-Up positioned itself as a tasty alternative to the dominant soft drink, colas.

One way to investigate how to position a product is by using a *positioning map*, which is a visual depiction of customer perceptions of competitive products, brands, or models. It is constructed by surveying customers about various product attributes and developing dimensions and a graph indicating the relative position of competitors. Figure 5.6 presents a sample positioning map for automobiles that offers marketers a way of assessing whether their brands are positioned appropriately. For example, if Chrysler or Buick wants to be positioned in the minds of consumers as serious competitors to Lexus, then their strategies need to be changed to move up on this dimension. After the new strategies are implemented, a new positioning map could be developed to see if the brands moved up as desired.

FIGURE 5.6
Positioning Map for Automobiles

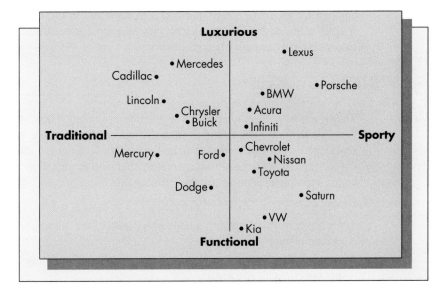

79

Dividing markets into segments and then selecting the best ones to serve is one of the cornerstones of sound marketing practice. However, there are situations when target marketing has been criticized as being unethical.

- R. J. Reynolds Tobacco Company planned to target African American consumers with a new brand of menthol cigarettes, Uptown. This brand was to be advertised with suggestions of glamour, high fashion, and night life. After criticism for targeting a vulnerable population, the company canceled plans for the brand.

- RJR planned to target white, 18- to 24-year-old "virile" females with a new cigarette brand, Dakota. It was criticized for targeting young, poorly educated, blue-collar women; and although it expanded the market to include males, Dakota failed in test markets and was withdrawn.

- Heileman Brewing Company planned to market a new brand of malt liquor called Power-Master. Malt liquor is disproportionately consumed by African Americans and in low-income neighborhoods. Criticism of this strategy led the brand to be withdrawn.

- The food industry has been criticized for many years for promoting high-fat-content foods to children.

One study suggests that whether targeting a group of consumers is unethical depends on two dimensions. The first is the degree to which the product can harm the consumers, and the second is the vulnerability of the group. Thus, to market harmful products to vulnerable target markets is likely to be considered unethical and could result in boycotts, negative word of mouth, and possibly litigation or legislation.

Source: Kevin Freking, "Marketing to Minors," *Wisconsin State Journal,* July 31, 2008, p. A7; N. Craig Smith and Elizabeth Cooper-Martin, "Ethics and Target Marketing: The Role of Product Harm and Consumer Vulnerability," *Journal of Marketing,* July 1997, pp. 1–20.

Some experts argue that different positioning strategies should be used depending on whether the firm is a market leader or follower and that followers usually should not attempt to position directly against the industry leader.[6] The main point here is that in segmenting markets, some segments might have to be forgone because a market-leading competitive product already dominates in sales and in the minds of customers. Thus, a smaller or less desirable target market may have to be selected since competing with market leaders is costly and not often successful.

DECIDE SEGMENTATION STRATEGY

The firm is now ready to select its segmentation strategy. There are four basic alternatives. First, the firm may decide not to enter the market. For example, analysis to this stage may reveal there is no viable market niche for the firm's offering. Second, the firm may decide not to segment but to be a mass marketer. There are at least three situations when this may be the appropriate decision for the firm:

1. The market is so small that marketing to a portion of it is not profitable.
2. Heavy users make up such a large proportion of the sales volume that they are the only relevant target.
3. The brand is the dominant brand in the market, and targeting to a few segments would not benefit sales and profits.

FIGURE 5.7
Selecting Target
Markets: Some
Questions Marketing
Managers Should
Answer

In order to select the best target markets, marketing managers must evaluate market segments on a number of dimensions. Below is a list of questions managers should answer before selecting target markets.

Measurability Questions

1. What are the appropriate bases for segmenting this market and are these bases readily measurable?
2. Are secondary data available on these bases so that the market segment can be identified and measured inexpensively?
3. If primary data are needed, is there sufficient return on investment to do the research?
4. Are specific names and addresses of people in this market segment needed; or is general knowledge of their existence, number, and geographic location sufficient?
5. Can purchases of people in this market segment be readily measured and tracked?

Meaningfulness Questions

1. How many people are in this market segment and how frequently will they purchase our product?
2. What market share can we expect in this segment?
3. What is the growth potential of this segment?
4. How strong is competition for this market segment and how is it likely to change in the future?
5. How satisfied are customers in this market segment with current product offerings?

Marketability Questions

1. Can this market segment be reached with our current channels of distribution?
2. If new channels are needed, can we establish them efficiently?
3. What specific promotion media do these people read, listen to, or watch?
4. Can we afford to promote to these people in the appropriate media to reach them?
5. Are people in this market segment willing to pay a price that is profitable for the company?
6. Can we produce a product for this market segment and do so profitably?

Third, the firm may decide to market to one segment. And fourth, the firm may decide to market to more than one segment and design a separate marketing mix for each. In any case, the firm must have some criteria on which to base its segmentation strategy decisions. Three important criteria on which to base such decisions are that a viable segment must be (1) measurable, (2) meaningful, and (3) marketable.

1. *Measurable.* For a segment to be selected, the firm must be capable of measuring its size and characteristics. For instance, one of the difficulties with segmenting on the basis of social class is that the concept and its divisions are not clearly defined and measured. Alternatively, income is a much easier concept to measure.
2. *Meaningful.* A meaningful segment is one that is large enough to have sufficient sales and growth potential to offer long-run profits for the firm.
3. *Marketable.* A marketable segment is one that can be reached and served by the firm in an efficient manner.

Figure 5.7 offers a list of questions marketing managers should answer when deciding whether a market segment meets these criteria. Segments that do so are viable target markets for the firm's offering. The firm must now give further attention to completing its marketing mix.

DESIGN MARKETING MIX STRATEGY

The firm is now in a position to complete its marketing plan by finalizing the marketing mix or mixes to be used for each segment. Clearly, selection of the target market and designing the marketing mix go hand in hand, and thus many marketing mix decisions should have already been carefully considered. To illustrate, the target market selected may be price sensitive, so some consideration has already been given to price levels, and clearly product positioning has many implications for promotion and channel decisions. Thus, while we place marketing mix design at the end of the model, many of these decisions are made in *conjunction* with target market selection. In the next six chapters of this text, marketing mix decisions will be discussed in detail.

SUMMARY

The purpose of this chapter was to provide an overview of market segmentation. Market segmentation was defined as the process of dividing a market into groups of similar consumers and selecting the most appropriate group(s) for the firm to serve. Market segmentation was analyzed as a six-stage process: (1) to delineate the firm's current situation, (2) to determine consumer needs and wants, (3) to divide the market on relevant dimensions, (4) to develop product positioning, (5) to decide segmentation strategy, and (6) to design marketing mix strategy.

Additional Resources

Bolton, Ruth N., and Matthew B. Myers. "Price-Based Global Market Segmentation for Services," *Journal of Marketing,* July 2003, pp. 108–28.
Dickson, Peter R., and James L. Ginter. "Market Segmentation, Product Differentiation, and Marketing Strategy." *Journal of Marketing,* April 1987, pp. 1–10.
Myers, James H. *Segmentation and Positioning for Strategic Marketing Decisions.* Chicago: American Marketing Association, 1996.
Yankelovich, Daniel, and David Meer. "Rediscovering Market Segmentation," *Harvard Business Review,* February 2006, pp. 122–31.

Key Terms and Concepts

A priori segmentation: Approach in which the marketing manager has decided on the appropriate basis for segmentation in advance of doing any research on the market.

Benefit segmentation: Approach that focuses on satisfying needs and wants by grouping consumers on the basis of the benefits they are seeking in a product.

Geodemographic segmentation: Approach that identifies specific households in a market by focusing on local neighborhood geography (such as zip codes) to create classifications of actual, addressable, mappable neighborhoods where consumers live and shop.

Market segmentation: The process of dividing a market into groups of similar consumers and selecting the most appropriate group(s) for the firm to serve.

Post hoc segmentation: Approach that groups people into segments on the basis of research findings rather than determining the basis prior to any research.

Positioning map: A visual depiction of consumer perceptions of competitive products, brands, or models.

Psychographic segmentation: Approach that focuses on consumer lifestyles as the basis for segmentation. Consumers are asked a variety of questions about their lifestyles (commonly, their activities, interests, and opinions) and then grouped on the basis of the similarity of their responses.

Target market: The group or segment a company selects to serve.

VALS: A product of SRI Consulting Business Intelligence; the best known psychographic approach; stands for "values and lifestyles."

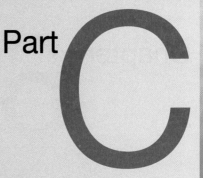

Part C

The Marketing Mix

Section I Essentials of Marketing Management

Chapter 6

Product and Brand Strategy

Product strategy is a critical element of marketing and business strategy, since it is through the sale of products and services that companies survive and grow. This chapter discusses four important areas of concern in developing product strategies. First, some basic issues are discussed, including product definition, product classification, product quality and value, product mix and product line, branding and brand equity, and packaging. Second, the product life cycle and its implications for product strategy are explained. Third, the product audit is reviewed, and finally, three ways to organize for product management are outlined. These include the marketing manager system, brand manager system, and cross-functional teams.

BASIC ISSUES IN PRODUCT MANAGEMENT

Successful marketing depends on understanding the nature of products and basic decision areas in product management. In this section, we discuss the definition and classification of products, the importance of product quality and value, and the nature of a product mix and product lines. Also considered is the role of branding and packaging.

Product Definition

The way in which the product variable is defined can have important implications for the survival, profitability, and long-run growth of the firm. For example, the same product can be viewed at least three different ways. First, it can be viewed in terms of the *tangible product*—the physical entity or service that is offered to the buyer. Second, it can be viewed in terms of the *extended product*—the tangible product along with the whole cluster of services that accompany it. For example, a manufacturer of computer software may offer a 24-hour hotline to answer questions users may have or to offer free or reduced-cost software updates, free replacement of damaged software, and a subscription to a newsletter that documents new applications of the software. Third, it can be viewed in terms of the *generic product*—the essential benefits the buyer expects to receive from the product. For example, many personal care products bring to the purchaser feelings of self-enhancement and security in addition to the tangible benefits they offer.

From the standpoint of the marketing manager, to define the product solely in terms of the tangible product is to fall into the error of "marketing myopia." Executives who are guilty of committing this error define their company's product too narrowly, since they overemphasize the physical object itself. The classic example of this mistake can be found in railroad passenger

Part C   The Marketing Mix

1. An audit of the firm's actual and potential resources
   a. Financial strength
   b. Access to raw materials
   c. Plant and equipment
   d. Operating personnel
   e. Management
   f. Engineering and technical skills
   g. Patents and licenses
2. Approaches to current markets
   a. More of the same products
   b. Variations of present products in terms of grades, sizes, and packages
   c. New products to replace or supplement current lines
   d. Product deletions
3. Approaches to new or potential markets
   a. Geographical expansion of domestic sales
   b. New socioeconomic or ethnic groups
   c. Overseas markets
   d. New uses of present products
   e. Complementary goods
   f. Mergers and acquisitions
4. State of competition
   a. New entries into the industry
   b. Product imitation
   c. Competitive mergers or acquisitions

service. Although no amount of product improvement could have staved off its decline, if the industry had defined itself as being in the transportation business, rather than the railroad business, it might still be profitable today. On the positive side, toothpaste manufacturers have been willing to exercise flexibility in defining their product. For years toothpaste was an oral hygiene product in which emphasis was placed solely on fighting tooth decay and bad breath (e.g., Crest with fluoride). More recently, many manufacturers have recognized the need to market toothpaste as a cosmetic item (to clean teeth of stains), as a defense against gum disease (to reduce the buildup of tartar above the gumline), as an aid for denture wearers, and as a breath freshener. As a result, special-purpose brands have been designed to serve these particular needs, such as Ultra Brite, Close-Up, Aqua-Fresh, Aim, Dental Care, and the wide variety of baking soda, tartar-control formula, and gel toothpastes offered under existing brand names.

In line with the marketing concept philosophy, a reasonable definition of product is that it is *the sum of the physical, psychological, and sociological satisfactions the buyer derives from purchase, ownership, and consumption.* From this standpoint, products are customer-satisfying objects that include such things as accessories, packaging, and service.

Product Classification

A product classification scheme can be useful to the marketing manager as an analytical device to assist in planning marketing strategy and programs. A basic assumption underlying such classifications is that products with common attributes can be marketed in a similar fashion. In general, products are classed according to two basic criteria: (1) end use or market, and (2) degree of processing or physical transformation.

1. *Agricultural products and raw materials.* These are goods grown or extracted from the land or sea, such as iron ore, wheat, and sand. In general, these products are fairly homogeneous, sold in large volume, and have low value per unit or in bulk weight.
2. *Organizational goods.* Such products are purchased by business firms for the purpose of producing other goods or for running the business. This category includes the following:
   a. Raw materials and semifinished goods.
   b. Major and minor equipment, such as basic machinery, tools, and other processing facilities.

    c. Parts or components, which become an integral element of some other finished good.

    d. Supplies or items used to operate the business but that do not become part of the final product.

3. *Consumer goods*. Consumer goods can be divided into three classes:

    a. Convenience goods, such as food, which are purchased frequently with minimum effort. Impulse goods would also fall into this category.

    b. Shopping goods, such as appliances, which are purchased after some time and energy are spent comparing the various offerings.

    c. Specialty goods, which are unique in some way so the consumer will make a special purchase effort to obtain them.

In general, the buying motive, buying habits, and character of the market are different for organizational goods vis-à-vis consumer goods. A primary purchasing motive for organizational goods is, of course, profit. As mentioned in a previous chapter, organizational goods are usually purchased as means to an end and not as an end in themselves. This is another way of saying that the demand for organizational goods is a derived demand. Organizational goods are often purchased directly from the original source with few middlemen, because many of these goods can be bought in large quantities; they have high unit value; technical advice on installation and use is required; and the product is ordered according to the user's specifications. Many organizational goods are subject to multiple-purchase influence, and a long period of negotiation is often required.

The market for organizational goods has certain attributes that distinguish it from the consumer goods market. Much of the market is concentrated geographically, as in the case of steel, auto, or shoe manufacturing. Certain products have a limited number of buyers; this is known as a *vertical market,* which means that (1) it is narrow, because customers are restricted to a few industries; and (2) it is deep, in that a large percentage of the producers in the market use the product. Some products, such as desktop computers, have a *horizontal market,* which means that the goods are purchased by all types of firms in many different industries. In general, buyers of organizational goods are reasonably well informed. As noted previously, heavy reliance is often placed on price, quality control, and reliability of supply source.

In terms of consumer products, many marketing scholars have found the convenience, shopping, and specialty classification inadequate and have attempted either to refine it or to derive an entirely new typology. None of these attempts appears to have met with complete success. Perhaps there is no best way to deal with this problem. From the standpoint of the marketing manager, product classification is useful to the extent that it assists in providing guidelines for developing an appropriate marketing mix. For example, convenience goods generally require broadcast promotion and long channels of distribution as opposed to shopping goods, which generally require more targeted promotion and somewhat shorter channels of distribution.

Product Quality and Value

Quality can be defined as the degree of excellence or superiority that an organization's product possesses.[1] Quality can encompass both the tangible and intangible aspects of a firm's products or services. In a technical sense, quality can refer to physical traits such as features, performance, reliability, durability, aesthetics, serviceability, and conformance to specifications. Although quality can be evaluated from many perspectives, the customer is the key perceiver of quality because his or her purchase decision determines the success of the organization's product or service and often the fate of the organization itself.

Many organizations have formalized their interest in providing quality products by undertaking total-quality management (TQM) programs. TQM is an organizationwide commitment to satisfying customers by continuously improving every business process involved in delivering products or services. Instead of merely correcting defects when they occur, organizations that practice TQM train and commit employees to continually look for ways to do things better so defects and problems don't arise in the first place. The result of this process is higher-quality products being produced at a lower cost. Indeed, the emphasis on quality has risen to such a level that over 70 countries have adopted the ISO 9000 quality system of standards, a standardized approach for evaluating a supplier's quality system, which can be applied to virtually any business.[2]

The term *quality* is often confused with the concept of value. Value encompasses not only quality but also price. *Value* can be defined as what the customer gets in exchange for what the customer gives. In other words, a customer, in most cases, receives a product in exchange for having paid the supplier for the product. A customer's perception of the value associated with a product is generally based both on the degree to which the product meets his or her specifications and the price that the customer will have to pay to acquire the product. Some organizations are beginning to shift their primary focus from one that solely emphasizes quality to one that also equally encompasses the customer's viewpoint of the price/quality trade-off. Organizations that are successful at this process derive their competitive advantage from the provision of customer value. In other words, they offer goods and services that meet or exceed customer needs at a fair price. Recall that Chapter 1 described various strategies based on value.

Product Mix and Product Line

A firm's *product mix* is the full set of products offered for sale by the organization; A product mix may consist of several *product lines,* or groups of products that share common characteristics, distribution channels, customers, or uses. A firm's product mix is described by its width and depth. *Width* of the product mix refers to the number of product lines handled by the organization. For example, one division of General Mills has a widespread mix consisting of five different product lines: ready-to-eat cereals, convenience foods, snack foods, baking products, and dairy products. *Depth* refers to the average number of products in each line. In its ready-to-eat cereals line, General Mills has eight different products. It has five different products in its line of convenience foods. Thus, the organization has a wide product mix and deep product lines.

An integral component of product line planning revolves around the question of how many product variants should be included in the line.[3] Manufacturing costs are usually minimized through large-volume production runs, and distribution costs tend to be lower if only one product is sold, stocked, and serviced. At a given level of sales, profits will usually be highest if those sales have been achieved with a single product. However, many firms offer many product variants.

Organizations offer varying products within a given product line for three reasons. First, potential customers rarely agree on a single set of specifications regarding their "ideal product," differing greatly in the importance and value they place on specific attributes. For example, in the laundry detergent market, there is a marked split between preferences for powder versus liquid detergent. Second, customers prefer variety. For example, a person may like Italian food but does not want to only eat spaghetti. Therefore, an Italian restaurant will offer the customer a wide variety of Italian dishes to choose from. Third, the dynamics of competition lead to multiproduct lines. As competitors seek to increase market share, they find it advantageous to introduce new products that subsegment an existing market segment by offering benefits more precisely tailored to the specific needs of a portion of that segment. For example, Proctor & Gamble offers Jif peanut butter in a low-salt version to target a specific subsegment of the peanut butter market.

All too often, organizations pursue product line additions with little regard for consequences.[4] However, in reaching a decision on product line additions, organizations need to evaluate whether (1) total profits will decrease or (2) the quality/value associated with current products will suffer. If the answer to either of the above is yes, then the organization

A. CLASSES OF CONSUMER GOODS—SOME CHARACTERISTICS AND MARKETING CONSIDERATIONS

Characteristics and Marketing Considerations	Type of Product		
	Convenience	Shopping	Specialty
Characteristics			
Time and effort devoted by consumer to shopping	Very little	Considerable	Cannot generalize; consumer may go to nearby store and buy with minimum effort or may have to go to distant store and spend much time and effort
Time spent planning the purchase	Very little	Considerable	Considerable
How soon want is satisfied after it arises	Immediately	Relatively long time	Relatively long time
Are price and quality compared?	No	Yes	No
Price	Usually low	High	High
Frequency of purchase	Usually frequent	Infrequent	Infrequent
Importance	Unimportant	Often very important	Cannot generalize
Marketing considerations			
Length of channel	Long	Short	Short to very short
Importance of retailer	Any single store is relatively unimportant	Important	Very important
Number of outlets	As many as possible	Few	Few; often only one in a market
Stock turnover	High	Lower	Lower
Gross margin	Low	High	High
Responsibility for advertising	Producer	Retailer	Joint responsibility
Importance of point-of-purchase display	Very important	Less important	Less important
Brand or store name important	Brand name	Store name	Both
Importance of packaging	Very important	Less important	Less important

Source: Michael J. Etzel, Bruce J. Walker, and William J. Stanton, *Fundamentals of Marketing*, 13th ed. (Burr Ridge IL: McGraw-Hill/Irwin, 2004), pp. 211, 214.

should not proceed with the addition. Closely related to product line additions are issues associated with branding. These are covered next.

Branding and Brand Equity

For some organizations, the primary focus of strategy development is placed on brand building, developing, and nurturing activities.[5] Factors that serve to increase the strength of a brand include[6] (1) product quality when products do what they do very well (e.g., Windex and Easy-Off); (2) consistent advertising and other marketing communications in which brands tell their story often and well (e.g., Pepsi and Visa); (3) distribution intensity whereby customers see the brand wherever they shop (e.g., Marlboro); and (4) brand personality where the brand stands for something (e.g., Disney). The strength of the Coca-Cola brand, for example, is widely attributed to its universal availability, universal awareness, and trademark protection, which came as a result of strategic actions taken by the parent organization.[7]

B. CLASSES OF ORGANIZATIONAL PRODUCTS—SOME CHARACTERISTICS AND MARKETING CONSIDERATIONS

Characteristics and Marketing Considerations	Type of Product				
	Raw Materials	Fabricating Parts and Materials	Installations	Accessory Equipment	Operating Supplies
Example	Iron ore	Engine blocks	Blast furnaces	Storage racks	Paper clips
Characteristics					
Unit price	Very low	Low	Very high	Medium	Low
Length of life	Very short	Depends on final product	Very long	Long	Short
Quantities purchased	Large	Large	Very small	Small	Small
Frequency of purchase	Frequent delivery; long-term purchase contract	Infrequent purchase, but frequent delivery	Very infrequent	Medium frequency	Frequent
Standardization of competitive products	Very much; grading is important	Very much	Very little; custom made	Little	Much
Quantity of supply	Limited; supply can be increased slowly or not at all	Usually no problem	No problem	Usually no problem	Usually no problem
Marketing considerations					
Nature of channel	Short; no middlemen	Short; middlemen for small buyers	Short; no middlemen	Middlemen used	Middlemen used
Negotiation period	Hard to generalize	Medium	Long	Medium	Short
Price competition	Important	Important	Not important	Not main factor	Important
Presale/postsale service	Not important	Important	Very important	Important	Very little
Promotional activity	Very little	Moderate	Sales people very important	Important	Not too important
Brand preference	None	Generally low	High	High	Low
Advance buying contract	Important; long-term contracts used	Important; long-term contracts used	Not usually used	Not usually used	Not usually used

The brand name is perhaps the single most important element on the package, serving as a unique identifier. Specifically, a *brand* is a name, term, design, symbol, or any other feature that identifies one seller's good or service as distinct from those of other sellers. The legal term for brand is *trademark*.[8] A good brand name can evoke feelings of trust, confidence, security, strength, and many other desirable characteristics.[9] To illustrate, consider the case of Bayer aspirin. Bayer can be sold at up to two times the price of generic aspirin due to the strength of its brand image.

Rank	Previous Rank	Brand	Country of Origin	Sector	Brand Value ($M)
1	1	Coca Cola	US	Beverages	70,452
2	2	IBM	US	Business services	64,727
3	3	Microsoft	US	Computer software	60,895
4	7	Google	US	Internet services	43,557
5	4	GE	US	Diversified	42,808
6	6	McDonalds	US	Restaurants	33,578
7	9	Intel	US	Electronics	32,015
8	5	Nokia	Finland	Electronics	29,495
9	10	Disney	US	Media	28,731
10	11	Hewlett-Packard	US	Electronics	26,867
11	8	Toyota	Japan	Automotive	26,192
12	12	Mercedes-Benz	Germany	Automotive	25,179
13	13	Gillette	US	FMCG	23,298
14	14	Cisco	US	Business services	23,219
15	15	BMW	Germany	Automotive	22,322
16	16	Louis Vuitton	France	Luxury	21,860
17	20	Apple	US	Electronics	21,143
18	17	Marlboro	US	Tobacco	19,961
19	19	Samsung	South Korea	Electronics	19,491
20	18	Honda	Japan	Automotive	18,506

Source: Interbrand, "The Best Global Brands," 2010.

Many companies make use of manufacturer branding strategies in carrying out market and product development strategies. The *line extension* approach uses a brand name to facilitate entry into a new market segment (e.g., Diet Coke and Liquid Tide). An alternative to line extension is brand extension. In *brand extension,* a current brand name is used to enter a completely different product class (e.g., Jello pudding pops, Ivory shampoo).[10]

A third form of branding is *franchise extension* or *family branding,* whereby a company attaches the corporate name to a product to enter either a new market segment or a different product class (e.g., Honda lawnmower, Toyota Lexus). A final type of branding strategy that is becoming more and more common is dual branding. A *dual branding* (also known as joint or cobranding) strategy is one in which two or more branded products are integrated (e.g., Bacardi rum and Coca-Cola, Long John Silver's and A&W Root Beer, Archway cookies and Kellogg cereal, US Airways and Bank of America Visa). The logic behind this strategy is that if one brand name on a product gives a certain signal of quality, then the presence of a second brand name on the product should result in a signal that is at least as powerful as, if not more powerful than, the signal in the case of the single brand name. Each of the preceding four approaches is an attempt by companies to gain a competitive advantage by making use of its or others' established reputation, or both.

Companies may also choose to assign different brand names to each product. This is known as *multibranding* strategy. By doing so, the firm makes a conscious decision to allow the product to succeed or fail on its own merits. Major advantages of using multiple brand names are that (1) the firm can distance products from other offerings it markets; (2) the image of one product (or set of products) is not associated with other products the company markets; (3) the product(s) can be targeted at a specific market segment; and (4) should the product(s) fail, the probability of failure impacting on other company products is minimized.

For example, many consumers are unaware that a number of different brands of laundry detergent are all marketed by Procter & Gamble. The major disadvantage of this strategy is that because new names are assigned, there is no consumer brand awareness and significant amounts of money must be spent familiarizing customers with new brands.

Increasingly, companies are finding that brand names are one of the most valuable assets they possess. Successful extensions of an existing brand can lead to additional loyalty and associated profits. Conversely, a wrong extension can cause damaging associations, as perceptions linked to the brand name are transferred back from one product to the other.[11] *Brand equity* can be viewed as the set of assets (or liabilities) linked to the brand that add (or subtract) value.[12] The value of these assets is dependent upon the consequences or results of the marketplace's relationship with a brand. Figure 6.1 lists the elements of brand equity. Brand equity is determined by the consumer and is the culmination of the consumer's assessment of the product, the company that manufactures and markets the product, and all other variables that impact on the product between manufacture and consumer consumption.

Before leaving the topic of manufacturer brands, it is important to note that, as with consumer products, organizational products also can possess brand equity. However, several differences do exist between the two sectors.[13] First, organizational products are usually branded with firm names. As a result, loyalty (or disloyalty) to the brand tends to be of a more global nature, extending across all the firm's product lines. Second, because firm versus brand loyalty exists, attempts to position new products in a manner differing from existing products may prove to be difficult, if not impossible. Finally, loyalty to organizational products encompasses not only the firm and its products but also the distribution channel members employed to distribute the product. Therefore, attempts to establish or change brand image must also take into account distributor image.

FIGURE 6.1
Elements of Brand Equity

Source: David A. Aaker, *Managing Brand Equity.* © 1991, New York, by David A. Aaker. Reprinted with the permission of Free Press, a division of Simon & Schuster. See David A. Aaker, *Building Strong Brands* (New York: Free Press, 1995), for his seminal work on branding as well as David A. Aaker, *Brand Portfolio Strategy: Creating Relevance, Differentiation, Energy, Leverage, and Clarity* (New York: Free Press, 2004). David A. Aaker, *Strategic Market Management* (Hoboken, NJ: John Wiley, 2008), Chapter 9.

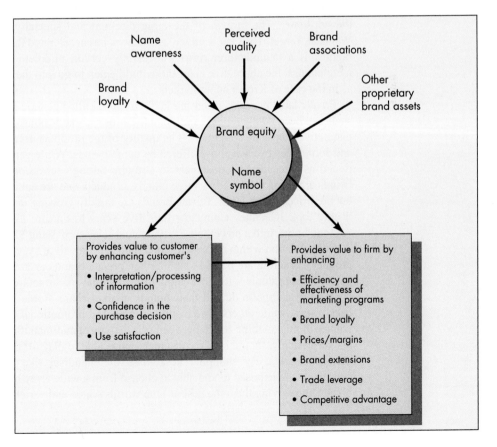

1. The name should suggest the product benefits. Names such as Easy Off (oven cleaner) and PowerBook (laptop computer) clearly suggest the benefits of purchasing the product.
2. The name should be memorable, distinctive, and positive. Many automobiles such as Mustang, Eagle, Firebird, and Bronco have strong names.
3. The name should fit the company or product image. Sharp (audio and video functions), Mustard's Last Stand (hot dogs), and Paddy O'Furniture (patio furniture) are some examples.
4. The name should have no legal restrictions. For example, the U.S. Food and Drug Administration discourages the use of word *heart* in food brand names. Also since brand names often need a corresponding address on the Internet, the choice may be complicated because millions of domain names have already been selected.
5. The name should be simple (such as Bold detergent and Sure deodorant), and emotional (Beautiful, Opium, and Obsession perfumes).

Source: Adapted from Roger A. Kerin, Steven W. Hartley, Eric N. Berkowitz, and William Rudelins, *Marketing,* 10th ed. (Burr Ridge, IL: McGraw-Hill/Irwin 2011), Chapter 11. Also see Kevin Lane Keller, *Strategic Brand Management,* 3rd ed. (Upper Saddle River, NJ: Prentice Hall, 2008), chap. 4.

As a related branding strategy, many retail firms produce or market their products under a so-called private label. For example, Kmart has phased in its own store-brand products to compete with the national brands. There's Nature's Classics, a line of fancy snacks and cookies; Oral Pure, a line of dental care products; Prevail house cleaners; B.E., a Gap-style line of weekend wear; and Benchmark, a line of "made in the U.S.A." tools. Such a strategy is highly important in industries where middlemen have gained control over distribution to the consumer. The growth of the large discount and specialty stores, such as Kmart, Walmart, Target, The Gap, Limited, and others, has accelerated the development of private brands. If a manufacturer refuses to supply certain middlemen with private branded merchandise, the alternative is for these middlemen to go into the manufacturing business, as in the case of Kroger supermarkets.

Private label products differ markedly from so-called generic products that sport labels such as "beer," "cigarettes," and "potato chips." Today's house brands are packaged in distinctively upscale containers. The quality of the products used as house brands equals and sometimes exceeds those offered by name brands. While generic products were positioned as a means for consumers to struggle through recessionary times, private label brands are being marketed as value brands, products that are equivalent to national brands but are priced much lower. Private brands are rapidly growing in popularity. For example, it only took JCPenney Company, Inc., five years to nurture its private-label jeans, the Arizona brand, into a powerhouse with annual sales surpassing $500 million.

Consolidation within the supermarket industry, growth of super centers, and heightened product marketing are poised to strengthen private brands even further.[14] However, these gains will not come without a fight from national manufacturers who are undertaking aggressive actions to defend their brands' market share. Some have significantly rolled back prices, while others have instituted increased promotional campaigns. The ultimate winner in this ongoing battle between private (store) and manufacturer (national) brands, not surprisingly, should be the consumer who is able to play off these store brands against national brands. By shopping at a mass merchandiser like Walmart or Walgreens, consumers are exposed to and able to choose from a wide array of both national and store brands, thus giving them the best of both worlds: value and variety.

Many different factors work together to make a strong brand. Brand managers often focus on only one or two of these factors. Here is a list of several characteristics shared by the world's strongest brands that can be used to assess the strengths of a brand and to identify points of improvement.

Characteristic	Examples
Delivers benefits desired by customers.	Starbucks offers "coffee house experience," not just coffee beans, and monitors bean selection and roasting to preserve quality.
Stays relevant.	Gillette continuously invests in major product improvements (MACH3), while using a consistent slogan: "The best a man can get."
Prices are based on value.	P&G reduced operating costs and passed on savings as "everyday low pricing," thus growing margins.
Well-positioned relative to competitors.	Saturn competes on excellent customer service, Mercedes on product superiority. Visa stresses being "everywhere you want to be."
Is consistent.	Michelob tried several different positionings and campaigns between 1970 and 1995, while watching sales slip.
The brand portfolio makes sense.	The Gap has Gap, Banana Republic, and Old Navy stores for different market segments; BMW has the 3-, 5-, and 7-series.
Marketing activities are coordinated.	Coca-Cola uses ads, promotions, catalogs, sponsorships, and interactive media.
What the brand means to customers is well understood.	Bic couldn't sell perfume in lighter-shaped bottles; Gillette uses different brand names such as Oral-B for toothbrushes to avoid this problem.
Is supported over the long run.	Coors cut back promotional support in favor of Coors Light and Zima, and lost about 50% of its sales over a four-year period.
Sources of brand equity are monitored.	Disney studies revealed that its characters were becoming "overexposed" and sometimes used inappropriately. It cut back on licensing and other promotional activity as a result.

Source: Kevin Lane Keller, "The Brand Report Card," *Harvard Business Review,* January-February 2000, pp. 147–157. Merle Crawford and Anthony DiBenedetto, *New Product Management*, 10th ed. (Burr Ridge, IL: McGraw-Hill/Irwin, 2011), p. 418.

Opportunity to Add Value	Some Decision Factors	Examples
Promoting	Link product to promotion	The bunny on the Energizer battery package is a reminder that it "keeps going and going."
	Branding at point of purchase or consumption	Coke's logo greets almost everyone each time the refrigerator is opened.
	Product information	Nabisco's nutrition label helps consumers decide which cookie to buy, and a UPC code reduces checkout time and errors.
Protecting	For shipping and storing	Sony's MP3 player is kept safe by Styrofoam inserts.
	From tampering	Tylenol's safety seal prevents tampering.
	From shoplifting	Cardboard hang-tag on Gillette razor blades is too large to hide in hand.
	From spoiling	Kraft's shredded cheese has a resealable zipper package to keep it fresh.
Enhancing product	The environment	Tide detergent bottle can be recycled.
	Convenience in use	Squeezable tube of Yoplait Go-Gurt is easy to eat on the go and in new situations.
	Added product functions	Plastic tub is useful for refrigerator leftovers after the Cool Whip is gone.

Source: William D. Perreault Jr., Joseph P. Cannon, and E. Jerome McCarthy, *Basic Marketing: A Marketing Strategy Planning Approach,* 18th ed. (Burr Ridge, Il: McGraw-Hill/Irwin, 2011), p. 241.

Packaging

Distinctive or unique packaging is one method of differentiating a relatively homogeneous product. To illustrate, shelf-stable microwave dinners, pumps rather than tubes of toothpaste or bars of soap, and different sizes and designs of tissue packages are attempts to differentiate a product through packaging changes and to satisfy consumer needs at the same time.

In other cases, packaging changes have succeeded in creating new attributes of value in a brand. A growing number of manufacturers are using green labels or packaging their products totally in green wrap to signify low- or no-fat content.[15] Frito-Lay, Quaker Oats, ConAgra, Keebler, Pepperidge Farm, Nabisco, and Sunshine Biscuits are all examples of companies involved in this endeavor.

Finally, packaging changes can make products urgently salable to a targeted segment. For example, the products in the Gillette Series grooming line, including shave cream, razors, aftershave, and skin conditioner, come in ribbed, rounded, metallic-gray shapes, looking at once vaguely sexual and like precision engineering.[16]

Marketing managers must consider both the consumer and costs in making packaging decisions. On one hand, the package must be capable of protecting the product through the channel of distribution to the consumer. In addition, it is desirable for packages to have a convenient size and be easy to open for the consumer. For example, single-serving soups and zip-lock packaging in cereal boxes are attempts by manufacturers to serve consumers better. Hopefully, the package is also attractive and informative, capable of being used as a competitive weapon to project a product's image. However, maximizing these objectives may increase the cost of the product to such an extent that consumers are no longer willing to purchase it. Thus, the marketing manager must determine the optimal protection, convenience, positioning, and promotional strengths of packages, subject to cost constraints.

PRODUCT LIFE CYCLE

A firm's product strategy must take into account the fact that products have a life cycle. Figure 6.2 illustrates this life-cycle concept. Products are introduced, grow, mature, and decline. This cycle varies according to industry, product, technology, and market. Marketing executives need to be aware of the life-cycle concept because it can be a valuable aid in developing marketing strategies.

During the introduction phase of the cycle, there are usually high production and marketing costs, and since sales are only beginning to materialize, profits are low or nonexistent. Profits increase and are positively correlated with sales during the growth stage as the market begins trying and adopting the product. As the product matures, profits for the initiating firm do not keep pace with sales because of competition. Here the seller may be forced to "remarket" the

FIGURE 6.2
The Product Life
Cycle

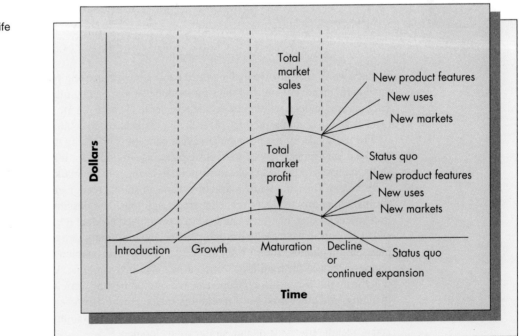

	Life-Cycle Stage			
Strategy Dimension	**Introduction**	**Growth**	**Maturity**	**Decline**
Basic objectives	Establish a market for product type; persuade early adopters to buy	Build sales and market share; develop preference for brand	Defend brand's share of market; seek growth by luring customers from competitors	Limit costs or seek ways to revive sales and profits
Product	Provide high quality; select a good brand; get patent or trademark protection	Provide high quality; add services to enhance value	Improve quality; add features to distinguish brand from competitors' brands	Continue providing high quality to maintain brand's reputation; seek ways to make the product new again
Pricing	Often high to recover development costs; sometimes low to build demand rapidly	Somewhat high because of heavy demand	Low, reflecting heavy competition	Low to sell off remaining inventory or high to serve a niche market
Channels	Limited number of channels	Greater number of channels to meet demand	Greater number of channels and more incentives to resellers	Limited number of channels
Promotion	Aimed at early adopters; messages designed to educate about product type; incentives such as samples and coupons to induce trial	Aimed at wider audience; messages focus on brand benefits; for consumer products, emphasis on advertising	Messages focus on differentiating brand from its competitors' brands; heavy use of incentives such as coupons to induce buyers to switch brands	Minimal, to keep costs down

product, which may involve making price concessions, increasing product quality, or expanding outlays on advertising and sales promotion just to maintain market share. At some point sales decline, and the seller must decide whether to (1) drop the product, (2) alter the product, (3) seek new uses for the product, (4) seek new markets, or (5) continue with more of the same.

The usefulness of the product life-cycle concept is primarily that it forces management to take a long-range view of marketing planning. In doing so, it should become clear that shifts in phases of the life cycle correspond to changes in the market situation, competition, and demand. Thus, the astute marketing manager should recognize the necessity of altering the marketing mix to meet these changing conditions. It is possible for managers to undertake strategies that, in effect, can lead to a revitalized product life cycle. For example, past advancements in technology led to the replacement of rotary dial telephones by touch-tone, push-button phones. Today, even newer technology has enabled the cordless and cellular phone to replace the traditional touch-tone, push-button phone. When applied with sound judgment, the life-cycle concept can aid in forecasting, pricing, advertising, product planning, and other aspects of marketing management. However, the marketing manager must also recognize that the life cycle is purely a tool for assisting in strategy development and not let the life cycle dictate strategy development.[17]

As useful as the product life cycle can be to managers, it does have limitations that require it to be used cautiously in developing strategy. For one thing, the length of time a product will remain in each stage is unknown and can't be predicted with accuracy. Thus, while each stage will likely occur for a successful product, marketers can't forecast when one stage will end and another will begin in order to adapt their strategies at the appropriate time. Also, they may misjudge when a stage is ending and implement an inappropriate strategy. For example, marketers who believe their products are ending the maturity stage may cut promotion costs and thus push the product into decline, whereas the product might have continued to sell if promotion had been maintained and altered.

Another limitation is that not all products go through the product life cycle in the same way. For example, many products are failures and do not have anything approaching a complete life cycle. Several variations of the life cycle also exist, two of which are fashions and fads.

Fashions are accepted and popular product styles. Their life cycle involves a distinctiveness stage in which trendsetters adopt the style, followed by an emulation stage in which more customers purchase the style to be the trendsetters. Next is the economic stage, in which the style becomes widely available at mass-market prices. Many fashions, such as skirt length and designer jeans, lose popularity, then regain it and repeat the fashion of cycle. The fashion cycle is clearly visible in clothing, cosmetics, tattoos, and body piercing.

Fads are products that experience an intense but brief period of popularity. Their life cycle resembles the basic product life cycle but in a very compressed form. It is usually so brief that competitors have no chance to capitalize on the fad. Some fads may repeat their popularity after long lapses.

Product Adoption and Diffusion

Obviously not all customers immediately purchase a product in the introductory stage of the product life cycle. The shape of the life-cycle curve indicates that most sales occur after the product has been available for awhile. The spread of a product through the population is known as the diffusion of innovation, as illustrated in Figure 6.3, which presents five adopter categories.

The first category is *innovators,* those who are the first to buy a new product. When innovators are consumers, they tend to be people who are venturesome and willing to take risks. When innovators are organizational buyers, they tend to be organizations that seek to remain at the cutting edge through the use of the latest technology and ideas.

FIGURE 6.3
Adopter Categories

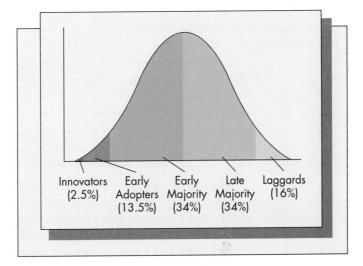

If the experience of innovators is favorable, *early adopters* begin to buy. These buyers, who are respected social leaders and above average in education, influence the next group. Influenced by what early adopters have, the rest of the market begins to get interested in the product. The biggest category of buyers is divided into groups called the early majority and late majority. Members of the *early majority* tend to avoid risk and to make purchases carefully. They also have many informal contacts. Members of the *late majority* not only avoid risks, but are cautious and skeptical about new ideas. Eventually, the product becomes commonplace, and even laggards are ready to buy. *Laggards* are reluctant to make changes and are comfortable with traditional products. They also have a fear of debt, but may eventually purchase a well-established brand.

THE PRODUCT AUDIT

The product audit is a marketing management technique whereby the company's current product offerings are reviewed to ascertain whether each product should be continued as is, improved, modified, or deleted. The audit is a task that should be carried out at regular intervals as a matter of policy. Product audits are the responsibility of the product manager unless specifically delegated to someone else.

Deletions

In today's environment, a growing number of products are being introduced each year that are competing for limited shelf space. This growth is primarily due to (1) new knowledge being applied faster, and (2) the decrease in time between product introductions (by a given organization).[18] In addition, companies are not consistently removing products from the market at the same time they are introducing new products. The result is a situation in which too many products are fighting for too little shelf space. One of the main purposes of the product audit is to detect sick products and then bury them. Rather than let the retailer or distributor decide which products should remain, organizations themselves should take the lead in developing criteria for deciding which products should stay and which should be deleted. Some of the more obvious factors to be considered are

Sales trends. How have sales moved over time? What has happened to market share? Why have sales declined? What changes in sales have occurred in competitive products both in our line and in those of other manufacturers?

Profit contribution. What has been the profit contribution of this product to the company? If profits have declined, how are these tied to price? Have selling, promotion, and distribution costs risen out of proportion to sales? Does the product require excessive management time and effort?

Product life cycle. Has the product reached a level of maturity and saturation in the market? Has new technology been developed that poses a threat to the product? Are more effective substitutes on the market? Has the product outgrown its usefulness? Can the resources used on this product be put to better use?

Customer migration patterns. If the product is deleted, will customers of this product switch to other substitute products marketed by our firm? In total, will profits associated with our line increase due to favorable switching patterns?

The above factors should be used as guidelines for making the final decision to delete a product. Deletion decisions are very difficult to make because of their potential impact on customers and the firm. For example, eliminating a product may force a company to lay off some employees. There are other factors to consider as well, such as keeping consumers supplied with replacement parts and repair service and maintaining the goodwill of distributors who have an inventory of the product. The deletion plan should also provide for clearing out of stock in question.

Product Improvement

One of the other important objectives of the audit is to ascertain whether to alter the product in some way or to leave things as they are. Altering the product means changing one or more of its attributes or marketing dimensions. *Attributes* refer mainly to product features, design, package, and so forth. *Marketing dimensions* refer to such things as price, promotion strategy, and channels of distribution.

It is possible to look at the product audit as a management device for controlling the product strategy. Here, control means feedback on product performance and corrective action in the form of product improvement. Product improvement is a top-level management decision, but the information needed to make the improvement decision may come from the consumer or the middlemen. Advertising agencies or consultants often make suggestions. Reports by the sales force should be structured in a way to provide management with certain types of product information; in fact, these reports can be the firm's most valuable product-improvement tool. Implementing a product improvement decision will often require the coordinated efforts of several specialists, plus some research. For example, product design improvement decisions involve engineering, manufacturing, accounting, and marketing. When a firm becomes aware that a product's design can be improved, it is not always clear how consumers will react to the various alterations. To illustrate, in blind taste tests, the Coca-Cola Company found that consumers overwhelmingly preferred the taste of a reformulated, sweeter new Coke over old Coke. However, when placed on the market in labeled containers, new Coke turned out to be a failure due to consumers' emotional attachments to the classic Coke. Consequently, it is advisable to conduct some market tests in realistic settings.

A discussion of product improvement would not be complete without taking into account the benefits associated with benchmarking, especially as they relate to the notion of the extended product, the tangible product along with the whole cluster of services that accompany it.[19] The formal definition of *benchmarking* is the continuous process of measuring products, services, and practices against those of the toughest competitors or companies renowned as leaders. In other words, benchmarking involves learning about best practices from best-performing companies—how they are achieving strong performance. It is an effective tool organizations use to improve on existing products, activities, functions, or processes. Major corporations such as IBM, AT&T, DuPont, Ford, Eastman Kodak, Miliken, Motorola, and Xerox all have numerous benchmarking studies in progress. Benchmarking can assist companies in many product improvement efforts, including (1) boosting product quality, (2) developing more user-friendly products, (3) improving customer order-processing activities, and (4) shortening delivery lead times. In the case of benchmarking, companies can achieve great success by copying others. Thus, by its very nature, benchmarking becomes an essential element in the ongoing product auditing process.

ORGANIZING FOR PRODUCT MANAGEMENT

Whether managing existing products or developing new products (the subject of the next chapter), organizations that are successful have one factor in common: They actively manage both types. Obviously, if a firm has only one product, it gets everyone's attention. But as the number of products grow and the need to develop new products becomes evident, some rational management system is necessary.

Under a *marketing-manager system,* one person is responsible for overseeing an entire product line with all of the functional areas of marketing such as research, advertising, sales promotion, sales, and product planning. This type of system is popular in organizations with a line or lines of similar products or one dominant product line. Sometimes referred to as category management, the marketing manager system is seen as being superior to a brand manager system because one manager oversees all brands within a particular line, thus avoiding brand competition. Organizations such as PepsiCo, Purex, Eastman Kodak, and Levi Strauss use some form of marketing-manager system.

Under a *brand-manager system,* a manager focuses on a single product or a very small group of new and existing products. Typically, this person is responsible for everything from marketing research and package design to advertising. Often called a product-management system, the brand-manager system has been criticized on several dimensions. First, brand managers often have difficulty because they do not have authority commensurate with their responsibilities. Second, they often pay inadequate attention to new products. Finally, they are often more concerned with their own brand's profitability than with the profitability of all of the organization's brands. These criticisms are not aimed at people but at the system itself, which may force brand managers into the above behaviors. Despite its drawbacks, organizations such as RJR Nabisco and Black & Decker have used this system.

Successful *new* products often come from organizations that try to bring all the capabilities of the organization to bear on the problems of customers. Obviously, this requires the cooperation of all the various functional departments in the organization (see Figure 6.4). Thus, the use of *cross-functional teams* has become an important way to manage the development of new products. A *venture team* is a popular method used in such organizations as Xerox, Polaroid, Exxon, IBM, Monsanto, and Motorola. A venture team is a cross-functional team responsible for all the tasks involved in the development of a new product. Once the new product is already launched, the team may turn over responsibility for managing the product to a brand manager or product manager or it may manage the new product as a separate business.

The use of cross-functional teams in product management and new product development is increasing for a very simple reason: Organizations need the contributions of all functions and therefore require their cooperation. Cross-functional teams operate

FIGURE 6.4

Some Requirements for the Effective Use of Cross-Functional Teams in Product Management and New Product Development

A growing number of organizations have begun using cross-functional teams for product management and new product development. Having representatives from various departments clearly has its advantages, but most important, effective teams must have the nurture and support of management. Some requirements for effective teams are

1. *Commitment of top management and provision of clear goals.* Organizations that successfully use cross-functional teams in product management or development have managers who are deeply committed to the team concept. As a result, high-performance teams have a clear understanding of the product management and development goals of the organization. The importance of these goals encourages individuals to defer their own functional or departmental concerns to team goals.

2. *Trust among members.* For cross-functional teams to work, a high level of trust must exist among members. The climate of trust within a team seems to be highly dependent on members' perception of management's trust of the group as a whole.

3. *Cross-functional cooperation.* If a team is to take responsibility and assume the risk of product development, its members will need detailed information about the overall operation of the organization. It often requires that functional units be willing to share information that previously was not shared with other departments.

4. *Time and training.* Effective cross-functional teams need time to mature. They require massive planning and intense and prompt access to resources, financial and other. Because members have to put aside functional and departmental loyalties and concerns, training is usually necessary.

independently of the organization's functional departments but include members from each function. A team might include a member from engineering, marketing, finance, service, and designers. Some organizations even include important outsiders (e.g., parts suppliers) on cross-functional teams. Figure 6.4 presents some important prerequisites for the use of cross-functional teams in managing existing products and developing new products.

SUMMARY

This chapter has been concerned with a central element of marketing management—product strategy. The first part of the chapter discussed some basic issues in product strategy, including product definition and classification, product quality and value, product mix and product lines, branding and brand equity, and packaging. The product life cycle was discussed as well as the product audit. Finally, three methods of organizing for product management were presented. Although product considerations are extremely important, remember that the product is only one element of the marketing mix. Focusing on product decisions alone, without consideration of the other marketing mix variables, would be an ineffective approach to marketing strategy.

Additional Resources

DeLuca, Luigi M., and Kwaku Atuahene. "Market Knowledge Dimensions and Cross Functional Collaboration: Examining the Different Routes to Product Innovation Performance." *Journal of Marketing,* January 2007, pp. 95–112.

Gladwell, Malcolm. *The Tipping Point.* NY: Book Bag Books, 2006.

Keough, Donald R. *The Ten Commandments of Business Failure.* NY: Portfolio Books, 2008.

Knapp, Duane. *The Brand Promise.* NY: McGraw-Hill, 2008.

Lindstrom, Martin. *Brand Sense: Build Powerful Brands Through Touch, Taste, Smell, Sight, and Sound.* NY: Free Press, 2005.

Pullig, Chris, Carolyn J. Simmons, and Richard G. Netemeyer. "Brand Dilution: When Do New Brands Hurt Existing Brands?" *Journal of Marketing,* April 2006, pp. 52–64.

Rust, Roland, Debra Viana Thompson, and Rebecca Thompson. "Defeating Feature Fatigue." *Harvard Business Review,* February 2006, pp. 98–109.

Key Terms and Concepts

Brand: A name, term, design, symbol, or any other feature that identifies one seller's good or service as distinct from those of other sellers. The legal term for brand is *trademark.*

Brand equity: The set of assets (or liabilities) linked to the brand that add (or subtract) value. The value of these assets is dependent upon the consequences or results of the market place's relationship with the brand.

Brand extension: A strategy that uses a current brand name to enter a completely different product class.

Brand-manager system: Type of product management system in which a manager focuses on a single product or a very small group of new and existing products. The brand manager is responsible for everything from marketing research and package design to advertising.

Cross-functional teams: Teams requiring the membership and cooperation of all the various functional departments in the organization to create successful new products.

Dual branding: A strategy in which two or more branded products are integrated. This strategy is sometimes called joint or cobranding.

Extended product: The tangible product along with the whole cluster of services that accompany it; one of the three ways a product can be viewed.

Fads: A product that experiences an intense but often very brief period of popularity. The faster it becomes popular, the faster it will become unpopular. A few fads may repeat their popularity after long absences.

Family branding: Sometimes called franchise extension; an organization's attachment of the corporate name to a product to enter either a new market segment or a different product class.

Fashions: Accepted and popular products that go through a repetitive cycle of popularity, lost popularity, and regained popularity, repeating the cycle again.

Generic product: Product that includes the essential benefits the buyer expects to receive; one of the three ways a product can be viewed.

Horizontal marketing: Market that exists for an organizational product when it is purchased by all types of firms in many different industries.

Marketing-manager system: Type of product management system popular in organizations with a line or lines of similar products or one dominant line. One person is responsible for overseeing an entire product line with all of the functional areas of marketing such as research, advertising, sales promotion, sales, and product planning.

Multibranding: A strategy that assigns different brand names to each product. The organization makes a conscious decision to allow the products to succeed or fail on their own merits.

Product: The sum of the physical, psychological, and sociological satisfactions the buyer derives from purchase, ownership, and consumption. This definition is consistent with the marketing concept.

Product adoption and diffusion: The spread of a product through the population; encompasses five stages of adopters: innovators, early adopters, early majority, late majority, and laggards.

Product life cycle: The concept that many products go through a cycle; that is, they are introduced, grow, mature, and decline. While the cycle varies according to industry, product, technology and market, it is a valuable aid in developing product and marketing strategies.

Product line: A group of products that share common characteristics, distribution channels, customers, or uses.

Product line extension: A strategy of line extension that uses a well-known brand name to enter into a new market segment.

Product mix: The full set of products offered for sale by an organization; described by its width and depth.

Product mix depth: The average number of products in each product line.

Product mix width: The number of individual product lines offered by the organization.

Quality: The degree of excellence or superiority that an organization's product or service possesses. It can encompass both the tangible and intangible aspects of a product or service. Although quality can be evaluated from many perspectives, the customer's perception of quality is crucial.

Tangible product: The physical entity or service that is offered to the buyer; one of the three ways a product can be viewed.

Value: Encompasses not only quality but also price. Value is what the customer gets for what the customer gives.

Venture team: A cross-functional team responsible for all of the tasks involved in the development of a new product. When the new product is launched, the team usually turns over responsibility for managing the product to a brand manager or product manager or it may manage the new product as a separate business.

Vertical market: Market for organizational products that have a limited number of buyers. A vertical market is narrow because customers are restricted to a few industries and is deep in that a large percentage of the producers in the market use the product.

Chapter

7

New Product Planning and Development

New products are a vital part of a firm's competitive growth strategy. Leaders of successful firms know that it is not enough to develop new products on a sporadic basis. What counts is a climate of product development that leads to one triumph after another. It is commonplace for major companies to have 50 percent or more of their current sales in products introduced within the last 10 years.[1]

Some additional facts about new products are important to remember:

- Many new products are failures. Estimates of new product failures range from 33 percent to 90 percent, depending on industry.
- New product sales grow far more rapidly than sales of current products, potentially providing a surprisingly large boost to a company's growth rate.
- Companies vary widely in the effectiveness of their new product programs.
- A major obstacle to effectively predicting new product demand is limited vision.
- Common elements appear in the management practices that generally distinguish the relative degree of efficiency and success between companies.

In one recent year, almost 22,000 products were introduced in supermarkets, drugstores, mass merchandisers, and health food stores.[2] Of these, only a small percentage (less than 20 percent) met sales goals. The cost of introducing a new brand in some consumer markets can range from $50 million to hundreds of millions of dollars. In addition to the outlay cost of product failures, there are also opportunity costs. These opportunity costs refer not only to the alternative uses of funds spent on product failures but also to the time spent in unprofitable product development.

Product development can take many years. For example, Hills Brothers (now owned by Nestlé) spent 22 years in developing its instant coffee, while it took General Foods (now owned by Altria) 10 years to develop Maxim. However, the success of one new product is no guarantee that additional low-cost brand extensions will be successful. For example, on the positive side, Gillette was able to leverage the research and monies spent on the original Sensor to successfully develop and launch the Sensor razor for women and the Sensor Excel razor. On the negative side, Maxwell House (Altria), Folgers (Procter & Gamble), and Nestlé are still struggling to develop commercially successful lines of fresh whole bean coffee, having been beaten to the punch by smaller companies such as Starbucks, Millstone Coffee, Inc., and Brothers Gourmet Coffees.[3]

Good management, with heavy emphasis on planning, organization, and interaction among the various functional units (e.g., marketing, manufacturing, engineering, R&D), seems to be the key factor contributing to a firm's success in launching new products. The primary reason found for new product failure is an inability on the part of the selling company to match its offerings to the needs of the customer. This inability to satisfy customer needs can be attributed to three main sources: inadequacy of upfront intelligence efforts, failure on the part of the company to stick close to what the company does best, and the inability to provide better value than competing products and technologies.

NEW PRODUCT STRATEGY

When developing new products, the first question must be, In how many ways can a product be new? Authors C. Merle Crawford and Anthony DiBenedetto have developed a useful definition of new products based on the following categories.[4]

1. *New-to-the-world products.* Products that are inventions and create a whole new market. For example, Sony Walkman, Polaroid camera, the Palm Pilot, the laser printer, in-line skates.
2. *New-to-the-firm products.* Products that take the firm into a category new to it but not to the world. Examples are Canon's laser printer, AT&T's Universal Credit Card, Hallmark gift items, P&G's first shampoo.
3. *Additions to existing product lines.* These are products that extend existing product lines to current markets such as Bud Light, Apple's iMac and Tide's liquid detergent.
4. *Improvements and revisions of existing products.* These are current products that are made better. Virtually every product on the market has been improved, often many times.
5. *Repositionings.* Products that are retargeted for a new use or application. Arm & Hammer baking soda is a classic example, being repositioned as a drain deodorant, refrigerator freshener, toothpaste, deodorant, and so on. Aspirin has been repositioned as a safeguard against heart attacks.
6. *Cost reductions.* These are new products that simply replace existing products in a line, providing the customer similar performance but at a lower cost.

The new product categories listed above raise the issue of imitation products, strictly me-too or improved versions of existing products. If a firm introduces a form of dry beer that is new to them but is identical or similar to other beers on the market, is it a new product? The answer is yes, because it is new to the firm. Managers should not get the idea that to imitate is bad and to innovate is good, for most of the best-selling products on the market today are improvements over another company's original invention. The best strategy is the one that will maximize company goals. It should be noted that Crawford and DiBenedetto's categories don't encompass variations such as new to a country, new channel of distribution, packaging improvement, and different resources or method of manufacture, which they consider to be variations of the six categories, especially as these variations relate to additions to product lines.

A second broader approach to the new product question is the one developed by H. Igor Ansoff in the form of growth vectors.[5] This is the matrix first introduced in Chapter 1 that indicates the direction in which the organization is moving with respect to its current products and markets. It is shown again in Figure 7.1.

Market penetration denotes a growth direction through the increase in market share for present product markets. *Product development* refers to creating new products to replace existing ones. Firms using either market penetration or product development strategies are attempting to capitalize on existing markets and combat competitive entry and/or further market incursions. *Market development* refers to finding new customers for existing

FIGURE 7.1
Organizational
Growth Strategies

Products Markets	Present	New
Present	Market penetration	Product development
New	Market development	Diversification

products. *Diversification* refers to developing new products and cultivating new markets. Firms using market development and diversification strategies are seeking to establish footholds in new markets or preempt competition in emerging market segments.

As shown in Figure 7.1, market penetration and market development strategies use present products. A goal of these types of strategies is to either increase frequency of consumption or increase the number of customers using the firm's product(s). A strategic focus is placed on altering the breadth and depth of the firm's existing product lines. Product development and diversification can be characterized as product mix strategies. New products, as defined in the growth vector matrix, usually require the firm to make significant investments in research and development and may require major changes in its organizational structure. Firms are not confined to pursuing a single direction. For example, Miller Brewing Co. has decided four key strategies should dictate its activities for the next decade, including (1) building its premium-brand franchises through investment spending, (2) continuing to develop value-added new products with clear consumer benefits, (3) leveraging local markets to build its brand franchise, and (4) building business globally.[6] Success for Miller depends on pursuing strategies that encompass all areas of the growth vector matrix.

It has already been stated that new products are the lifeblood of successful business firms. Thus, the critical product policy question is not whether to develop new products but in what direction to move. One way of dealing with this problem is to formulate standards or norms that new products must meet if they are to be considered candidates for launching. In other words, as part of its new product policy, management must ask itself the basic question, What is the potential contribution of each anticipated new product to the company?

Each company must answer this question in accordance with its long-term goals, corporate mission, resources, and so forth. Unfortunately, some of the reasons commonly given to justify the launching of new products are so general that they become meaningless. Phrases such as *additional profits, increased growth,* or *cyclical stability* must be translated into more specific objectives. For example, one objective may be to reduce manufacturing overhead costs by using plant capacity better. This may be accomplished by using the new product as an off-season filler. Naturally, the new product proposal would also have to include production and accounting data to back up this cost argument.

In every new product proposal some attention must be given to the ultimate economic contribution of each new product candidate. If the argument is that a certain type of product is needed to keep up with competition or to establish leadership in the market, it is fair to ask, Why? To put the question another way, top management can ask: What will be the effect on the firm's long-run profit picture if we do not develop and launch this or that new product? Policy-making criteria on new products should specify (1) a working definition of the profit concept acceptable to top management, (2) a minimum level or floor of profits, (3) the availability and cost of capital to develop a new product, and (4) a specified time period in which the new product must recoup its operating costs and begin contributing to profits.

It is critical that firms not become solely preoccupied with a short-term focus on earnings associated with new products. For example, in some industrial markets, a 20-year

1. A superior differentiated product that is unique by virtue of features, benefits, quality, and value.
2. A market-driven and customer focused new product development process.
3. Predevelopment work prior to beginning the development process.
4. Clear and early product definition.
5. Appropriate internal organizational structure.
6. A product that is familiar to the company's current products and markets.
7. A new product development process that uses profiles of previous product successes.
8. Controls on the new product development process that ensure sound execution.
9. Sound execution rather than speed.
10. Support for the new product through friendly, courteous, prompt, and efficient customer service.

Source: Based on Robert G. Cooper, "What Distinguishes the Top Performing New Products in Financial Services," *Journal of Product Innovation Management,* September 1994, pp. 281–99; and "The New Product System: The Industry Experience," *Journal of Product Innovation Management,* June 1992, pp. 113–27; and William O. Beardon, Thomas N, Ingram, and Raymond W. LaForge, *Marketing: Principles and Perspectives,* 5th ed. (Burr Ridge, IL: McGraw-Hill/Irwin, 2007), p. 219.

spread has been found between the development and wide-spread adoption of products, on average. Indeed, an advantage that some Japanese firms appear to possess is that their management is free from the pressure of steady improvement in earnings per share that plagues American managers who emphasize short-term profits. Japanese managers believe that market share will lead to customer loyalty, which in turn will lead to profits generated from repeat purchases. Through a continual introduction of new products, firms will succeed in building share. This share growth will then ultimately result in earnings growth and profitability that the stock market will support through higher share prices over the long term.

NEW PRODUCT PLANNING AND DEVELOPMENT PROCESS

Ideally, products that generate a maximum dollar profit with a minimum amount of risk should be developed and marketed. However, it is very difficult for planners to implement this idea because of the number and nature of the variables involved. What is needed is a systematic, formalized process for new product planning. Although such a process does not provide management with any magic answers, it can increase the probability of new product success. Initially, the firm must establish some new product policy guidelines that include the product fields of primary interest, organizational responsibilities for managing the various stages in new product development, and criteria for making go-ahead decisions. After these guidelines are established, a process such as the one shown in Figure 7.2 should be useful in new product development.

Idea Generation

Every product starts as an idea. But all new product ideas do not have equal merit or potential for economic or commercial success. Some estimates indicate that as many as 60 or 70 ideas are necessary to yield one successful product. This is an average figure, but it serves to illustrate that new product ideas have a high mortality rate. In terms of money, almost three-fourths of all the dollars of new product expense go to unsuccessful products.

FIGURE 7.2
The New Product
Development Process

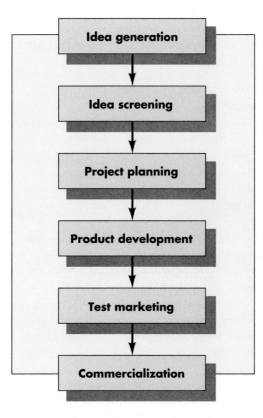

Idea generation

Idea screening

Project planning

Product development

Test marketing

Commercialization

The problem at this stage is to ensure that all new product ideas available to the company at least have a chance to be heard and evaluated. Ideas are the raw materials for product development, and the whole planning process depends on the quality of the idea generation and screening process. Since idea generation is the least costly stage in the new product development process (in terms of investment in funds, time, personnel, and escalation of commitment), it makes sense that an emphasis be placed first on recognizing available sources of new product ideas and then on funneling these ideas to appropriate decision makers for screening.

Top-management support is critical to providing an atmosphere that stimulates new product activity. Many times, great ideas come from some very unusual sources. A top-management structure that is unwilling to take risks will avoid radical new product and other innovation activities and instead concentrate solely on minor areas of improvement such as line extensions. To facilitate top-management support, it is essential that new product development be focused on meeting market needs.

Both technology push and market pull research activities play an important role in new product ideas and development. By taking a broad view of customer needs and wants, basic and applied research (technology push) can lead to ideas that will yield high profits to the firm. For example, Compaq bet millions (and won) on PC network servers in the early 1990s even though business customers said they would never abandon their mainframes. In a similar vein, Chrysler forged ahead with the original minivan despite research showing people disliked the odd-looking vehicle.[7] Marketing, on the other hand, is more responsible for gathering and disseminating information gained from customers and other contacts. This information relates mainly to specific features and functions of the product that can be improved upon or market needs that current products are not satisfying (market pull). For example, product ideas at Rubbermaid often come from employees roaming the aisles at

Marissa Mayer joined Google in early 1999 as a programmer when the workforce totaled 20. By 2007 Google had 5,700 employees and expected sales of $16 billion.

As Director of Consumer Web Products Marissa is a champion of innovation, and she favors new product launches that are early and often.

HOW GOOGLE INNOVATES

The search leader has earned a reputation as one of the most innovative companies in the world of technology. These are illustrative of the ways Google hatches new ideas:

FREE (THINKING) TIME

Google gives all engineers one day a week to develop their own pet projects, no matter how far these projects are from the company's central mission. If work gets in the way of free days for a few weeks, they accumulate. Google News came out of this process.

THE IDEA LIST

Anyone at Google can post thoughts for new technologies of businesses on an ideas mailing list, available companywide for input and vetting. But beware: Newbies who suggest familiar or poorly thought-out ideas can face an intellectual pummeling.

OPEN OFFICE HOURS

Think back to your professors' office hours in college. That's pretty much what key managers, including Mayer, do two or three times a week, to discuss new ideas. One success born of this approach was Google's personalized home page.

BIG BRAINSTORMS

As it has grown, Google has cut back on brainstorming sessions. Mayer still holds them eight times a year, but limits hers to 100 engineers. Six concepts are pitched and discussed for ten minutes each. The goal: To build on the initial idea with at least one complementary idea per minute.

ACQUIRE GOOD IDEAS

Although Google strongly prefers to develop technology in-house, it has also been willing to snap up small companies with interesting initiatives. In 2004 it bought Keyhole, including the technology that let Google offer sophisticated maps with satellite imagery.

Source: "Managing Googles's Idea Factory," *Business Week,* October 3, 2005, pp. 88–90. David Cravens and Nigel F. Piercy, *Strategic Marketing,* 9th ed. (Burr Ridge, Il: McGraw-Hill/Irwin, 2009), p. 240.

hardware stores and conversations with family and friends.[8] Both technology push and market pull approaches are essential to the generation of new product ideas.

Some firms use mechanisms such as "out-rotation," outsider involvement, and rewards to foster cooperation between design engineers and marketers.[9] Out-rotation involves placing employees in positions that require direct contact with customers, competitors, and other key outside groups. For example, Hewlett-Packard regularly rotates design engineers to retail sales positions on a temporary basis. Other organizations actively involve "outsiders" in planning or reward engineers for making external customer contacts. Regardless of method used, the primary lesson is to keep the communications flow going in all directions throughout the organization.

Idea Screening

The primary function of the idea screening process is twofold: first, to eliminate ideas for new products that could not be profitably marketed by the firm, and second, to expand viable ideas into full product concepts. New product ideas may be eliminated either because they are outside the fields of the firm's interest or because the firm does not have the necessary resources or technology to produce the product at a profit. Generally speaking, the organization has to consider three categories of risk (and its associated risk tolerance) in the idea screening phase prior to reaching a decision:[10]

1. *Strategic risk.* Strategic risk involves the risk of not matching the role or purpose of a new product with a specific strategic need or issue of the organization. If an organization feels it necessary to develop certain types of radical innovations or products new to the company in order to carry out long-term strategies, then management must be willing to dedicate necessary resources and time to pursue these type projects.

2. *Market risk.* Market risk is the risk that a new product won't meet a market need in a value-added, differentiated way. As products are being developed, customer requirements change and new technologies evolve. Management must be willing and able to shift its new product efforts to keep pace with change.

3. *Internal risk.* Internal risk is the risk that a new product won't be developed within the desired time and budget. Up front, management must decide the level of commitment it will extend in terms of time and budgetary expenditures to adequately ensure the completion of specific projects. Concurrently, progress goals must be established so that "proceed" or "do not proceed" decisions can be reached regarding continuation of projects.

In evaluating these risks, firms should not act too hastily in discounting new product ideas solely because of a lack of resources or expertise. Instead, firms should consider forming joint or strategic alliances with other firms. A strategic alliance is a long-term partnership between two organizations designed to accomplish the strategic goals of both parties. Potential benefits to be gained from alliances include (1) increased access to technology, funding, and information; (2) market expansion and greater penetration of current markets; and (3) de-escalated competitive rivalries. Motorola is a company that has prospered by forming numerous joint ventures with both American and foreign companies.[11]

Ideas that appear to have adequate profit potential and offer the firm a competitive advantage in the market should be accepted for further study.

Project Planning

This stage of the process involves several steps. It is here that the new product proposal is evaluated further and responsibility for the project is assigned to a project team. The proposal is analyzed in terms of production, marketing, financial, and competitive factors. A development budget is established, and some preliminary marketing and technical research is undertaken. The product is actually designed in a rough form. Alternative product features and component specifications are outlined. Finally, a project plan is written up, which includes estimates of future development, production, and marketing costs along with capital requirements and manpower needs. A schedule or timetable is also included. Finally, the project proposal is given to top management for a go or no-go decision.

Various alternatives exist for creating and managing the project teams. Two of the better-known methods are the establishment of a *skunkworks,* whereby a project team can work in relative privacy away from the rest of the organization, and a *rugby* or *relay approach,* whereby groups in different areas of the company are simultaneously working on the project.[12] The common tie that binds these and other successful approaches together is the degree of interaction that develops among the marketing, engineering, production, and other critical staff. The earlier in the process that interactive, cooperative efforts begin, the higher is the likelihood that development efforts will be successful. A key component contributing to the success of many companies' product development efforts relates to the emphasis placed on creating *cross-functional teams* early in the development process. Both of the above methods use cross-functional teams. Members from many different departments come together to jointly establish new product development goals and priorities and to develop

1. Customers
   a. Customer requests
   b. Customer complaints/compliments
   c. Market surveys
   d. Focus groups
2. Competitors
   a. Monitoring competitors' developments
   b. Monitoring testing of competitors' products
   c. Monitoring industry movements
3. Distribution channels
   a. Suppliers
   b. Distributors
   c. Retailers
   d. Trade shows
4. Research and engineering
   a. Product testing
   b. Product endorsement
   c. Brainstorming meetings
   d. Accidental discovery
5. Other internal sources
   a. Management
   b. Sales force
   c. Employee suggestions
   d. Innovation group meetings
   e. Stockholders
6. Other external sources
   a. Consultants
   b. Academic journals
   c. Periodicals and other press

new product development schedules. Frequently, marketing and/or sales personnel are called in to lead these teams.[13]

Product Development

At this juncture, the product idea has been evaluated from the standpoint of engineering, manufacturing, finance, and marketing. If it has met all expectations, it is considered a candidate for further research and testing. In the laboratory, the product is converted into a finished good and tested. A development report to management is prepared that spells out in fine detail: (1) results of the studies by the engineering department, (2) required plan design, (3) production facilities design, (4) tooling requirements, (5) marketing test plan, (6) financial program survey, and (7) estimated release date.[14]

Test Marketing

Up until now the product has been a company secret. Now management goes outside the company and submits the product candidate for customer approval. Test-market programs are conducted in line with the general plans for launching the product. Test marketing is a controlled experiment in a limited geographical area to test the new product or in some cases certain aspects of the marketing strategy, such as packaging or advertising.

The main goal of a test market is to evaluate and adjust, as necessary, the general marketing strategy to be used and the appropriate marketing mix. Additionally, producers can use the early interaction with buyers, occurring in test markets, to begin exploration of issues related to the next generation of product development.[15] Especially in cases where new technologies and markets are emerging, firms can benefit greatly from knowledge gained in test markets. Throughout the test market process, findings are being analyzed and forecasts of volume developed. In summary, a well-done test market procedure can reduce the risks that include not only lost marketing and sales dollars but also capital—the expense of installing production lines or building a new factory. Upon completion of a successful test market phase, the marketing plan can be finalized and the product prepared for launch.

Participant*	Activity	Participant*	Activity
1. Project Manager	Leader Integrator Translator Mediator Judge Arbitrator Coordinator	4. Strategist	Longer range Managerial Entire program
2. Product champion	Supporter Spokesperson Pusher Won't concede	5. Inventor	Creative scientist Basement inventor Idea source
3. Sponsor	Senior manager Supporter Endorses Assures hearing Mentor Increases output	6. Rationalist 7. Facilitator	Objectivity Reality Reason Financial Boosts productivity

*The participant role may be either formal or informal.

Source: Merle Crawford and Anthony DiBenedetto, *New Products Management,* 10th ed. (Burr Ridge, IL: McGraw-Hill/Irwin, 2011), p. 348.

Commercialization

This is the launching step in which the firm commits to introducing the product into the marketplace. During this stage, heavy emphasis is placed on the organization structure and management talent needed to implement the marketing strategy. Emphasis is also given to following up on such things as bugs in the design, production costs, quality control, and inventory requirements. Procedures and responsibility for evaluating the success of the new product by comparison with projections are also finalized.

The Importance of Time

Over the course of the last five years, companies have placed an increasing emphasis on shortening their products' time to market. *Time to market* can be defined as the elapsed time between product definition and product availability. It has been well documented that companies that are first in bringing their products to market enjoy a competitive advantage both in terms of profits and market share.[16] Successful time-based innovations can be attributed to the use of short production runs, whereby products can be improved on an incremental basis, and the use of cross-functional teams, decentralized work scheduling and monitoring, and a responsive system for gathering and analyzing customer feedback.

Several U.S. companies, including Procter & Gamble, have taken steps to speed up the new product development cycle by giving managers, at the product class and brand family level, more decision-making power. Increasingly, companies are bypassing time-consuming regional test markets, when feasible, in favor of national launches. It is becoming important, more than ever, that firms do a successful job of developing new products right the first time. To accomplish this, companies must have the right people with the right skills and talents in key positions within the new product framework.

111

Customer Acceptance Measures	Product Level Performance
Customer acceptance (use)	Product cost
Customer satisfaction	Time to launch
Revenue (dollar sales)	Product performance
Market share	Quality guidelines
Unit volume	
Financial Performance	**Other**
Time to break even	Nonfinancial measures peculiar to the new product being launched.
Margins	Example: competitive effect, image change, morale change.
Profitability (IRR, ROI)	

Source: Merle Crawford and Anthony DiBenedetto, *New Products Management,* 10th ed. (Burr Ridge, Il: McGraw-Hill/Irwin, 2011), p. 375.

SOME IMPORTANT NEW PRODUCT DECISIONS

In the development of new products, marketers have several important decisions to make about the characteristics of the product itself. These include quality level, product features, product design, and product safety levels.

Quality Level

Both consumers and organizational buyers consider the level of product quality when making purchase decisions for both new and existing products. At a minimum, buyers want products that will perform the functions they are supposed to and do so reasonably well. Some customers are willing to accept lower quality if product use is not demanding and the price is lower. Some homeowners might prefer Sears brand hand tools over the higher-quality Craftsman brand since they are lower priced and may be used only occasionally. Industrial buyers of nuts and bolts for automobiles seldom use the highest quality used in aircraft since cars are used in less demanding situations.

In designing new products, marketers must consider what criteria potential customers use to determine their perceptions of quality. While these will vary by product, Figure 7.3 presents eight general criteria.

FIGURE 7.3
Some Criteria for Determining Perceptions of Quality

Source: Adopted from David A. Garvin, "Competing on the Eight Dimensions of Quality," *Harvard Business Review,* November–December 1987. For a discussion of some determinants of quality for service businesses, see chapter 12, "The Marketing of Services."

1. *Performance*—How well does the product do what it is supposed to do?
2. *Features*—Does the product have any unique features that are desirable?
3. *Reliability*—Is the product likely to function well and not break down over a reasonable time period?
4. *Conformance*—Does the product conform to established standards for such things as safety?
5. *Durability*—How long will the product last before it will be worn out and have to be replaced?
6. *Serviceability*—How quickly and easily can any problems be corrected?
7. *Aesthetics*—How appealing is the product to the appropriate senses of sight, taste, smell, feel, and/or sound?
8. *Overall Evaluation*—Considering everything about the product, including its physical characteristics, manufacturer, brand image, packaging, and price, how good is this product?

When specialized knowledge is needed to satisfy the needs of customers, cross-functional teams can greatly improve product development success. Such teams bring together complementary skills in one of three areas: technical or functional expertise, problem-solving and decision-making skills, and interpersonal skills.

1. *Technical or functional skills.* It would make little sense for a marketer to design technical specifications for a new type of cellular phone. Likewise, it would make little sense for an engineer to try to guess what features consumers find most important in choosing what type of phone to purchase. In this case, a product development group that consists solely of marketers or engineers would be less likely to succeed than a cross-functional team using the complementary skills of both.

2. *Problem-solving and decision-making skills.* Cross-functional teams possess the ability to identify problems and opportunities the entire organization faces, identify feasible new product alternatives, and make the necessary choices quicker. Most industrial functional units are not able to perform all of these tasks effectively. However, it is likely that the necessary skills are present in a well-chosen cross-functional team and that these skills can be used in the organization's best interests.

3. *Interpersonal skills.* Common understanding and knowledge of problems faced and decisions needed for effective product development cannot arise without effective communication and constructive conflict. What is needed is risk-taking, helpful criticism, objectivity, active listening, support, and recognition of the interests and achievements of others. An effective, cross-functional team is made up of members who, in total, possess all of these skills. Individual members, at various times, will be called on to use their interpersonal skill to move the team forward. The use of the complementary interpersonal skills of team members can lead to extraordinary results for organizations.

An important indicator of a number of the criteria listed in Figure 7.3 is the presence and extent of a new product *warranty*. A warranty is the producer's statement of what it will do to compensate the buyer if the product is defective or does not work properly. In many instances, the courts also hold that businesses have implied warranties or unstated promises to compensate buyers if their products fail to perform up to the basic standards of the industry or to the level promised. Certainly an organization that wants to emphasize high quality will offer customers more than implied warranties enforced by the courts.

Finally, many marketers offer a guarantee instead of or in addition to a warranty on new products. A *guarantee* is an assurance that the product is as represented and will perform properly. Typically if the product fails to perform, the organization making the guarantee replaces the product or refunds the customer's money. Guarantees imply to some buyers that the manufacturer is confident of the new products' quality.

Product Features

A *product feature* is a fact or particular specification about a product (e.g., "less calories than all other soft drinks," "more vitamin C than any other multiple vitamin"). Marketers select new product features by determining what it is that customers want their products to offer. Effective marketers attempt not only to ask potential customers what they want, but to learn what these customers are likely to need. Such marketers may identify a need for new features that target markets have not yet thought of and may not yet even understand.

Product Design

Many well-designed products are easy to use as intended and pleasing to the senses. Designing new products with both ease of use and aesthetic appeal can be difficult, but it can clearly differentiate a new product from competitors. Good design can add great value to a new product. A well-designed product can please customers without necessarily costing more to make. This is especially likely to happen when the organization uses cross-functional teams to develop its products. If employees from engineering, marketing, and manufacturing work together on what the product will look like and how it will operate, they are more likely to create a design that is easy and economical to make as well as use.

Product Safety

Clearly, new products must have a reasonable level of safety. Safety is both an ethical and practical issue. Ethically, customers should not be harmed by using a product as intended. The practical issue is that when users get harmed by a product, they may stop buying, tell others about their experience, or sue the company that made or sold it.

Some products are inherently dangerous and can result in injury to users. However, it may be so expensive to make them safer that buyers could not afford to buy them. Such products include automobiles, farm equipment and other machinery, and guns. Other products such as patented medicines can harm a small portion of users. Hopefully, the benefits such products offer outweigh their risks.

CAUSES OF NEW PRODUCT FAILURE

Many new products with satisfactory potential have failed to make the grade for reasons related to execution and control problems. What follows is a brief list of some of the more important marketing causes of new product failures after the products have been carefully screened, developed, and marketed.[17]

1. No competitive point of difference, unexpected reactions from competitors, or both.
2. Poor positioning.
3. Poor quality of product.
4. Nondelivery of promised benefits of product.
5. Too little marketing support.
6. Poor perceived price/quality (value) relationship.
7. Faulty estimates of market potential and other marketing research mistakes.
8. Faulty estimates of production and marketing costs.
9. Improper channels of distribution selected.
10. Rapid change in the market (economy) after the product was introduced.

Some of these problems are beyond the control of management, but it is clear that successful new product planning requires large amounts of reliable information in diverse areas. Each department assigned functional responsibility for product development automatically becomes an input to the information system that the new product decision maker needs. For example, when a firm is developing a new product, it is wise for both engineers and marketers to consider both the kind of market to be entered (e.g., consumer, organizational, international) and specific target segments. These decisions will be of paramount influence on the design and cost of the finished good, which will, of course, directly influence price, sales, and profits.

1. *Not listening* to the "voice of the customer." Product managers assume they know more than customers or that doing marketing research will not be worth the cost or time.
2. *Skipping steps* in the new-product process. (See Figure 7-2.)
3. *Trying to generate* quick revenue by releasing a poorly conceived product to market.
4. *"Groupthink"* in product development committees. This popular problem occurs in groups when members "go along" to "get along" rather than be seen as nay sayers or non-team players.
5. *Not identifying* the lessons from previous failures.

Sources: Adapted from Pierre Loewe and Jennifer Domeniquini, "Overcoming the Barriers to Effective Innovation," *Strategy and Leadership* 34, no. 1 (2006), pp. 24–31; Dan P. Lovallo and Oliver Sibony, "Distortions and Deceptions in Strategic Decisions," *The McKinsey Quarterly,* no. 1 (2006), pp. 19–29; Eyal Biyalogorsky, William Boulding, and Richard Staelin, "Stuck in The Past: Why Managers Persist with New Product Failures," *Journal of Marketing,* April 2006, pp. 108–21; Jena MacGregor, "How Failure Breeds Success," *Business Week,* July 10, 2006, pp. 42–52; and Roger A. Kerin, Steven W. Hartley, and William Rudelius, *Marketing,* 10th ed. (Burr Ridge, IL: McGraw-Hill/Irwin, 2011), pp. 254–55.

Need for Research

In many respects it can be argued that the keystone activity of any new product planning system is research—not just marketing research, but technical research as well. Regardless of the way the new product planning function is organized in the company, top management's new product development decisions require data that provide a base for making more intelligent choices. New product project reports ought to be more than a collection of "expert" opinions. Top management has a responsibility to ask certain questions, and the new product planning team has an obligation to generate answers to these questions based on research that provides marketing, economic, engineering, and production information. This need will be more clearly understood if some of the specific questions commonly raised in evaluating product ideas are examined:

1. What is the anticipated market demand over time? Are the potential applications for the product restricted?
2. Can the item be patented? Are there any antitrust problems?
3. Can the product be sold through present channels and the current sales force? What number of new salespersons will be needed? What additional sales training will be required?
4. At different volume levels, what will be the unit manufacturing costs?
5. What is the most appropriate package to use in terms of color, material, design, and so forth?
6. What is the estimated return on investment?
7. What is the appropriate pricing strategy?

While this list is not intended to be exhaustive, it serves to illustrate the serious need for reliable information. Note also that some of the essential facts required to answer these questions can be obtained only through time-consuming and expensive marketing research studies. Other data can be generated in the engineering laboratories or pulled from accounting records. Certain types of information must be based on assumptions, which may or may not hold true, and on expectations about what will happen in the future, as in the case of anticipated competitive reaction or the projected level of sales.

SUMMARY

This chapter has focused on the nature of new product planning and development. Attention has been given to the management process required to have an effective program for new product development. It should be obvious that this is one of the most important and difficult aspects of marketing management. The problem is so complex that, unless management develops a plan for dealing with the problem, it is likely to operate at a severe competitive disadvantage in the marketplace.

Additional Resources

Bender, Michael. *A Manager's Guide to Project Management.* Upper Saddle River, NJ: FT Press, 2010.

Biyalogorsky, Eyal, William Boulding, and Richard Staelin. "Stuck In The Past: Why Managers Persist in New Product Failures." *Journal of Marketing,* April 2006, pp. 108–122.

Estrin, Judy. *Closing The Innovation Gap.* NY: McGraw-Hill, 2009.

Macintosh, Julie. *Dethroning the King.* NY: John Wiley and Sons, 2011.

Mack, Ben. *Think Two Products Ahead.* NY: John Wiley, 2007.

Moeller, Leslie H., and Edward Landry. *The Four Pillars of Profit Driven Marketing.* NY: McGraw-Hill, 2009.

Key Terms and Concepts

Commercialization: Stage of the new product development process that involves the actual launch of the product and the implementation of the marketing strategy.

Cross-functional teams: Members from many different departments coming together to jointly establish new product development goals and priorities and to develop schedules.

Diversification: A strategy that seeks to develop new products and cultivate new customers. It often leads the organization into new businesses, sometimes through acquisition.

Guarantee: An assurance by the producer that the product is as represented and will perform properly. If not, the organization making the guarantee replaces the product or refunds the customer's money.

Idea generation: Stage of the new product development process at which the goal is to ensure that all new product ideas considered by the organization have the opportunity to be heard and evaluated because the success of the process will depend greatly on the quality of the ideas generated.

Idea screening: Evaluation of an idea based on strategic risk, market risk, and internal risk for the purpose of eliminating ideas that could not be profitably marketed and expanding viable ideas into full product concepts.

Market development: A strategy that seeks to find new customers for existing products. An organization pursuing this strategy seeks to establish footholds in new markets or preempt competition in emerging market segments.

Market penetration: A strategy that denotes a growth direction through the increase in market share of present products in present markets. An organization pursuing this strategy hopes to capitalize on existing markets and combat competitive entry or incursions.

New product development process: Stages include idea generation, idea screening, project planning, product development, test marketing, commercialization.

Product development: A strategy that seeks to create new products to replace existing ones. An organization pursuing this strategy hopes to capitalize on existing markets and combat competitive entry or incursions.

Product development stage: Stage of the new product development process at which the product idea has met all expectations and is considered a candidate for further research and testing. In the laboratory, the product is converted into a finished good and tested.

Project planning: Stage of the new product development process at which the idea is evaluated further and responsibility for the project is assigned to a project team. The idea is evaluated in terms of production, marketing, financial, and competitive factors. A development budget is established, and preliminary marketing and technical research is undertaken.

Rugby or relay: An approach to creating and managing product development teams that involves groups in different areas of the organization working simultaneously on the project.

Skunkworks: An approach to creating and managing product development teams that involves team members working in relative privacy, away from the rest of the organization.

Test marketing: Stage of new product development process at which the product is no longer a company secret. Test marketing is a controlled experiment in a limited geographical area to test the new product as well as elements of the marketing mix.

Time to market: The elapsed time between product definition and product availability. It is important because history has shown that organizations that are first in bringing their product to market often gain a competitive advantage in terms of profits and market share.

Warranty: The statement of the producer of what it will do to compensate the buyer if the product is defective or does not perform properly.

Chapter

Integrated Marketing Communications

Communicating with customers will be the broad subject of the next two chapters that focus on various elements of promotion. To simplify our discussion, the topic has been divided into two basic categories: nonpersonal communication (Chapter 8) and personal communication (Chapter 9). This chapter also discusses the necessity to integrate the various elements of marketing communication.

STRATEGIC GOALS OF MARKETING COMMUNICATION

Marketers seek to communicate with target customers for the obvious goal of increased sales and profits. Accordingly, they seek to accomplish several strategic goals with their marketing communications efforts.

Create Awareness

Obviously, we cannot purchase a product if we are not aware of it. An important strategic goal must be to generate awareness of the firm as well as its products. Marketing communications designed to create awareness are especially important for new products and brands in order to stimulate trial purchases. As an organization expands globally, creating awareness must be a critical goal of marketing communications.

Build Positive Images

When products or brands have distinct images in the minds of customers, the customers better understand the value that is being offered. Positive images can even create value for customers by adding meaning to products. Retail stores and other organizations also use communications to build positive images. A major way marketers create positive and distinct images is through marketing communications.

Identify Prospects

Identifying prospects is becoming an increasingly important goal of marketing communications because modern technology makes information gathering much more practical, even in large consumer markets. Marketers can maintain records of consumers who have

France 26.1 million visitors		Germany 32.6 million visitors		Japan 53.8 million visitors	
1. Google Sites	18.2	Google Sites	23.0	Yahoo sites	40.7
2. Microsoft sites	16.4	Microsoft sites	17.7	Google sites	32.0
3. France Telecom	14.0	eBay	17.4	Microsoft sites	30.0
4. Illaid/Free.fr	12.9	United-Internet sites	16.2	Rakuten Inc.	28.5
5. Grope Pages Jaunes	11.4	Time Warner Network	14.6	NTT group	24.6
6. eBay	11.4	Wikipedia sites	12.6	FC2 Inc.	24.1
7. Yahoo sites	10.9	T-Online sites	12.1	Nifty Corp.	22.0
8. Skyrock Network	9.5	Yahoo sites	11.2	Wikipedia sites	20.6
9. Groupe PPR	8.9	Otto Grupe	11.1	Livedoor	19.7
10. Wikipedia sites	8.5	Karstadt-Quelle	10.1	Amazon sites	18.4

Source: Philip R. Cateora, Mary C. Gilly, and John I. Graham, *International Marketing,* 15th ed. (Burr Ridge, Il: McGraw-Hill/Irwin, 2011), p. 484.

expressed an interest in a product, then more efficiently direct future communications. Technology now enables marketers to stay very close to their customers. Web sites are used to gather information about prospects, and supermarkets use point-of-sale terminals to dispense coupons selected on the basis of a customer's past purchases.

Build Channel Relationships

An important goal of marketing communications is to build a relationship with the organization's channel members. When producers use marketing communications to generate awareness, they are also helping the retailers who carry the product. Producers may also arrange with retailers to distribute coupons, set up special displays, or hold promotional events in their stores, all of which benefit retailers and wholesalers. Retailers support manufacturers when they feature brands in their ads to attract buyers. Because of such efforts, all members of the channel benefit. Cooperating in these marketing communication efforts can build stronger channel relationships.

Retain Customers

Loyal customers are a major asset for every business. It costs far more to attract a new customer than to retain an existing customer. Marketing communications can support efforts to create value for existing customers. Interactive modes of communication—including salespeople and Web sites—can play an important role in retaining customers. They can serve as sources of information about product usage and new products being developed. They can also gather information from customers about what they value, as well as their experiences using the products. This two-way communication can assist marketers in increasing the value of what they offer to existing customers, which will influence retention.

THE PROMOTION MIX

The promotion mix concept refers to the combination and types of nonpersonal and personal communication the organization puts forth during a specified period.[1] There are five elements of the promotion mix, four of which are nonpersonal forms of communication (advertising, sales promotion, public relations, and direct marketing), and one, personal selling, which is a personal form of communication. Let's briefly examine each one.

1. *Advertising* is a paid form of nonpersonal communications about an organization, its products, or its activities that is transmitted through a mass medium to a target audience. The mass medium might be television, radio, newspapers, Internet, magazines, outdoor displays, car cards, or directories.

2. *Sales promotion* is an activity or material that offers customers, sales personnel, or resellers a direct inducement for purchasing a product. This inducement, which adds value to or incentive for the product, might take the form of a coupon, sweepstakes, refund, or display.

3. *Public relations* is a nonpersonal form of communication that seeks to influence the attitudes, feelings, and opinions of customers, noncustomers, stockholders, suppliers, employees, and political bodies about the organization. A popular form is *publicity,* which is a nonpaid form of nonpersonal communication about the organization and its products that is transmitted through a mass medium in the form of a news story. Obviously, marketers seek positive publicity.

4. *Direct marketing* uses direct forms of communication with customers. It can take the form of direct mail, online marketing, catalogs, telemarketing, and direct response advertising. Similar to personal selling, it may consist of an interactive dialog between the marketer and the customer. Its objective is to generate orders, visits to retail outlets, or requests for further information. Obviously, personal selling is a form of direct marketing, but because it is a very personal form of communication, we place it in its own category.

5. *Personal selling* is face-to-face communication with potential buyers to inform them about and persuade them to buy an organization's product. It will be examined in detail in the next chapter.

Obviously, marketers strive for the right mix of promotional elements to ensure that their product is well received. For example, if the product is a new soft drink, promotional effort is likely to rely more on advertising, sales promotion, and public relations (publicity) in order to (1) make potential buyers aware of the product, (2) inform these buyers about the benefits of the product, (3) convince buyers of the product's value, and (4) entice buyers to purchase the product. If the product is more established but the objective is to stabilize sales during a nonpeak season, the promotion mix will likely contain short-run incentives (sales promotions) for people to buy the product immediately. Finally, if the product is a new complex technology that requires a great deal of explanation, the promotional mix will likely focus heavily on personal selling so that potential buyers can have their questions answered.

As seen by the previous examples, a firm's promotion mix is likely to change over time. The mix must be continually adapted to reflect changes in the market, competition, the product's life cycle, and the adoption of new strategies. In essence, the firm should take into account three basic factors when devising its promotion mix: (1) the role of promotion in the overall marketing mix, (2) the nature of the product, and (3) the nature of the market.

INTEGRATED MARKETING COMMUNICATIONS

In many organizations, elements of the promotion mix are often managed by specialists in different parts of the organization or, in some cases, outside the organization when an advertising agency is used. For example, advertising plans might be developed jointly by

FIGURE 8.1

How Various
Promotion Tools
Might Contribute to
the Purchase of a
Hypothetical Product

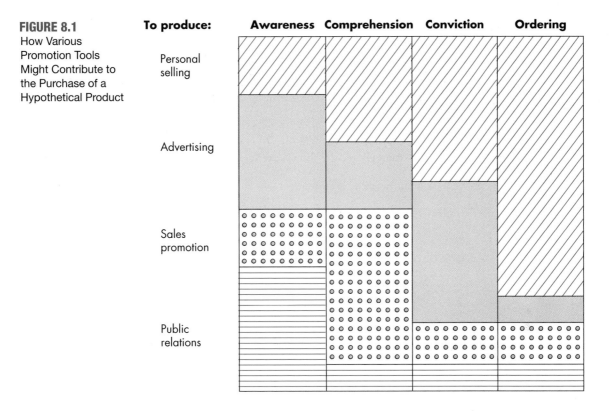

the advertising department and the advertising agency; plans for the sales force might be developed by managers of the sales force; and sales promotions might be developed independently of the advertising and sales plans. Thus, it is not surprising that the concept of *integrated marketing communications* has evolved in recent years.

The idea of integrated marketing communications is easy to understand and certainly has a great deal of commonsense validity. But like so many concepts in marketing, it is difficult to implement. The goal of integrated marketing communications is to develop marketing communications programs that coordinate and integrate all elements of promotion—advertising, sales promotion, personal selling, and publicity—so that the organization presents a consistent message. Integrated marketing communication seeks to manage all sources of brand or company contacts with existing and potential customers.

The concept of integrated marketing communication is illustrated in Figure 8.1. It is generally agreed that potential buyers usually go through a process of (1) *awareness* of the product or service, (2) *comprehension* of what it can do and its important features, (3) *conviction* that it has value for them, and (4) *ordering*. Consequently, the firm's marketing communication tools must encourage and allow the potential buyer to experience the various stages. Figure 8.1 illustrates the role of various marketing communication tools for a hypothetical product.

The goal of integrated marketing communication is an important one, and many believe it is critical for success in today's crowded marketplace. As with many management concepts, implementation is slower than many would like to see. Internal "turf" battles within organizations and the reluctance of some advertising agencies to willingly broaden their role beyond advertising are two factors that are hindering the successful implementation of integrated marketing communication.

These levels demonstrate how Integrated Marketing Communications programs range from narrowly focused corporate monologues to broad, interactive dialogues that result in a corporate culture that permeates an organization and drives everything it does, internally and externally.

Level	Name	Focus	Examples
1	Unified image	One look; one voice; strong brand image focus	3M
2	Consistent voice	Consistent tone and look; coordinated messages to various audiences (customers, suppliers, etc.)	Hallmark, Coca-Cola, Walmart
3	Good listener	Solicits two-way communication, enabling feedback through toll-free numbers, surveys, trade shows, etc.; focus on long-term relationships	Dove, Saturn
4	World-class citizen	Social, environmental consciousness; strong company culture; focus on wider community	Ben and Jerry's, Apple, Google, Honda

Source: Tom Duncan, "Integrated Marketing? It's Synergy," *Advertising Age,* March 8,1993, p. 22; and William F. Arens, Michael F. Weigold, and Christian Arens, *Contemporary Advertising and Integrated Marketing Communications,* 13th ed. (Burr Ridge, Il: McGraw-Hill/Irwin, 2011), p. 274.

ADVERTISING: PLANNING AND STRATEGY

Advertising seeks to promote the seller's product by means of printed and electronic media. This is justified on the grounds that messages can reach large numbers of people and make them aware and persuade and remind them about the firm's offerings.

From a marketing management perspective, advertising is an important strategic device for maintaining a competitive advantage in the marketplace. Advertising budgets represent a large and growing element in the cost of goods and services. In a year it is possible for large multi-product firms to spend $1.5 to $2 billion advertising their products, and it is common to spend $74 to $100 million on one individual brand. Clearly, advertising must be carefully planned.

Objectives of Advertising

There are at least three different viewpoints about the contribution of advertising to the economic health of the firm. The generalist viewpoint is primarily concerned with sales, profits, return on investment, and so forth. At the other extreme, the specialist viewpoint is represented by advertising experts who are primarily concerned with measuring the effects of specific ads or campaigns; here primary attention is given to organizations that offer services that measure different aspects of the effects of advertising such as the Nielsen Index, Starch Reports, Arbitron Index, and Simmons Reports. A middle view, one that might be classified as more of a marketing management approach, understands and appreciates the other two viewpoints but, in addition, sees advertising as a competitive weapon. Emphasis in this approach is given to the strategic aspects of the advertising function.[2]

Building on what was said earlier, objectives for advertising can be assigned that focus on creating *awareness,* aiding *comprehension,* developing *conviction,* and encouraging

Element	Ethical and Legal Concerns
Advertising	• Using deceptive advertising • Reinforcing unfavorable ethnic/racial/sex stereotypes • Encouraging materialism and excessive consumption
Public relations	• Lack of sincerity (paying lip service to worthwhile causes) • Using economic power to gain favorable publicity • Orchestrating news events to present a false appearance of widespread support for the company position
Sales promotion	• Offering misleading consumer promotions • Paying slotting allowances to gain retail shelf space • Using unauthorized mailing lists to reach consumers
Personal selling	• Using high-pressure selling • Failing to disclose product limitations/safety concerns • Misrepresenting product health
Direct marketing communications	• Invading privacy with telemarketing • Using consumer database information without consumers' authorization • Creating economic waste with unwanted direct mail

Source: William O. Bearden, Thomas N. Ingram, and Raymond W. LaForge, *Marketing: Principles and Perspectives,* 5th ed. (Burr Ridge, IL: McGraw-Hill/Irwin, 2007), p. 383.

ordering. Within each category, more specific objectives can be developed that take into account time and degree of success desired. Obviously, compared to the large number of people that advertising makes aware of the product or service, the number actually motivated to purchase is usually quite small.

In the long run and often in the short run, advertising is justified on the basis of the revenue it produces. Revenue in this case may refer to either sales or profits. Economic theory assumes that firms are profit maximizers, and the advertising outlays should be increased in every market and medium up to the point where the additional cost of gaining more business equals the incremental profits. Since most business firms do not have the data required to use the marginal analysis approach, they usually employ less-sophisticated decision-making models. Evidence also shows that many managers advertise to maximize sales on the assumption that higher sales mean more profits (which may or may not be true).

The point to be made here is that the ultimate objective of the business advertiser is to make sales and profits. To achieve this objective, customers must purchase and repurchase the advertised product. Toward this end, an approach to advertising is needed that provides for intelligent decision making. This approach must recognize the need for measuring the results of advertising, and these measurements must be as valid and reliable as possible. Marketing managers must also be aware that advertising not only complements other forms of communication but is subject to the law of diminishing returns. This means that for any advertised product, it can be assumed a point is eventually reached at which additional advertising produces little or no additional sales.

ADVERTISING DECISIONS

In line with what has just been said, the marketing manager must make two key decisions. The first decision deals with determining the size of the advertising budget, and the second deals with how the advertising budget should be allocated. Although these decisions are highly interrelated, we deal with them separately to achieve a better understanding of the problems involved. Today's most successful brands of consumer goods were built by heavy advertising and marketing investment long ago. Many marketers have lost sight of the connection between advertising spending and market share. They practice the art of discounting: cutting ad budgets to fund price promotions or fatten quarterly earnings. Companies employing these tactics may benefit in the short term but may be at a severe competitive disadvantage in the long term.

Marketers at some companies, however, know that brand equity and consumer preference for brands drive market share. They understand the balance of advertising and promotion expenditures needed to build brands and gain share, market by market, regardless of growth trends in the product categories where they compete. For example, Procter & Gamble has built its Jif and Folger's brands from single-digit shares to being among category leaders. In peanut butter and coffee, P&G invests more in advertising and less in discounting than its major competitors. What P&G and other smart marketers such as Kellogg, General Mills, Coke, and PepsiCo hold in common is an awareness of a key factor in advertising: consistent investment spending. They do not raid their ad budgets to increase earnings for a few quarters, nor do they view advertising as a discretionary cost.

The Expenditure Question

Most firms determine how much to spend on advertising by one of the following methods.

Percent of Sales

This is one of the most popular rule-of-thumb methods, and its appeal is found in its simplicity. The firm simply takes a percentage figure and applies it to either past or future sales. For example, suppose next year's sales are estimated to be $1 million. Using the criterion of 2 percent of sales, the ad budget would be $20,000. This approach is usually justified by its advocates in terms of the following argument: (1) Advertising is needed to generate sales; (2) a number of cents (i.e., the percentage used) out of each dollar of sales should be devoted to advertising in order to generate needed sales; and (3) the percentage is easily adjusted and can be readily understood by other executives. The percent-of-sales approach is popular in retailing.

Per-Unit Expenditure

Closely related to the above technique is one in which a fixed monetary amount is spent on advertising for each unit of the product expected to be sold. This method is popular with higher-priced merchandise, such as automobiles or appliances. For instance, if a company is marketing color televisions priced at $500, it may decide that it should spend $30 per set on advertising. Since this $30 is a fixed amount for each unit, this method amounts to the same thing as the percent-of-sales method. The big difference is in the rationale used to justify each of the methods. The per-unit expenditure method attempts to determine the retail price by using production costs as a base. Here the seller realizes that a reasonably competitive price must be established for the product in question and therefore attempts to cost out the gross margin. All this means is that, if the suggested retail price is to be $500 and manufacturing costs are $250, a gross margin of $250 is available to cover certain expenses, such as transportation, personal selling, advertising, and dealer profit. Some of these expense items are flexible, such as advertising, while others are nearly fixed, as in the case of transportation. The basic problem with this method and the percentage-of-sales method is that they view advertising as a function of sales, rather than sales as a function of advertising.

All You Can Afford

Here the advertising budget is established as a predetermined share of profits or financial resources. The availability of current revenues sets the upper limit of the ad budget. The only advantage to this approach is that it sets reasonable limits on the expenditures for advertising. However, from the standpoint of sound marketing practice, this method is undesirable because there is no necessary connection between liquidity and advertising opportunity. Any firm that limits its advertising outlays to the amount of available funds will probably miss opportunities for increasing sales and profits.

Competitive Parity

This approach is often used in conjunction with other approaches, such as the percent-of-sales method. The basic philosophy underlying this approach is that advertising is defensive. Advertising budgets are based on those of competitors or other members of the industry. From a strategy standpoint, this is a "followership" technique that assumes that the other firms in the industry know what they are doing and have similar goals. Competitive parity is not a preferred method, although some executives feel it is a safe approach. This may or may not be true depending in part on the relative market share of competing firms and their growth objectives.

The Research Approach

Here the advertising budget is argued for and presented on the basis of research findings. Advertising media are studied in terms of their productivity by the use of media reports and research studies. Costs are also estimated and compared with study results. A typical experiment is one in which three or more test markets are selected. The first test market is used as a control, either with no advertising or with normal levels of advertising. Advertising with various levels of intensity is used in the other markets, and comparisons are made to see what effect different levels of intensity have. The marketing manager then evaluates the costs and benefits of the different approaches and intensity levels to determine the overall budget. Although the research approach is generally more expensive than some other models, it is a more rational approach to the expenditure decision.

The Task Approach

Well-planned advertising programs usually make use of the task approach, which initially formulates the advertising goals and defines the tasks to accomplish these goals. Once this is done, management determines how much it will cost to accomplish each task and adds up the total. This approach is often in conjunction with the research approach.

The Allocation Question

This question deals with the problem of deciding on the most effective way of spending advertising dollars. A general answer to the question is that management's choice of strategies and objectives determines the media and appeals to be used. In other words, the firm's or product division's overall marketing plan will function as a general guideline for answering the allocation question.

From a practical standpoint, however, the allocation question can be framed in terms of message and media decisions. A successful ad campaign has two related tasks: (1) say the right things in the ads themselves, and (2) use the appropriate media in the right amounts at the right time to reach the target market.

Effective advertising should follow a plan. There is no one best way to go about planning an advertising campaign, but in general, marketers should have good answers to the following eight questions:

1. *The management question:* Who will manage the advertising program?
2. *The money question:* How much should be spent on advertising as opposed to other forms of communication?
3. *The market question:* To whom should the advertising be directed?
4. *The message question:* What should the ads say about the product?
5. *The media question:* What types and combinations of media should be used?
6. *The macroscheduling question:* How long should the advertising campaign be in effect before changing ads or themes?
7. *The microscheduling question:* At what times and dates would it be best for ads to appear during the course of the campaign?
8. *The measurement question:* How will the effectiveness of the advertising campaign be measured and how will the campaign be evaluated and controlled?

Message Strategy

The advertising process involves creating messages with words, ideas, sounds, and other forms of audiovisual stimuli that are designed to affect consumer (or distributor) behavior. It follows that much of advertising is a communication process. To be effective, the advertising message should meet two general criteria: (1) It should take into account the basic principles of communication, and (2) it should be predicated upon a good theory of consumer motivation and behavior.

The basic communication process involves three elements: (1) the sender or source of the communication, (2) the communication or message, and (3) the receiver or audience. Advertising agencies are considered experts in the communications field and are employed by most large firms to create meaningful messages and assist in their dissemination. Translating the product idea or marketing message into an effective ad is termed *encoding*. In advertising, the goal of encoding is to generate ads that the audience understands. For this to occur, the audience must be able to *decode* the message in the ad so that the perceived content of the message is the same as the intended content of the message. From a practical standpoint, all this means is that advertising messages must be sent to consumers in an understandable and meaningful way.

Advertising messages, of course, must be transmitted and carried by particular communication channels commonly known as advertising media. These media or channels vary in efficiency, selectivity, and cost. Some channels are preferred to others because they have less "noise," and thus messages are more easily received and understood. For example, a particular newspaper ad must compete with other ads, pictures, or stories on the same page. In the case of radio or TV, while only one firm's message is usually broadcast at a time, other distractions (noise) can hamper clear communications, such as driving while listening to the radio.

The relationship between advertising and consumer behavior is quite obvious. For many products and services, advertising is an influence that may affect the consumer's decision to purchase a particular product or brand. It is clear that consumers are subjected to many selling influences, and the question arises about how important advertising is or can be. In this case, the advertising expert must operate on some theory of consumer behavior. The reader will recall from the discussion of consumer behavior that the buyer was viewed as progressing through various stages from an unsatisfied need through and beyond a

Newspapers

Advantages

1. Flexible and timely.
2. Intense coverage of local markets.
3. Broad acceptance and use.
4. High believability of printed word.

Disadvantages

1. Short life.
2. Read hastily.
3. Small "pass-along" audience.

Radio

Advantages

1. Mass use (over 25 million radios sold annually).
2. Audience selectivity via station format.
3. Low cost (per unit of time).
4. Geographic flexibility.

Disadvantages

1. Audio presentation only.
2. Less attention than TV.
3. Chaotic buying (nonstandardized rate structures).
4. Short life.

Outdoor

Advantages

1. Flexible.
2. Relative absence of competing advertisements.
3. Repeat exposure.
4. Relatively inexpensive.

Disadvantages

1. Creative limitations.
2. Many distractions for viewer.
3. Public attack (ecological implications).
4. No selectivity of audience.

Television

Advantages

1. Combination of sight, sound, and motion.
2. Appeals to senses.
3. Mass audience coverage.
4. Psychology of attention.

Disadvantages

1. Nonselectivity of audience.
2. Fleeting impressions.
3. Short life.
4. Expensive.

Magazines

Advantages

1. High geographic and demographic selectivity.
2. Psychology of attention.
3. Quality of reproduction.
4. Pass-along readership.

Disadvantages

1. Long closing periods (six to eight weeks prior to publication).
2. Some waste circulation.
3. No guarantee of position (unless premium is paid).

Direct Mail

Advantages

1. Audience selectivity.
2. Flexible.
3. No competition from competing advertisements.
4. Personalized.

Disadvantages

1. Relatively high cost.
2. Consumers often pay little attention and throw it away.

Internet

Advantages

1. Interactive.
2. Low cost per exposure.
3. Ads can be placed in interest sections.
4. Timely.
5. High information content possible.
6. New favorable medium.

Disadvantages

1. Low attention getting.
2. Short message life.
3. Reader selects exposure.
4. May be perceived as intruding.
5. Subject to download speeds.

purchase decision. The end goal of an advertisement and its associated campaign is to move the buyer to a decision to purchase the advertised brand. By doing so, the advertisement will have succeeded in moving the consumer to the trial and repeat purchase stage of the consumer behavior process, which is the end goal of advertising strategy.

The planning of an advertising campaign and the creation of persuasive messages require a mixture of marketing skill and creative know-how. Relative to the dimension of marketing skills, some important pieces of marketing information are needed before launching an ad campaign. Most of this information must be generated by the firm and kept up-to-date. Listed below are some of the critical types of information an advertiser should have.

1. *Who* the firm's customers and potential customers are: their demographic, economic, and psychological characteristics and any other factors affecting their likelihood of buying.
2. *How many* such customers there are.
3. *How much* of the firm's type and brand of product they are currently buying and can reasonably be expected to buy in the short-term and long-term future.
4. *Which* individuals, other than customers and potential customers, *influence* purchasing decisions.
5. *Where* they buy the firm's brand of product.
6. *When* they buy, and frequency of purchase.
7. *Which* competitive brands they buy and frequency of purchase.
8. *How* they use the product.
9. *Why* they buy particular types and brands of products.

Media Mix

Media selection is no easy task. To start with, there are numerous types and combinations of media to choose from. Marketing Insight 8–5 presents a brief summary of the advantages and disadvantages of some of the major advertising media.

In the advertising industry, a common measure of efficiency or productivity is cost per thousand, or CPMs. This figure generally refers to the dollar cost of reaching 1,000 prospects, and its chief advantage lies in its simplicity and allowance for a common base of comparison between differing media types. The major disadvantage of the use of CPMs also relates to its simplicity. For example, the same commercial placed in two different television programs, having the same viewership and the same audience profile, may very well generate different responses depending on the level of viewer involvement. This "positive effects" theory states that the more the viewers are involved in a television program, the stronger they will respond to commercials. In essence, involving programs produce engaged respondents who demonstrate more favorable responses to advertising messages.

Generally, such measures as circulation, audience size, and sets in use per commercial minute are used in the calculation. Of course, different relative rankings of media can occur, depending on the measure used. A related problem deals with what is meant by "effectively reaching" the prospect.[3] *Reach,* in general, is the number of different targeted audience members exposed at least once to the advertiser's message within a predetermined time frame. Just as important as the number of different people exposed (reach) is the number of times, on average, that they are exposed to an advertisement within a given time period. This rate of exposure is called *average frequency.* Since marketers all have budget constraints, they must decide whether to increase reach at the expense of average frequency or average frequency at the expense of reach. In essence, the marketer's dilemma is to develop a media schedule that both (1) exposes a sufficient number of targeted customers (reach) to the firm's product and (2) exposes them enough times (average frequency) to the product to produce the desired effect. The desired effect can come in the

Advertising can be found everywhere these days—even places where we least expect it.

Aerial Banners and Lights

Banners carrying ad messages can be pulled by low-flying planes. After dark, traveling aerial lights can display messages of up to 90 characters. Slow-flying helicopters can carry 40- by 80-foot signs lit by thousands of bulbs.

Blimps

In addition to Goodyear, blimps now carry ads for many companies, including Citibank, Coca-Cola, and Fuji Film, among others. Computer operated lighting systems allow the blimps to advertise at night.

In-Flight Ads

Many airlines' in-flight audio and video entertainment runs ads. The travel industry and advertisers that want to reach business fliers are the primary users.

Newspaper Bags

The protective bags of newspapers are used for full-color advertising and can be enhanced by adding product samples. This method is desirable because it does not have to compete with other advertisers.

Transit Terminal Domination

The latest version of saturation bombing has come to large transit hubs around the country. One advertiser buys up all or most of the message space in one confined site banishing all competition. This greatly increases the chances of being seen even by the most harried passers by.

Electronic Billboards

Most modern sports stadiums and arenas sell ad space on giant electronic displays.

Inflatables

Giant inflatable beer cans, mascots, and even cereal boxes are used for advertising purposes.

Painted Vehicles

Buses, trucks, and cars are completely decorated with larger than life illustrations and messages to attract attention. Some vehicles are 'wrapped' with a material that covers the entire vehicle to present the greatest visual impact.

Reactrix Brand Play

In small theaters and other spaces, Reactrix creates highly entertaining branding displays that respond to the physical movement of the audience.

Trash Receptacles

Uniquely designed and decorated trash bins, boxes, and baskets bear advertising logos and messages. Some major cities now offer advertising space on concrete litter receptacles at major commercial intersections.

Kiosks

Stand-alone kiosks can be painted with eye-catching designs and messages. Unique constructions can be attached to the top and sides to draw attention. Electronic displays running presentation software can show colorful fast-action video clips, slide images, and interactive text. These systems can also play synchronized sounds and music.

Lavatory Advertising

Numerous venues allow advertising in lavatories. Print ads can be found on the inner side of stalls and above urinals in some men's restrooms.

Gobo/Cookie Advertising

The gobo (or cookie) is a piece of metal stenciled with a logo through which light is projected against a wall or other suitable background. This is ideal for huge outdoor or indoor events.

Train Cars

Train cars are wrapped with advertisements instead of graffiti these days. In Chicago an eight-car commuter train was wrapped with Illinois lottery ads.

Grocery Receipts

Today most major supermarket chains print coupons on the back of grocery receipts. The coupons feature discounts at local retailers.

Source: William F. Arens, Michael F. Weigold, and Christian Arens, *Contemporary Advertising*, 13th ed. (Burr Ridge, IL: McGraw-Hill/Irwin, 2011), p. 304.

FIGURE 8.2   Example of Sales Promotion Activities

Source: William D. Perreault, Jr. and E. Jerome McCarthy, *Basic Marketing: A Marketing Strategy Planning Approach,* 18th ed. (Burr Ridge, IL: McGraw-Hill/Irwin, 2011), chap. 14.

Aimed at final consumers or users	Aimed at middlemen	Aimed at company's own sales force
Contests	Price deals	Contests
Coupons	Promotion allowances	Bonuses
Aisle displays	Sales contests	Meetings
Samples	Calendars	Portfolios
Trade shows	Gifts	Displays
Point-of-purchasing materials	Trade shows	Sales aids
Banners and streamers	Meetings	Training materials
Frequent buyer programs	Catalogs	
Sponsored events	Merchandising aids	
	Videos	

form of reaching goals associated with any or all of the categories of advertising objectives (the prospect becomes aware of the product, takes action, etc.) covered earlier in the chapter.

SALES PROMOTION

Over the past two decades, the popularity of sales promotion has been increasing. Two reasons for this increased popularity are undoubtedly the increased pressure on management for short-term results and the emergence of new purchase tracking technology. For example, many supermarket cash registers are now equipped with a device that dispenses coupons to a customer at the point of purchase. The type, variety, and cash amount of the coupon will vary from customer to customer based on their purchases. In essence, it is now possible for the Coca-Cola Company to dispense coupons only to those customers who purchase Pepsi Cola, thus avoiding spending promotional dollars on already-loyal Coke drinkers. Figure 8.2 presents some popular targets of sales promotion and the methods used.

Push versus Pull Marketing

Push and pull marketing strategies comprise the two options available to marketers interested in getting their product into the hands of customers. They are illustrated in Figure 8.3. *Push strategies* involve aiming promotional efforts at distributors, retailers, and sales personnel to gain their cooperation in ordering, stocking, and accelerating the sales of a product. For example, a local rock band may visit local DJs seeking air play for their record, offer distributors special prices to carry the CD, and offer retailers special allowances for putting up posters or special counter displays. These activities, which are usually in the form of price allowances, distribution allowances, and advertising dollar allowances, are designed to "push" the CD toward the customer.[4]

Pull strategies involve aiming promotional efforts directly at customers to encourage them to ask the retailer for the product. In the past few years drug manufacturers have begun to advertise prescription drugs directly to consumers. Customers are encouraged to "Ask Your Doctor" about Viagra or Paxil. These activities, which can include advertising and sales promotion, are designed to "pull" a product through the channel from manufacturer to buyer.

FIGURE 8.3   Push versus Pull Strategies in Marketing Communications

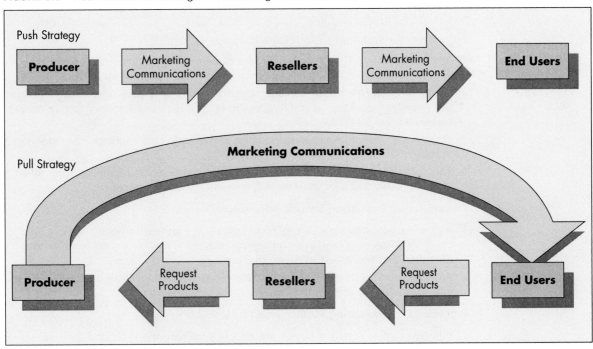

Trade Sales Promotions

Trade promotions are those promotions aimed at distributors and retailers of products who make up the distribution channel. The major objectives of trade promotions are to (1) convince retailers to carry the manufacturer's products, (2) reduce the manufacturer's inventories and increase the distributor's or retailer's inventories, (3) support advertising and consumer sales promotions, (4) encourage retailers either to give the product more favorable shelf space or to place more emphasis on selling the product, and (5) serve as a reward for past sales efforts.

Promotions built around price discounts and advertising or other allowances are likely to have higher distributor/retailer participation levels than other type promotions because a direct economic incentive is attached to the promotion.[5] The importance attached to individual types of promotions may vary by the size of distributor/retailer. For example, small retailers do not consider contests, sweepstakes, and sales quotas as being important to their decision to participate in promotions; getting the full benefit of such promotions is difficult due to their size. Marketers must keep in mind that not all distributors or retailers will have the same reaction to promotions offered. The manufacturer must carefully consider differences in attitudes when designing and implementing trade promotion programs.

Consumer Promotions

Consumer promotions can fulfill several distinct objectives for the manufacturer. Some of the more commonly sought-after objectives include (1) inducing the consumer to try the product, (2) rewarding the consumer for brand loyalty, (3) encouraging the consumer to trade up or purchase larger sizes of a product, (4) stimulating the consumer to make repeat purchases of the product, (5) reacting to competitor efforts, and (6) reinforcing and serving as a complement to advertising and personal selling efforts.

Procedures for Evaluating Specific Advertisements

1. *Recognition tests.* Estimate the percentage of people claiming to have read a magazine who recognize the ad when it is shown to them (e.g., Starch Message Report Service).
2. *Recall tests.* Estimate the percentage of people claiming to have read a magazine who can (unaided) recall the ad and its contents (e.g., Gallup and Robinson Impact Service, various services for TV ads as well).
3. *Opinion tests.* Potential audience members are asked to rank alternative advertisements as most interesting, most believable, best liked.
4. *Theater tests.* Theater audience is asked for brand preferences before and after an ad is shown in context of a TV show (e.g., Schwerin TV Testing Service).

Procedures for Evaluating Specific Advertising Objectives

1. *Awareness.* Potential buyers are asked to indicate brands that come to mind in a product category. A message used in an ad campaign is given and buyers are asked to identify the brand that was advertised using that message.
2. *Attitude.* Potential buyers are asked to rate competing or individual brands on determinant attributes, benefits, and characterizations using rating scales.

Procedures for Evaluating Motivational Impact

1. *Intention to buy.* Potential buyers are asked to indicate the likelihood they will buy a brand (on a scale from "definitely will not" to "definitely will").
2. *Market test.* Sales changes in different markets are monitored to compare the effects of different messages, budget levels.

Source: Joseph Guiltinan and Gordon Paul, *Marketing Management,* 6th ed., © 1997, New York, McGraw-Hill, Inc., p. 274. Reproduced by permission of The McGraw-Hill Companies.

Figure 8.4 presents a brief description of some of the most commonly used forms of consumer promotion activities.

What Sales Promotion Can and Can't Do

Advocates of sales promotion often point to its growing popularity as a justification for the argument that we don't need advertising; sales promotion itself will suffice. Marketers should bear in mind that sales promotion is only one part of a well-constructed integrated marketing communications program. While sales promotion is proven to be effective in achieving the objectives listed in the previous sections, there are several compelling reasons why it should not be used as the sole promotional tool. These reasons include sales promotion's inability (1) to generate long-term buyer commitment to a brand in many cases; (2) to change, except on a temporary basis, declining sales of a product; (3) to convince buyers to purchase an otherwise unacceptable product; and (4) to make up for a lack of advertising or sales support for a product. In addition, promotions can often fuel the flames of competitive retaliation far more than other marketing activities. When the competition gets drawn into the promotion war, the effect can be a significant slowing of the sharp sales increases predicted by the initiator of the promotion. Worse yet, promotions can often devalue the image of the promoted brand in the consumer's eyes.

FIGURE 8.4
Some Commonly
Used Forms of
Consumer
Promotions

• *Sampling*	Customers are offered regular trial sizes of the product either free or at a nominal price.
• *Price deals*	Customers are offered discounts from the product's regular price.
• *Bonus packs*	Additional amounts of the product are given to buyers when they purchase the product.
• *Rebates and refunds*	Customers are given reimbursements for purchasing the product either on the spot or through the mail.
• *Sweepstakes and contests*	Prizes are available either through chance selection or games of skill.
• *Premiums*	A reward or gift can come from purchasing a product.
• *Coupons*	Probably the most familiar and widely used of all consumer promotions, now often available at point of purchase.

The dilemma marketers face is how to cut back on sales promotions without losing market share to competitors. In an effort to overcome this problem, some consumer products companies are instituting new pricing policies to try to cut back on the amount of sales promotions used. For example, Procter & Gamble and General Mills have instituted everyday low-price strategies for many of their products. The intent of this type of policy is to give retailers a lower list price in exchange for cutting trade promotions. While the net cost of the product to retailers remains unchanged, retailers are losing promotional dollars that they controlled. In many situations, although trade allowances are supposed to be used for encouraging retail sales, it is not uncommon for retailers to take a portion of the trade allowance money as profit. The rationale behind companies' (such as Procter & Gamble and General Mills) efforts to cut back on trade and other promotions is (1) not to force brand-loyal customers to pay unusually high prices when a product isn't on special; (2) to allow consumers to benefit from a lower average shelf price, since retailers will no longer have discretion over the use of allowance dollars; and (3) to improve efficiencies in manufacturing and distribution systems because retailers will lose the incentive to do heavy forward buying of discounted items.

In addition to developing pricing policies to cut back on short-term promotions, some consumer products companies are starting to institute *frequency marketing programs* in which they reward consumers for purchases of products or services over a sustained period of time.[6] These programs are not technically considered sales promotions due to their ongoing nature. Frequency marketing originated in 1981 when American Airlines launched its frequent-flyer program with the intention of securing the loyalty of business travelers.

PUBLIC RELATIONS

As noted earlier in the chapter, public relations is a nonpersonal form of communication that tries to influence the overall image of the organization and its products and services among its various stakeholder groups. Public relations managers prefer to focus on communicating positive news about the organization, but they must also be available to minimize the negative impacts of a crisis or problem. We have already noted that the most popular and frequently used public relations tool is publicity. There are several forms of publicity:

1. *News release.* An announcement regarding changes in the organization or the product line, sometimes called a *press release.* The objective is to inform members of the media of a newsworthy event in the hope that they will convert it into a story.

When Directed at Consumers

1. To obtain the trial of a product.
2. To introduce a new or improved product.
3. To encourage repeat or greater usage by current users.
4. To bring more customers into retail stores.
5. To increase the total number of users of an established product.

When Directed at Salespeople

1. To motivate the sales force.
2. To educate the sales force about product improvements.
3. To stabilize a fluctuating sales pattern.

When Directed at Resellers

1. To increase reseller inventories.
2. To obtain displays and other support for products.
3. To improve product distribution.
4. To obtain more and better shelf space.

2. *News conference.* A meeting held for representatives of the media so that the organization can announce major news events such as new products, technologies, mergers, acquisitions, and special events, or, in the case of a crisis or problem, present its position and plans for dealing with the situation.
3. *Sponsorship.* Providing support for and associating the organization's name with events, programs, or even people such as amateur athletes or teams. Besides publicity, sponsorship can also include advertising and sales promotion activities. Many organizations sponsor sporting events, art festivals, and public radio and television programs.
4. *Public service announcements.* Many nonprofit organizations rely on the media to donate time for advertising for contributions and donors. Many nonprofit organizations cannot afford the cost of advertising or in some cases are prohibited from doing so.

DIRECT MARKETING

We already know that with direct marketing the organization communicates directly with customers either online or through direct mail, catalogs, direct response advertising, or personal selling (the subject of the next chapter).

Direct marketing methods are certainly not new. In fact, several of them will be discussed later in the book as methods of nonstore retailing. What is new is the ability to design and use them more efficiently and effectively because of the availability of computers and databases. Technology has clearly been the catalyst in the tremendous growth in direct marketing activities in the last decade. Because of technology, it is now possible for marketers to customize communication efforts and literally create one-to-one connections and dialogues with customers. This would be especially true for those organizations that have successfully implemented an integrated marketing communications program.

Another obvious catalyst for growth in direct marketing has been consumers' increased use of the Internet for purchasing many types of products. The projected growth rates for online expenditures continue to rise. As growth continues in the number of households with Internet access and in the number of businesses with Web sites and product or service offerings via the Internet, it will likely fuel even greater growth in direct marketing.

For the American consumer facing a "poverty of time," direct marketing offers many benefits. In addition to saving time, consumers often save money, get better service, and enjoy increased privacy; many even find it entertaining. For the marketer, sales revenues are the obvious benefit but not the only one. Direct marketing activities are often very effective in generating sales leads when a customer asks for more information about a product or service and can also increase store traffic when potential buyers are encouraged to visit a dealership or retail store.

SUMMARY

This chapter has been concerned with integrated marketing communications. Remember that advertising and sales promotion are only two of the ways by which sellers can affect the demand for their product. Advertising and sales promotion are only part of the firm's promotion mix, and in turn, the promotion mix is only part of the overall marketing mix. Thus, advertising and sales promotion begin with the marketing plan and not with the advertising and sales promotion plans. Ignoring this point can produce ineffective and expensive promotional programs because of a lack of coordination with other elements of the marketing mix.

Additional Resources

Burns, Brian C., and Tom U. Snyder. *Selling in a New Market Space.* NY: McGraw-Hill, 2010.

Mullin, Jeanniery, and David Daniels. *Email Marketing.* Indianapolis: Wiley Publishers, 2009.

Percival, Sean. *My Space Marketing: Creating a Social Network to Boom Your Business.* Indianapolis: Que Books, 2009.

Postman, Joel. *SocialCorp: Social Media Goes Corporate.* Berkeley CA: New Riders, 2009.

Reich, Brian, and Don Soloman. *Media Rules: Mastering Today's Technology to Connect With and Keep Your Audience.* Hoboken NJ: John Wiley and Sons, 2008.

Vollmer, Christopher, and Geoffrey Precourt. *Always On: Advertising and Marketing Media in an Era of Consumer Control.* NY: McGraw-Hill, 2008.

Key Terms and Concepts

Advertising: A paid form of nonpersonal communications about an organization, its product, or its activities that is transmitted through a mass medium to a target audience.

Average frequency: The number of times customers, on average, are exposed to an advertisement within a given time period.

Consumer promotions: Promotions directed at consumers designed to induce the customer to try the product, reward brand loyalty, encourage the consumer to trade-up or purchase larger sizes, stimulate repeat purchases, and reinforce other advertising or personal selling efforts.

Cost per thousand: A common measure of efficiency or productivity in advertising, cost per thousand (CPM) refers to the dollar cost of reaching 1,000 prospects.

Direct marketing: Direct communication with customers through direct mail, online marketing, catalogs, telemarketing, and direct response advertising.

Expenditure question: The methods used to decide how much to spend on advertising, ranging from simple (a percent of sales), to more complex (the task approach which determines goals and how much it will cost to accomplish each goal).

Frequency marketing programs: Programs designed to reward customers for purchases of a product or service over a sustained period of time.

Integrated marketing communications: Marketing communications programs that coordinate and integrate all elements of the promotion mix so that the organization presents a consistent message. It seeks to manage all sources of brand or company contacts with existing and potential customers.

Objectives of advertising: Creating awareness, aiding comprehension, developing conviction, and encouraging ordering. Within each category more specific objectives can be developed that take into account time and degree of success desired.

Personal selling: Face-to-face communication with potential buyers to inform them about and persuade them to purchase an organization's product.

Promotion mix: The combination and types of nonpersonal and personal communication an organization puts forth during a specified period. There are five elements of the promotion mix, four of which are nonpersonal forms of communication (advertising, sales promotion, public relations, and direct marketing), and one, personal selling, which is a personal form of communication.

Public relations: Efforts directed at influencing the attitudes, feelings, and opinions of customers, noncustomers, stockholders, suppliers, employees, and political bodies about the organization. A popular form is publicity.

Pull strategy: Promotional efforts directed at customers to encourage them to ask the retailer for the product. They are designed to "pull" a product through the distribution channel from manufacturer to buyer.

Push strategy: Promotional efforts directed at distributors, retailers, and sales personnel to gain their cooperation in ordering, stocking, and supporting the sales of a product. As such they "push" the product toward the customer.

Reach: The number of targeted audience members exposed at least once to an advertiser's message within a predetermined time frame.

Sales promotion: An activity or material that offers customers, sales personnel, or resellers a direct inducement for purchasing a product.

Trade promotions: Promotions aimed at distributors and retailers of products who make up the distribution channel.

Appendix

Major Federal Agencies Involved in Control of Advertising

Agency	Function
Federal Trade Commission	Regulates commerce between states; controls unfair business practices; takes action on false and deceptive advertising; most important agency in regulation of advertising and promotion.
Food and Drug Administration	Regulatory division of the Department of Health, Education, and Welfare; controls marketing of food, drugs, cosmetics, medical devices, and potentially hazardous consumer products.
Federal Communications Commission	Regulates advertising indirectly, primarily through the power to grant or withdraw broadcasting licenses.
Postal Service	Regulates material that goes through the mails, primarily in areas of obscenity, lottery, and fraud.
Alcohol and Tobacco Tax Division	Part of the Treasury Department; has broad powers to regulate deceptive and misleading advertising of liquor and tobacco.
Grain Division	Unit of the Department of Agriculture responsible for policing seed advertising.
Securities and Exchange Commission	Regulates advertising of securities.

Information Source	Description
Patent Office	Regulates registration of trademarks.
Library of Congress	Controls protection of copyrights.
Department of Justice	Enforces all federal laws through prosecuting cases referred to it by other government agencies.

9

Personal Selling, Relationship Building, and Sales Management

Personal selling, unlike advertising or sales promotion, involves direct relationships between the seller and the prospect or customer. In a formal sense, personal selling can be defined as a two-way flow of communication between a potential buyer and a salesperson that is designed to accomplish at least three tasks: (1) identify the potential buyer's needs; (2) match those needs to one or more of the firm's products or services; and (3) on the basis of this match, convince the buyer to purchase the product.[1] The personal selling element of the promotion mix can encompass diverse forms of direct interaction between a salesperson and a potential buyer, including face-to-face, telephone, written, and computer communication. The behavioral scientist would most likely characterize personal selling as a type of personal influence. Operationally, it is a complex communication process, one still not fully understood by marketers.

IMPORTANCE OF PERSONAL SELLING

The importance of the personal selling function depends partially on the nature of the product. As a general rule, goods that are new and different, technically complex, or expensive require more personal selling effort. The salesperson plays a key role in providing the consumer with information about such products to reduce the risks involved in purchase and use. Insurance, for example, is a complex and technical product that often needs significant amounts of personal selling. In addition, many organizational products cannot be presold, and the salesperson has a key role to play in finalizing the sale.

It is important to remember that, for many companies, the salesperson represents the customer's main link to the firm. In fact, to some, the salesperson is the company. Therefore, it is imperative that the company take advantage of this unique link. Through the efforts of the successful salesperson, a company can build relationships with customers that continue long beyond the initial sale. It is the salesperson who serves as the conduit through which information regarding product flaws, improvements, applications, or new uses can pass from the customer to the marketing department. To illustrate the importance of using salespeople as an information resource, consider this fact: In some industries, customer information serves as a major source for up to 90 percent of new product and process ideas.

Along with techniques described in the previous chapter, personal selling provides the push needed to get middlemen to carry new products, increase their amount of goods purchased, and devote more effort in merchandising a product or brand.

In summary, personal selling is an integral part of the marketing system, fulfilling two vital duties (in addition to the core sales task itself): one for customers and one for companies.[2] First, the salesperson dispenses knowledge to buyers. Lacking relevant information, customers are likely to make poor buying decisions. For example, computer users would not learn about new equipment and new programming techniques without the assistance of computer sales representatives. Doctors would have difficulty finding out about new drugs and procedures were it not for pharmaceutical salespeople. Second, salespeople act as a source of marketing intelligence for management. Marketing success depends on satisfying customer needs. If present products don't fulfill customer needs, then profitable opportunities may exist for new or improved products. If problems with a company's product exist, then management must be quickly apprised of the fact. In either situation, salespeople are in the best position to act as the intermediary through which valuable information can be passed back and forth between product providers and buyers.

THE SALES PROCESS

Personal selling is as much an art as it is a science. The word *art* is used to describe that portion of the selling process that is highly creative in nature and difficult to explain. This does not mean there is little control over the personal selling element in the promotion mix. It does imply that, all other things equal, the trained salesperson can outsell the untrained one.

Before management selects and trains salespeople, it should have an understanding of the sales process. Obviously, the sales process will differ according to the size of the company, the nature of the product, the market, and so forth, but some elements are common to almost all selling situations. For the purposes of this text, the term *sales process* refers to two basic factors: (1) the objectives the salesperson is trying to achieve while engaged in selling activities; and (2) the sequence of stages or steps the salesperson should follow in trying to achieve the specific objectives (the relationship-building process).

Objectives of the Sales Force

Much like the concepts covered in the previous chapter, personal selling can be viewed as a strategic means to gain competitive advantage in the marketplace. For example, most organizations include service representatives as part of their sales team to ensure that customer concerns with present products are addressed and remedied at the same time new business is being solicited.

In a similar manner, marketing management understands that while, ultimately, personal selling must be justified on the basis of the revenue and profits it produces, other categories of objectives are generally assigned to the personal selling function as part of the overall promotion mix.[3] These objectives are

1. *Information provision.* Especially in the case of new products or customers, the salesperson needs to fully explain all attributes of the product or service, answer any questions, and probe for additional questions.
2. *Persuasion.* Once the initial product or service information is provided, the salesperson needs to focus on the following objectives:
   - Clearly distinguish attributes of the firm's products or services from those of competitors.
   - Maximize the number of sales as a percent of presentations.
   - Convert undecided customers into first-time buyers.

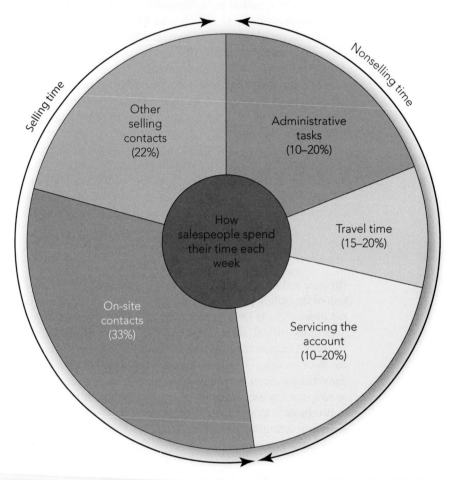

Source: Roger Kerin, Stephen W. Hartley, and William Rudalius, *Marketing,* 10th ed. (Burr Ridge, IL.: McGraw-Hill/Irwin, 2011), p. 524.

- Convert first-time customers into repeat purchasers.
- Sell additional or complementary items to repeat customers.
- Tend to the needs of dissatisfied customers.

3. *After-sale service.* Whether the sale represents a first-time or repeat purchase, the salesperson needs to ensure the following objectives are met:

- Delivery or installation of the product or service that meets or exceeds customer expectations.
- Immediate follow-up calls and visits to address unresolved or new concerns.
- Reassurance of product or service superiority through demonstrable actions.
- Build relationships.

The Sales Relationship-Building Process

For many years, the traditional approach to selling emphasized the first-time sale of a product or service as the culmination of the sales process. As emphasized in Chapter 1, the

FIGURE 9.1
The Sales
Relationship-Building
Process

Source: Adapted from material discussed in Stephen B. Castleberry, and John F. Tanner, *Selling: Building Partnerships,* 8th ed. (Burr Ridge, IL: Irwin/McGraw-Hill, 2011), p. 151.

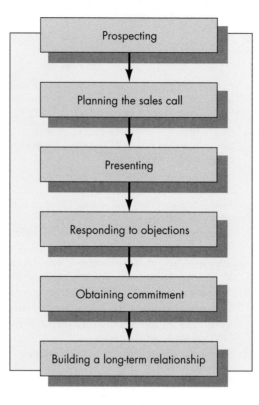

marketing concept and accompanying approach to personal selling view the initial sale as merely the first step in a long-term relationship-building process, not as the end goal. As we shall see later in this chapter, long-term relationships between the buyer and seller can be considered partnerships because the buyer and seller have an ongoing, mutually beneficial affiliation, with each party having concern for the other party's well-being.[4] The relationship-building process, which is designed to meet the objectives listed in the previous section, contains six sequential stages (Figure 9.1). These stages are (1) prospecting, (2) planning the sales call, (3) presentation, (4) responding to objections, (5) obtaining commitment/closing the sale, and (6) building a long-term relationship. What follows is a brief description of each of the stages.

Prospecting

The process of locating potential customers is called *prospecting.* The prospecting activity is critical to the success of organizations in maintaining or increasing sales volume. Continual prospecting is necessary for several reasons, including the fact that customers (1) switch to other suppliers, (2) move out of the organization's market area, (3) go out of business because of bankruptcy, (4) are acquired by another firm, or (5) have only a one-time need for the product or service. In addition, the organization's buying contracts with present customers may be replaced and organizations that wish to grow must increase their customer base. Prospecting in some fields is more important than in others. For example, a stockbroker, real estate agent, or partner in an accounting firm with no effective prospecting plan usually doesn't last long in the business. In these positions, it may take as many as 100 contacts to gain 10 prospects who will listen to presentations from which one to two sales may result. On the other hand, a Procter & Gamble sales representative in a certain geographic area would likely know all the potential retailers for Crest toothpaste.

Source	How Used
Satisfied customers	Current and previous customers are contacted for additional business and leads.
Endless chain	Salesperson attempts to secure at least one additional lead from each person he or she interviews.
Networking	Salesperson uses personal relationships with those who are connected and cooperative to secure leads.
Center of influence	Salesperson cultivates well-known, influential people in the territory who are willing to supply lead information.
The Internet	Salesperson uses Web sites, e-mail, Listservs, bulletin boards, forums, round-tables, and newsgroups to secure leads.
Ads, direct mail, catalogs, and publicity	Salespeople use these forms of promotional activities to generate leads.
Shows, fairs, and merchandise markets	Salespeople use trade shows, conventions, fairs, and merchandise markets for lead generation.
Seminars	Salespeople use seminars for prospects to generate leads.
Lists and directories	Salesperson uses secondary data sources, which can be free or fee-based.
Data mining and CRM systems	Salespeople use sophisticated data analysis software and the company's CRM system to generate leads.
Cold calling	Salesperson tries to generate leads by calling on totally unfamiliar organizations.
Spotters	Salesperson pays someone for lead information.
Telemarketing	Salesperson uses phone and/or telemarketing staff to generate leads.
Sales letters	Salesperson writes personal letters to potential leads.
Other sources	Salesperson uses noncompeting salespeople, people in his or her own firm, friends, and so on, to secure information.

Source: Stephen B. Castleberry, and John F. Tanner Jr., *Selling: Building Partnerships,* 8th ed. (Burr Ridge, IL: McGraw-Hill/Irwin, 2011), p. 155.

The prospecting process usually involves two major activities that are undertaken on a continual, concurrent basis. First, prospects must be located. When names and addresses of prospects are not available, as is usually the case when firms enter new markets or a new salesperson is hired, they can be generated by randomly calling on businesses or households or by employing mass appeals (through advertising). This process, called *random lead generation,* usually requires a high number of contacts to gain a sale. A *lead* is a potential prospect that may or may not have the potential to be a true prospect, a candidate, to whom a sale could be made.

For most professional, experienced salespeople, a more systematic approach to generating leads from predetermined target markets is used. This approach, aptly named *selected-lead generation,* uses existing contacts and knowledge to generate new prospects. In general, the best source of prospects is referrals from satisfied customers. The more satisfied one's customers are, the higher the quality of leads a salesperson will receive from them. Marketing Insight 9–2 lists some common sources of leads and how they are used to generate new contacts.

The second step in the prospecting process involves screening. Once leads are generated, the salesperson must determine whether the prospect is a true prospect. This qualifying process usually entails gathering information, which leads to answering five questions:

1. Does the lead have a want or need that can be satisfied by the purchase of the firm's products or services?
2. Does the lead have the ability to pay?

3. Does the lead have the authority to pay?
4. Can the lead be approached favorably?
5. Is the lead eligible to buy?

Depending on the analysis of answers to these questions, the determination of whether a lead is a true prospect can be made. In seeking and qualifying leads, it is important to recognize that responsibility for these activities should not be totally assumed by individual salespeople. Rather, companies should develop a consistent, organized program, recognizing that the job of developing prospects belongs to the entire company, not just the sales force.

Planning the Sales Call

Salespeople will readily admit that their number one problem is getting through the door for an appointment with a prospect. Customers have become sophisticated in their buying strategies. Consequently, salespeople have to be equally sophisticated in developing their selling strategies.

While a full discussion on the topic of planning sales calls is beyond the scope of this text, what follows are brief descriptions of some key areas of knowledge salespeople should possess prior to embarking on sales calls.

1. They should have thorough knowledge of the company they represent, including its past history. This includes the philosophy of management as well as the firm's basic operating policies.
2. They should have thorough knowledge of their products and/or product lines. This is particularly true when selling organizational products. When selling very technical products, many firms require their salespeople to have training as engineers.
3. They should have good working knowledge of competitors' products. This is a vital requirement because the successful salesperson will have to know the strengths and weaknesses of those products that are in competition for market share.
4. They should have in-depth knowledge of the market for their merchandise. *The market* here refers not only to a particular sales territory but also to the general market, including the economic factors that affect the demand for their goods.
5. They should have accurate knowledge of the buyer or the prospect to whom they are selling. Under the marketing concept, knowledge of the customer is a vital requirement.

Presenting

Successful salespeople have learned the importance of making a good impression. One of the most important ways of improving the buyer's impression is for the salesperson to be well prepared in the knowledge areas discussed above. Some salespeople actually develop a checklist of things to take to the presentation so that nothing is forgotten. Just as important is the development of good interpersonal skills; they are a key ingredient of effective selling. Salespeople who can adapt their selling style to individual buyer needs and styles have a much stronger overall performance than less-flexible counterparts.

Responding to Objections

To assume the buyer will passively listen and positively respond to a sales presentation by placing an immediate order would be unrealistic. Salespeople can expect to hear objections (issues or concerns raised by the buyer) at any time during the presentation and subsequent relationship. Objections can be raised when the salesperson attempts to secure appointments, during the presentation, when the salesperson attempts to obtain commitment, or during the after-sale follow-up.

When sales prospects raise an objection, it is a sign that they are not ready to buy and need an acceptable response to the objection before the buying decision can be made. In response to an objection, the salesperson should not challenge the respondent. Rather, the salesperson's objective should be to present the necessary information so that the prospect is able to make intelligent decisions based on that information.

Obtaining Commitment

At some point, if all objections have been resolved, the salesperson must ask for commitment. It's a rare moment when a customer will ask to buy. Consequently, knowing how and when to close a sale is one of a salesperson's most indispensable skills.

It should be noted that not all sales calls end in commitment, a successful closing. If commitment is not obtained, salespeople should analyze the reasons and determine whether (1) more sales calls are necessary to obtain commitment; or (2) currently, there just does not exist a good match between customer needs and seller offerings. If the salesperson determines that more calls are necessary, then he or she should leave the meeting with a clear action plan, which is agreeable to the customer, for the next visit.

Building a Long-Term Relationship

Focusing on building and maintaining long-term relationships with customers has become an important goal for salespeople. As marketers realize that it can cost five times as much to acquire a new customer than to service an existing one, the importance of customer retention and relationship building has become very clear.[5] Terry Vavra focuses on the value of current customers to the organization and has developed the concept of *aftermarketing,* which focuses the organization's attention on providing continuing satisfaction and reinforcement to individuals or organizations that are past or current customers. The goal of aftermarketing is to build lasting relationships with customers.[6] Successful aftermarketing efforts require that many specific activities be undertaken by the salesperson and others in the organization. These activities include

1. Establishing and maintaining a customer information file.
2. Monitoring order processing.
3. Ensuring initial proper use of the purchased product or service.
4. Providing ongoing guidance and suggestions.
5. Analyzing customer feedback and responding quickly to customer questions and complaints.
6. Continually conducting customer satisfaction research and responding to it.

As seen by the preceding discussion, there are no magic secrets of successful selling. The difference between good salespeople and mediocre ones is often the result of training plus experience. Training is no substitute for experience; the two complement each other. The difficulty with trying to discuss the selling job in terms of basic principles is that experienced, successful salespeople will always be able to find exceptions to these principles.

Relationships Can Lead to Partnerships

When the interaction between a salesperson and a customer does not end with the sale, the beginnings of a relationship are present. Many salespeople are finding that building relationships and even partnering with customers is becoming increasingly important.

When a buyer and a salesperson have a close personal relationship, they both begin to rely on each other and communicate honestly. When each has a problem, they work together to solve it. Such market relationships are known as *functional relationships.* An important trust begins to exist between the parties. As with any relationship, each often

1. *Improved sales productivity.* When the product or system being purchased is for the whole organization, different specialists handle different parts of the job. This usually results in a more effective and efficient sales process.

2. *More flexibility and quicker decisions.* To thrive in today's increasingly competitive markets, buying organizations often require selling organizations to produce small runs of tailored products on a very tight schedule. Cross-functional sales teams enable sellers to be more flexible because all functional units are involved in the sales process, which also enables the seller to make quicker decisions in response to buyer demands.

3. *Better decisions.* In most cases, the use of cross-functional teams composed of individuals with varied backgrounds in the company will lead to more innovative forms of thought and superior decisions than would be the case of an individual acting alone. Improved decisions would benefit both the buyer and the seller.

4. *Increased customer satisfaction.* The ultimate measure of the success of cross-functional sales teams comes with increased customer satisfaction, cemented relationships, and repeat business. The energy, flexibility, and commitment associated with cross-functional sales teams have led many organizations to adopt the approach.

gives and takes when the situation calls for it in order to keep the relationship intact. The reader may have such a relationship with a long-term medical or dental practitioner or hair cutter.

When organizations move beyond functional relationships, they develop *strategic partnerships,* or *strategic alliances.* These are long-term, formal relationships in which both parties make significant commitments and investments in each other in order to pursue mutual goals and to improve the profitability of each other. While a functional relationship is based on trust, a strategic partnership or alliance moves beyond trust. The partners in the relationship actually invest in each other. Obviously, the reasons for forming strategic partnerships vary. Some do it to create joint opportunities (banks, insurance companies, and brokerage firms), to gain access to new markets [United Parcel Service of America (UPS) and Mail Boxes Etc.], to develop new technology or exploit joint opportunities (IBM and Apple), or to gain a marketing advantage over competitors (United Airlines and Starbucks Coffee, American Airlines and Career Track).

People Who Support the Sales Force

In many instances, sales personnel will require some assistance at various stages of the sales process. These support personnel do not seek the order. Their purpose is to focus on the long-term relationship and increase the likelihood of sales in the long run.

Missionary salespeople are used in certain industries such as pharmaceuticals to focus solely on promotion of existing products and introduction of new products. They may call on physicians to convince them to prescribe a new drug or on pharmacies to convince them to promote a new cold remedy with a large display during the cold and flu season.

A *technical sales specialist* supports the sales staff by providing training or other technical assistance to the prospect. This individual may follow up an expression of interest to the salesperson from a prospect, especially when the product is to be used to solve certain technical problems of the buyer. Some organizations will provide training to the front-line staff of the buying organization who will be expected to sell the product to their customers.

1. *Ego strength:* A healthy self-esteem that allows one to bounce back from rejection.
2. *A sense of urgency:* Wanting to get it done now.
3. *Ego drive:* A combination of competitiveness and self-esteem.
4. *Assertiveness:* The ability to be firm, lead the sales process, and get one's point across confidently.
5. *Willingness to take risk:* Willingness to innovate and take a chance.
6. *Sociable:* Outgoing, talkative, friendly, and interested in others.
7. *Abstract reasoning:* Ability to understand concepts and ideas.
8. *Skepticism:* A slight lack of trust and suspicion of others.
9. *Creativity:* The ability to think differently.
10. *Empathy:* The ability to place oneself in someone else's shoes.

Source: Research conducted by Sales and Marketing Management involving 209 salespeople representing 189 companies in 37 industries and reported in George E. Belch and Michael A. Belch, *Advertising and Promotion,* 8th ed. (Burr Ridge, IL: McGraw-Hill/Irwin, 2009), p. 600.

Finally, when the product is extremely high priced and is being sold to the whole organization, *cross-functional sales teams* are often used. Since products increase in technical complexity, and units of the buying organization require specialized knowledge before a buying decision can be made, team selling has increased in popularity. For example, a manufacturer's sales team might be made up of people from sales, engineering, customer service, and finance, depending on the needs of the customer. A bank's sales team might consist of people from the commercial lending, investments, small business, and trust departments.

MANAGING THE SALES AND RELATIONSHIP-BUILDING PROCESS

Every personal sale can be divided into two parts: the part done by the salespeople and the part done for the salespeople by the company. For example, from the standpoint of the product, the company should provide the salesperson with a product skillfully designed, thoroughly tested, attractively packaged, adequately advertised, and priced to compare favorably with competitive products. Salespeople have the responsibility of being thoroughly acquainted with the product, its selling features, and points of superiority and possess a sincere belief in the value of the product. From a sales management standpoint, the company's part of the sale involves the following:

1. Efficient and effective sales tools, including continuous sales training, promotional literature, samples, trade shows, product information, and adequate advertising.
2. An efficient delivery and reorder system to ensure that customers will receive the merchandise as promised.
3. An equitable compensation plan that rewards performance, motivates the salesperson, and promotes company loyalty. It should also reimburse the salesperson for all reasonable expenses incurred while doing the job.
4. Adequate supervision and evaluation of performance as a means of helping salespeople do a better job not only for the company but for themselves as well.

The Sales Management Task

Marketing managers and sales managers must make some very important decisions regarding how the sales force should be organized. Most companies organize their sales efforts either by geography, product, or customer. These are illustrated in Figure 9.2.

In a *geographic structure,* individual salespeople are assigned geographic territories to cover. A salesperson calls on all prospects in the territory and usually represents all of the company's products. A geographic structure provides the practical benefit of limiting the distance each salesperson must travel to see customers and prospects.

In a *product structure,* each salesperson is assigned to prospects and customers for a particular product or product line. A product structure is useful when the sales force must have specific technical knowledge about products in order to sell effectively. However, this structure can result in a duplication of sales efforts because more than one salesperson can call on the same customer. Consequently, it tends to be expensive.

A *customer structure* assigns a salesperson or selling team to serve a single customer or single type of customer. This structure works best when different types of buyers have large or significantly different needs. When this structure involves devoting all of a salesperson's time to a single customer, it is expensive but can result in large sales and satisfied customers.

In a variation of the customer structure, a company may employ *major account management,* or the use of team selling to focus on major customers to establish long-term relationships.[7] Procter & Gamble, whose sales force used to be organized by product, has

FIGURE 9.2
Organizing the
Sales Force

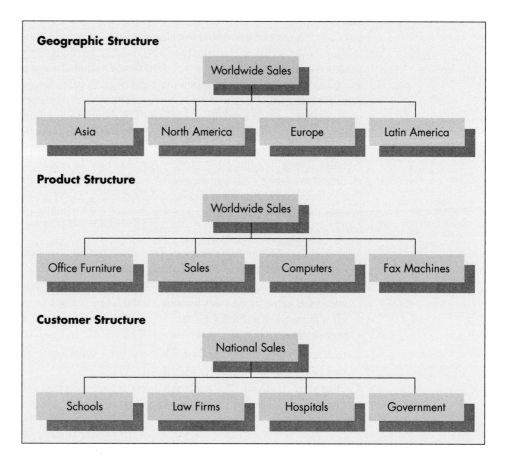

shifted to major account management. Assigning resources to particular customers has proved to be more flexible and customer focused for the company.

The customer-organized structure is well suited for the use of cross-functional teams. However, geographic and product territories can also be effective. The key is that sales management and the sales force must concentrate on learning and meeting customers' wants and needs better than competitors do.

Controlling the Sales Force

There are two obvious reasons why it is critical that the sales force be properly controlled. First, personal selling can be the largest marketing expense component in the final price of the product. Second, unless the sales force is somehow directed, motivated, and audited on a continual basis, it is likely to be less efficient than it is capable of being. Controlling the sales force involves four key functions: (1) forecasting sales, (2) establishing sales territories and quotas, (3) analyzing expenses, and (4) motivating and compensating performance.

Forecasting Sales

Sales planning begins with a forecast of sales for some future period or periods. From a practical standpoint, these forecasts are made on a short-term basis of a year or less, although long-range forecasts of one to five years are made for purposes other than managing the sales force, such as financing, production, and development. Generally speaking, forecasting is the marketing manager's responsibility. In large firms, because of the complexity of the task, it is usually delegated to a specialized unit, such as the marketing research department. Forecast data should be integrated into the firm's marketing information system for use by sales managers and other executives. For many companies, the sales forecast is the key instrument in the planning and control of operations.

The *sales forecast* is an estimate of how much of the company's output, either in dollars or in units, can be sold during a specified future period under a proposed marketing plan and under an assumed set of economic conditions. A sales forecast has several important uses: (1) It is used to establish sales quotas; (2) it is used to plan personal selling efforts as well as other types of promotional activities in the marketing mix; (3) it is used to budget selling expenses; and (4) it is used to plan and coordinate production, logistics, inventories, personnel, and so forth.

Sales forecasting has become very sophisticated in recent years, especially with the increased availability of computer software. It should be mentioned, however, that a forecast is never a substitute for sound business judgment. At the present time no single method of sales forecasting gives uniformly accurate results with infallible precision. Outlined next are some commonly used sales forecasting methods.[8]

1. *Jury of executive opinion method.* This combines and averages the views of top management representing marketing, production, finance, purchasing, and administration.
2. *Sales force composite method.* This is similar to the first method in that it obtains the combined views of the sales force about the future outlook for sales. In some companies all salespeople, or district managers, submit estimates of the future sales in their territory or district.
3. *Customer expectations method.* This approach involves asking customers or product users about the quantity they expect to purchase.
4. *Time-series analysis.* This approach involves analyzing past sales data and the impact of factors that influence sales (long-term growth trends, cyclical fluctuations, seasonal variations).

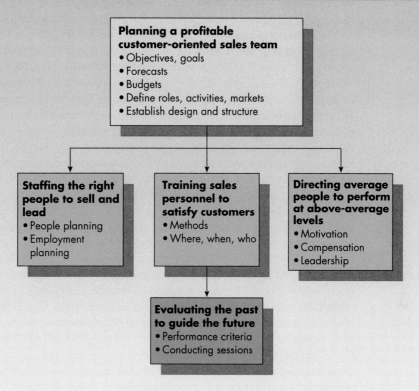

Source: Charles M. Futrell, *Fundamentals of Selling: Customers for Life Through Service,* 12th ed. (Burr Ridge, IL: McGraw-Hill/Irwin, 2011), p. 500.

5. *Correlation analysis.* This involves measuring the relationship between the dependent variable, sales, and one or more independent variables that can explain increases or decreases in sales volumes.

6. *Other quantitative techniques.* Numerous statistical and mathematical techniques can be used to predict or estimate future sales. Two of the more important techniques are (*a*) growth functions, which are mathematical expressions specifying the relationship between demand and time; and (*b*) simulation models, in which a statistical model of the industry is developed and programmed to compute values for the key parameters of the model.

Establishing Sales Territories and Quotas

The establishment of sales territories and sales quotas represents management's need to match personal selling effort with sales potential (or opportunity). Soundly designed sales territories can improve how the market is served.[9] It is much easier to pinpoint customers and prospects and to determine who should call on them when the market is geographically divided than when the market is considered a large aggregate of potential accounts. The geographic segments should represent small clusters of customers or prospects within some physical proximity. Implied here is the notion that there are some distinct economic advantages to dividing the market into smaller segments. Salespeople restricted to a geographic area are likely to get more sales in the territory. Instead of simply servicing the "easy" and larger accounts, they are prone to develop small accounts. Of course, there are criteria other than geography for establishing territories. One important criterion is product specialization. In this case, salespeople are specialists relative to particular product or customer situations.

The question of managing sales territories cannot be discussed meaningfully without saying something about sales quotas. In general, quotas represent goals assigned to salespeople. As such, quotas provide three main benefits. First, they provide incentives for salespeople. For example, the definite objective of selling $500,000 worth of computer equipment is more motivating to most salespeople than the indefinite charge to go out and sell computer equipment. Sales bonuses and commissions based on quotas can also be motivational. Second, quotas provide a quantitative standard against which the performance of individual sales representatives or other marketing units can be measured. They allow management to pinpoint individuals and units that are performing above average and those experiencing difficulty. Third, quotas can be used not only to evaluate salespersons' performances but also to evaluate and control their efforts. As part of their job, salespeople are expected to engage in various activities besides calling on established accounts. These activities might include calling on new accounts, collecting past-due accounts, and planning and developing sales presentations. Activity quotas allow the company to monitor whether salespeople are engaging in these activities to the extent desired.

Sales quotas represent specific sales goals assigned to each territory or unit over a designated time period. The most common method of establishing quotas for territories is to relate sales to forecasted sales potential. For example, if the Ajax Drug Company's territory M has an estimated industry sales potential for a particular product of $400,000 for the year, the quota might be set at 25 percent of that potential, or $100,000. The 25 percent figure represents the market share Ajax estimates to be a reasonable target. This $100,000 quota may represent an increase of $20,000 in sales over last year (assuming constant prices) that is expected from new business.

In establishing sales quotas for its individual territories or sales personnel, management needs to take into account three key factors. First, all territories will not have equal potential and, therefore, compensation must be adjusted accordingly. Second, all salespeople will not have equal ability and assignments may have to be made accordingly. Third, the sales task in each territory may differ from time period to time period. For instance, the nature of some territories may require that salespeople spend more time seeking new accounts, rather than servicing established accounts, especially in the case of so-called new territories. The point to be made here is that quotas can vary, not only by territory but also by assigned tasks. The effective sales manager should assign quotas not only for dollar sales but also for each major selling function. Figure 9.3 is an example of how this is done for the Medi-Test Company, where each activity is assigned a quota and a weight reflecting its relative importance.

Analyzing Expenses

Sales forecasts should include a sales expense budget. In some companies, sales expense budgets are developed from the bottom up. Each territorial or district manager submits estimates of expenses and forecasted sales quotas. These estimates are usually prepared for a period of a year and then broken down into quarters and months. The sales manager then reviews the budget requests from the field offices and from staff departments.

Motivating and Compensating Performance

An important task for the sales manager is motivating and compensating the sales force. These two tasks are major determinants of sales force productivity. Managing people is always a challenge and involves personal interaction with members of the sales force, time in the field visiting customers, free-flowing communication with the sales force, either by e-mail or telephone, and providing feedback on a regular basis as well as coaching and developing incentive programs through which job promotions or increased earnings can be achieved.[10]

EFFORT-ORIENTED MEASURES

1. Number of sales calls made.
2. Number of maintenance-repairs-operations (MRO) calls made.
3. Number of complaints handled.
4. Number of checks on reseller stocks.
5. Uncontrollable lost job time.
6. Number of inquiries followed up.
7. Number of demonstrations completed.

RESULTS-ORIENTED MEASURES

1. Sales volume (total or by product or model).
2. Sales volume as a percentage of quota.
3. Sales profitability (dollar gross margin or contribution).
4. Number of new accounts.
5. Number of stockouts.
6. Number of distributors participating in programs.
7. Number of lost accounts.
8. Percentage volume increase in key accounts.
9. Number of customer complaints.
10. Distributor sales-inventory ratios.

Source: Adapted from Thomas N. Ingram, Raymond W. Laforge, and Charles H. Schwepker, Jr., *Sales Management: Analysis and Decision Making,* 9th ed. (Mason, OH: Thomson Southwestern, 2009), chap. 15; and Thayer C. Taylor, "SFA: The Newest Orthodoxy," *Sales and Marketing Management,* February 1993, pp. 26–28.

There are two basic types of compensation: salary and commission. *Salary* usually refers to a specific amount of monetary compensation at an agreed rate for definite time periods. *Commission* is usually monetary compensation provided for each unit of sales and expressed as a percentage of sales. The base on which commissions are computed may be volume of sales in units of product, gross sales in dollars, net sales after returns,

FIGURE 9.3
Medi-Test Company
Sales Activity
Evaluation

Territory: Southern Salesperson: Marsha Smith					
Functions	**(1)** Quota	**(2)** Actual	**(3)** Percent (2 ÷ 1)	**(4)** Weight	**(5)** Score (3 × 4)
Sales volume					
Old business	$380,000	$300,000	79	0.7	55.3
New business	$ 20,000	$ 20,000	100	0.5	50.0
Calls on prospects					
Doctors	20	15	75	0.2	15.0
Druggists	80	60	75	0.2	15.0
Wholesalers	15	15	100	0.2	20.0
Hospitals	10	10	100	0.2	20.0
				2.0	175.3

Performance index = 175.3

FIGURE 9.4
Types of Sales Force
Incentives and Some
Possible Performance
Outcomes

Source: Some of the
material was adapted from
Gilbert A. Churchill Jr., Neil
M. Ford, and Orville C.
Walker, *Sales Force
Management,* 5th ed. (Burr
Ridge, IL: Irwin/McGraw-Hill,
1997), p. 490.

Types of Incentives	Some Possible Outcomes
• Positive evaluation feedback.	• Increase in sales volume.
• Company-wide recognition.	• Sale of more profitable products.
• Bonus.	• Attention on selling new products.
• Salary increases.	• Achieving greater market penetration.
• Pay for new product idea.	• Increased number of sales calls.
• Education allowance.	• Larger average orders.
• Time off.	• Attracting new customers.
• Fringe benefits.	• Improved service of existing customers.
• Stock options.	• Reduction in customer turnover.
• Retirement plan.	• Reduction in selling costs.
• Profit sharing.	• Full-line balanced selling.

sales volume in excess of a quota, or net profits. Very often, several compensation approaches are combined. For example, a salesperson might be paid a base salary, a commission on sales exceeding a volume figure, and a percentage share of the company's profits for that year.

In addition to straight dollar compensation, there are numerous other forms of incentives that can be used to motivate the sales force. Some of these types of incentives and their potential performance outcomes are listed in Figure 9.4.

SUMMARY

This chapter has attempted to outline and explain the personal selling aspect of the promotion mix. An emphasis was placed on describing the importance of the relationship-building aspect of the personal selling process. For organizations that wish to continue to grow and prosper, personal selling plays an integral part in the marketing of products and services. As long as production continues to expand through the development of new and highly technical products, personal selling will continue to be an important part of marketing strategy.

Additional Resources

Ash, Mary Kay. *The Mary Kay Way: Timeless Principles from America's Greatest Woman Entrepreneur.* Hoboken NJ: John Wiley and Sons, 2008.

Gonzalez, Gabriel R., Douglas Hoffman, and Thomas N. Ingram. "Improving Relationship Selling through Failure Analysis and Recovery Efforts: A Framework and Call to Action." *Journal of Personal Selling and Sales Management.* Spring 2005, pp. 24–32.

Hunter, Gary K., and William D. Perreault. "Making Sales Technology Effective." *Journal of Marketing,* January 2007, pp. 16–34.

Pradeep, A. K., *The Buying Brain: Secrets for Selling the Subconscious Mind.* NY: John Wiley and Sons, 2010.

Schroder, Richard M., *From a Good Sales Call to a Great Sales Call.* NY: McGraw-Hill, 2011.

Key Terms and Concepts

After marketing: A concept that focuses attention on the value of current customers to the organization and on providing continuing satisfaction and reinforcement to them as well as past customers. The goal is to build lasting relationships with customers.

Correlation analysis: A method used in sales forecasting that involves measuring the relationship between the dependent variable, sales, and one or more independent variables that can explain increases or decreases in sales volume.

Cross-functional sales teams: A team that might include people from sales, engineering, customer service, and finance, depending on the needs of the customer. When the product is extremely high priced and is being sold to the whole organization, cross-functional sales teams are often used.

Customer organization structure: A structure that assigns a salesperson or team to serve a single customer or type of customer that has large or significant needs.

Geographic organization structure: Structure in which individual salespeople are assigned geographic territories. The salesperson calls on all prospects in the territory and usually represents all of the company's products.

Lead: A prospect that may or may not have the potential to be a true prospect, a candidate, to whom a sale could be made.

Major account organization structure: A variation of the customer organization structure, in which a company may assign a salesperson or a team to focus on major customers to foster long-term relationships.

Missionary salesperson: Used in many industries to focus solely on the promotion of existing products and introduction of new products.

Objectives of the sales force: Ultimately, revenue and sales. Other objectives include information provision, persuasion, and after-sale service.

Product organization structure: Structure in which each salesperson is assigned customers and prospects for a particular product or product line. This structure is useful when the sales force must have specific technical knowledge about products in order to sell effectively.

Prospecting: The process of locating potential customers. The process usually involves random lead generation which usually requires a high number of contacts to gain a sale or selected lead generation which uses existing contacts and knowledge to generate new prospects.

Sales forecast: An estimate of how much of the organization's output, either in dollars or in units, can be sold during a specific period under a proposed marketing plan and under an assumed set of economic conditions. It has many important uses in sales management, marketing planning, and strategic planning.

Sales relationship-building process: Process that views the initial sale as the first step in a long-term relationship-building process, not as the end goal. It contains six sequential stages: (1) prospecting, (2) planning the sales call, (3) presenting, (4) responding to objections, (5) obtaining commitment/closing the sale, and (6) building a long-term relationship.

Strategic alliance: Also called strategic partnership, long-term, formal relationships in which both parties make significant commitments and investments in each other in order to pursue mutual goals and to improve the profitability of each other. The partners in a strategic alliance actually invest in each other.

Technical sales specialist: Often used when the product is to be used to solve technical problems of the buyer. They support the salesperson by providing training or other technical assistance to the prospect.

Time series analyses: A method used in forecasting sales that involves analyzing past sales data and the impact of factors that influence sales (long-term growth trends, cyclical fluctuations, seasonal variations).

Chapter 10

Distribution Strategy

Channel of distribution decisions involve numerous interrelated variables that must be integrated into the total marketing mix. Because of the time and money required to set up an efficient channel, and since channels are often hard to change once they are set up, these decisions are critical to the success of the firm.

This chapter is concerned with the development and management of channels of distribution and the process of goods distribution in complex, highly competitive, and specialized economies. It should be noted at the outset that channels of distribution provide the ultimate consumer or organizational buyer with time, place, and possession utility. Thus, an efficient channel is one that delivers the product when and where it is wanted at a minimum total cost.

THE NEED FOR MARKETING INTERMEDIARIES

A *channel of distribution* is the combination of institutions through which a seller markets products to organizational buyers or ultimate consumers. The need for other institutions or intermediaries in the delivery of goods is sometimes questioned, particularly since the profits they make are viewed as adding to the cost of the product. However, this reasoning is generally fallacious, since producers use marketing intermediaries because the intermediary can perform functions more cheaply and more efficiently than the producer can. This notion of efficiency is critical when the characteristics of advanced economies are considered.

For example, the U.S. economy is characterized by heterogeneity in terms of both supply and demand. In terms of numbers alone, there are over 7 million establishments with employees comprising the supply segment of the economy, and there are nearly 110 million households making up the demand side. Clearly, if each of these units had to deal on a one-to-one basis to obtain needed goods and services, and there were no intermediaries to collect and disperse assortments of goods, the system would be totally inefficient. Thus, the primary role of intermediaries is to bring supply and demand together in an efficient and orderly fashion.

CLASSIFICATION OF MARKETING INTERMEDIARIES AND FUNCTIONS

There are a great many types of marketing intermediaries, many of which are so specialized by function and industry that they need not be discussed here. Figure 10.1 presents the major types of marketing intermediaries common to many industries. Although there is some overlap in this classification, these categories are based on the marketing

FIGURE 10.1
Major Types
of Marketing
Intermediaries

Source: Based on Peter D.
Bennett, ed., *Dictionary of
Marketing Terms*, 2d ed.
(Chicago: American Marketing
Association, 1995).

Middleman—an independent business concern that operates as a link between producers and ultimate consumers or organizational buyers.

Merchant middleman—a middleman who buys the goods outright and takes title to them.

Agent—a business unit that negotiates purchases, sales, or both but does not take title to the goods in which it deals.

Wholesaler—a merchant establishment operated by a concern that is primarily engaged in buying, taking title to, usually storing and physically handling goods in large quantities, and reselling the goods (usually in smaller quantities) to retailers or to organizational buyers.

Retailer—a merchant middleman who is engaged primarily in selling to ultimate consumers.

Broker—a middleman who serves as a go-between for the buyer or seller. The broker assumes no title risks, does not usually have physical custody of products, and is not looked upon as a permanent representative of either the buyer or the seller.

Manufacturers' agent—an agent who generally operates on an extended contractual basis, often sells within an exclusive territory, handles noncompeting but related lines of goods, and possesses limited authority with regard to prices and terms of sale.

Distributor—a wholesale middleman especially in lines where selective or exclusive distribution is common at the wholesaler level in which the manufacturer expects strong promotional support; often a synonym for wholesaler.

Jobber—a middleman who buys from manufacturers and sells to retailers; a wholesaler.

Facilitating agent—a business firm that assists in the performance of distribution tasks other than buying, selling, and transferring title (i.e., transportation companies, warehouses, etc.)

functions performed; that is, various intermediaries perform different marketing functions and to different degrees. Figure 10.2 is a listing of the more common marketing functions performed in the channel.

It should be remembered that whether or not a manufacturer uses intermediaries to perform these functions, the functions have to be performed by someone. In other words, the managerial question is not whether to perform the functions, but who will perform them and to what degree.

FIGURE 10.2
Major Functions
Performed in
Channels of
Distribution

Source: Roger A. Kerin,
Steven W. Hartley, and
William Rudelius, *Marketing*,
10th ed. (Burr Ridge, IL:
McGraw-Hill/Irwin, 2011),
p. 381.

Transactional Function

Buying: Purchasing products for resale or as an agent for supply of a product.

Selling: Contacting potential customers, promoting products, and soliciting orders.

Risk taking: Assuming business risks in the ownership of inventory that can become obsolete or deteriorate.

Logistical Function

Assorting: Creating product assortments from several sources to serve customers.

Storing: Assembling and protecting products at a convenient location to offer better customer service.

Sorting: Purchasing in large quantities and breaking into smaller amounts desired by customers.

Transporting: Physically moving products to customers.

Facilitating Function

Financing: Extending credit to customers.

Grading: Inspecting, testing, or judging products, and assigning them quality grades.

Marketing information and research: Providing information to customers and suppliers, including competitive conditions and trends.

CHANNELS OF DISTRIBUTION

As previously noted, a channel of distribution is the combination of institutions through which a seller markets products to the user or ultimate consumer. Some of these links assume the risks of ownership; others do not. The conventional channel of distribution patterns for consumer goods markets are shown in Figure 10.3.

Some manufacturers use *direct channels,* selling directly to a market. For example, Gateway sold computers through the mail without the use of other intermediaries. Using a direct channel, called *direct marketing,* increased in popularity as marketers found that products could be sold directly using a variety of methods. These include direct mail, tele-marketing, direct-action advertising, catalog selling, cable selling, online selling, and direct selling through demonstrations at home or place of work. These will be discussed in more detail later in this chapter.

In other cases, one or more intermediaries may be used in the distribution process. For example, Hewlett-Packard sells its computers and printers through retailers such as Best Buy and Office Max. A common channel for consumer goods is one in which the manufacturer sells through wholesalers and retailers. For instance, a cold remedy manufacturer may sell to drug wholesalers who, in turn, sell a vast array of drug products to various retail outlets. Small manufacturers may also use agents, since they do not have sufficient capital for their own sales forces. Agents are commonly used intermediaries in the jewelry industry. The final channel in Figure 10.3 is used primarily when small wholesalers and retailers are involved. Channels with one or more intermediaries are referred to as *indirect channels.*

In contrast to consumer products, the direct channel is often used in the distribution of organizational goods. The reason for this stems from the structure of most organizational markets, which often have relatively few but extremely large customers. Also, many organizational products, such as computer systems, need a great deal of presale and postsale service. Distributors are used in organizational markets when there is a large number of buyers but each purchases a small amount of a product. As in the consumer market, agents are used

FIGURE 10.3   Conventional Channels of Distribution of Consumer Goods

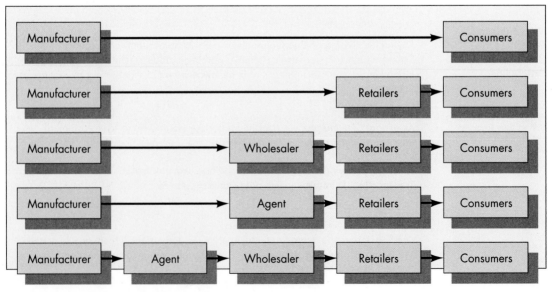

FIGURE 10.4   Conventional Channels of Distribution for Organizational Goods

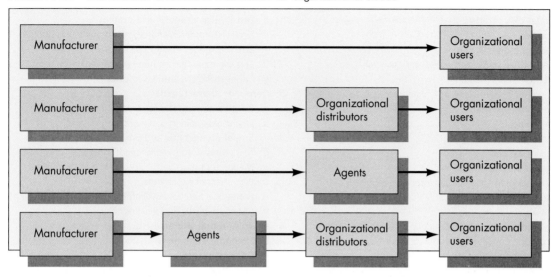

in organizational markets in cases where manufacturers do not wish to have their own sales forces. Such an arrangement may be used by small manufacturers or when the market is geographically dispersed. The final channel arrangement in Figure 10.4 may also be used by a small manufacturer or when the market consists of many small customers. Under such conditions, it may not be economical for sellers to have their own sales organization.

SELECTING CHANNELS OF DISTRIBUTION

Given the numerous types of channel intermediaries and functions that must be performed, the task of selecting and designing a channel of distribution may at first appear to be overwhelming. However, in many industries, channels of distribution have developed over many years and have become somewhat traditional. In such cases, the producer may be limited to this type of channel to operate in the industry. This is not to say that a traditional channel is always the most efficient and that there are no opportunities for innovation. But the fact that such a channel is widely accepted in the industry suggests it is highly efficient. A primary constraint in these cases and in cases where no traditional channel exists is that of availability of the various types of middlemen. All too often in the early stages of channel design, executives map out elaborate channel networks only to find out later that no such independent intermediaries exist for the firm's product in selected geographic areas. Even if they do exist, they may not be willing to accept the seller's products. In general, there are six basic considerations in the initial development of channel strategy. These are outlined in Figure 10.5.

It should be noted that for a particular product any one of these characteristics greatly influences choice of channels. To illustrate, highly perishable products generally require direct channels, or a firm with little financial strength may require intermediaries to perform almost all of the marketing functions.

Specific Considerations

The above characteristics play an important part in framing the channel selection decision. Based on them, the choice of channels can be further refined in terms of

FIGURE 10.5 General Considerations in Channel Planning

1. **Customer characteristics.**
   a. Number.
   b. Geographic dispersion.
   c. Preferred channels and outlets for purchase.
   d. Purchasing patterns.
   e. Use of new channels (e.g., online purchasing).
2. **Product characteristics.**
   a. Unit value.
   b. Perishability.
   c. Bulkiness.
   d. Degree of standardization.
   e. Installation and maintenance services required.
3. **Intermediary characteristics.**
   a. Availability.
   b. Willingness to accept product or product line.
   c. Geographic market served.
   d. Marketing functions performed.
   e. Potential for conflict.
   f. Potential for long-term relationship.
   g. Competitive products sold.
   h. Financial condition.
   i. Other strengths and weaknesses.
4. **Competitor characteristics.**
   a. Number.
   b. Relative size and market share.
   c. Distribution channels and strategy.
   d. Financial condition and estimated marketing budget.
   e. Size of product mix and product lines.
   f. Overall marketing strategy employed.
   g. Other strengths and weaknesses.
5. **Company characteristics.**
   a. Relative size and market share.
   b. Financial condition and marketing budget.
   c. Size of product mix and product lines.
   d. Marketing strategy employed.
   e. Marketing objectives.
   f. Past channel experience.
   g. Marketing functions willing to perform.
   h. Other strengths and weaknesses.
6. **Environmental characteristics.**
   a. Economic conditions.
   b. Legal regulations and restrictions.
   c. Political issues.
   d. Global and domestic cultural differences and changes.
   e. Technological changes.
   f. Other opportunities and threats.

(1) distribution coverage required, (2) degree of control desired, (3) total distribution cost, and (4) channel flexibility.

Distribution Coverage Required

Because of the characteristics of the product, the environment needed to sell the product, and the needs and expectations of the potential buyer, products will vary in the intensity of distribution coverage they require. Distribution coverage can be viewed along a continuum ranging from intensive to selective to exclusive distribution.

Intensive Distribution   Here the manufacturer attempts to gain exposure through as many wholesalers and retailers as possible. Most convenience goods require intensive distribution based on the characteristics of the product (low unit value) and the needs and expectations of the buyer (high frequency of purchase and convenience).

Selective Distribution   Here the manufacturer limits the use of intermediaries to the ones believed to be the best available in a geographic area. This may be based on the service organization available, the sales organization, or the reputation of the intermediary. Thus, appliances, home furnishings, and better clothing are usually distributed selectively. For appliances, the intermediary's service organization could be a key factor, while for better clothing and home furnishings, the intermediary's reputation would be an important consideration.

Exclusive Distribution   Here the manufacturer severely limits distribution, and intermediaries are provided exclusive rights within a particular territory. The characteristics of the product are a determining factor here. Where the product requires certain specialized selling effort or investment in unique facilities or large inventories, this arrangement is usually selected. Retail paint stores are an example of such a distribution arrangement.

THE PERFECT INTERMEDIARY

1. Has access to the market that the manufacturer wants to reach.
2. Carries adequate stocks of the manufacturer's products and a satisfactory assortment of other products.
3. Has an effective promotional program—advertising, personal selling, and product displays. Promotional demands placed on the manufacturer are in line with what the manufacturer intends to do.
4. Provides services to customers—credit, delivery, installation, and product repair—and honors the product warranty conditions.
5. Pays its bills on time and has capable management.

THE PERFECT MANUFACTURER

1. Provides a desirable assortment of products—well designed, properly priced, attractively packaged, and delivered on time and in adequate quantities.
2. Builds product demand for these products by advertising them.
3. Furnishes promotional assistance to its middlemen.
4. Provides managerial assistance for its middlemen.
5. Honors product warranties and provides repair and installation service.

THE PERFECT COMBINATION

1. Probably doesn't exist.

Degree of Control Desired

In selecting channels of distribution, the seller must make decisions concerning the degree of control desired over the marketing of the firm's products. Some manufacturers prefer to keep as much control over their products as possible. Ordinarily, the degree of control achieved by the seller is proportionate to the directness of the channel. One Eastern brewery, for instance, owns its own fleet of trucks and operates a wholly owned delivery system direct to grocery and liquor stores. Its market is very concentrated geographically, with many small buyers, so such a system is economically feasible. However, all other brewers in the area sell through distributors.

When more indirect channels are used, the manufacturer must surrender some control over the marketing of the firm's product. However, attempts are commonly made to maintain a degree of control through some other indirect means, such as sharing promotional expenditures, providing sales training, or other operational aids, such as accounting systems, inventory systems, or marketing research data on the dealer's trading area.

Total Distribution Cost

The total distribution cost concept has developed out of the more general topic of systems theory. The concept suggests that a channel of distribution should be viewed as a total system composed of interdependent subsystems, and that the objective of the system (channel) manager should be to optimize total system performance. In terms of distribution costs, it generally is assumed that the total system should be designed to minimize costs for a given level of service. The following is a representative list of the major distribution costs to be minimized:

1. Transportation.
2. Order processing.

3. Cost of lost business (an opportunity cost due to inability to meet customer demand).
4. Inventory carrying costs, including:
    a. Storage-space charges.
    b. Cost of capital invested.
    c. Taxes.
    d. Insurance.
    e. Obsolescence and deterioration.
5. Packaging.
6. Materials handling.

The important qualification to the total-cost concept is the statement "other things being equal." The purpose of the total-cost concept is to emphasize total system performance to avoid suboptimization. However, other important factors must be considered, not the least of which are level of customer service, sales, profits, and interface with the total marketing mix.

Channel Flexibility

A final consideration relates to the ability of the manufacturer to adapt to changing conditions. To illustrate, much of the population has moved from inner cities to suburbs, and thus buyers make most of their purchases in shopping centers and malls. If a manufacturer had long-term exclusive dealership with retailers in the inner city, the ability to adapt to this population shift could have been severely limited.

MANAGING A CHANNEL OF DISTRIBUTION

Once the seller has decided on the type of channel structure to use and selected the individual members, the entire coalition should operate as a total system. From a behavioral perspective, the system can be viewed as a social system since each member interacts with the others, each member plays a role vis-à-vis the others, and each has certain expectations of the other. Thus, the behavioral perspective views a channel of distribution as more than a series of markets or participants extending from production to consumption.

Relationship Marketing in Channels

For many years in theory and practice, marketing has taken a competitive view of channels of distribution. In other words, since channel members had different goals and strategies, it was believed that the major focus should be on concepts such as power and conflict. Research interests focused on issues concerning bases of power, antecedents and consequences of conflict, and conflict resolution.

More recently, however, a new view of channels has developed. Perhaps because of the success of Japanese companies in the 1980s, it was recognized that much could be gained by developing long-term commitments and harmony among channel members. This view is called *relationship marketing,* which can be defined as "marketing with the conscious aim to develop and manage long-term and/or trusting relationships with customers, distributors, suppliers, or other parties in the marketing environment."[1]

It is well documented in the marketing literature that long-term relationships throughout the channel often lead to higher-quality products with lower costs. These benefits may account for the increased use of vertical marketing systems.[2]

Vertical Marketing Systems

To this point in the chapter the discussion has focused primarily on conventional channels of distribution. In conventional channels, each firm is relatively independent of the other

FIGURE 10.6
Major Types of
Vertical Marketing
Systems

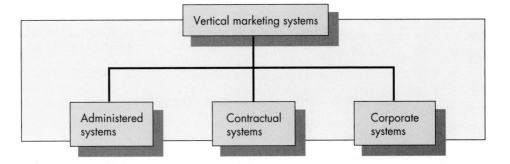

members in the channel. However, one of the important developments in channel management in recent years is the increasing use of vertical marketing systems.

Vertical marketing systems are channels in which members are more dependent on one another and develop long-term working relationships in order to improve the efficiency and effectiveness of the system. Figure 10.6 shows the major types of vertical marketing systems, which include administered, contractual, and corporate systems.[3]

Administered Systems

Administered vertical marketing systems are the most similar to conventional channels. However, in these systems there is a higher degree of interorganizational planning and management than in a conventional channel. The dependence in these systems can result from the existence of a strong channel leader such that other channel members work closely with this company in order to maintain a long-term relationship. While any level of channel member may be the leader of an administered system, Walmart, Kmart, and Sears are excellent examples of retailers that have established administered systems with many of their suppliers.

Contractual Systems

Contractual vertical marketing systems involve independent production and distribution companies entering into formal contracts to perform designated marketing functions. Three major types of contractual vertical marketing systems are the retail cooperative organization, wholesaler-sponsored voluntary chain, and various franchising programs.

In a retail cooperative organization, a group of independent retailers unite and agree to pool buying and managerial resources to improve competitive position. In a wholesaler-sponsored voluntary chain, a wholesaler contracts with a number of retailers and performs channel functions for them. Usually, retailers agree to concentrate a major portion of their purchasing with the sponsoring wholesaler and to sell advertised products at the same price. The most visible type of contractual vertical marketing systems involves a variety of franchise programs. Franchises involve a parent company (the franchisor) and an independent firm (the franchisee) entering into a contractual relationship to set up and operate a business in a particular way. Many products and services reach consumers through franchise systems, including automobiles (Ford), gasoline (Mobil), hotels and motels (Holiday Inn), restaurants (McDonald's), car rentals (Avis), and soft drinks (Pepsi). In fact, some analysts predict that within the next 10 years, franchises will account for 50 percent of all retail sales.

Corporate Systems

Corporate vertical marketing systems involve single ownership of two or more levels of a channel. A manufacturer's purchasing wholesalers or retailers is called *forward integration*.

A franchise is a means by which a producer of products or services achieves a direct channel of distribution without wholly owning or managing the physical facilities in the market. In effect, the franchisor provides the franchisee with the franchisor's knowledge, manufacturing, and marketing techniques for a financial return.

INGREDIENTS OF A FRANCHISED BUSINESS

Six key ingredients should be included within a well-balanced franchise offered to a franchisee. These are given in order of importance.

- *Technical knowledge* in its practical form is supplied through an intensive course of study.
- *Managerial techniques* based on proven and time-tested programs are imparted to the franchisee on a continuing basis, even after the business has been started or taken over by the franchisee.
- *Commercial knowledge* involving prescribed methods of buying and selling is explained and codified. Most products to be obtained, processed, and sold to the franchisee are supplied by the franchisor.
- *Financial instruction* on managing funds and accounts is given to the franchisee during the indoctrination period.
- *Accounting controls* are set up by the franchisor for the franchisee.
- *Protective safeguards* are included in the intensive training of the franchisee for employees and customers, including the quality of the product, as well as the safeguards for assets through adequate insurance controls.

ELEMENTS OF AN IDEAL FRANCHISE PROGRAM

- *High gross margin.* In order for the franchisee to be able to afford a high franchise fee (which the franchisor needs), it is necessary to operate on a high gross margin percentage. This explains the widespread application of franchising in the food and service industries.
- *In-store value added.* Franchising works best in those product categories in which the product is at least partially processed in the store. Such environments require constant on-site supervision—a chronic problem for company-owned stores using a hired manager. Owners simply are willing to work harder over longer hours.
- *Secret processes.* Concepts, formulas, or products that the franchisee can't duplicate without joining the franchise program.
- *Real estate profits.* The franchisor uses income from ownership of property as a significant revenue source.
- *Simplicity.* The most successful franchises have been those that operate on automatic pilot: All the key decisions have been thought through, and the owner merely implements the decisions.

Source: Partially adapted from Philip D. White and Albert D. Bates, "Franchising Will Remain Retailing Fixture, but Its Salad Days Have Long Since Gone," *Marketing News,* February 17, 1984, p. 14; and Scott Shane and Chester Spell, "Factors for New Franchise Success," *Sloan Management Review,* Spring 1998, pp. 43–50. Also see Stephen Spinelli, Jr., Robert M. Rosenberg, and Sue Birley, *Franchising* (Upper Saddle River, NJ: Prentice-Hall PTR, 2004).

Wholesalers or retailers' purchasing channel members above them is called *backward integration.* Firms may choose to develop corporate vertical marketing systems in order to compete more effectively with other marketing systems, to obtain scale economies, and to increase channel cooperation and avoid channel conflict.

WHOLESALING

As noted, wholesalers are merchants that are primarily engaged in buying, taking title to, usually storing and physically handling goods in large quantities, and reselling the goods (usually in smaller quantities) to retailers or to industrial or business users.[4] Wholesalers are also called distributors in some industries, particularly when they have exclusive distribution rights, such as in the beer industry. Other wholesalers that do not take title to goods are called agents, brokers, or manufacturers' representatives in various industries. There are over 890,000 wholesalers in the United States.

Wholesalers create value for suppliers, retailers, and users of goods by performing distribution functions efficiently and effectively. They may transport and warehouse goods, exhibit them at trade shows, and offer advice to retailers concerning which lines of products are selling best in other areas. Producers use wholesalers to reach large markets and extend geographic coverage for their goods. Wholesalers may lower the costs for other channel members by efficiently carrying out such activities as physically moving goods to convenient locations, assuming the risk of managing large inventories of diverse products, and delivering products as needed to replenish retail shelves.

While producers may actively seek out wholesalers for their goods, wholesalers also try to attract producers to use their services. To do so, they may offer to perform all the distribution functions or tailor their services to include only the functions that producers do not have the ability to perform effectively. Naturally, wholesalers especially seek producers of major brands for which sales and profit potential are likely to be the greatest. Wholesalers may compete with other wholesalers to attract producers by offering lower costs for the functions they perform. Wholesalers with excellent track records that do not carry directly competing products and brands, that have appropriate locations and facilities, and that have relationships with major retail customers can more easily attract manufacturers of successful products. Also, wholesalers that serve large markets may be more attractive since producers may be able to reduce the number of wholesalers they deal with and thereby lower their costs. Long-term profitable producer–wholesaler relationships are enhanced by trust, doing a good job for one another, and open communication about problems and opportunities.

Wholesalers also need to attract retailers and organizational customers to buy from them. In many cases, wholesalers have exclusive contracts to distribute products in a particular trading area. For popular products and brands with large market shares, the wholesaler's task is simplified because retailers want to carry them. For example, distributors of Coke and Pepsi can attract retailers easily because the products sell so well and consumers expect to find them in many retail outlets. Retail supermarkets and convenience stores would be at a competitive disadvantage without these brands.

However, for new or small market-share products and brands, particularly those of less well-known manufacturers, wholesalers may have to do considerable marketing to get retailers to stock them. Wholesalers may get placement for such products and brands in retail stores because they have previously developed strong long-term working relationships with them. Alternatively, wholesalers may have to carefully explain the marketing plan for the product, why it should be successful, and why carrying the product will benefit the retailer.

While there are still many successful wholesalers, the share of products they sell is likely to continue to decrease. This is because large retail chains such as Walmart have gained such market power that they can buy directly from manufacturers and bypass wholesalers altogether. The survival of wholesalers depends on their ability to meet the needs of both manufacturers and retailers by performing distribution functions more efficiently and effectively than a channel designed without them.

BENEFITS FOR MANUFACTURERS

- Provide the ability to reach diverse geographic markets cost effectively.
- Provide information about retailers and end users in various markets.
- Reduce costs through greater efficiency and effectiveness in distribution functions performed.
- Reduce potential losses by assuming risks and offering expertise.

BENEFITS FOR RETAILERS

- Provide potentially profitable products otherwise unavailable for resale in retail area.
- Provide information about industries, manufacturers, and other retailers.
- Reduce costs by providing an assortment of goods from different manufacturers.
- Reduce costs through greater efficiency in distribution functions performed.

BENEFITS FOR END USERS

- Increase the product alternatives available in local markets.
- Reduce retail prices by the efficiency and effectiveness contributed to the channel.
- Improve product selection by providing information to retailers about the best products to offer end users.

STORE AND NONSTORE RETAILING

As noted, retailers are merchants who are primarily engaged in selling to ultimate consumers. The more than 1.9 million retailers in the United States can be classified in many ways. For example, they are broken down in the North American Industry Classification System (NAICS) codes into eight general categories and a number of subcategories based on the types of merchandise they sell.[5]

Marketers have a number of decisions to make to determine the best way to retail their products. For example, decisions have to be made about whether to use stores to sell merchandise, and if so, whether to sell through company-owned stores, franchised outlets, or independent stores or chains. Decisions have to be made about whether to sell through nonstore methods, such as the Internet, and if so, which methods of nonstore retailing should be used. Each of these decisions brings about a number of others such as what types of stores to use, how many of them, what locations should be selected, and what specific types of nonstore retailing to use.

Store Retailing

About 90 percent of retail purchases are made through stores. This makes them an appropriate retail method for most types of products and services. Retailers vary not only in the types of merchandise they carry but also in the breadth and depth of their product assortments and the amount of service they provide. In general, *mass merchandisers* carry broad product assortments and compete on two bases. Supermarkets (Kroger) and department stores (Macy's) compete with other retailers on the basis of offering a good selection in a number of different categories, whereas supercenters (Walmart Supercenters), warehouse clubs (Costco), discount stores (Walmart), and off-price retailers (T.J. Maxx) compete more on the basis of offering lower prices on products in their large assortments. Manufacturers of many types of consumer goods must get distribution in one or more types of mass merchandisers to be successful.

Specialty stores handle deep assortments in a limited number of product categories. Specialty stores include limited-line stores that offer a large assortment of a few related product lines (The Gap), single-line stores that emphasize a single product (Batteries Plus), and category killers (Best Buy), which are large, low-priced limited-line retail chains that attempt to dominate a particular product category. If a product type is sold primarily through specialty stores and sales are concentrated in category killer chains, manufacturers may have to sell through them to reach customers.

Convenience stores (7-Eleven) are retailers whose primary advantages to consumers are location convenience, close-in parking, and easy entry and exit. They stock products that consumers want to buy in a hurry, such as milk or soft drinks, and charge higher prices for the purchase convenience. They are an important retail outlet for many types of convenience goods.

In selecting the types of stores and specific stores and chains to resell their products, manufacturers (and wholesalers) have a variety of factors to consider. They want stores and chains that reach their target market and have good reputations with consumers. They want stores and chains that handle distribution functions efficiently and effectively, order large quantities, pay invoices quickly, display their merchandise well, and allow them to make good profits. Selling products in the right stores and chains increases sales, and selling in prestigious stores can increase the equity of a brand and the price that can be charged. The locations of retail stores, the types of people who shop at them, and the professionalism of the salespeople and clerks who work in them all affect the success of the stores and the products they sell. In addition to the merchandise offered, store advertising, and price levels, the characteristics of the store itself—including layout, colors, smells, noises, lights, signs, and shelf space and displays—influence the success of both the stores and the products they offer.

Nonstore Retailing

Although stores dominate sales for most products, there are still opportunities to market products successfully in other ways. Five nonstore methods of retailing include catalogs and direct mail, vending machines, television home shopping, direct sales, and electronic exchanges.[6]

Catalogs and Direct Mail

Catalogs and direct mail dominate nonstore retailing. The advantages of this type of nonstore retailing for marketers are that consumers can be targeted effectively and reached in their homes or at work, overhead costs are decreased, and assortments of specialty merchandise can be presented with attractive pictures and in-depth descriptions of features and benefits. Catalogs can also remain in homes or offices for a lengthy time period, making available potential sales. Catalogs can offer specialty products for unique markets that are geographically dispersed in a cost-effective manner. Although consumers cannot experience products directly as they can in stores, catalog retailers with reputations for quality and generous return policies can reduce consumers' risks. For example, Levenger, which sells pens, desks, and "other tools for serious readers," sends consumers a postage-paid label to return unwanted merchandise. Many consumers enjoy the time savings of catalog shopping and are willing to pay higher prices to use it.

Vending Machines

Vending machines are a relatively limited method of retail merchandising, and most vending machine sales are for beverages, food, and candy. The advantages for marketers include the following: They are available for sales 24 hours a day, they can be placed in a variety of high-traffic locations, and marketers can charge higher prices. While uses of vending machines for such things as airline insurance and concert and game tickets are not unusual, this method has limited potential for most products.

Television Home Shopping

Television home shopping includes cable channels dedicated to shopping, infomercials, and direct-response advertising shown on cable and broadcast networks. Home Shopping Network and QVC are the leaders in this market, and the major products sold are inexpensive jewelry, apparel, cosmetics, and exercise equipment. While this method allows better visual display than catalogs, potential customers must be watching at the time the merchandise is offered; if not, they have no way of knowing about the product or purchasing it.

Direct Sales

Direct sales are made by salespeople to consumers in their homes or offices or by telephone. The most common products purchased this way are cosmetics, fragrances, decorative accessories, vacuum cleaners, home appliances, cooking utensils, kitchenware, jewelry, food and nutritional products, and educational materials. Avon, Mary Kay, and Tupperware are probably the best-known retail users of this channel. Salespeople can demonstrate products effectively and provide detailed feature and benefit information. A limitation of this method is that consumers are often too busy to spend their time this way and do not want to pay the higher prices needed to cover the high costs of this method of retailing.

Electronic Exchanges and Multichannel Marketing

Electronic exchanges or sales made online are the fastest growing method of retailing and in some years, sales have grown 20 to 25 percent per year. Some analysts suggest that in a few years, over 12 percent of all retail sales will be online. Companies like Amazon.com and Priceline.com have created profitable businesses by selling online and both business-to-business and business-to-consumer sales have grown to be profitable for a number of companies.

While the growth of electronic exchanges is partly due to the success of new, entrepreneurial companies, much of the growth can be attributed to large, established companies using a multichannel marketing strategy. *Multichannel marketing* involves the use of both traditional channels and electronic exchanges to better serve customers and build relationships with them. For example, JCPenney offers merchandise and information about it in its brick-and-mortar stores, in its mailed paper catalogs, and online to better serve its customers. In fact, its best customers purchase from all three. Similarly, other companies like Eddie Bauer, Bass Pro Shop, and Cabela's offer customers the opportunity to purchase from its stores, its catalogs, and online.

Figure 10.7 lists some of the advantages and disadvantages of electronic exchanges for marketers. In examining this figure, it is important to recognize that there are some differences in the advantages and disadvantages depending on whether the marketer is a small, entrepreneurial venture or a large, established company. Since electronic exchange offers low-entry barriers, this is an advantage for a small company that wants to get into a market and compete for business with less capital. However, for large, established companies, this

When developing commercial Web sites, it is important to consider what customers experience when searching for information, evaluating alternative products, and purchasing them. Below are some basic questions that Web site designers should consider.

INFORMATION SEARCH

1. Ease of navigation—is it easy to move throughout the Web site?
2. Speed of page downloads—does each page load quickly enough?
3. Effectiveness of search features—are search features returning the information users are looking for?
4. Frequency of product updates—is product information updated often enough to meet user needs?

EVALUATION OF ALTERNATIVES

1. Ease of product comparisons—is it easy to compare different products offered on the Web site?
2. Product descriptions—are product descriptions accurate, clear, and comprehensive enough to allow customers to make informed decisions?
3. Contacting customer service representatives—are customer service phone numbers easy to locate?
4. In-stock status—are out-of-stock products flagged before the customer proceeds to the checkout process?

PURCHASE

1. Security and privacy issues—do users feel comfortable transmitting personal information?
2. Checkout process—are users able to move through the checkout process in a reasonable amount of time?
3. Payment options—are payment options offered that nonbuyers desire?
4. Delivery options—are delivery options offered that nonbuyers desire?
5. Ordering instructions—are ordering instructions easy to understand?

Source: Based on Douglas K. Hoffman and John E. G. Bateson, *Services Marketing: Concepts, Strategies, and Cases.* 3rd ed. (Mason, OH: Thomson South Western, 2006), p. 86.

is less of an advantage since they have the capital to invest; low-entry barriers create more competition for them from smaller companies.

Similarly, large companies with established names and brand equity can more easily market products that customers would ordinarily want to examine before purchase (touch-and-feel products) than can smaller companies with less brand equity. For example, companies like Lands' End, J.C. Penney, and Walmart are more successful in attracting customers electronically because customers know the companies and their offerings better and perceive less risk in purchasing from them than from a new or unknown electronic marketer. This does not mean that newer companies that sell only by electronic means cannot compete for business. Companies such as Amazon.com and Priceline.com have created well-known Web sites and have generated considerable sales and profits.

In sum, electronic exchanges are an established alternative for marketing products and services. They do provide customers with a wealth of product information and large product assortments that are readily available. Many electronic marketers have found ways to deliver superior customer value and become profitable and many others are close to doing so.[7]

FIGURE 10.7
Electronic
Commerce:
Advantages and
Disadvantages for
Marketers

Advantages for Marketers

Reduces the need for stores, paper catalogs, and salespeople; can be cost efficient.

Allows good visual presentation and full description of product features and benefits.

Allows vast assortments of products to be offered efficiently.

Allows strategic elements, such as product offerings, prices, and promotion appeals, to be changed quickly.

Allows products to be offered globally in an efficient manner.

Allows products to be offered 24 hours a day, 365 days a year.

Fosters the development of one-on-one, interactive relationships with customers.

Provides an efficient means for developing a customer database and doing online marketing research.

Disadvantages for Marketers

Strong price competition online often squeezes profit margins.

Low entry barriers lead some e-marketers to overemphasize order-taking and not develop sufficient infrastructure for order fulfillment.

Customers must go to the Web site rather than having marketers seek them out via salespeople and advertising; advertising their Web sites is prohibitively expensive for many small e-marketers.

Limits the market to customers who are willing and able to purchase electronically; many countries still have a small population of computer-literate people.

Not as good for selling touch-and-feel products as opposed to look-and-buy products unless there is strong brand/store/site equity (Dell computers/Walmart/Amazon.com) or the products are homogeneous (books, CDs, plane tickets, etc.).

Often less effective and efficient in business-to-consumer markets than in business-to-business markets.

SUMMARY

This chapter introduced the distribution of goods and services in a complex, highly competitive, highly specialized economy. It emphasized the vital need for marketing intermediaries to bring about exchanges between buyers and sellers in a reasonably efficient manner. The chapter examined various types of intermediaries and the distribution functions they perform as well as topics in the selection and management of distribution channels. Finally, both wholesaling and store and nonstore retailing were discussed.

Additional Resources

Chopra, Sunil, and Peter Meindl. *Supply Chain Management.* 3rd ed. Upper River Saddle, NJ: Prentice Hall, 2007.

Coughlin, Anne T.; Erin Anderson; Louis W. Stern; and Adel I. El-Ansary. *Marketing Channels.* 7th ed. Upper Saddle River, NJ: Prentice Hall, 2006.

Levy, Michael, and Barton A. Weitz. *Retailing Management.* 8th ed. Burr Ridge, IL: Irwin/McGraw-Hill, 2012.

Rosenbloom, Bert. *Marketing Channels: A Management View.* 8th ed. Mason, OH: Thomson South-Western, 2012.

Simchi-Levi, David; Philip Kaminsky, and Edith Simchi-Levi. *Designing and Managing the Supply Chain.* 3rd ed. Burr Ridge, IL: McGraw-Hill, 2008.

Key Terms and Concepts

Note: For definitions of the major types of marketing intermediaries, see Figure 10.1 and for the major functions performed in channels of distribution, see Figure 10.2 at the beginning of this chapter.

Administered system: A vertical marketing system with a higher degree of interorganizational planning than a conventional channel often brought about by having a strong channel leader.

Backward integration: The purchase by wholesalers or retailers of channel members above them.

Channel of distribution: The combination of institutions through which a seller markets products to organizational buyers or ultimate consumers.

Contractual system: A vertical marketing system that involves independent production and distribution companies entering into formal contracts to perform designated marketing functions.

Convenience stores: Retailers whose primary advantages to consumers are location convenience, close-in parking, and easy entry and exit. They typically stock a limited number of items that consumers want to buy in a hurry, such as milk or soft drinks and include stores like 7-Eleven and PDQ.

Corporate system: A vertical marketing system involving single ownership of two or more levels of a channel such as a manufacturer owning a wholesale operation.

Direct channels: Channels in which the manufacturer sells directly to a market without the use of intermediaries.

Direct marketing: A direct channel in which the seller uses direct mail, telemarketing, direct-action advertising, catalog selling, cable selling, online selling, or direct selling through demonstrations at home or place of work to reach buyers.

Exclusive distribution: An approach to distribution that involves the manufacturer providing exclusive rights to intermediaries in particular territories.

Forward integration: A manufacturer's purchase of wholesalers or retailers who distribute its products.

Indirect channels: Distribution channels with one or more intermediaries.

Intensive distribution: An approach to distribution that involves using as many wholesalers and retailers as possible to get broad distribution. It is commonly used with convenience goods.

Mass merchandisers: Large retailers that carry broad product assortments and compete on the basis of a good selection in a number of different categories (e.g. Macy's, Kroger) or on the basis of lower prices on products in their large assortment (e.g. Walmart, Costco).

Multichannel marketing: The use of traditional channels, such as stores and catalogs, along with electronic exchanges to better serve customers and build relationships with them.

Relationship marketing: Marketing with the conscious aim to develop and manage long-term and/or trusting relationships with customers, distributors, suppliers, or other parties in the marketing environment.

Selective distribution: An approach to distribution in which the manufacturer limits the use of intermediaries to the best available in a geographic area. The intermediaries are commonly selected on the basis of the service or sales organization available or reputation.

Specialty stores: Stores that handle deep assortments in a limited number of product categories, such as The Gap, Batteries Plus, or Best Buy.

Total distribution costs: Concept that suggests that a channel of distribution should be viewed as a total system composed of interdependent subsystems and that the objective of the system (channel) manager should be to optimize total system performance. This typically means the total system should minimize costs for a given level of service.

Vertical marketing systems: Channels in which members are more dependent on one another and develop long-term working relationships in order to improve the efficiency and effectiveness of the system.

Chapter

11

Pricing Strategy

One of the most important and complex decisions a firm has to make relates to pricing its products or services. If consumers or organizational buyers perceive a price to be too high, they may purchase competitive brands or substitute products, leading to a loss of sales and profits for the firm. If the price is too low, sales might increase, but profitability may suffer. Thus, pricing decisions must be given careful consideration when a firm is introducing a new product or planning a short- or long-term price change.

This chapter discusses demand, supply, and environmental influences that affect pricing decisions and emphasizes that all three must be considered for effective pricing. However, as will be discussed in the chapter, many firms price their products without explicitly considering all of these influences.

DEMAND INFLUENCES ON PRICING DECISIONS

Demand influences on pricing decisions concern primarily the nature of the target market and expected reactions of consumers to a given price or change in price. There are three primary considerations here: demographic factors, psychological factors, and price elasticity.

Demographic Factors

In the initial selection of the target market that a firm intends to serve, a number of demographic factors are usually considered. Demographic factors that are particularly important for pricing decisions include the following:

1. Number of potential buyers.
2. Location of potential buyers.
3. Position of potential buyers (organizational buyers or final consumers).
4. Expected consumption rates of potential buyers.
5. Economic strength of potential buyers.

These factors help determine market potential and are useful for estimating expected sales at various price levels.

Psychological Factors

Psychological factors related to pricing concern primarily how consumers will perceive various prices or price changes. For example, marketing managers should be concerned with such questions as these:

1. Will potential buyers use price as an indicator of product quality?
2. Will potential buyers be favorably attracted by odd pricing (e.g. 99¢, $3,999)?

Most analyses of the price of a product focus on the amount of money a buyer must pay to purchase. However, there are other costs involved that can strongly influence purchase decisions. Below are three types of costs marketing analysts should consider when making pricing decisions.

Time Costs. Time is valuable to most people. Time involved in purchasing products often could be used for more pleasant activities. Waiting in a long checkout line or waiting for a pizza to be delivered can be considered a waste of time too. Many people are willing to pay more money to reduce the time they have to wait to get a product. Vending machine sales often depend on buyers who will pay more money to get a product sooner and with less hassle. People who want a product immediately are often willing to finance the purchase on a credit card to reduce the time waiting to get it.

Psychological Costs. The mental energy and stress in making important purchases and accepting the risks of products not performing as expected can make buyers uncomfortable. Purchasing complex or expensive products can involve investigating and evaluating lots of information and worrying about making the right choices. Car dealers that offer "no haggle" sales do so in order to lower buyers' psychological costs of negotiating.

Behavioral Costs. Buying products and services usually requires some level of physical activity. These costs can increase if buyers have to drive a long way to make a purchase, park far away in a large mall parking lot and have to walk to the store, hunt through many aisles looking for products, and stand for long periods waiting to check out. One way buyers reduce this cost is by shopping and buying from catalogs or the Internet even if they have to pay more money because of shipping charges.

If buyers in a target market are sensitive to these costs, it is possible for marketers to get a competitive advantage by reducing them. These strategies include such things as selling through multiple channels, free shipping, fast delivery, in-store credit, no-hassle return policies, and money-back guarantees. Another strategy is to reduce the monetary price of products in order to compensate for higher time, psychological, or behavioral costs. For example, Walmart's lower monetary prices help offset the additional costs to buyers of having to drive longer distances to get to the stores that are located on the outskirts of most markets.

3. Will potential buyers perceive the price as too high relative to the service the product gives them or relative to competition?

4. Are potential buyers prestige oriented and therefore willing to pay higher prices to fulfill this need?

5. How much will potential buyers be willing to pay for the product?

While psychological factors have a significant effect on the success of a pricing strategy and ultimately on marketing strategy, answers to the above questions may require considerable marketing research. In fact, a review of buyers' subjective perceptions of price concluded that very little is known about how price affects buyers' perceptions of alternative purchase offers and how these perceptions affect purchase response.[1] However, some tentative generalizations about how buyers perceive price have been formulated. For example, research has found that persons who choose high-priced items usually perceive large quality variations within product categories and see the consequences of a poor choice as being undesirable. They believe that quality is related to price and see themselves as good judges of product quality. In general, the reverse is true for persons who select low-priced items in the same product categories. Thus, although information on psychological factors involved in purchasing may be difficult to obtain, marketing managers must at least consider the effects of such factors on their desired target market and marketing strategy.[2]

There are three types of psychological pricing strategies. First there is *prestige pricing,* in which a high price is charged to create a signal that the product is exceptionally fine. Prestige pricing is commonly used for some brands of cars, clothing, perfume, jewelry, cosmetics, wine and liquor, and crystal and china. Second, there is *odd pricing,* or odd-even pricing, in which prices are set a few dollars or a few cents below a round number. For example, Frito-Lay's potato chips are priced at 69 cents a bag rather than 70 cents to encourage consumers to think of them as less expensive (60 some-odd cents rather than 70 cents). Hertz economy cars are rented for $129 rather than $130 to appear less expensive. Third, there is *bundle pricing,* in which several products are sold together at a single price to suggest a good value. For example, travel agencies offer vacation packages that include travel, accommodations, and entertainment at a single price to connote value and convenience for customers.

Price Elasticity

Both demographic and psychological factors affect price elasticity. *Price elasticity* is a measure of consumers' price sensitivity, which is estimated by dividing relative changes in the quantity sold by the relative changes in price:

$$e = \frac{\text{Percent change in quantity demanded}}{\text{Percent change in price}}$$

Although price elasticity is difficult to measure, two basic methods are commonly used to estimate it. First, price elasticity can be estimated from historical data or from price/quantity data across different sales districts. Second, price elasticity can be estimated by sampling a group of consumers from the target market and polling them concerning various price/quantity relationships. Both of these approaches provide estimates of price elasticity; but the former approach is limited to the consideration of price changes, whereas the latter is often expensive and there is some question as to the validity of subjects' responses. However, even a crude estimate of price elasticity is a useful input to pricing decisions.[3]

SUPPLY INFLUENCES ON PRICING DECISIONS

For the purpose of this text, supply influences on pricing decisions can be discussed in terms of three basic factors. These factors relate to the objectives, costs, and nature of the product.

Pricing Objectives

Pricing objectives should be derived from overall marketing objectives, which in turn should be derived from corporate objectives. Since it is traditionally assumed that business firms operate to maximize profits in the long run, it is often thought that the basic pricing objective is solely concerned with long-run profits. However, the profit maximization norm does not provide the operating marketing manager with a single, unequivocal guideline for selecting prices. In addition, the marketing manager does not have perfect cost, revenue, and market information to be able to evaluate whether or not this objective is being reached. In practice, then, many other objectives are employed as guidelines for pricing decisions. In some cases, these objectives may be considered as operational approaches to achieve long-run profit maximization.

Research has found that the most common pricing objectives are (1) pricing to achieve a target return on investment, (2) stabilization of price and margin, (3) pricing to achieve a target market share, and (4) pricing to meet or prevent competition.

There are two common pricing strategies at the retail level: EDLP, which stands for "everyday low pricing," and high/low, which means that the retailer charges prices that are sometimes above competitors' but promotes frequent sales that lower prices below them. Four successful U.S. retailers—Home Depot, Walmart, Office Depot, and Toys 'R' Us—have adopted EDLP, while many fashion, grocery, and drug stores use high/low. Below is a list of the advantages of each of these pricing strategies.

ADVANTAGES OF EDLP

- *Assures customers of low prices.* Many customers are skeptical about initial retail prices. They have become conditioned to buying only on sale—the main characteristic of a high/low pricing strategy. The EDLP strategy lets customers know that they will get the same low prices every time they patronize the EDLP retailer. Customers do not have to read the ads and wait for items they want to go on sale.

- *Reduces advertising and operating expenses.* The stable prices caused by EDLP limit the need for the weekly sale advertising used in the high/low strategy. In addition, EDLP retailers do not have to incur the labor costs of changing price tags and signs and putting up sale signs.

- *Reduces stockouts and improves inventory management.* The EDLP approach reduces the large variations in demand caused by frequent sales with large markdowns. As a result, retailers can manage their inventories with more certainty. Fewer stockouts mean more satisfied customers, resulting in higher sales. In addition, a more predictable customer demand pattern enables the retailer to improve inventory turnover by reducing the average inventory needed for special promotions and backup stock.

ADVANTAGES OF HIGH/LOW

- *Increases profits.* High/low pricing allows retailers to charge higher prices to customers who are not price-sensitive and will pay the "high" price and to charge lower prices to price-sensitive customers who will wait for the "low" sale price.

- *Creates excitement.* A "get them while they last" atmosphere often occurs during a sale. Sales draw a lot of customers, and a lot of customers create excitement. Some retailers augment low prices and advertising with special in-store activities, such as product demonstrations, giveaways, and celebrity appearances.

- *Sells merchandise.* Sales allow retailers to get rid of slow-selling merchandise.

Source: Based on Michael Levy and Barton A. Weitz, *Retailing Management,* 8th ed. (Burr Ridge, IL: McGraw-Hill/Irwin, 2012), p. 373.

Cost Considerations in Pricing

The price of a product usually must cover costs of production, promotion, and distribution, plus a profit, for the offering to be of value to the firm. In addition, when products are priced on the basis of costs plus a fair profit, there is an implicit assumption that this sum represents the economic value of the product in the marketplace.

Cost-oriented pricing is the most common approach in practice, and there are at least three basic variations: markup pricing, cost-plus pricing, and rate-of-return pricing. *Markup pricing* is commonly used in retailing: A percentage is added to the retailer's invoice price to determine the final selling price. Closely related to markup pricing is *cost-plus pricing,* in which the costs of producing a product or completing a project are totaled and a profit amount or percentage is added on. Cost-plus pricing is most often used to describe the pricing of jobs that are nonroutine and difficult to "cost" in advance, such as construction and military weapon development.

The following formulas are used to calculate breakeven points in units and in dollars:

$$BEP_{(in\ units)} = \frac{FC}{(SP - VC)}$$

$$BEP_{(in\ dollars)} = \frac{FC}{1 - (VC/SP)}$$

where

FC = Fixed cost
VC = Variable cost
SP = Selling price

If, as is generally the case, a firm wants to know how many units or sales dollars are necessary to generate a given amount of profit, profit (P) is simply added to fixed costs in the formulas. In addition, if the firm has estimates of expected sales and fixed and variable costs, the selling price can be solved for. (A more detailed discussion of breakeven analysis is provided in the financial analysis section of this book.)

Rate-of-return pricing is commonly used by manufacturers. With this method, price is determined by adding a desired rate of return on investment to total costs. Generally, a breakeven analysis is performed for expected production and sales levels and a rate of return is added on. For example, suppose a firm estimated production and sales to be 75,000 units at a total cost of $300,000. If the firm desired a before-tax return of 20 percent, the selling price would be $(300,000 + 0.20 \times 300,000) \div 75,000 = \$4.80$.

Cost-oriented approaches to pricing have the advantage of simplicity, and many practitioners believe that they generally yield a good price decision. However, such approaches have been criticized for two basic reasons. First, cost approaches give little or no consideration to demand factors. For example, the price determined by markup or cost-plus methods has no necessary relationship to what people will be willing to pay for the product. In the case of rate-of-return pricing, little emphasis is placed on estimating sales volume. Even if it were, rate-of-return pricing involves circular reasoning, since unit cost depends on sales volume but sales volume depends on selling price. Second, cost approaches fail to reflect competition adequately. Only in industries where all firms use this approach and have similar costs and markups can this approach yield similar prices and minimize price competition. Thus, in many industries, cost-oriented pricing could lead to severe price competition, which could eliminate smaller firms. Therefore, although costs are a highly important consideration in price decisions, numerous other factors need to be examined.

Product Considerations in Pricing

Although numerous product characteristics can affect pricing, three of the most important are (1) perishability, (2) distinctiveness, and (3) stage in the product life cycle.

Perishability

Some products, such as fresh meat, bakery goods, and some raw materials are physically perishable and must be priced to sell before they spoil. Typically, this involves discounting the products as they approach being no longer fit for sale. Products can also be perishable in the sense that demand for them is confined to a specific time period. For example, high fashion and fad products lose most of their value when they go out of style and marketers have the difficult task of forecasting demand at specific prices and judging the time period of customer interest. While the time period of interest for other seasonal products, such as winter coats or Christmas trees, is easier to estimate, marketers must still determine the appropriate price and discount structure to maximize profits and avoid inventory losses or carrying costs.

Distinctiveness

Marketers try to distinguish their products from those of competitors and if successful, can often charge higher prices for them. While such things as styling, features, ingredients, and service can be used to try to make a product distinctive, competitors can copy such physical changes. Thus, it is through branding and brand equity that products are commonly made distinctive in customers' minds. For example, prestigious brands like Rolex, Tiffany's, and Lexus can be priced higher in large measure because of brand equity. Of course, higher prices also help create and reinforce the brand equity of prestigious products.

Life Cycle

The stage of the life cycle that a product is in can have important pricing implications. With regard to the life cycle, two approaches to pricing are skimming and penetration price policies. A *skimming policy* is one in which the seller charges a relatively high price on a new product. Generally, this policy is used when the firm has a temporary monopoly and when demand for the product is price inelastic. In later stages of the life cycle, as competition moves in and other market factors change, the price may then be lowered. Flat screen TV's and cell phones are examples of this. A *penetration policy* is one in which the seller charges a relatively low price on a new product. Generally, this policy is used when the firm expects competition to move in rapidly and when demand for the product is, at least in the short run, price elastic. This policy is also used to obtain large economies of scale and as a major instrument for rapid creation of a mass market. A low price and profit margin may also discourage competition. In later stages of the life cycle, the price may have to be altered to meet changes in the market.

ENVIRONMENTAL INFLUENCES ON PRICING DECISIONS

Environmental influences on pricing include variables that the marketing manager cannot control. Two of the most important of these are competition and government regulation.

Competition

In setting or changing prices, the firm must consider its competition and how competition will react to the price of the product. Initially, consideration must be given to such factors as

1. Number of competitors.
2. Market shares, growth, and profitability of competitors.
3. Strengths and weaknesses of competitors.
4. Likely entry of new firms into the industry.
5. Degree of vertical integration of competitors.
6. Number of products sold by competitors.
7. Cost structure of competitors.
8. Historical reaction of competitors to price changes.

These factors help determine whether the firm's selling price should be at, below, or above competition. Pricing a product at competition (i.e., the average price charged by the industry) is called *going-rate pricing* and is popular for homogeneous products, since this approach represents the collective wisdom of the industry and is not disruptive of industry harmony. An example of pricing below competition can be found in *sealed-bid pricing,* in which the firm is bidding directly against competition for project contracts. Although cost and profits are initially calculated, the firm attempts to bid below competitors to obtain the job contract. A firm may price above competition because it has a superior product or because the firm is the price leader in the industry.

Government Regulations

Prices of certain goods and services are regulated by state and federal governments. Public utilities are examples of state regulation of prices. However, for most marketing managers, federal laws that make certain pricing practices illegal are of primary consideration in pricing decisions. The list below is a summary of some of the more important legal constraints on pricing. Of course, since most marketing managers are not trained as lawyers, they usually seek legal counsel when developing pricing strategies to ensure conformity to state and federal legislation.

1. *Price fixing* is illegal per se. Sellers must not make any agreements with competitors or distributors concerning the final price of the goods. The Sherman Antitrust Act is the primary device used to outlaw horizontal price fixing. Section 5 of the Federal Trade Commission Act has been used to outlaw price fixing as an unfair business practice.

2. *Deceptive pricing* practices are outlawed under Section 5 of the Federal Trade Commission Act. An example of deceptive pricing would be to mark merchandise with an exceptionally high price and then claim that the lower selling price actually used represents a legitimate price reduction.

3. *Price discrimination* (the practice of charging different prices to different buyers for goods of like grade and quality) that lessens competition or is deemed injurious to it is outlawed by the Robinson-Patman Act. Price discrimination is not illegal per se, but sellers cannot charge competing buyers different prices for essentially the same products if the effect of such sales is injurious to competition. Price differentials can be legally justified on certain grounds, especially if the price differences reflect cost differences. This is particularly true of quantity discounts.

4. *Predatory pricing* involves charging a very low price for a product with the intent of driving competitors out of business. It is illegal under the Sherman Act and Federal Trade Commission Act.[4]

A GENERAL PRICING MODEL

It should be clear that effective pricing decisions involve considerations of many factors, and different industries may have different pricing practices. Although no single model will fit all pricing decisions, Figure 11.1 presents a general model for developing prices for products and services.[5] While all pricing decisions cannot be made strictly on the basis of this model, it does break pricing strategy into a set of manageable stages that are integrated into the overall marketing strategy.

Set Pricing Objectives

Given a product or service designed for a specific target market, the pricing process begins with a clear statement of the pricing objectives. These objectives guide the pricing strategy and should be designed to support the overall marketing strategy. Because pricing strategy

FIGURE 11.1
A General Pricing
Model

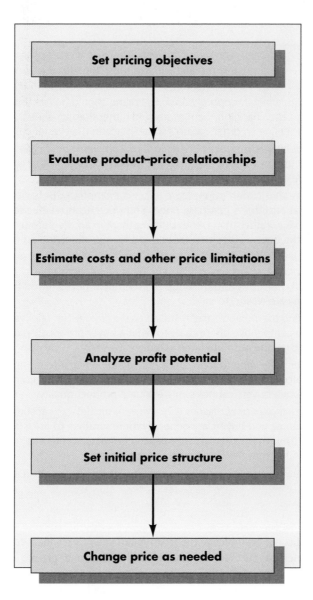

has a direct bearing on demand for a product and the profit obtained, efforts to set prices must be coordinated with other functional areas. For example, production will have to be able to meet demand at a given price, and finance will have to manage funds flowing in and out of the organization at predicted levels of production.

Evaluate Product–Price Relationships

As noted, the distinctiveness, perishability, and stage of the life cycle a product is in all affect pricing. In addition, marketers need to consider what value the product has for customers and how price will influence product positioning. There are three basic value positions. First, a product could be priced relatively high for a product class because it offers value in the form of high quality, special features, or prestige. Second, a product could be priced at about average for the product class because it offers value in the form of good quality for a reasonable price. Third, a product could be priced relatively low for a product class because it offers value in the form of acceptable quality at a low price. A Porsche or

1. *Base pricing strategies on sound research.* Although a recent study found that few companies do serious pricing research, it is a must for sound pricing strategies. Research is needed to understand the factors that influence supply and demand.

2. *Continuously monitor pricing decisions.* Pricing should be treated as a process of developing prices and changing them as needed rather than an annual budgeting exercise. Price decisions define an organization's value image in the eyes of customers and competitors.

3. *Recognize that buyers may have difficulty in computing price differences.* Buyers do not constantly monitor the prices of many products and will not necessarily quickly recognize the value in a price deal.

4. *Recognize that customers evaluate prices comparatively.* Behavioral pricing research suggests that customers compare prices and price deals relative to internal or external reference prices rather than just evaluating them in an absolute sense. An internal reference price is the price a customer has in mind for a product and an external reference price is one the customer has seen in advertising, a catalog, or on a store sign or price tag.

5. *Recognize that buyers typically have a range of acceptable prices.* Buyers often have an upper and lower threshold or range of acceptable prices rather than only one acceptable price they are willing to pay.

6. *Understand the importance of relative price to buyers.* The relative price of a product compared to competitive offerings or to what a buyer previously paid for it may be more important than the absolute price asked.

7. *Understand the importance of price information.* Price information can affect preferences and choices for different models in a product line or for competitive offerings, particularly when buyers cannot easily evaluate product quality.

8. *Recognize that price elasticities vary.* Price elasticities vary according to the direction of a price change, and buyers are generally more sensitive to price increases than to price decreases. Thus, it is easier to lose sales to current customers by increasing prices than it is to gain sales from new buyers by reducing them.

Source: Based on Kent B. Monroe and Jennifer L. Cox, "Pricing Practices That Endanger Profits," *Marketing Management*, September/October 2001, pp. 42–46.

Nike Air Max are examples of the first type of value; a Honda Accord or Keds tennis shoes are examples of the second; and Hyundai cars and private label canvas shoes are examples of the third. Setting prices so that targeted customers will perceive products to offer greater value than competitive offerings is called *value pricing*.

In addition, research is needed to estimate how much of a particular product the target market will purchase at various price levels—price elasticity. This estimate provides valuable information about what the target market thinks about the product and what it is worth to them.

Estimate Costs and Other Price Limitations

The costs to produce and market products provide a lower bound for pricing decisions and a baseline from which to compute profit potential. If a product cannot be produced and marketed at a price to cover its costs and provide reasonable profits in the long run, then it should not be produced in its designed form. One possibility is to redesign the product so that its costs are lower. In fact, some companies first determine the price customers are willing to pay for a product and then design it so that it can be produced and marketed at a cost that allows targeted profits.

Other price limitations that need to be considered are government regulations and the prices that competitors charge for similar and substitute products. Also, likely competitive reactions that could influence the price of a new product or a price change in an existing one need to be considered.

Analyze Profit Potential

Analysis in the preceding stages should result in a range of prices that could be charged. Marketers must then estimate the likely profit in pricing at levels in this range. At this stage, it is important to recognize that it may be necessary to offer channel members quantity discounts, promotional allowances, and slotting allowances to encourage them to actively market the product. *Quantity discounts* are discounts for purchasing a large number of units. *Promotional allowances* are often in the form of price reductions in exchange for the channel member performing various promotional activities, such as featuring the product in store advertising or on in-store displays. *Slotting allowances* are payments to retailers to get them to stock items on their shelves. All of these can increase sales but also add marketing cost to the manufacturer and affect profits.

Set Initial Price Structure

Since all of the supply, demand, and environmental factors have been considered, a marketer can now set the initial price structure. The price structure takes into account the price to various channel members, such as wholesalers and retailers, as well as the recommended price to final consumers or organizational buyers.

Change Price as Needed

There are many reasons why an initial price structure may need to be changed. Channel members may bargain for greater margins, competitors may lower their prices, or costs may increase with inflation. In the short term, discounts and allowances may have to be larger or more frequent than planned to get greater marketing effort to increase demand to profitable levels. In the long term, price structures tend to increase for most products as production and marketing costs increase.

SUMMARY

Pricing decisions that integrate the firm's costs with marketing strategy, business conditions, competition, demand, product variables, channels of distribution, and general resources can determine the success or failure of a business. This places a very heavy burden on the price maker. Modern-day marketing managers cannot ignore the complexity or the importance of price management. Pricing strategies must be continually reviewed and must take into account that the firm is a dynamic entity operating in a very competitive environment. There are many ways for money to flow out of a firm in the form of costs, but often there is only one way to bring in revenues and that is by the price-product mechanism.

Additional Resources

Macdivitt, Harry, and Mike Wilkinson. *Value-Based Pricing.* New York: McGraw-Hill, 2012.
Mazumdar, Tridib; S. P. Raj, and Indrajit Sinha. "Reference Price Research: Review and Propositions." *Journal of Marketing,* October 2005, pp. 84–102.
Monroe, Kent B. *Pricing: Making Profitable Decisions*. 3d ed. New York: McGraw-Hill, 2003.
Nagle, Thomas T., John Hogan, and Joseph Zale. *The Strategy and Tactics of Pricing.* 5th ed. Englewood Cliffs, NJ: Prentice Hall, 2011.
Smith, Tim. *Pricing Strategy.* Mason, OH: Southwestern, 2012.
Winer, Russell S. *Pricing.* Cambridge, MA: Marketing Science Institute, 2005.

Key Terms and Concepts

Bundle pricing: A form of psychological pricing that involves selling several products together at a single price in order to suggest a good value.

Cost-plus pricing: A cost-oriented pricing approach that involves totaling up the costs of producing a product or completing a project and then adding on a percentage or fixed profit amount. This approach is used when costs are difficult to estimate in advance such as military weapon development.

Deceptive pricing: Illegal under the Federal Trade Commission Act, an approach that involves price deals that mislead the consumer. For example, putting a fake price on a product much higher than the product sells for in the market, crossing it out, and then offering the product at the market price and claiming a price reduction could easily mislead consumers.

Going-rate pricing: Pricing a product at the average charged in the industry.

Markup pricing: A cost-oriented pricing approach that involves adding a percentage to the invoice price in order to determine the final selling price . For example, if a retailer used a 50 percent markup on a product that was bought from a wholesaler for $1, the selling price to the consumer would be $1.50.

Odd pricing: Also called odd-even pricing, a form of psychological pricing in which the prices are set at one or a few cents or dollars below a round number in order to create the perception that the price is low, for example, 99 cents or $129 rather than $1 or $130.

Penetration pricing policy: Approach to pricing in which the seller charges a relatively low price on a new product initially in order to grow a market, gain market share, and discourage competition from entering the market.

Prestige pricing: A form of psychological pricing that involves charging a high price to create a signal that the product is exceptionally fine.

Predatory pricing: Practice that involves charging a very low price for a product with the intent of driving competitors out of business. It is illegal under the Sherman Act and Federal Trade Commission Act.

Price discrimination: The practice of charging different prices to different buyers for goods of like grade and quality which is illegal under the Robinson-Patman Act if it lessens or is deemed injurious to competition.

Price elasticity: A measure of consumers' price sensitivity which is estimated by dividing relative changes in the quantity sold by relative changes in price. If demand is elastic, a slight lowering of price will result in a relatively large increase in quantity demanded.

Price fixing: An unfair business practice outlawed by the Sherman Antitrust Act and the Federal Trade Commission Act that involves competitors in a market colluding to set the final price of a product.

Promotional allowance: Price reduction offered to channel members in exchange for performing various promotional activities such as featuring the product in store advertising or on in-store displays.

Quantity discounts: Discounts offered for purchasing a large number of units.

Rate-of-return pricing: Cost-oriented approach to pricing that involves adding a desired rate of return on investment to total costs. Generally, a breakeven analysis is performed for expected production and sales levels and a rate of return is added on.

Sealed-bid pricing: Bidding process in which each seller submits a sealed bid and attempts to price below competition in order to get the contract. Many large construction and military projects are bid this way.

Skimming pricing policy: Approach to pricing in which the seller charges a relatively high price on a new product initially in order to recover costs and make profits rapidly and then lowers the price at a later date to make sales to more price-sensitive buyers.

Slotting allowances: Payments to retailers to get them to stock items on their shelves, a common tactic for getting new products into stores.

Value pricing: Setting prices so that targeted customers will perceive products to offer greater value than competitive offerings. For existing products, this can be accomplished by offering more product or service while maintaining or decreasing the dollar price.

Part D

Marketing in Special Fields

Chapter 12

The Marketing of Services

Over the course of the past 40 years, the fastest-growing segment of the American economy has not been the production of tangibles but the performance of services. Spending on services has increased to such an extent that today it captures more than 50 cents of the consumer's dollar. In addition, the service sector in the United States produces a balance-of-trade surplus and is expected to be responsible for all net job growth in the forseeable future.[1] The dominance of the service sector is not limited to the United States. The service sector accounts for more than half the GNP and employs more than half the labor force in most Latin American and Caribbean countries. Over the course of the next decade, the service sector will spawn whole new legions of doctors, nurses, medical technologists, physical therapists, home health aids, and social workers to administer to the needs of an aging population, along with armies of food servers, child care providers, and cleaning people to cater to the wants of two-income families. Also rising to the forefront will be a swelling class of technical workers, including computer engineers, systems analysts, and paralegals.

Many marketing textbooks still devote little attention to program development for the marketing of services, especially those in the rapidly changing areas of health care, finance, and travel. This omission is usually based on the assumption that the marketing of products and services is basically the same, and, therefore, the techniques discussed under products apply as well to the marketing of services. Basically, this assumption is true. Whether selling goods or services, the marketer must be concerned with developing a marketing strategy centered on the four controllable decision variables that comprise the marketing mix: the product (or service), the price, the distribution system, and promotion. In addition, the use of marketing research is as valuable to service marketers as it is to product marketers. However, because services possess certain distinguishing characteristics, the task of determining the marketing mix ingredients for a service marketing strategy may raise different and more difficult problems than those encountered in marketing products.

The purpose of this chapter is fourfold. First, the reader will become acquainted with the special characteristics of services and their strategy implications. Second, key concepts associated with providing quality services will be discussed. Third, obstacles will be described that in the past impeded and still continue to impede development of services marketing. Finally, current trends and strategies of innovation in services marketing will be explored. With this approach, the material in the other chapters of the book can be integrated to give a better understanding of the marketing of services.

Before proceeding, some attention must be given to what we refer to when using the term *services*. Probably the most frustrating aspect of the available literature on services is that the definition of what constitutes a service remains unclear. The fact is that no common definition and boundaries have been developed to delimit the field of services. The American Marketing Association has defined services as follows:[2]

1. *Service products,* such as a bank loan or home security, that are intangible, or at least substantially so. If totally intangible, they are exchanged directly from producer to user, cannot be transported or stored, and are almost instantly perishable. Service products are often difficult to identify, since they come into existence at the same time they are bought and consumed. They are composed of intangible elements that are inseparable; they usually involve customer participation in some important way, cannot be sold in the sense of ownership transfer, and have no title. Today, however, most products are partly tangible and partly intangible, and the dominant form is used to classify them as either goods or services (all are products). These common, hybrid forms, whatever they are called, may or may not have the attributes just given for totally intangible services.

2. *Services,* as a term, is also used to describe activities performed by sellers and others that accompany the sale of a product and that aid in its exchange or its utilization (e.g., shoe fitting, financing, an 800 number). Such services are either presale or postsale and supplement the product but do not comprise it.

The first definition includes what can be considered almost pure services, such as insurance, banking, entertainment, airlines, health care, telecommunications, and hotels; the second definition includes such services as wrapping, financing an automobile, providing warranties on computer equipment, and the like because these services exist in connection with the sale of a product or another service. This suggests that marketers of goods are also marketers of services. For example, one could argue that McDonald's is not in the hamburger business. Its hamburgers are actually not very different from those of the competition. McDonald's is in the service business.

More and more manufacturers are also exploiting their service capabilities as stand-alone revenue producers. For example, General Motors, Ford, and Chrysler all offer financing services. Ford and General Motors have extended their financial services offerings to include a MasterCard, which offers discounts on purchases of their automobiles.

The reader can imagine from his or her own experience that some purchases are very tangible (a coffeemaker) while others are very much intangible (a course in marketing). Others have elements of both (lunch on a flight from New York to Chicago). In other words, in reality there is a goods–service continuum, with many purchases including both tangible goods and intangible services. Figure 12.1 illustrates such a continuum. On the goods side of the continuum, the buyer owns an object after the purchase. On the services side of the continuum, when the transaction is over, the buyer leaves with an experience and a feeling. When the course in marketing is over or the flight from New York to Chicago is completed, the student or passenger leaves with a feeling.

The examples of services on the right side of Figure 12.1 are mostly or entirely intangible. They do not exist in the physical realm. They cannot appeal to the five senses.

FIGURE 12.1
The Goods–Service
Continuum

Tangible	← ———— Mixed ————→	Intangible
Golf clubs	Green fees with sleeve of balls included	Green fees
Car	Oil change	Taxi ride
Suit	Suit with alterations	Alterations
Airplane	Air flight with lunch	Air flight

IMPORTANT CHARACTERISTICS OF SERVICES

Services possess several unique characteristics that often have a significant impact on marketing program development. These special features of services may cause unique problems and often result in marketing mix decisions that are substantially different from those found in connection with the marketing of goods. Some of the more important of these characteristics are intangibility, inseparability, perishability and fluctuating demand, a client relationship, customer effort, and uniformity. They are presented in Figure 12.2.

Intangibility

The obvious basic difference between goods and services is the intangibility of services, and many of the problems encountered in the marketing of services are due to intangibility. To illustrate, how does an airline make tangible a trip from Philadelphia to San Francisco? These problems are unique to service marketing.

The fact that many services cannot appeal to a buyer's sense of touch, taste, smell, sight, or hearing before purchase places a burden on the marketing organization. For example, hotels that promise a good night's sleep to their customers cannot actually show this service in a tangible way. Obviously, this burden is most heavily felt in a firm's promotional program, but, as will be discussed later, it may affect other areas. Depending on the type of service, the intangibility factor may dictate use of direct channels because of the need for personal contact between the buyer and seller. Since a service firm is actually selling an idea or experience, not a product, it must tell the buyer what the service will do because it is often difficult to illustrate, demonstrate, or display the service in use. For example, the hotel must somehow describe to the consumer how a stay at the hotel will leave the customer feeling well rested and ready to begin a new day.

The above discussion alludes to two strategy elements firms should employ when trying to overcome the problems associated with service intangibility. First, tangible aspects associated with the service should be stressed. For example, advertisements for airlines should emphasize (through text and visuals) the newness of the aircraft, the roominess of the

FIGURE 12.2 Unique Characteristics Distinguishing Services from Goods

Characteristic	Services	Goods
Intangibility	The customer owns only memories, outcomes, or feelings such as an airline flight, greater knowledge, or styled hair.	The customer owns objects that can be used, resold, or given to others.
Inseparability	Services often cannot be separated from the person providing them. They are often produced and consumed at the same time.	Goods are usually produced and sold by different people.
Perishability	Services can be used only at the time they are offered. They cannot be inventoried, stored, or transported.	Goods can be placed in inventory for use at another time.
Client Relationship	Services often involve a long-term personal relationship between buyer and seller.	Goods often involve an impersonal short-term relationship although in many instances relationship strength and duration are increasing.
Customer Effort	Customers are often heavily involved in the production.	Customer's involvement may be limited to buying the completed product and using it.
Uniformity	Because of inseparability and high involvement on the part of the buyer, each service may be unique, with the quality likely to vary.	Variations in quality and variance from standards can be corrected before customers purchase products.

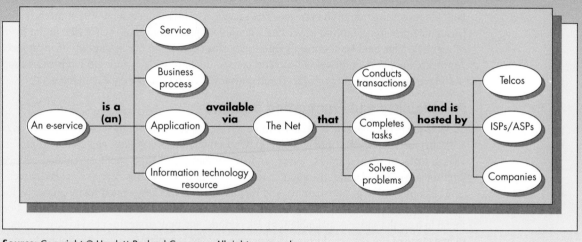

cabin, and the friendliness of the flight attendants. Second, end benefits resulting from completion of the service encounter should be accentuated. In the case of air travel, an individual's ability to make an important meeting or arrive home in time for a special occasion could be the derived benefit.

Inseparability

In many cases, a service cannot be separated from the person of the seller. In other words, the service must often be produced and marketed simultaneously. Because of the simultaneous production and marketing of most services, the main concern of the marketer is usually the creation of time and place utility. For example, the bank teller produces the service of receiving a deposit and markets other appropriate bank services at the same time. Many services, therefore, are tailored and not mass produced. Often, because a company's employees are "the company" at the point of contact, they must be given wide latitude and assistance in determining how best to tailor a specific service to meet customer needs.

The implication of inseparability on issues dealing with the selection of channels of distribution and service quality is quite important. Inseparable services cannot be inventoried, and thus direct sale is the only feasible channel of distribution. Service quality cannot sometimes be completely standardized due to the inability to completely mechanize the service encounter. However, some industries, through innovative uses of technology, have been able to overcome or, at least, alleviate challenges associated with the inseparability characteristic.

For example, in the financial services industry, automated teller machines (ATMs) and home banking, through use of computers and telephones, have contributed greatly to eliminating the need for the customer to directly interact with a bank teller. Further, many banks are developing computer applications to allow tellers and other service representatives to think like expert problem solvers. These applications allow for platform banking, a means of enabling bank representatives in any location to bring up on a screen all the information the bank has about the customer. Every face-to-face contact with a customer can mean an opportunity to make a sale and, more importantly, further the relationship with the customer. Of course, the bank representative is still of critical importance as the one who might recognize by the customer's expression or words that this visit is not the appropriate time to be marketing additional services.

In addition to technology, tangible representations of the service can serve to overcome the inseparability problem. For example, in the insurance industry, a contract serves as the tangible representation of the service. The service itself remains inseparable from the seller (insurance provider), but the buyer has a tangible representation of the service in the form of a policy. This enables the use of intermediaries (agents) in the marketing of insurance. Another example is in the use of a credit card—the card itself is a tangible representation of the service that is being produced and consumed each time the card is being used.

Perishability and Fluctuating Demand

Services are perishable and markets for most services fluctuate either by season (tourism), days (airlines), or time of day (movie theaters). Unused telephone capacity and electrical power; vacant seats on planes, trains, buses, and in stadiums; and time spent by catalog service representatives waiting for customers to reach them all represent business that is lost forever.

The combination of perishability and fluctuating demand has created many problems for marketers of services. Specifically, in the areas of staffing and distribution, avenues must be found to have the services available for peak periods, and new strategies need to be developed to make use of the service during slack periods. Some organizations are attempting to cope with these problems through the use of pricing strategy. *Off-peak pricing* consists of charging different prices during different times or days in order to stimulate demand during slow periods. Discounts given for weekend calling, Saturday night stay-overs, early-bird dinners, or winter cruises are all examples of efforts service providers make to redistribute demand.

Other organizations are dealing with issues related to peak period demand through the use of technology. To illustrate, a well-designed voice mail system allows companies and callers to cut down on missed phone calls, eliminates long waits on hold, and delivers clear, consistent messages. In the catalog industry, automated call routing (ACR) is used to route incoming calls to available service representatives in the order in which they were received. Finally, in the utilities industry, many electric utilities no longer have to generate capacity that will meet peak electrical demand. Instead, they rely on buying unused power from other utilities in other regions of the country.

Client Relationship

In the marketing of a great many services, a client relationship, as opposed to a customer relationship, exists between the buyer and the seller. In other words, the buyer views the seller as someone who has knowledge that is of value. Examples of this type of relationship are the physician-patient, college professor–student, accountant–small business owner, and broker-investor. The buyer, many times, abides by the advice offered or suggestions provided by the seller, and these relationships may be of an ongoing nature. Also, since many service firms are client-serving organizations, they may approach the marketing function in a more professional manner, as seen in health care, finance, legal, governmental, and educational services.

Professionals face at least two marketing challenges. First, in many cases, fear or hostility is brought to the transaction because the customer is uncertain about how genuine the professional's concern for his or her satisfaction is. For example, many unpleasant reasons exist for consulting doctors, lawyers, bankers, or even visiting a college professor. These could include having surgery, being sued, having to take out a loan, or doing poorly on an exam. Second, even high-quality service delivery by the professional can lead to dissatisfied customers. For a physician, the ability to provide high-quality medical care may be overshadowed by a brusque, unfriendly personality. For a college professor, the demand on students to contact or visit him or her only during office hours, coupled with students' own hectic work schedules, can diminish the impact of the professor's classroom presentations. It is vitally important that the professional service provider strive to build long-term positive relationships with clients.

Type of Service	Type of Customer	Principal Expectations
Automobile repair	Consumers	*Be competent.* Fix it right the first time.
		Explain things. Explain why the customer needs the suggested repairs—provide an itemized list.
		Be respectful. "Don't treat me like an idiot."
Automobile insurance	Consumers	*Keep me informed.* "I shouldn't have to learn about insurance law changes from the newspaper."
		Be on my side. "I don't want them to treat me like I am a criminal just because I have a claim."
		Play fair. "Don't drop me when something goes wrong."
		Protect me from catastrophe. "Make sure my estate is covered in the event of a major accident."
		Provide prompt service. "I want a fast settlement of my claims."
Hotel	Consumers	*Provide a clean room.* "Don't have a deep-pile carpet that can't be completely cleaned . . . You can literally see germs down there."
		Provide a secure room. Good deadbolts and a peephole on the door.
		Treat me like a guest. "It is almost like they're looking you over to decide whether or not they're going to let you have a room."
		Keep your promise. "They said the room would be ready at the promised time, but it wasn't."
Property and casualty insurance	Business customers	*Fulfill obligations.* Pay up.
		Learn my business and work with me. "I expect them to know me and my company."
		Protect me from catastrophe. Cover risk exposure so there is no single big loss.
		Provide prompt service. Fast claim service.
Equipment repair	Business customers	*Share my sense of urgency.* Speed of response. "One time I had to buy a second piece of equipment because of the huge downtime with the first piece."
		Be prepared. Have all the parts ready.
Truck and tractor rental/leasing	Business customers	*Keep the equipment running.* Have equipment working all the time—that is the key.
		Be flexible. "The leasing company should have the leasing flexibility to rent us equipment when we need it."
		Provide full service. Get rid of all the paperwork and headaches.

Source: A. Parasuraman, Leonard L. Berry, and Valarie A. Zeithaml, "Understanding Customer Expectations of Service," *Sloan Management Review,* Spring 1991, pp. 39–48.

Customer Effort

Customers are often involved to a relatively great degree in the production of many types of service. In some restaurants you clean your table. You may carry your luggage to a cart parked next to a baggage compartment of the plane. If you wish to enjoy an exhibit at a local art museum, you must walk around the facility and pay careful attention to what is on display. If an organization purchases the services of an advertising agency, employees will have to work with the agency, review its ideas, and make the final selections.

Obviously, not every service requires the same degree of customer effort. Your effort with a credit card service may be little beyond taking it from your wallet to make a purchase and writing a check once a month to pay the bill.

Uniformity

The quality of services can vary more than the quality of goods. Producers of goods have procedures to prevent, identify, and correct defects. If these procedures are working, customers are unlikely to purchase defective products. This is not the case with most services. Because they are often human performances and often customized to the needs of the buyer, quality can vary. Each trip to the bank or airline flight or university course can be a different experience. Many service jobs such as nursing, teaching, and career counseling require a positive attitude; how employees feel influences their performance.

PROVIDING QUALITY SERVICES

In today's increasingly competitive environment, quality service is critical to organizational success. Unlike products in which quality is often measured against standards, service quality is measured against performance.[3] Since services are frequently produced in the presence of a customer, are labor intensive, and are not able to be stored or objectively examined, the definition of what constitutes good service quality can be difficult and, in fact, continually changes in the face of choices.[4] Customers determine the value of service quality in relation to available alternatives and their particular needs. In general, problems in the determination of good service quality are attributable to differences in the expectations, perceptions, and experiences regarding the encounter between the service provider and consumer. These gaps can be classified as follows:

1. The gap between consumer expectations and management perceptions of consumer expectations.
2. The gap between management perceptions of consumer expectations and the firm's service quality specifications.
3. The gap between service quality specifications and actual service quality.
4. The gap between actual service delivery and external communications about the service.

In essence, the customer perceives the level of service quality as being a function of the magnitude and direction of the gap between expected service and perceived service. Management of a company may not even realize that they are delivering poor-quality service due to differences in the way managers and consumers view acceptable quality levels. To overcome this problem and to avoid losing customers, firms must be aware of the determinants of service quality. A brief description of these determinants follows.

1. *Tangibles* include the physical evidence of the service. For example, employees are always visible in a hotel lobby dusting or otherwise cleaning up. Likewise, clean, shiny, up-to-date medical equipment or aircraft are examples of tangible elements.
2. *Reliability* involves the consistency and dependability of the service performance. For example, does a bank or phone company always send out accurate customer statements? Likewise, does the plumber always fix the problem on his or her first visit?
3. *Responsiveness* concerns the willingness or readiness of employees or professionals to provide service. For example, will a physician see patients on the same day they call in to say they are ill? Will a college professor return a student's call the same day?

Throughout this book we have stressed the importance of building long-term relationships in which the initial sale is viewed as a beginning step in a process, not an end or goal. For marketers of services, relationship marketing can present a special set of challenges which require a different new view of the business and a change in strategy.

For decades, most service marketers were concerned with attracting new customers. Promotion programs and convenient locations focused on the acquisition of new customers. During the last two decades, however, service marketers are beginning to think about marketing in a fundamentally new way. The idea is that marketing is about *having customers,* not merely *acquiring customers.* Service marketers now understand that attracting new customers is only the first step in the process, that making existing customers better customers is marketing too. In other words, service marketers understand the importance of relationship marketing. It is fundamentally different from the traditional view of marketing in service organizations.

Traditional Service Marketing	*Relationship Service Marketing*
1. Marketing focuses on attracting new "customers."	1. Marketing focuses on "clients." Customer attraction is a beginning step.
2. Emphasis on selling the service the customer requests.	2. Emphasis on establishing and building a long-term relationship.
3. Need satisfaction is approached from the standpoint of the "part." For example, haircut, checking account, airline ticket.	3. Need satisfaction is approached from the standpoint of the "whole." For example, total hair care, day spa, personal banker, travel management.
4. Primary sales contact is through process driven providers. For example, airline ticket agent, bank teller.	4. Primary sales contact is through a trained marketing professional. For example, travel agent, personal banker.
5. Profitability is assessed on individual services. For example, individual haircut.	5. Profitability is assessed on the total relationship. For example, haircut plus shampoos, conditioners, brushes, combs, dryers, etc.

Source: Based on the work of James H. Donnelly Jr., Leonard L. Berry, and Thomas W. Thompson.

4. *Assurance* refers to the knowledge and competence of service providers and the ability to convey trust and confidence. This determinant encompasses the provider's name and reputation; possession of necessary skills; and trustworthiness, believability, and honesty. For example, a bank will guarantee same-day loan processing; a doctor is highly trained in a particular specialty.

5. *Empathy* refers to the service provider's efforts to understand the customer's needs and then to provide, as best as possible, individualized service delivery. For example, flight attendants on a customer's regular route learn what type of beverages the customer drinks and what magazines the customer reads.

Each of these determinants plays an important role in how the customer views the service quality of a firm. Turning service quality into a powerful competitive weapon requires continuously striving for service superiority—consistently performing above the adequate service level and capitalizing on opportunities for exceeding the desired service level. Relentless efforts to continually improve service performance may well be rewarded by improvements in customer attitudes toward the firm: from customer frustration to customer preference to customer loyalty. What should be obvious is that to be successful, a service firm must have both an effective means to measure customer satisfaction and dedicated employees to provide high-quality service.

Customer Satisfaction Measurement

As mentioned above, satisfied customers can become loyal customers. Service quality and customer satisfaction are of growing concern to business organizations throughout the world, and research on these topics generally focuses on two key issues: (1) understanding the expectations and requirements of the customer, and (2) determining how well a company and its major competitors are succeeding in satisfying these expectations and requirements.[5]

As such, an organization's approach to measuring service quality through customer satisfaction measurement (CSM) and effectively implementing programs derived from results of such studies can spell the difference between success and failure. Research on market leaders' CSMs found they had the following aspects in common:

1. Marketing and sales employees were primarily responsible (with customer input) for designing CSM programs and questionnaires.
2. Top management and the marketing function championed the programs.
3. Measurement involved a combination of qualitative and quantitative research methods that primarily included mail questionnaires, telephone surveys, and focus groups.
4. Evaluations included both the company's and competitors' satisfaction performance.
5. Results of all research were made available to employees, but not necessarily to customers.
6. Research was performed on a continual basis.
7. Customer satisfaction was incorporated into the strategic focus of the company via the mission statement.
8. There was a commitment to increasing service quality and customer satisfaction from employees at all levels within the organization.

The Importance of Internal Marketing

Properly performed customer satisfaction research can yield a wealth of strategic information about customers, the sponsoring company, and competitors. However, service quality goes beyond the relationship between a customer and a company. Rather, as shown by the last aspect listed, it is the personal relationship between a customer and the particular employee that the customer happens to be dealing with at the time of the service encounter that ultimately determines service quality. The importance of having customer-oriented, frontline people cannot be overstated.[6] If frontline service personnel are unfriendly, unhelpful, uncooperative, or uninterested in the customer, the customer will tend to project that same attitude to the company as a whole. The character and personality of an organization reflects the character and personality of its top management. Management must develop programs that will stimulate employee commitment to customer service. To be successful, these programs must contain five critical components:

1. *A careful selection process in hiring frontline employees.* To do this, management has to clearly define the skills the service person must bring to the job.[7] For example, Fairfield Inn often considers as many as 25 candidates for each housekeeping or front-desk position.[8]
2. *A clear, concrete message* that conveys a particular service strategy that frontline people can begin to act on. People delivering service need to know how their work fits in the broader scheme of business operations.[9] They need to have a cause because servicing others is just too demanding and frustrating to be done well each day without one.[10]
3. *Significant modeling by managers,* that is, managers demonstrating the behavior that they intend to reward employees for performing. For example, some airline executives regularly travel economy class to talk to customers and solicit ideas for improvement.[11]

Practicing relationship marketing is a challenge for service organizations because there are important differences between "customers" and "clients." The notion of "client" is critical for relationship marketing to succeed in a service organization.

Customers	*Clients*
1. Customers may be nameless.	1. Clients must have names.
2. Customers are served as part of a large mass of people.	2. Clients are served on an individual basis.
3. Customers are statistics; their needs are reflected in market summaries. For example, the most popular ice cream for people over 50 in 2008 was vanilla.	3. Clients are individual entities. Specific information about them is stored in a database. For example, Mr. Smith wants only morning flights, first class seats, vegetarian meals, aisle seats, airport motels, and mid-size rental cars.
4. Customers are served by the first available person. For example, airline ticket agent, bank teller.	4. Clients are served by a trained professional who has been assigned to them. For example, travel agent, personal banker.
5. Customers have no strong reason to feel any loyalty or allegience to the service provider.	5. Clients often have a strong relationship with the service provider.

Source: Based on the work of James H. Donnelly Jr, Leonard L. Berry, and Thomas W. Thompson.

4. *An energetic follow-through process,* in which managers provide the training, support, and incentives necessary to give the employees the capability and willingness to provide quality service.[12]

5. *An emphasis on teaching employees to have good attitudes.* This type of training usually focuses on specific social techniques, such as eye contact, smiling, tone of voice, and standards of dress.

However, organizing and implementing such programs will only lead to temporary results unless managers practice a strategy of internal marketing. We define *internal marketing* as the continual process by which managers actively encourage, stimulate, and support employee commitment to the company, the company's goods and services, and the company's customers. Emphasis should be placed on the word *continual.* Managers who consistently pitch in to help when needed, constantly provide encouragement and words of praise to employees, strive to help employees understand the benefits of performing their jobs well, and emphasize the importance of employee actions on both company and employee results are practitioners of internal marketing. In service marketing, successful internal marketing efforts, leading to employee commitment to service quality, are a key to success.

Federal Express serves as a prime example of the benefits accruing to a company that successfully practices internal marketing.[13] Federal Express is the first service organization to win the Malcolm Baldrige National Quality Award. The company's motto is "people, service, and profits." Behind its purple, white, and orange planes and uniforms are self-managing work teams, gainsharing plans, and empowered employees seemingly consumed with providing flexible and creative services to customers with varying needs. Federal

Express is a high-involvement, horizontally coordinated organization that encourages employees to use their judgment above and beyond the rulebook.

OVERCOMING THE OBSTACLES IN SERVICE MARKETING

The factors of intangibility and inseparability, as well as difficulties in coming up with objective definitions of acceptable service quality, make comprehension of service marketing difficult. However, in view of the size and importance of services in our economy, considerable innovation and ingenuity are needed to make high-quality services available at convenient locations for consumers as well as businesspeople. In fact, the area of service marketing probably offers more opportunities for imagination and creative innovation than does goods marketing. Unfortunately, many service firms still lag in the area of creative marketing. Even today, those service firms that have done a relatively good job have been slow in recognizing opportunities in all aspects of their marketing programs. Four reasons, connected to past practices, can be given for the lack of innovative marketing on the part of service marketers: (1) a limited view of marketing, (2) a lack of strong competition, (3) a lack of creative management, and (4) no obsolescence.

Limited View of Marketing

Because of the nature of their service, many firms depended to a great degree on population growth to expand sales. A popular example here is the telephone company, which did not establish a marketing department until 1955. It was then that the company realized it had to be concerned not only with population growth but also with meeting the needs of a growing population. Increases in educational levels and the standard of living also bring about the need for new and diversified services.

Service firms must meet these changing needs by developing new services and new channels and altering existing channels to meet the changing composition and needs of the population. For many service industries, growth has come as a result of finding new channels of distribution. For example, some banks and other financial service companies were able to grow and tap into new markets by establishing limited-service kiosks in malls and supermarkets. Airlines have successfully brought in a whole new class of travelers by offering advance-purchase discounted fares. Traditionally, users of these fares either drove or used other means of transportation to reach their destination.

While many service firms have succeeded in adopting a marketing perspective, others have been slow to respond. It was not until deregulation of the telecommunications industry took place in 1984 that the telephone companies began taking a broadened view of marketing. Even today, critics point to the obsession with inventing new technology versus using current technology in meeting customer needs as a weakness of these companies.

Limited Competition

A second major cause of the lack of innovative marketing in many service industries was the lack of competition. Many service industries such as banking, railroads, and public utilities have, throughout most of their histories, faced very little competition; some have even been regulated monopolies. Obviously, in an environment characterized by little competition, there was not likely to be a great deal of innovative marketing. However, two major forces have changed this situation. First, in the past two decades the banking, financial services, railroad, cable, airline, telecommunications industries, and utilities have all been deregulated in varying degrees. With deregulation has come a need to be able to compete effectively. Second, service marketing has taken on an international focus.

On the Internet, you cannot have a more convenient location than your competition. Everyone is just a click away. It is critical that it is easy to do business with your company in order to attract and retain customers. Following are some ways to improve e-service.

1. A customer should be able to buy something in seven clicks or less beginning from the home page. Many experts believe the ideal should be four clicks.
2. Images should load quickly. Research shows that eight seconds is the longest people will wait before they move on to another site.
3. From a product section of your site, customers should be able to get from your home page to a product page in that section in one click.
4. Shopping should be easy. Searching, browsing, checking out, returning items, and getting assistance from a live person must be simple.
5. Customers should have the choice to register their personal information (e.g., address and credit card information) or to enter this information each time they purchase.
6. A customer should be able to check out in no more than three steps.
7. Delivery should be on time.

Source: Ron Zemke, *E-Service: 24 Ways to Keep Your Customers—When the Competition Is Just a Click Away* (New York: Amazon, 2001).

Today, many foreign companies are competing in domestic service markets. Foreign interests own several banks, many hotels (including Holiday Inn), and shares in major airlines (including Northwest and US Airways). Likewise, American companies are expanding overseas as markets open up. For example, Merrill Lynch & Co. purchased Smith New Court PLC, a large British security firm, to become the world's largest brokerage firm.

Noncreative Management

For many years, the managements of service industries have been criticized for not being progressive and creative. Railroad management has long been criticized for being slow to innovate. More recently, however, railroads have become leading innovators in the field of freight transportation, introducing such innovations as piggyback service and containerization, and in passenger service, introducing luxury overnight accommodations on trains with exotic names such as the Zephyr. Some other service industries, however, have been slow to develop new services or to innovate in the marketing of their existing services. In fact, as a whole, U.S. firms lag behind their Japanese and German competitors not only in collecting customer satisfaction data but also in designing services that address customers' needs.[14]

No Obsolescence

A great advantage for many service industries is the fact that many services, because of their intangibility, are less subject to obsolescence than goods. While this is an obvious advantage, it has also led some service firms to be sluggish in their approach to marketing. Manufacturers of goods may constantly change their marketing plans and seek new and more efficient ways to produce and distribute their products. Since service firms are often not faced with obsolescence, they often failed to recognize the need for change. This failure has led to wholesale changes in many industries as new operators who possessed marketing skills revolutionized the manner in which the service is performed and provided. Many barbershops and hair dressers have gone out of business due to an inability to compete against hairstyling salons. Many accountants have lost clients to tax preparation services, such as H&R Block, that specialize in doing one task well and have used technology, including Internet filing services, to their advantage. Likewise, the old, big movie house has become a relic of the past as entrepreneurs realized the advantages to be gained from building and operating theater complexes that contain several minitheaters in or near suburban malls.

THE SERVICE CHALLENGE

Despite traditional thinking and practices on the part of many marketing managers and writers concerning the similarities between the operation of manufacturing and services organizations, the past decade has seen the growth of many innovative ways of meeting the service challenge. The service challenge is the quest to (1) constantly develop new services that will better meet customer needs, (2) improve on the quality and variety of existing services, and (3) provide and distribute these services in a manner that best serves the customer. This next section illustrates the challenges facing companies in various service industries and examples of marketing strategies they employ to meet the service challenge.

Banking

"Banking is vital to a healthy economy. Banks are not." This is the message that a banking expert delivered to a group of his peers.[15] Needless to say, the days when banking was considered a dead-end career, but one that offered stable employment for marketers, are long gone. Perhaps banking best exemplifies the changes that are taking place as service organizations strive to become practitioners of the "marketing concept." Buy or be bought is the new watchword in the banking industry, which is experiencing the biggest wave of consolidation in its history.

Banking is becoming an increasingly technology-driven business. The main reason is that more and more financial services, from loans to credit cards, are being marketed through computers and telephones instead of through branches. Banks large enough to afford big technology investments can reach customers nationwide even though their physical franchise may be limited. For example, most consumers possess credit cards from banks they have never physically visited. Further, the advent of new electronic delivery systems (via computer) for consumer and small-business banking could, within the next decade, greatly reduce the number of branch banks needed. To prevent a loss of a large portion of their customer base, many of the leading banks, such as Chase Manhattan and Citibank, are aligning themselves with software and hardware manufacturers to develop home banking systems.

Banks have also learned the value of bundling services. Many now offer an account that combines checking, savings, credit card, and auto loan features. Benefits to the customer include free ATM transactions, interest-bearing checking accounts, no-fee credit cards, and the convenience of one-stop banking. In addition, they offer preapproved auto loans and cash-flow statements. Most banks also target some marketing activities toward senior citizens, which may include discount coupons for entertainment, travel newsletters, and lower monthly minimum required balances.

Competition between banks and other financial institutions will continue to intensify. The survivors will be those that have best mastered the art of services marketing.

Health Care

The distribution of health care services is of vital concern. In health care delivery, the inseparability characteristic presents more of a handicap than in other service industries because users (patients) literally place themselves in the hands of the seller. Although direct personal contact between producer and user is often necessary, new and more efficient means of distribution seem to be evolving.

Up until the past few decades, medical care has been traditionally associated with the solo practice, fee-for-service system. Recently, several alternative delivery systems have been developed, most notably the health maintenance organization (HMO). This type of delivery system stresses the creation of group health care clinics using teams of salaried health practitioners (physicians, pharmacists, technicians, and so forth) that serve a specified, enrolled membership on a prepaid basis. The primary benefits to the customer (patient) from membership in an HMO are (1) the ability to have all ailments treated at one facility, (2) payment of a fixed fee for services, and (3) the encouragement of preventive versus remedial treatments. The success of the HMO concept in traditional medical care has inspired similar programs to be developed for dental and eye care.

In the pharmaceutical field, Chronimed of Minnetonka, Minnesota, has focused on providing great customer service as its avenue to success.[16] The company supplies 100,000 patients across the United States with specialized medications that local pharmacies can't afford to stock. Chronimed's skill is twofold. First, it provides needed drugs by mail to organ transplant recipients and patients with diabetes or AIDS. Second, it employs a team of 50 pharmacists and assistants who provide much-needed information about the medications they dispense, such as details about drug interaction and side effects. As evidenced by the above examples, health care companies, regardless of the specific area in which they compete, are becoming more and more market oriented as they try to differentiate their offerings from those of the competition.

Insurance

In recent years, the insurance industry has exploded with new product and service offerings. Not too long ago, customers were faced with limited options in choosing life, hospital, or auto insurance. Now there is a wide array of insurance policies to choose from, including universal life policies, which double as retirement savings; nursing care insurance; reversible mortgages, which allow people to take equity from their house while still living in it; and other offerings aimed at serving an aging population. To illustrate, Prudential Insurance Company offers a program whereby terminally ill policyholders are allowed to withdraw funds against the face value of their policy while still alive. In addition to insurance services, most insurance companies now offer a full range of financial services, including auto loans, mortgages, mutual funds, and certificates of deposit.

Distribution of insurance services has also been growing. The vending machines found in airports for flight insurance have been finding their way into other areas. Travel auto insurance is now available in many motel chains and through the AAA. Group insurance written through employers and labor unions also has been extremely successful. In each instance, the insurance industry has used intermediaries to distribute its services.

Travel

The travel industry, most notably the airlines, has been a leader in the use of technology. Computerized reservation systems allow customers to book plane tickets from home or work. Nearly all airlines are using Internet sites to dispense flight and fare information. Airlines are in the midst of implementing ticketless travel programs in which passengers purchase tickets, select their seats, and pick up boarding passes and luggage tags at machines resembling ATMs.[17] Technology has also allowed airlines to make strategic pricing decisions through the use of yield management. In yield management, certain seats on aircraft are discounted and certain ones aren't. Through the use of elaborate computer programs, managers are able to determine who their customer segments are and who is likely to purchase airline tickets when and to where.

Despite its success in employing technology to attract additional customers and offer added convenience, the airline industry has operated in somewhat dire straits, plagued by

"I'm a nice customer. You all know me. I'm the one who never complains, no matter what kind of service I get.

"I'll go into a restaurant, and I'll sit while the waitress gossips with a friend and never bothers to look to see if my hamburger is ready to go. Sometimes a party who came in after I did gets my hamburger, but I don't say a word in complaint when the waitress tells me, 'Oh, I'm sorry. I'll order another for you.' I just wait.

It's the same when I go to a bank. I don't throw my weight around. I try to be thoughtful of the other person. If I get poor service I'm as polite as can be. I don't believe rudeness in return is the answer.

"The other day I stopped in at the neighborhood gas station. I waited for almost five minutes before the attendant took care of me. And when he did, he spilled gas and wiped the car windows with an oily rag. I didn't expect him to thank me for stopping by—and he didn't. Naturally, I didn't complain about the service.

"I never kick. I never nag. I never criticize. And I wouldn't dream of making a scene, as I've seen some people do in public places. I think that's uncalled for. No, I'm the nice customer. And I'll tell you what else I am.

"I'm the customer who never comes back!

"In fact, a nice customer like me, multiplied by others of my kind, can just about ruin a business. There are a lot of nice people in the world, just like me. When we get pushed far enough, we go on down the street to another store, another bank, where they're smart enough to hire help who have been trained to appreciate nice customers.

"He laughs loudest, they say, who laughs last. I laugh when I see you frantically spending your money on expensive advertising to get me back, when you could have had me in the first place for a few kind words and a smile and some good services.

"I don't care what business you're in. Maybe you live in a different town; maybe I've never heard of you. But if you're going broke or your business is bad, maybe there are enough people like me, who do know you. I'm your customer who never comes back."

Source: Unknown.

---

problems associated with overcapacity, high labor costs, and low perceived service quality. The decade of the 90s could be considered the most turbulent ever encountered by U.S. commercial airlines.[18] During this time, some airlines either went out of business (Midway, Eastern, and Pan Am) or were in and out of bankruptcy proceedings (Continental, America West, and TWA); and most others operated at a loss. In the early 2000s, both United Airlines and Delta Airlines faced bankruptcy.

A notable exception to the fate that befell most carriers is Southwest Airlines, which has finally convinced its peers that a carrier can be consistently profitable by offering cheap fares on short-distance routes. Now, big carriers such as Continental and United have created their own Southwest look-alikes to supplement their long-haul, full-service, high-fare operations. Southwest's secret to success (which other airlines may or may not be able to imitate) is the high level of employee morale everyone associated with the company exhibits. This has come as a direct result of upper management's internal marketing efforts.

Implications for Service Marketers

The preceding sections emphasized the use of all components of the marketing mix. Many service industries have been criticized for an overdependence on advertising. The overdependence on one or two elements of the marketing mix is a mistake that service marketers cannot afford. The sum total of the marketing mix elements represents the total impact of the firm's marketing strategy. The slack created by severely restricting one element cannot be compensated by heavier emphasis on another, since each element in the marketing mix is designed to address specific problems and achieve specific objectives.

Services must be made available to prospective users, which implies distribution in the marketing sense of the word. The revised concept of the distribution of services points out that service marketers must distinguish conceptually between the production and distribution of services. The problem of making services more widely available must not be ignored.

The above sections also pointed out the critical role of new service development. In several of the examples described, indirect distribution of the service was made possible because "products" were developed that included a tangible representation of the service. This development facilitates the use of intermediaries, because the service can now be separated from the producer. In addition, the development of new services paves the way for companies to expand and segment their markets. With the use of varying service bundles, new technology, and alternative means of distributing the service, companies are now able to practice targeted marketing.

SUMMARY

This chapter has dealt with the complex topic of service marketing. While the marketing of services has much in common with the marketing of products, unique problems in the area require highly creative marketing management skills. Many of the problems in the service area can be traced to the intangible and inseparable nature of services and the difficulties involved in measuring service quality. However, considerable progress has been made in understanding and reacting to these difficult problems, particularly in the area of distribution. In view of the major role services play in our economy, it is important for marketing practitioners to better understand and appreciate the unique problems of service marketing.

Additional Resources

Berry, Leonard L. *Discovering the Soul of Service.* NY: Free Press, 2000.

Berry, Leonard L. and Kent D. Seltman. *Management Lessons from Mayo Clinic.* NY: McGraw-Hill, 2008.

Collier, Marsha. *The Ultimate Online Customer Service Guide.* NY: John Wiley and Sons, 2011.

Fullerton, Sam. *Sports Marketing.* Burr Ridge, IL: McGraw-Hill/Irwin, 2007.

Gronroos, Christian. *Service Management and Marketing.* 3rd ed. NY: John Wiley and Sons, 2007.

Hoffman, K. Douglas, and John E. G. Bateson. *Service Marketing.* Mason, OH: Thomson Southwestern, 2009.

Keiningham, Timothy, and Terry Vavra. *The Customer Delight Principle.* NY: McGraw-Hill, 2001.

Schultz, Mike, and John E. Doerr. *Professional Service Marketing.* NY: John Wiley and Sons, 2009.

Key Terms and Concepts

Client relationship: Relationship in which the buyer of services views the seller as someone who has knowledge that is of value; may be of an ongoing nature.

Customer effort: For many services, the involvement of customers to some degree in the production of the service (e.g., some restaurants, airline baggage).

Inseparability: An important characteristic of services, the impossibility of separating a service from the person of the seller. In other words, services must often be produced and consumed simultaneously.

Intangibility: An important difference between goods and services is the intangibility of services which means that most services cannot appeal to a buyer's sense of touch, taste, smell, sight or hearing before purchase, intangibility places a burden on the marketing organization.

Internal marketing: The continual process by which managers actively encourage, stimulate, and support employee commitment to the organization and its customers.

Off-peak pricing: The different prices service marketers charge during different times or days in order to stimulate demand during slow periods and hopefully, smooth out demand for the service.

Perishability and fluctuating demand: Services are perishable which means that unused capacity represents business that is lost forever. The demand for many services also fluctuates by season, day of the week, or time of the day.

Quality service: Customers' perception of quality as a function of (1) *tangibles* which include physical evidence of the service; (2) *reliability* which involves the consistency and dependability of the service performance; (3) *responsiveness* which is the willingness or readiness of employees or professionals to provide service; (4) *assurance* which refers to the knowledge and competence of service providers and the ability to convey trust and confidence; and (5) *empathy* which is the service provider's efforts to understand the customer's needs.

Services: Activities performed by sellers and others that accompany the sale of a product and that aid in its exchange or its utilization (e.g. financing, an 800 number).

Service products: Products that are intangible, or at least substantially so. If totally intangible, they are exchanged directly from producer to user (e.g. hair cut, medical service), cannot be transported or stored, and are almost instantly perishable. Service products are often difficult to identify since they come into existence at the same time they are bought and consumed.

Uniformity: An important characteristic of services is that their quality can vary more than the quality of goods. Because they are often human performances and often customized to the needs of the buyer, (eg. haircut), uniformity is difficult to achieve and quality can vary.

Chapter

13

Global Marketing

A growing number of U.S. corporations have transversed geographical boundaries and become truly multinational in nature. For most other domestic companies, the question is no longer, Should we go international? Instead, the questions relate to when, how, and where the companies should enter the international marketplace. The past 15 years have seen the reality of a truly world market unfold.

Firms invest in foreign countries for the same basic reasons they invest in their own country. These reasons vary from firm to firm but fall under the categories of achieving offensive or defensive goals. Offensive goals are to (1) increase long-term growth and profit prospects; (2) maximize total sales revenue; (3) take advantage of economies of scale; and (4) improve overall market position. As many American markets reach saturation, American firms look to foreign markets as outlets for surplus production capacity, sources of new customers, increased profit margins, and improved returns on investment. For example, the ability to expand the number of locations of McDonald's restaurants in the United States is becoming severely limited. Yet, on any given day, only 0.5 percent of the world's population visits McDonald's. Indeed, in the recent past, of the 50 most profitable McDonald's outlets, 25 were located in Hong Kong. For PepsiCo, the results are similar. Its restaurant division operates over 10,000 Kentucky Fried Chicken, Pizza Hut, and Taco Bell outlets abroad.

Multinational firms also invest in other countries to achieve defensive goals. Chief among these goals are the desire to (1) compete with foreign companies on their own turf instead of in the United States, (2) gain access to technological innovations that are developed in other countries, (3) take advantage of significant differences in operating costs between countries, (4) preempt competitors' global moves, and (5) avoid being locked out of future markets by arriving too late.

Such well-known companies as Zenith, Pillsbury, Shell Oil, CBS Records, and Firestone Tire & Rubber are now owned by non-U.S. interests. Since 1980, the share of the U.S. high-tech market held by foreign products has grown from less than 8 percent to over 50 percent. In such diverse industries as power tools, tractors, television, and banking, U.S. companies have lost the dominant position they once held. By investing solely in domestic operations or not being willing to adapt products to foreign markets, U.S. companies are more susceptible to foreign incursions. For example, there has been a great uproar over Japan's practice of not opening up its domestic automobile market to U.S. companies. However, not too many years ago, a great majority of the American cars shipped to Japan still had the steering wheel located on the left side of the vehicle—the opposite of where it should be for the Japanese market.

In many ways, marketing globally is the same as marketing at home. Regardless of which part of the world the firm sells in, the marketing program must still be built around

Company	Global Revenues (billions)	Percent Revenues from Outside the U.S.
Walmart	$401.1	24.6%
Ford Motor	146.3	51.9
General Electric	182.5	53.7
CitiGroup	52.8	74.8
Hewlett-Packard	118.4	68.2
Boeing	60.9	38.9
Intel	37.6	85.4
Coca-Cola	31.9	77.0
Apple	36.5	46.0
Starbucks	10.4	20.8

Source: Philip R. Cateora, Mary C. Gilly, and John L. Graham, *International Marketing*, 15th ed. (Burr Ridge, IL: McGraw-Hill/Irwin, 2011), p.10.

a sound product or service that is properly priced, promoted, and distributed to a carefully analyzed target market. In other words, the marketing manager has the same controllable decision variables in both domestic and nondomestic markets.

Although the development of a marketing program may be the same in either domestic or nondomestic markets, special problems may be involved in the implementation of marketing programs in nondomestic markets. These problems often arise because of the environmental differences that exist among various countries that marketing managers may be unfamiliar with.

In this chapter, marketing management in a global context will be examined. Methods of organizing global versus domestic markets, global market research tasks, methods of entry strategies into global markets, and potential marketing strategies for a multinational firm will be discussed. In examining each of these areas, the reader will find a common thread—knowledge of the local cultural environment—that appears to be a major prerequisite for success in each area.

With the proper adaptations, many companies have the capabilities and resources needed to compete successfully in the global marketplace. To illustrate, companies as diverse as Kellogg's, Avon, Eli Lilly, and Sun Microsystems all generate a large percentage of their sales from foreign operations. Smaller companies can also be successful. For example, Nemix, Inc., of Bell Gardens, California, is a franchisee of Church's Fried Chicken. Small by world standards, this company has succeeded in developing a fully vertical operation in Poland, doing everything from raising chickens to operating restaurants.[1]

THE COMPETITIVE ADVANTAGE OF NATIONS

As each year passes, it becomes more and more clear that some industries and companies succeed on a global scale while others do not. Harvard Business School professor Michael Porter introduced what he calls the "diamond" of national advantage to explain a nation's competitive advantage and why some companies and industries become global business leaders. Figure 13.1 presents Porter's model. The diamond presents four factors that determine the competitive advantage or disadvantage of a nation.

1. *Factor conditions.* The nation's ability to turn its natural resources, skilled labor, and infrastructure into a competitive advantage.

FIGURE 13.1
Porter's Diamond of
National Advantage

Source: Michael E. Porter,
*The Competitive Advantage
of Nations* (New York: Fress
Press, 1990), pp. 577–615.

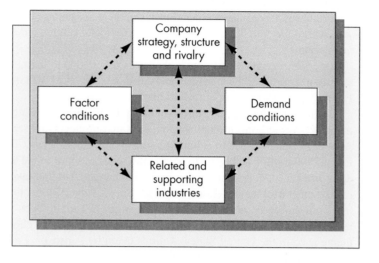

2. *Demand conditions.* The nature of domestic demand and the sophistication of domestic customers for the industry's product or service.

3. *Related and supporting industries.* The existence or absence in the country of supplier and related industries that are also internationally competitive.

4. *Company strategy, structure, and rivalry.* The conditions in the nation that govern how companies are created, organized, and managed, and how intensely they compete domestically.

Before Porter developed his model, he studied companies in more than 100 industries. While the most successful companies differed in many ways and employed different strategies, a very important common theme emerged: A company that succeeds on a global scale, first succeeded in intense domestic competition. His model is a dynamic model and illustrates how over time, a nation can build up and maintain its competitive advantage in any industry.

ORGANIZING FOR GLOBAL MARKETING

When compared with the tasks it faces at home, a firm attempting to establish a global marketing organization faces a much higher degree of risk and uncertainty. In a foreign market, management is often less familiar with the cultural, political, and economic situation. Many of these problems arise as a result of conditions specific to the foreign country. Managers are also faced with the decisions concerning how to organize the multinational company.

Problems with Entering Foreign Markets

While numerous problems could be cited, attention here will focus on those that firms most often face when entering foreign markets.

Cultural Misunderstanding

Differences in the cultural environment of foreign countries may be misunderstood or not even recognized because of the tendency for marketing managers to use their own cultural values and priorities as a frame of reference. Some of the most common areas of difference lie in the way dissimilar cultures perceive time, thought patterns, personal space, material possessions, family roles and relationships, personal achievement, competitiveness, individuality, social behavior, and other interrelated issues.[2] Another important source of misunderstandings is in the perceptions of managers about the people with whom they are dealing. Feelings of superiority can lead to changed communication mannerisms.

American managers must make the necessary efforts to learn, understand, and adapt to the cultural norms of the managers and customers they deal with in other parts of the world. Failure to do so will result in missed market opportunities.

On the other hand, companies should not shy away from attempting to enter global markets because conventional wisdom says that products and service will not succeed in some regions purely due to cultural reasons. For example, PepsiCo's Pepsi division entered into a $500 million offensive to try to grab a larger share of the $6 billion Brazilian soft-drink market.[3] Understanding the dramatic changes that had taken place in Brazil, Pepsi repositioned itself as the choice of a new Brazil. Advertisements for the Pepsi brand feature young people enumerating recent changes in Brazil. Does this campaign sound familiar? It should since it's a takeoff on the popular "Pepsi, the choice of a new generation" theme used in the United States. Actions taken by PepsiCo's Frito-Lay unit serve as another example of a successful adaptation to cultural differences.[4] In China, Frito-Lay introduced its popular Cheetos snack food. The twist to this effort lies in the fact that the Chinese are not big consumers of dairy products. In China, Cheetos are cheeseless, instead consisting of flavors such as "Savory American Cream" and "Zesty Japanese Steak." As a result of these and other adaptations, it's no wonder that PepsiCo ranks among the leaders in the global food and beverage industry.

Political Uncertainty

Governments are unstable in many countries, and social unrest and even armed conflict must sometimes be reckoned with. Other nations are newly emerging and anxious to seek their independence. These and similar problems can greatly hinder a firm seeking to establish its position in foreign markets. For example, at the turn of the century, firms scaled back their investment plans in Russia due to, among other reasons, (1) a business environment plagued by mobsters, (2) politics badly corrupted by the botched invasion of Chechnya, and (3) an economy troubled by runaway inflation and a plummeting ruble.[5] This is not to say investment in Russia is a poor choice. Rather, in situations like this, caution must be used and companies must have a keen understanding of the risks involved in undertaking sizable investments.

Import Restrictions

Tariffs, import quotas, and other types of import restrictions hinder global business. These are usually established to promote self-sufficiency and can be a huge roadblock for the multinational firm. For example, a number of countries, including South Korea, Taiwan, Thailand, and Japan, have placed import restrictions on a variety of goods produced in America, including telecommunications equipment, rice, wood products, automobiles, and produce. In other cases, governments may not impose restrictions that are commonly adhered to in the United States. For example, Chrysler pulled out of a proposed investment deal in China, worth billions of dollars, because the Chinese government refused to protect its right to limit access to technological information.

Exchange Controls and Ownership Restrictions

Some nations establish limits on the amount of earned and invested funds that can be withdrawn from it. These exchange controls are usually established by nations that are experiencing balance-of-payment problems. In addition, many nations have a requirement that the majority ownership of a company operating there be held by nationals. These and other types of currency and ownership regulations are important considerations in the decision

BODY LANGUAGE

- Standing with your hands on your hips is a gesture of defiance in Indonesia.
- Carrying on a conversation with your hands in your pockets makes a poor impression in France, Belgium, Finland, and Sweden.
- Shaking your head from side to side means yes in Bulgaria and Sri Lanka.
- Crossing your legs to expose the sole of your shoe is really taboo in Muslim countries. In fact, to call a person a "shoe" is a deep insult.

PHYSICAL CONTACT

- Patting a child on the head is a grave offense in Thailand or Singapore, since the head is revered as the location of the soul.
- In an Oriental culture, touching another person is considered an invasion of privacy; in Southern European and Arabic countries, it is a sign of warmth and friendship.

PROMPTNESS

- Be on time when invited for dinner in Denmark or in China.
- In Latin countries, your host or business associate would be surprised if you arrived at the appointed hour.

EATING AND COOKING

- It is rude to leave anything on your plate when eating in Norway, Malaysia, or Singapore.
- In Egypt, it is rude *not* to leave something.
- In Italy and Spain, cooking is done with oil.
- In Germany and Great Britain, margarine and butter are used.

OTHER SOCIAL CUSTOMS

- In Sweden, nudity and sexual permissiveness are quite all right, but drinking is really frowned on.
- In Spain, there is a very negative attitude toward life insurance. By receiving insurance benefits, a wife feels that she is profiting from her husband's death.
- In Western European countries, many consumers still are reluctant to buy anything (other than a house) on credit. Even for an automobile, they will pay cash.

Source: William J. Stanton, Michael J. Etzel, and Bruce J. Walker, *Fundamentals of Marketing*, 13th ed. (Burr Ridge IL: McGraw-Hill/Irwin, 2004), p. 544.

to expand into a foreign market. For example, up until a few years ago, foreign holdings in business ventures in India were limited to a maximum of 40 percent. Once this ban was lifted, numerous global companies such as Sony, Whirlpool, JVC, Grundig, Panasonic, Kellogg's, Levi Strauss, Pizza Hut, and Domino's rushed to invest in this market.[6]

Economic Conditions

As noted earlier, nations' economies are becoming increasingly intertwined, and business cycles tend to follow similar patterns. However, there are differences, mainly due to political upheaval or social changes, and these may be significant. In determining whether to invest, marketers need to perform in-depth analyses of a country's stage of economic development, the buying power of its populace, and the strength of its currency. For example, when the North American Free Trade Agreement (NAFTA) was signed, many American companies rushed to invest in Mexico, building production facilities and retail outlets. These companies assumed that signing the agreement would stabilize Mexico's economy. In the long term, these investments may pay off. However, many companies lost millions of dollars there due to the devaluation of the peso. Indeed, the crash of the peso caused the retail giant Walmart to scale back a $1 billion investment project to open stores throughout Mexico.

Organizing the Multinational Company

There are two kinds of global companies—the multidomestic corporation and the global corporation.[7] The *multidomestic company* pursues different strategies in each of its foreign markets. It could have as many different product variations, brand names, and advertising campaigns as countries in which it operates. Each overseas subsidiary is autonomous. Local managers are given the authority to make the necessary decisions and are held accountable for results. In effect, the company competes on a market-by-market basis. Honeywell and General Foods are U.S. firms that have operated this way.

The *global company,* on the other hand, views the world as one market and pits its resources against the competition in an integrated fashion. It emphasizes cultural similarities across countries and universal consumer needs and wants rather than differences. It standardizes marketing activities when there are cultural similarities and adapts them when the cultures are different. Since there is no one clear-cut way to organize a global company, three alternative structures are normally used: (1) worldwide product divisions, each responsible for selling its own products throughout the world; (2) divisions responsible for all products sold within a geographic region; and (3) a matrix system that combines elements of both of these arrangements. Many organizations, such as IBM, Caterpillar, Timex, General Electric, Siemens, and Mitsubishi, are structured in a global fashion.

Most companies are realizing the need to take a global approach to managing their businesses. However, recognizing the need and actually implementing a truly global approach are two different tasks. For some companies, industry conditions dictate that they take a global perspective. The ability to actually implement a global approach to managing international operations, however, largely depends on factors unique to the company. Globalization, as a competitive strategy, is inherently more vulnerable to risk than a multidomestic or domestic strategy, due to the relative permanence of the organizational structure once established.

In determining whether or not to globalize a particular business, managers should look first at their industry.[8] Market, economic, environmental, and competitive factors all influence the potential gains to be realized by following a global strategy. Factors constituting the external environment that are conducive to a global strategy are:

1. *Market factors.* Homogeneous market needs, global customers, shorter product life cycles, transferable brands and advertising, and the ability to globalize distribution channels.
2. *Economic factors.* Worldwide economies of scale in manufacturing and distribution, steep learning curves, worldwide sourcing efficiencies, rising product development costs, and significant differences in host-country costs.
3. *Environmental factors.* Improving communications, favorable government policies, and the increasing speed of technological change.
4. *Competitive factors.* Competitive interdependencies among countries, global moves of competitors, and opportunities to preempt a competitor's global moves.[9]

Many of the reasons given in the first part of the chapter about why a domestic company should become a multinational can also be used to support the argument that a firm should take a global perspective. This is because the integration of markets is forcing companies that wish to remain successful not only to become multinationals but also to take a global perspective in doing so. In the past, companies had the option of remaining domestic or going multinational due to the separation of markets. This is no longer the case.

Growth in global markets has created opportunities for building global brands. The advantages are many and so are the pitfalls. Here are 10 commandments that marketers can use when planning a global branding campaign.

1. *Understand similarities and differences in the global branding landscape.* The best brands retain consistency of theme and alter specific elements to suit each country.
2. *Don't take shortcuts in brand building.* Build brands in new markets from the "bottom up."
3. *Establish marketing infrastructure.* Most often, firms adopt or invest in foreign partners for manufacturing and distribution.
4. *Embrace integrated marketing communications.* Because advertising opportunities may be more limited, marketers must use other forms of communication such as sponsorship and public relations.
5. *Establish brand partnerships.* Most global brands have marketing partners ranging from joint venture partners to franchisees and distributors who provide access to distribution.
6. *Balance standardization and customization.* Know what to standardize and what to customize.
7. *Balance global and local control.* This is very important in the following areas: organization structure, entry strategies, coordination processes, and mechanisms.
8. *Establish operable guidelines.* Set the rules about how the brand will be positioned and marketed.
9. *Implement a global brand equity measurement system.* The ideal measurement system provides complete, up-to-date information on the brand and on all its competitors to the appropriate decision makers.
10. *Leverage brand elements.* If the meanings of the brand name and all related trademarked identifiers are clear, they can be an invaluable source of brand equity worldwide.

Source: Kevin Lane Keller, "The Ten Commandments of Global Branding," *MBA Bullet Point,* October 3–16, 2000, p. 3, and Kevin Lane Keller, *Strategic Brand Management,* 3rd ed. (Upper Saddle River, NJ: Prentice-Hall, 2008), chap. 14.

Several internal factors can either facilitate or impede a company's efforts to undertake a global approach to marketing strategies. These factors and their underlying dimensions are

1. *Structure.* The ease of installing a centralized global authority and the absence of rifts between present domestic and international divisions or operating units.
2. *Management processes.* The capabilities and resources available to perform global planning, budgeting, and coordination activities, coupled with the ability to conduct global performance reviews and implement global compensation plans.
3. *Culture.* The ability to project a global versus national identity, a worldwide versus domestic commitment to employees, and a willingness to tolerate interdependence among business units.
4. *People.* The availability of employable foreign nationals and the willingness of current employees to commit to multicountry careers, frequent travel, and having foreign superiors.

Overall, whether a company should undertake a multidomestic or global approach to organizing its international operations will largely depend on the nature of the company and its products, how different foreign cultures are from the domestic market, and the company's ability to implement a global perspective. Many large brands have failed in their quest to go global. The primary reason for this failure is rushing the process. Successful global brands carefully stake out their markets, allowing plenty of time to develop their overseas marketing efforts and evolve into global brands.

Indeed, in many cases, firms do not undertake either purely multidomestic or global approaches to marketing. Instead, they develop a hybrid approach whereby these global brands carry with them the same visual identity, the same strategic positioning, and the same advertising. In addition, local characteristics are factored in. Regardless of the approach undertaken, management and organizational skills that emphasize the need to handle diversity are the critical factors that determine the long-term success of any company's endeavors in the global marketplace.

PROGRAMMING FOR GLOBAL MARKETING

In this section of the chapter, the major areas in developing a global marketing program will be examined. As mentioned at the outset, marketing managers must organize the same controllable decision variables that exist in domestic markets. However, many firms that have been extremely successful in marketing in the United States have not been able to duplicate their success in foreign markets.

Global Marketing Research

Because the risks and uncertainties are so high, marketing research is equally important in foreign markets and in domestic markets and probably more so. Many companies encounter losing situations abroad because they do not know enough about the market.[10] They don't know how to get the information or find the cost of collecting the information too high. To be successful, organizations must collect and analyze pertinent information to support the basic go/no-go decision before getting to the issues addressed by conventional market research. Toward this end, in attempting to analyze foreign consumers and markets, at least four organizational issues must be considered.

Population Characteristics

Population characteristics are one of the major components of a market, and significant differences exist between and within foreign countries. If data are available, the marketing manager should be familiar with the total population and with the regional, urban, rural, and interurban distribution. Other demographic variables, such that the number and size of families, education, occupation, and religion, are also important. In many markets, these variables can have a significant impact on the success of a firm's marketing program. For example, in the United States, a cosmetics firm can be reasonably sure that the desire to use cosmetics is common among women of all income classes. However, in Latin America the same firm may be forced to segment its market by upper-, middle-, and lower-income groups, as well as by urban and rural areas. This is because upper-income women want high-quality cosmetics promoted in prestige media and sold through exclusive outlets. In some rural and less prosperous areas, cosmetics must be inexpensive; in other rural areas, women do not accept cosmetics.

Ability to Buy

To assess the ability of consumers in a foreign market to buy, four broad measures should be examined: (1) gross national product or per capita national income, (2) distribution of income, (3) rate of growth in buying power, and (4) extent of available financing. Since each of these vary in different areas of the world, the marketing opportunities available must be examined closely.

Many consumer goods companies have sought growth by expanding into global markets. For U.S. companies, this is sound strategy since 95 percent of the world's population and two-thirds of its purchasing power are located outside their country. The potential for success in global markets is enhanced when companies carefully research and analyze consumers in foreign countries, just as it is in domestic markets. Below are some suggestions for companies seeking to successfully market to global consumers.

- Research the cultural nuances and customs of the market. Be sure that the company and brand name translate favorably in the language of the target country, and if not, consider using an abbreviation or entirely different brand name for the market. Consider using marketing research firms or ad agencies that have detailed knowledge of the culture.

- Determine whether the product can be exported to the foreign country as is or whether it has to be modified to be useful and appealing to targeted consumers. Also, determine what changes need to be made to packaging and labeling to make the product appealing to the market.

- Research the prices of similar products in the target country or region. Determine the necessary retail price to make marketing it profitable in the country, and research whether a sufficient number of consumers would be willing to pay that price. Also, determine what the product has to offer that would make consumers willing to pay a higher price.

- On the basis of research, decide whether the targeted country or region will require a unique marketing strategy or whether the same general strategy can be used in all geographic areas.

- Research the ways consumers purchase similar products in the targeted country or region and whether the company's product can be sold effectively using this method of distribution. Also, determine if a method of distribution not currently being used in the country could create a competitive advantage for the product.

- Pretest integrated marketing communication efforts in the targeted country to ensure not only that messages are translated accurately but also that subtle differences in meaning are not problematic. Also, research the effectiveness of planned communication efforts.

Marketing consumer goods successfully in global markets requires a long-term commitment because it may take time to establish an identity in new markets. However, with improving technology and the evolution of a global economy, both large and small companies have found global marketing both feasible and profitable.

Source: Dom Del Prete, "Winning Strategies Lead to Global Marketing Success," *Marketing News,* August 18, 1997, pp. 1, 2. Also see Philip R. Cateora, Mary C. Gilly, and John L. Graham, *International Marketing,* 15th ed. (Burr Ridge, IL: McGraw-Hill/Irwin, 2011), chap. 8.

Willingness to Buy

The cultural framework of consumer motives and behavior is integral to the understanding of the foreign consumer. If data are available, cultural values and attitudes toward the material culture, social organizations, the supernatural, aesthetics, and language should be analyzed for their possible influence on each of the elements in the firm's marketing program. It is easy to see that such factors as the group's values concerning acquisition of material goods, the role of the family, the positions of men and women in society, and the various age groups and social classes can have an effect on marketing because each can influence consumer behavior.

In some areas tastes and habits seem to be converging, with different cultures becoming more and more integrated into one homogeneous culture, although still separated by national

Procter & Gamble: According to the P&G Web site, P&G products are developed as global R&D projects. P&G has 22 research centers in 13 countries from which they can draw expertise. As a good example of a global product, consider the Swiffer mop. P&G made use of its research centers in the United States and France to conduct market research and testing in support of this new product.

Apple: In the development of the iPod, Apple worked with about ten different firms and independent contractors throughout the world, and did product design and customer requirement definition in both the United States and Japan.

Ikea: The Swedish furniture retailer knows that its target market (middle-class strivers) crosses international and intercontinental lines, so it operates globally in a streamlined fashion. It identifies an unmet customer need (say a certain style of table at a given price point), commissions in-house and outsourced designers to compete for the best design, then its manufacturing partners worldwide compete for the rights to manufacture it. Excellent global logistics complete the value delivery to customers.

Bungie Studios: This boutique software company, now owned by Microsoft, developed the MS Halo gaming software series in the United States, but product-tested it in Europe and Asia. Like Ikea customers in the prior example, gamers are much alike the world over.

Source: Loida Rosario, "Borderless Innovation: The Impact of Globalization on NPD in Three Industries," *Visions,* June 2006. Merle Crawford and Anthony DiBenedetto, *New Products Management,* 10th ed. (Burr Ridge, IL: McGraw-Hill/Irwin, 2011), p. 10.

boundaries. This appears to be the case in Western Europe, where consumers are developing into a mass market. This convergence obviously will simplify the task for a marketer in this region. However, cultural differences still prevail among many areas of the world and strongly influence consumer behavior. Marketing organizations may have to do primary research in many foreign markets to obtain usable information about these issues.

Differences in Research Tasks and Processes

In addition to the dimensions mentioned above, the processes and tasks associated with carrying out the market research program may also differ from country to country. Many market researchers count on census data for in-depth demographic information. However, in foreign countries the market researcher is likely to encounter a variety of problems in using census data. These include[11]

1. *Language.* Some nations publish their census reports in English. Other countries offer census reports only in their native language; some do not take a census.

2. *Data content.* Data contained in a census vary from country to country and often omit items of interest to researchers. For example, most foreign nations do not include an income question on their census. Others do not include such items as marital status or education levels.

3. *Timeliness.* The United States takes a census every 10 years. Japan and Canada conduct one every five years. However, some northern European nations are abandoning the census as a data-collection tool and instead are relying on population registers to account for births, deaths, and changes in marital status or place of residence.

4. *Availability in the United States.* If a researcher requires detailed household demographics on foreign markets, the cost and time required to obtain the data will be significant. Unfortunately, census data for many countries do not exist. For some it will be difficult to obtain, although data about others can be found on the Internet.

Global Product Strategy

Global marketing research can help determine whether (1) there is an unsatisfied need for which a new product could be developed to serve a foreign market or (2) there is an unsatisfied need that could be met with an existing domestic product, either as is or adapted to the foreign market. In either case, product planning is necessary to determine the type of product to be offered and whether there is sufficient demand to warrant entry into a foreign market.

Most U.S. firms would not think of entering a domestic market without extensive product planning. However, some marketers have failed to do adequate product planning when entering foreign markets. An example of such a problem occurred when American manufacturers began to export refrigerators to Europe. The firms exported essentially the same models sold in the United States. However, the refrigerators were the wrong size, shape, and temperature range for some areas and had weak appeal in others—thus failing miserably. Although adaptation of the product to local conditions may have eliminated this failure, this adaptation is easier said than done. For example, even in the domestic market, overproliferation of product varieties and options can dilute economies of scale. This dilution results in higher production costs, which may make the price of serving each market segment with an adapted product prohibitive.

The solution to this problem is not easy. In some cases, changes need not be made at all or, if so, can be accomplished rather inexpensively. In other cases, the sales potential of the particular market may not warrant expensive product changes. For example, Pepsi's Radical Fruit line of juice drinks was introduced without adaptation on three continents. On the other hand, U.S. companies wishing to market software in foreign countries must undertake painstaking and costly efforts to convert the embedded code from English to foreign languages. This undertaking severely limits the potential markets where individual software products can be profitably marketed. In any case, management must examine these product-related problems carefully prior to making foreign market entry decisions.

Global Distribution Strategy

The role of the distribution network in facilitating the transfer of goods and titles and in the demand stimulation process is as important in foreign markets as it is at home. Figure 13.2

FIGURE 13.2
International Channel-of-Distribution Alternatives

Source: Philip R. Cateora, Mary C. Gilly, and John I. Graham, *International Marketing,* 15th ed. (Burr Ridge, IL: McGraw-Hill/Irwin, 2011), p. 430.

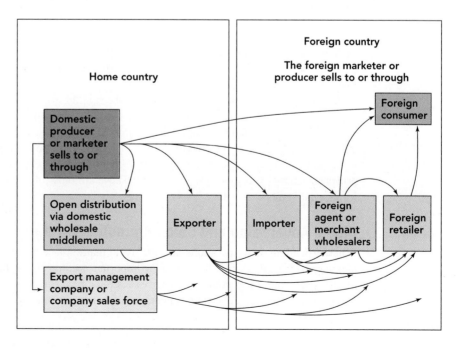

illustrates some of the most common channel arrangements in global marketing. They range from no control to almost complete control of the distribution system by manufacturers.

Global distribution strategy can be extremely challenging because sellers must influence two sets of channels: one in the home country and one in the foreign country. There are many possibilities as the figure clearly illustrates. The arrows indicate to whom the producers and various middlemen might sell in order to move products between countries.

Manufacturers can become more directly involved and, hence, have greater control over distribution, when they select agents and distributors located in foreign markets. Both perform similar functions, except that agents do not assume title to the manufacturers' products, while wholesalers do. If manufacturers should assume the functions of foreign agents or wholesalers and establish their own foreign branch, they greatly increase control over their global distribution system. Manufacturers' effectiveness will then depend on their own administrative organization rather than on independent intermediaries. If the foreign branch sells to other intermediaries, such as wholesalers and retailers, as is the case with most consumer goods, manufacturers again relinquish some control. However, since the manufacturers are located in the market area, they have greater potential to influence these intermediaries. For example, Volkswagen, Anheuser-Busch, and Procter & Gamble have each made substantial investments in building manufacturing facilities in Brazil. These investments allow the companies to begin making direct sales to dealers and retailers in the country.

The channel arrangement that enables manufacturers to exercise a great deal of control is where the manufacturer sells directly to organizational buyers or ultimate consumers. Although this arrangement is most common in the sale of organizational goods, some consumer goods companies have also pursued this arrangement.

Global Pricing Strategy

In domestic markets, pricing is a complex task. The basic approaches used in price determination in foreign markets are the same as those discussed earlier in the chapter on pricing. However, the pricing task is often more complicated in foreign markets because of additional problems associated with tariffs, antidumping laws, taxes, inflation, and currency conversion.

Import duties are probably the major constraint for global marketers and are encountered in many markets. Management must decide whether import duties will be paid by the firm or the foreign consumer, or whether they will be paid by both. This and similar constraints may force the firm to abandon an otherwise desirable pricing strategy or may force the firm out of a market altogether.

Another pricing problem arises because of the rigidity in price structures found in many foreign markets. Many foreign intermediaries are not aggressive in their pricing policies. They often prefer to maintain high unit margins at the expense of low sales volume rather than develop large sales volume by means of lower prices and smaller margins per unit. Many times this rigidity is encouraged by legislation that prevents retailers from cutting prices substantially at their own discretion. These are only a few of the pricing problems foreign marketers encounter.

Global Advertising and Sales Promotion Strategy

When expanding their operations into the world marketplace, most firms are aware of the language barriers that exist and realize the importance of translating their messages into the proper idiom. However, numerous other issues must be resolved as well, such as selecting appropriate media and advertising agencies in foreign markets.

There are many problems in selecting media in foreign markets. Often the media that are traditionally used in the domestic market are not available. For example, it was not until recently that national commercial TV became a reality in the former Soviet Union. If media are available, they may be so only on a limited basis or they may not reach the potential buyers. In addition to the problem of availability, other difficulties arise from the lack of accurate media information. There is no rate and data service or media directory that covers all the media available throughout the world. Where data are available, their accuracy is often questionable.

Another important promotion decision that must be made is the type of agency used to prepare and place the firm's advertisements. Along with the growth in multinational product companies, more multinational advertising agencies are available. Among the top 15 global advertising agencies, less than half are U.S. owned. Alliances and takeovers have stimulated growth in the formation of global agencies. The U.S. company can take either of two major approaches to choosing an agency. The first is to use a purely local agency in each area where the advertisement is to appear. The rationale for this approach is that a purely local agency employing only local nationals can better adapt the firm's message to the local culture.

The other approach is to use either a U.S.-based multinational agency or a multinational agency with U.S. offices to develop and implement the ad campaign. For example, the Coca-Cola Company uses one agency to create ads for the 80 nations in which Diet Coke is marketed. The use of these so-called super agencies is increasing (annual growth rates averaged over 30 percent in the last decade). By using global advertising agencies, companies are able to take advantage of economies of scale and other efficiencies. However, global agencies are not without their critics. Many managers believe that small, local agencies in emerging markets take a more entrepreneurial and fresher approach to advertising than do global agencies. Much discussion has developed over which approach is best, and it appears that both approaches can be used successfully.

The use of sales promotion can also lead to opportunities and problems for marketers in foreign markets. Sales promotions often contain certain characteristics that are more attractive than other elements of the promotion mix.[12] In less-wealthy countries, consumers tend to be even more interested in saving money through price discounts, sampling, or premiums. Sales promotion can also be used as a strategy for bypassing restrictions on advertising placed by some foreign governments. In addition, sales promotion can be an effective means for reaching people who live in rural locations where media support for advertising is virtually nonexistent.

ENTRY AND GROWTH STRATEGIES FOR GLOBAL MARKETING

A major decision facing companies that desire either to enter a foreign market or pursue growth within a specific market relates to the choice of entry or growth strategy. What type of strategy to employ depends on many factors, including the analysis of market opportunities, company capabilities, the degree of marketing involvement and commitment the company is willing to make, and the amount of risk that the company is able to tolerate.[13] A company can decide to (1) make minimal investments of funds and resources by limiting its efforts to exporting; (2) make large initial investments of resources and management effort to try to establish a long-term share of global markets; or (3) take an incremental approach whereby the company starts with a low-risk mode of entry that requires the least financial and other resource commitment and gradually increases its commitment over time. All three approaches can be profitable. In general, a company can initially enter a global market and, subsequently, pursue growth in the global marketplace in six ways:

1. *Exporting.* Exporting occurs when a company produces the product outside the final destination and then ships it there for sale. It is the easiest and most common approach for a company making its first international move. Exporting has two distinct advantages. First, it avoids the cost of establishing manufacturing operations in the host country; second, it may help a firm achieve experience-curve and location economies. By manufacturing the product in a centralized location and exporting it to other national markets, the firm may be able to realize substantial scale economies from its global sales volume. This method is what allowed Sony to dominate the global TV market. The major disadvantages related to exporting include (1) the sometimes higher cost associated with the process, (2) the necessity of the exporting firm to pay import duties or face trade barriers, and (3) the delegation of marketing responsibility for the product to foreign agents who may or may not be dependable.

2. *Licensing.* Companies can grant patent rights, trademark rights, and the right to use technological processes to foreign companies. This is the most common strategy for small and medium-size companies. The major advantage to licensing is that the firm does not have to bear the development costs and risks associated with opening up a foreign market. In addition, licensing can be an attractive option in unfamiliar or politically volatile markets. The major disadvantages are that (1) the firm does not have tight control over manufacturing, marketing, and strategy that is required for realizing economies of scale; and (2) there is the risk that foreign companies may capitalize on the licensed technology. RCA Corporation, for example, once licensed its color TV technology to a number of Japanese firms. These firms quickly assimilated the technology and used it to enter the U.S. market.

3. *Franchising.* Franchising is similar to licensing but tends to involve longer-term commitments. Also, franchising is commonly employed by service firms, as opposed to manufacturing firms. In a franchising agreement, the franchisor sells limited rights to use its brand name in return for a lump sum and share of the franchisee's future profits. In contrast to licensing agreements, the franchisee agrees to abide by strict operating procedures. Advantages and disadvantages associated with franchising are primarily the same as with licensing except to a lesser degree. In many cases, franchising offers an effective mix of centralized and decentralized decision making.

4. *Joint ventures.* A company may decide to share management with one or more collaborating foreign firms. Joint ventures are especially popular in industries that call for large investments, such as natural gas exploration and automobile manufacturing. Control of the joint venture may be split equally, or one party may control decision making. Joint ventures hold several advantages. First, a firm may be able to benefit from a partner's knowledge of the host country's competitive position, culture, language, political systems, and so forth. Second, the firm gains by sharing costs and risks of operating in a foreign market. Third, in many countries, political considerations make joint ventures the only feasible entry mode. Finally, joint ventures allow firms to take advantage of a partner's distribution system, technological know-how, or marketing skills. For example, General Mills teamed up with CPC International in an operation called International Dessert Partners to develop a major baking and dessert-mix business in Latin America. The venture combines General Mills' technology and Betty Crocker dessert products with CPC's marketing and distribution capabilities in Latin America. The major disadvantages associated with joint ventures are that (1) a firm may risk giving up control of proprietary knowledge to its partner; and (2) the firm may lose the tight control over a foreign subsidiary needed to engage in coordinated global attacks against rivals.

5. *Strategic alliances.* Although some consider strategic alliances a form of joint venture, we consider them a distinct entity for two reasons. First, strategic alliances are normally partnerships that two or more firms enter into to gain a competitive advantage on a worldwide versus local basis. Second, strategic alliances are usually of a much longer-term nature than are joint ventures. In strategic alliances, the partners share long-term goals and pledge almost total cooperation. Strategic alliances can be used to reduce manufacturing costs, accelerate technological diffusion and new product development, and overcome legal and trade barriers.[14] The major disadvantage associated with formation of a strategic alliance is the increased risk of competitive conflict between the partners.

6. *Direct ownership.* Some companies prefer to enter or grow in markets either through establishment of a wholly owned subsidiary or through acquisition. In either case, the firm owns 100 percent of the stock. The advantages to direct ownership are that the firm has (1) complete control over its technology and operations, (2) immediate access to foreign markets, (3) instant credibility and gains in the foreign country when acquisitions are the mode of entry or growth, and (4) the ability to install its own management team. Of course, the primary disadvantages of direct ownership are the huge costs and significant risks associated with this strategy. These problems may more than offset the advantages depending upon the country entered.

Regardless of the choice of methods used to gain entry into and grow within a foreign marketplace, companies must somehow integrate their operations. The complexities involved in operating on a worldwide basis dictate that firms decide on operating strategies. A critical decision that marketing managers must make relates to the extent of adaptation of the marketing mix elements for the foreign country in which the company operates. Depending on the area of the world under consideration and the particular product mix, different degrees of standardization/adaptation of the marketing mix elements may take place. As a guideline, standardization of one or more parts of the marketing mix is a function of many factors that individually and collectively affect companies' decision making.[15] It is more likely to succeed under the following conditions:

- When markets are economically similar.
- When worldwide customers, not countries, are the basis for segmenting markets.
- When customer behavior and lifestyles are similar.
- When the product is culturally compatible across the host country.
- When a firm's competitive position is similar in different markets.
- When competing against the same competitors, with similar market shares, in different countries, rather than competing against purely local companies.
- When the product is an organizational and high-technology product rather than a consumer product.
- When there are similarities in the physical, political, and legal environments of home and host countries.
- When the marketing infrastructure in the home and host countries is similar.

The decision to adapt or standardize marketing should be made only after a thorough analysis of the product-market mix has been undertaken. The company's end goal is to develop, manufacture, and market the products best suited to the actual and potential needs of the local (wherever that may be) customer and to the social and economic conditions of the marketplace. There can be subtle differences from country to country and from region to region in the ways a product is used and what customers expect from it.

SUMMARY

The world is truly becoming a global market. Many companies that avoid operating in the global arena are destined for failure. For those willing to undertake the challenges and risks necessary to become multinational organizations, long-term survival and growth are likely outcomes. The purpose of this chapter was to introduce the reader to the opportunities, problems, and challenges involved in global marketing.

Additional Resources

Bahl, Raghaw. *Super Power? The Amazing Race Between China's Hare and India's Tortoise.* NY: Portfolio/Penguin, 2010.

Behravesh, Nariman. *Spin Free Economics: A No-Nonsense Nonpartisan Guide to Today's Global Economic Debates.* NY: McGraw-Hill 2009.

Friedman, Thomas L. *The World is Flat.* NY: Farrar, Straus, and Giroux, 2005.

McEwen, William, Xiaoguang Fang, Zhang Chuanping, and Richard Bunkholder. "Inside the Mind of the Chinese Consumer." *Harvard Business Review,* March 2006, pp. 66–67.

Milanovic, Branko. *The Haves and the Have Nots.* NY: Basic Books, 2011.

Steenkamp, Jan-Benedict E.M., and Inge Geyskens. "How Country Characteristics Affect the Perceived Value of Web Sites." *Journal of Marketing,* July 2006, pp. 136–150.

Key Terms and Concepts

Diamond of national advantage: Developed by Michael Porter, an explanation of a nation's competitive advantage and why some companies and industries become global business leaders.

Direct ownership: An organization's strategy for entering and growing in global markets either through the establishment of a wholly owned subsidiary or through acquisition where it owns 100 percent of the stock.

Exporting: A strategy for entering global markets where a firm produces the product outside the final destination and then ships it there for sale. It is the easiest and most common approach to entering a foreign market.

Franchising: A market entry strategy that is similar to licensing but usually involves longer-term commitments. The franchisor sells limited rights to use its brand name in return for a lump sum and share of the franchisee's future profits. It is more commonly employed by service organizations than manufacturers.

Global company: A company that views the world as one market and employs its resources against the competition in an integrated fashion. It emphasizes cultural similarities across countries and universal consumer needs and wants rather than differences. It standardizes marketing activities where there are cultural similarities and adapts them when the cultures are different.

Joint venture: An organization's entry into a foreign market by sharing management with one or more collaborating foreign firms. Decision making may be shared equally or controlled by one party.

Licensing: Organization's granting of patent rights, trademark rights, and the right to use technological processes to foreign markets. By licensing, an organization does not have to bear the costs and risks associated with actually locating in a foreign market.

Multidomestic company: A company that pursues different strategies in each of its foreign markets. It could have as many different product variations, brand names, and advertising campaigns as countries in which it operates.

Strategic alliance: Partnerships where two or more firms invest in each other to gain competitive advantages on a worldwide versus local level. They are usually of a much longer-term nature than a joint venture.

Analyzing
Marketing Problems
and Cases

Case studies help bridge the gap between classroom learning and the practice of marketing management. They provide us with an opportunity to develop, sharpen, and test our analytical skills at

- Assessing situations.
- Sorting out and organizing key information.
- Asking the right questions.
- Defining opportunities and problems.
- Identifying and evaluating alternative courses of action.
- Interpreting data.
- Evaluating the results of past strategies.
- Developing and defending new strategies.
- Interacting with other managers.
- Making decisions under conditions of uncertainty.
- Critically evaluating the work of others.
- Responding to criticism.

Source: David W. Cravens, Charles W. Lamb, Jr., and Victoria L. Crittenden, *Strategic Marketing Management Cases,* 7th ed. (Burr Ridge, IL: McGraw-Hill/Irwin, 2002), p. 671.

The use of business cases was developed by faculty members of the Harvard Graduate School of Business Administration in the 1920s. Case studies have been widely accepted as one effective way of exposing students to strategic marketing processes.

Basically, cases represent detailed descriptions or reports of business situations. They are often written by a trained observer who was actually involved in the firm or organization and had some dealings with the problems under consideration. Cases generally entail both qualitative and quantitative data that the student must analyze to determine appropriate alternatives and solutions.

The primary purpose of the case method is to introduce a measure of realism into marketing management education. Rather than emphasizing the teaching of concepts, the case method focuses on application of concepts and sound logic to real-world business problems. In this way, students learn to bridge the gap between abstraction and application and to appreciate the value of both.

The primary purpose of this section is to offer a logical format for the analysis of case problems. Although there is no one format that can be successfully applied to all cases, the following framework is intended to be a logical sequence from which to develop sound analyses. This framework is presented for analysis of comprehensive marketing cases; however, the process should also be useful for shorter marketing cases, incidents, and problems.

A CASE ANALYSIS FRAMEWORK

A basic approach to case analysis involves a four-step process. First, the problem is defined. Second, alternative courses of action are formulated to solve the problem. Third, the alternatives are analyzed in terms of their strengths and weaknesses. And fourth, an alternative is accepted and a course of action is recommended. This basic approach is quite useful for students well versed in case analysis, particularly for shorter cases or incidents. However, for the newcomer, this framework may be oversimplified. Thus, the following expanded framework and checklists are intended to aid students in becoming proficient in case and problem analysis.

1. Analyze and Record the Current Situation

Whether the analysis of a firm's problems is done by a manager, student, or paid business consultant, the first step is to analyze the current situation. This does not mean writing up a history of the firm but entails the type of analysis described below. This approach is useful not only for getting a better grip on the situation but also for discovering both real and potential problems—central concerns of any case analysis.

Phase 1: The Environment

The first phase in analyzing a marketing problem or case is to consider the environment in which the firm is operating. The environment can be broken down into a number of different components such as the economic, social, political, and legal areas. Any of these may contain threats to a firm's success or opportunities for improving a firm's situation.

Phase 2: The Industry

The second phase involves analyzing the industry in which the firm operates. A framework provided by Michael Porter includes five competitive forces that need to be considered to do a complete industry analysis.[1] The framework is shown in Figure 1 and includes rivalry among existing competitors, threat of new entrants, and threat of substitute products. In addition, in this framework, buyers and suppliers are included as competitors because they can threaten the profitability of an industry or firm.

While rivalry among existing competitors is an issue in most cases, analysis and strategies for dealing with the other forces can also be critical. This is particularly so when a firm is considering entering a new industry and wants to forecast its potential success. Each of the five competitive forces is discussed below.

Rivalry among Existing Competitors   In most cases and business situations a firm needs to consider the current competitors in its industry in order to develop successful strategies. Strategies such as price competition, advertising battles, sales promotion offers, new product

FIGURE 1   Competitive Forces in an Industry

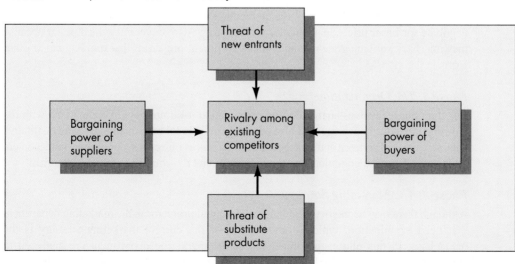

Source: Adapted from Michael E. Porter, "Industry Structure and Competitive Strategy: Keys to Profitability," *Financial Analysts Journal,* July–August 1980, p. 33.

introductions, and increased customer service are commonly used to attract customers from competitors.

To fully analyze existing rivalry, it is important to determine which firms are the major competitors and what are their annual sales, market share, growth profile, and strengths and weaknesses. Also, it is useful to analyze their current and past marketing strategies to try to forecast their likely reactions to a change in a competitive firm's strategy. Finally, it is important to consider any trends or changes in government regulation of an industry or changes in technology that could affect the success of a firm's strategy.

Threat of New Entrants   It is always possible for firms in other industries to try to compete in a new industry. New entrants are more likely in industries that have low entry barriers. *Entry barriers* include such things as a need for large financial resources, high brand equity for existing brands in an industry, or economies of scale obtained by existing firms in an industry. Also, existing firms in an industry may benefit from experience curves; that is, their cumulative experience in producing and marketing a product may reduce their per-unit costs below those of inexperienced firms. In general, the higher the entry barriers, the less likely outside firms are to enter an industry. For example, the entry barriers for starting up a new car company are much higher than for starting up an online software company.

Threat of Substitute Products   In a broad sense, all firms in an industry compete with industries producing substitute products. For example, in cultures where bicycles are the major means of transportation, bicycle manufacturers compete with substitute products such as motor scooters and automobiles. Substitutes limit the potential return in an industry by placing a ceiling on the prices a firm in the industry can profitably charge. The more attractive the price–performance alternative offered by substitutes, the tighter the lid on industry profits. For example, the price of candy, such as Raisinets chocolate-covered raisins, may limit the price that can be charged for granola bars.

Bargaining Power of Suppliers   Suppliers can be a competitive threat in an industry because they can raise the price of raw materials or reduce their quality. Powerful suppliers can reduce the profitability of an industry or firm if companies cannot raise their prices to cover price increases by suppliers. Also, suppliers may be a threat because they may forward integrate into an industry by purchasing a firm that they supply or other firms in the industry.

Bargaining Power of Buyers   Buyers can compete with an industry by forcing prices down, bargaining for higher quality or more services, and playing competitors off against each other. All these tactics can lower the profitability of a firm or industry. For example, because Walmart sells such a large percentage of many companies' products, it can negotiate for lower prices than smaller retailers can. Also, buyers may be a threat because they may backward integrate into an industry by purchasing firms that supply them or other firms in the industry.

Phase 3: The Organization

The third phase involves analysis of the organization itself not only in comparison with the industry and industry averages but also internally in terms of both quantitative and qualitative data. Key areas of concern at this stage are such factors as objectives, constraints, management philosophy, financial condition, and the organizational structure and culture of the firm.

Phase 4: The Marketing Strategy

Although there may be internal personnel or structural problems in the marketing department that need examination, typically an analysis of the current marketing strategy is the next phase. In this phase, the objectives of the marketing department are analyzed in comparison with those of the firm in terms of agreement, soundness, and attainability. Each element of the marketing mix as well as other areas, such as marketing research and

A common criticism of prepared cases goes something like this: "You repeated an awful lot of case material, but you really didn't analyze the case." Yet, at the same time, it is difficult to verbalize exactly what *analysis* means—that is, "I can't explain exactly what it is, but I know it when I see it!"

This is a common problem since the term *analysis* has many definitions and means different things in different contexts. In terms of case analysis, one thing that is clear is that analysis means going beyond simply describing the case information. It includes determining the implications of the case information for developing strategy. This determination may involve careful financial analysis of sales and profit data or thoughtful interpretation of the text of the case.

One way of thinking about analysis involves a series of three steps: synthesis, generalizations, and implications. A brief example of this process follows.

The high growth rate of frozen pizza sales has attracted a number of large food processors, including Pillsbury (Totino's), Quaker Oats (Celeste), American Home Products (Chef Boy-ar-dee), Nestlé (Stouffer's), General Mills (Saluto), and H. J. Heinz (La Pizzeria). The major independents are Jeno's, Tony's, and John's. Jeno's and Totino's are the market leaders, with market shares of about 19 percent each. Celeste and Tony's have about 8 to 9 percent each, and the others have about 5 percent or less.

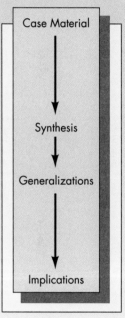

The frozen pizza market is a highly competitive and highly fragmented market.

In markets such as this, attempts to gain market share through lower consumer prices or heavy advertising are likely to be quickly copied by competitors and thus tend not to be very effective.

Lowering consumer prices and spending more on advertising are likely to be poor strategies. Perhaps increasing freezer space in retail outlets could be effective (this might be obtained through trade discounts). A superior product, for example, better-tasting pizza, microwave pizza, or increasing geographic coverage of the market, may be better strategies for obtaining market share.

Note that none of the three analysis steps includes any repetition of the case material. Rather, they all involve abstracting a meaning of the information and, by pairing it with marketing principles, coming up with the strategic implications of the information.

information systems, is analyzed in terms of whether it is internally consistent, synchronized with the goals of the department and firm, and focused on specific target markets. Although cases often are labeled in terms of their primary emphasis, such as "pricing" or "advertising," it is important to analyze the marketing strategy and entire marketing mix, since a change in one element will usually affect the entire marketing program.

In performing the analysis of the current situation, the data should be analyzed carefully to extract the relevant from the superfluous. Many cases contain information that is not relevant to the problem; it is the analyst's job to discard this information to get a clearer picture of the current situation. As the analysis proceeds, a watchful eye must be kept on each phase to determine (1) symptoms of problems, (2) current problems, and (3) potential problems. Symptoms of problems are indicators of a problem but are not problems in and of themselves. For example, a symptom of a problem may be a decline in sales in a particular sales territory. However, the problem is the root cause of the decline in sales—perhaps the field representative quit making sales calls and is relying on phone orders only.

The following is a checklist of the types of questions that should be asked when performing the analysis of the current situation.

Checklist for Analyzing the Current Situation

Phase 1: The Environment

1. What is the state of the economy and are there any trends that could affect the industry, firm, or marketing strategy?
2. What are current trends in cultural and social values and how do these affect the industry, firm, or marketing strategy?
3. What are current political values and trends and how do they affect the industry, firm, or marketing strategy?
4. Is there any current or pending federal, state, or local legislation that could change the industry, firm, or marketing strategy?
5. Overall, are there any threats or opportunities in the environment that could influence the industry, firm, or marketing strategy?

Phase 2: The Industry

1. What industry is the firm in?
2. Which firms are the major competitors in the industry and what are their annual sales, market share, and growth profile?
3. What strategies have competitors in the industry been using and what has been their success with them?
4. What are the relative strengths and weaknesses of competitors in the industry?
5. Is there a threat of new competitors coming into the industry and what are the major entry barriers?
6. Are there any substitute products for the industry and what are their advantages and disadvantages compared to this industry's products?
7. How much bargaining power do suppliers have in this industry and what is its impact on the firm and industry profits?
8. How much bargaining power do buyers have in this industry and what is its impact on the firm and industry profits?

Phase 3: The Organization

1. What are the objectives of the organization? Are they clearly stated? Attainable?
2. What are the strengths of the organization? Managerial expertise? Financial? Copyrights or patents?
3. What are the constraints and weaknesses of the organization?
4. Are there any real or potential sources of dysfunctional conflict in the structure of the organization?
5. How is the marketing department structured in the organization?

Phase 4: The Marketing Strategy

1. What are the objectives of the marketing strategy? Are they clearly stated? Are they consistent with the objectives of the firm? Is the entire marketing mix structured to meet these objectives?
2. What marketing concepts are at issue in the current strategy? Is the marketing strategy well planned and laid out? Is the strategy consistent with sound marketing principles? If the strategy takes exception to marketing principles, is there a good reason for it?

3. To what target market is the strategy directed? Is it well defined? Is the market large enough to be profitably served? Does the market have long-run potential?

4. What competitive advantage does the marketing strategy offer? If none, what can be done to gain a competitive advantage in the marketplace?

5. What products are being sold? What are the width, depth, and consistency of the firm's product lines? Does the firm need new products to fill out its product line? Should any product be deleted? What is the profitability of the various products?

6. What promotion mix is being used? Is promotion consistent with the products and product images? What could be done to improve the promotion mix?

7. What channels of distribution are being used? Do they deliver the product at the right time and right place to meet customer needs? Are the channels typical of those used in the industry? Could channels be made more efficient?

8. What pricing strategies are being used? How do prices compare with similar products of other firms? How are prices determined?

9. Are marketing research and information systematically integrated into the marketing strategy? Is the overall marketing strategy internally consistent?

The relevant information from this preliminary analysis is now formalized and recorded. At this point the analyst must be mindful of the difference between facts and opinions. Facts are objective statements, such as financial data, whereas opinions are subjective interpretations of facts or situations. The analyst must make certain not to place too much emphasis on opinions and to carefully consider any variables that may bias such opinions.

Regardless of how much information is contained in the case or how much additional information is collected, the analyst usually finds that it is impossible to specify a complete framework for the current situation. At this point, assumptions must be made. Clearly, since each analyst may make different assumptions, it is critical that assumptions be explicitly stated. When presenting a case, the analyst may wish to distribute copies of the assumption list to all class members. This avoids confusion about how the analyst perceives the current situation, and others can evaluate the reasonableness and necessity of the assumptions.

2. Analyze and Record Problems and Their Core Elements

After careful analysis, problems and their core elements should be explicitly stated and listed in order of importance. Finding and recording problems and their core elements can be difficult. It is not uncommon when reading a case for the first time for the student to view the case as a description of a situation in which there are no problems. However, careful analysis should reveal symptoms, which lead to problem recognition.

Recognizing and recording problems and their core elements is most critical for a meaningful case analysis. Obviously, if the root problems are not explicitly stated and understood, the remainder of the case analysis has little merit because the true issues are not being dealt with. The following checklist of questions is designed to assist in performing this step of the analysis.

Checklist for Analyzing Problems and Their Core Elements

1. What is the primary problem in the case? What are the secondary problems?

2. What proof exists that these are the central issues? How much of this proof is based on facts? On opinions? On assumptions?

3. What symptoms are there that suggest these are the real problems in the case?

4. How are the problems, as defined, related? Are they independent or are they the result of a deeper problem?

5. What are the ramifications of these problems in the short run? In the long run?

It is possible that a case could describe a company that is doing everything right and there are no serious problems in it. However, most of the time, analysis of a case will reveal one or more important shortcomings in the organization's marketing strategy. Below is a sample list of mistakes that marketers make that could be in a case.

1. The organization failed to offer products that customers want either because it did no research, did poor research, failed to interpret the research appropriately, or failed to react to it appropriately.
2. The organization underestimated the ability of competitors to gain market share and failed to react appropriately to successful competitive strategies.
3. The organization failed to react appropriately to changes in other aspects of the environment such as social, political, or legal changes.
4. The organization failed to keep up with or underestimated the impact of competitors' innovations in production and product development.
5. The organization did not position its products on dimensions that customers care about.
6. The organization overestimated the likely success of new products because of faulty sales forecasts or wishful thinking.
7. The organization expanded too rapidly into new markets or offered its products in too many outlets in existing markets.
8. The organization failed to raise prices when warranted or raised prices too much or too frequently.
9. The organization offered an inconsistent marketing mix that failed to provide a clear image of the product in the minds of customers.
10. The organization relied on promotion to sell an inferior product.
11. The organization failed to use the best channels to reach customers.
12. The organization underestimated the cost of competing effectively in an industry.

3. Formulate, Evaluate, and Record Alternative Courses of Action

This step is concerned with the question of what can be done to resolve the problem defined in the previous step. Generally, a number of alternative courses of action are available that could potentially help alleviate the problem condition. Three to seven are usually a reasonable number of alternatives to work with. Another approach is to brainstorm as many alternatives as possible initially and then reduce the list to a workable number.

Sound logic and reasoning are very important in this step. It is critical to avoid alternatives that could potentially alleviate the problem, but would create a greater new problem or require greater resources than the firm has at its disposal.

After serious analysis and listing of a number of alternatives, the next task is to evaluate them in terms of their costs and benefits. Costs are any output or effort the firm must exert to implement the alternative. Benefits are any input or value received by the firm. Costs to be considered are time, money, other resources, and opportunity costs; benefits are such things as sales, profits, brand equity, and customer satisfaction. The following checklist provides a guideline of questions to be used when performing this phase of the analysis.

Checklist for Formulating and Evaluating Alternative Courses of Action

1. What possible alternatives exist for solving the firm's problems?
2. What limits are there on the possible alternatives? Competence? Resources? Management preference? Ethical responsibility? Legal restrictions?

3. What major alternatives are now available to the firm? What marketing concepts are involved that affect these alternatives?

4. Are the listed alternatives reasonable, given the firm's situation? Are they logical? Are the alternatives consistent with the goals of the marketing program? Are they consistent with the firm's objectives?

5. What are the financial and other costs of each alternative? What are the benefits? What are the advantages and disadvantages of each alternative?

6. Which alternative best solves the problem and minimizes the creation of new problems, given the above constraints?

4. Select and Record the Chosen Alternative and Implementation Details

In light of the previous analysis, the alternative is now selected that best solves the problem with a minimum creation of new problems. It is important to record the logic and reasoning that precipitated the selection of a particular alternative. This includes articulating not only why the alternative was selected but also why the other alternatives were not selected.

No analysis is complete without an action-oriented decision and plan for implementing the decision. The accompanying checklist indicates the type of questions that should be answered in this stage of analysis.

Checklist for Selecting and Implementing the Chosen Alternative

1. What must be done to implement the alternative?
2. What personnel will be involved? What are the responsibilities of each?
3. When and where will the alternative be implemented?
4. What will be the probable outcome?
5. How will the success or failure of the alternative be measured?

PITFALLS TO AVOID IN CASE ANALYSIS

Following is a summary of some of the most common errors analysts make when analyzing cases. When evaluating your analysis or those of others, this list provides a useful guide for spotting potential shortcomings.

1. *Inadequate definition of the problem.* By far the most common error made in case analysis is attempting to recommend courses of action without first adequately defining or understanding the core problems. Whether presented orally or in a written report, a case analysis must begin with a focus on the central issues and problems represented in the case situation. Closely related is the error of analyzing symptoms without determining the root problem.

2. *The search for "the answer."* In case analysis, there are usually no clear-cut solutions. Keep in mind that the objective of case studies is learning through discussion and exploration. There is usually no one "official" or "correct" answer to a case. Rather, there are usually several reasonable alternative solutions.

3. *Not enough information.* Analysts often complain there is not enough information in some cases to make a good decision. However, there is justification for not presenting *all* of the information in a case. As in real life, a marketing manager or consultant seldom has all the information necessary to make an optimal decision. Thus, reasonable assumptions have to be made, and the challenge is to find intelligent solutions in spite of the limited information.

4. *Use of generalities.* In analyzing cases, specific recommendations are necessarily not generalities. For example, a suggestion to increase the price is a generality; a suggestion to increase the price by $1.07 is a specific.

A useful approach to gaining an understanding of the situation an organization is facing at a particular time is called *SWOT analysis.* SWOT stands for the organization's *strengths* and *weaknesses* and the *opportunities* and *threats* it faces in the environment. Below are some issues an analyst should address in performing a SWOT analysis.

POTENTIAL STRENGTHS AND COMPETITIVE ASSETS

- Competencies that are well matched to industry key success factors.
- Strong financial condition; ample financial resources to grow the business.
- Strong brand-name image/company reputation.
- Attractive customer base.
- Proprietary technology/superior technological skills/important patents.
- Superior intellectual capital.
- Skills in advertising and promotion.
- Strong bargaining power over suppliers or buyers.
- Product innovation capabilities.
- Proven capabilities in improving production processes.
- Good supply chain management capabilities.
- Good customer service capabilities.
- Superior product quality.
- Wide geographic coverage and/or strong global distribution capability.
- Alliances/joint ventures that provide access to valuable technology, competencies, and/or attractive geographic markets.
- A product that is strongly differentiated from those of rivals.
- Cost advantages over rivals.
- Core competencies in _____.
- A distinctive competence in _____.
- Resources that are hard to copy and for which there are no good substitutes.

POTENTIAL WEAKNESSES AND COMPETITIVE DEFICIENCIES

- Competencies that are not well-matched to industry key success factors.
- In the wrong strategic group.
- Losing market share because _____.
- Lack of attention to customer needs.
- Weak balance sheet, short on financial resources to grow the firm, too much debt.
- Higher overall unit costs relative to those of key competitors.
- Weak or unproven product innovation capabilities.
- A product/service with ho-hum attributes or features inferior to the offerings of rivals.
- Too narrow a product line relative to rivals.
- Weak brand image or reputation.
- Weaker dealer network than key rivals and/or lack of adequate global distribution capability.
- Behind on product quality, R&D, and/or technological know-how.
- Lack of management depth.
- Inferior intellectual capital relative to rivals.
- Plagued with internal operating problems or obsolete facilities.
- Too much underutilized plant capacity.
- No well-developed or proven core competencies.
- No distinctive competencies or competitively superior resources.

- Resources that are readily copied or for which there are good substitutes.
- No clear strategic direction.

POTENTIAL MARKET OPPORTUNITIES

- Openings to win market share from rivals.
- Sharply rising buyer demand for the industry's product.
- Serving additional customer groups or market segments.
- Expanding into new geographic markets.
- Expanding the company's product line to meet a broader range of customer needs.
- Utilizing existing company skills or technological know how to enter new product lines or new businesses.
- Online sales via the Internet.
- Integrating forward or backward.
- Falling trade barriers in attractive foreign markets.
- Acquiring rival firms or companies with attractive technological expertise or capabilities.
- Entering into alliances or joint ventures to expand the firm's market coverage or boost its competitive capability.
- Openings to exploit emerging new technologies.

POTENTIAL EXTERNAL THREATS TO A COMPANY'S FUTURE PROFITABILITY

- Increasing intensity of competition among industry rivals—may squeeze profit margins.
- Slowdowns in market growth.
- Likely entry of potent new competitors.
- Loss of sales, to substitute products.
- Growing bargaining power of customers or suppliers.
- Vulnerability to industry driving forces.
- Shift in buyer needs and tastes away from the industry's product.
- Adverse demographic changes that threaten to curtail demand for the industry's product.
- Adverse economic conditions that threaten critical suppliers or distributers.
- Changes in technology—particularly disruptive technology that can undermine the company's distinctive competencies.
- Restrictive foreign trade policies.
- Costly new regulatory requirements.
- Tight credit conditions.
- Rising prices on energy or other key inputs.

Source: Arthur A. Thompson, Margaret A. Peteraf, John E. Gamble, and A. J. Strickland III, *Crafting and Executing Strategy*, 18th ed. (Burr Ridge, IL: McGraw-Hill/Irwin, 2012), p. 106.

    5. *A different situation.* Analysts sometimes exert considerable time and effort contending that "If the situation were different, I'd know what course of action to take" or "If the marketing manager hadn't already fouled things up so badly, the firm wouldn't have a problem." Such reasoning ignores the fact that the events in the case have already happened and cannot be changed. Even though analysis or criticism of past events is necessary in diagnosing the problem, in the end, the present situation must be addressed and decisions must be made based on the given situations.

    6. *Narrow vision analysis.* Although cases are often labeled as a specific type of case, such as "pricing," "product," and so forth, this does not mean that other marketing variables

should be ignored. Too often analysts ignore the effects that a change in one marketing element will have on the others.

7. *Realism.* Too often analysts become so focused on solving a particular problem that their solutions become totally unrealistic. For instance, suggesting a $1 million advertising program for a firm with a capital structure of $50,000 is an unrealistic solution.

8. *The marketing research solution.* A quite common but unsatisfactory solution to case problems is marketing research; for example, "The firm should do this or that type of marketing research to find a solution to its problem." Although marketing research may be helpful as an intermediary step in some cases, marketing research does not solve problems or make decisions. In cases where marketing research is recommended, the cost and potential benefits should be fully specified in the case analysis.

9. *Rehashing the case material.* Analysts sometimes spend considerable effort rewriting a two- or three-page history of the firm as presented in the case. This is unnecessary since the instructor and other analysts are already familiar with this information.

10. *Premature conclusions.* Analysts sometimes jump to premature conclusions instead of waiting until their analysis is completed. Too many analysts jump to conclusions upon first reading the case and then proceed to interpret everything in the case as justifying their conclusions, even factors logically against it.

COMMUNICATING CASE ANALYSES

The final concern in case analysis deals with communicating the results of the analysis. The most comprehensive analysis has little value if it is not communicated effectively. Case analyses are communicated through two primary media—the written report and the oral presentation.

The Written Report

Since the structure of the written report will vary by the type of case analyzed, the purpose of this section is not to present a "one and only" way of writing up a case; it is to present some useful generalizations to aid analysts in case write-ups.

A good written report starts with an outline that organizes the structure of the analysis in a logical manner. The following is a general outline for a marketing case report.

  I. Title Page
 II. Table of Contents
III. Executive Summary (one- to two-page summary of the analysis and recommendations)
IV. Situation Analysis
   A. *Environment*
     1. Economic conditions and trends
     2. Cultural and social values and trends
     3. Political and legal issues
     4. Summary of environmental opportunities and threats
     5. Implications for strategy development
   B. *Industry*
     1. Classification and definition of industry
     2. Analysis of existing competitors
     3. Analysis of potential new entrants
     4. Analysis of substitute products
     5. Analysis of suppliers
     6. Analysis of buyers
     7. Summary of industry opportunities and threats
     8. Implications for strategy development

1. Read the case quickly to get an overview of the situation.
2. Read the case again thoroughly. Underline relevant information and take notes on potential areas of concern.
3. Review outside sources of information on the environment and the industry. Record relevant information and the source of this information.
4. Perform comparative analysis of the firm with the industry and industry averages.
5. Analyze the firm.
6. Analyze the marketing program.
7. Record the current situation in terms of relevant environmental, industry, firm, and marketing strategy parameters.
8. Make and record necessary assumptions to complete the situational framework.
9. Determine and record the major issues, problems, and their core elements.
10. Record proof that these are the major issues.
11. Record potential courses of action.
12. Evaluate each initially to determine constraints that preclude acceptability.
13. Evaluate remaining alternatives in terms of costs and benefits.
14. Record analysis of alternatives.
15. Select an alternative.
16. Record alternative and defense of its selection.
17. Record the who, what, when, where, how, and why of the alternative and its implementation.

C. *Organization*
 1. Objectives and constraints
 2. Financial condition
 3. Management philosophy
 4. Organizational structure
 5. Organizational culture
 6. Summary of the firm's strengths and weaknesses
 7. Implications for strategy development
D. *Marketing strategy*
 1. Objectives and constraints
 2. Analysis of sales, profits, and market share
 3. Analysis of target market(s)
 4. Analysis of marketing mix variables
 5. Summary of marketing strategy's strengths and weaknesses
 6. Implications for strategy development

V. **Problems Found in Situation Analysis**
 A. *Statement of primary problem(s)*
  1. Evidence of problem(s)
  2. Effects of problem(s)
 B. *Statement of secondary problem(s)*
  1. Evidence of problem(s)
  2. Effects of problem(s)

VI. **Strategic Alternatives for Solving Problems**
 A. *Description of strategic alternative 1*
  1. Benefits of alternative 1
  2. Costs of alternative 1

        B. *Description of strategic alternative 2*
           1. Benefits of alternative 2
           2. Costs of alternative 2
        C. *Description of strategic alternative 3*
           1. Benefits of alternative 3
           2. Costs of alternative 3
  VII. Selection of Strategic Alternative and Implementation
        A. *Statement of selected strategy*
        B. *Justification for selection of strategy*
        C. *Description of implementation of strategy*
 VIII. Summary
   IX. Appendices
        A. *Financial analysis*
        B. *Technical analysis*

Writing the case report entails filling out the details of the outline in prose form. Of course, not every case report requires all the headings listed above, and different headings may be required for some cases. Like any other skill, it takes practice to determine the appropriate headings and approach for writing particular cases. However, good case reports flow logically from topic to topic, are clearly written, are based on solid situation analysis, and demonstrate sound strategic thinking.

The Oral Presentation

Case analyses are often presented by an individual or team. As with the written report, a good outline is critical, and it is often useful to hand out the outline to each class member. Although there is no best way to present a case or to divide responsibility between team members, simply reading the written report is unacceptable because it encourages boredom and interferes with all-important class discussion.

The use of visual aids can be quite helpful in presenting class analyses. However, simply presenting financial statements contained in the case is a poor use of visual media. On the other hand, graphs of sales and profit curves can be more easily interpreted and can be quite useful for making specific points.

Oral presentation of cases is particularly helpful to analysts for learning the skill of speaking to a group. In particular, the ability to handle objections and disagreements without antagonizing others is a skill worth developing.

SUMMARY

From the discussion it should be obvious that good case analyses require a major commitment of time and effort. Individuals must be highly motivated and willing to get involved in the analysis and discussion if they expect to learn and succeed in a course where cases are used. Persons with only passive interest who perform "night before" analyses cheat themselves out of valuable learning experiences that can aid them in their careers.

Additional Resources

Aaker, David A. *Strategic Market Management.* 9th ed. Hoboken, NJ: Wiley, 2009.

Cravens, David W; Charles W. Lamb, Jr.; and Victoria L. Crittenden. *Strategic Marketing Management Cases.* 7th ed. Burr Ridge, IL: McGraw-Hill/Irwin, 2002, Appendix B.

Ellet, William. *The Case Study Handbook.* Boston: Harvard Business School Press, 2007.

Kevin, Roger A., and Robert A. Peterson. *Strategic Marketing Problems.* 12th ed. Upper Saddle River, NJ: Prentice Hall, 2010.

Marshall, Greg W., and Mark W. Johnston. *Marketing Management.* Burr Ridge, IL: McGraw-Hill/Irwin, 2010.

Financial Analysis
for Marketing Decisions

FINANCIAL ANALYSIS

Financial analysis is an important aspect of strategic marketing planning and should be an integral part of marketing problem and case analysis. In this section, we present several financial tools that are useful for analyzing marketing problems and cases. First, we investigate break-even analysis, which is concerned with determining the number of units or dollar sales, or both, necessary to break even on a project or to obtain a given level of profits. Second, we illustrate net present value analysis, which is a somewhat more sophisticated tool for analyzing marketing alternatives. Finally, we investigate ratio analysis, which can be a useful tool for determining the financial condition of the firm, including its ability to invest in a new or modified marketing program.

Break-Even Analysis

Break-even analysis is a common tool for investigating the potential profitability of a marketing alternative. The *break-even point* is that level of sales in either units or sales dollars at which a firm covers all of its costs. In other words, it is the level at which total sales revenue just equals the total costs necessary to achieve these sales.

To compute the break-even point, an analyst must have or be able to obtain three values. First, the analyst needs to know the selling price per unit of the product (SP). For example, suppose the Ajax Company plans to sell its new electric car through its own dealerships at a retail price of $5,000. Second, the analyst needs to know the level of fixed costs (FC). Fixed costs are all costs relevant to the project that do not change regardless of how many units are produced or sold. For instance, whether Ajax produces and sells 1 or 100,000 cars, Ajax executives will receive their salaries, land must be purchased for a plant, a plant must be constructed, and machinery must be purchased. Other fixed costs include such things as interest, lease payments, and sinking fund payments. Suppose Ajax has totaled all of its fixed costs and the sum is $1.5 million. Third, the analyst must know the variable costs per unit produced (VC). As the name implies, variable costs are those that vary directly with the number of units produced. For example, each car Ajax produces involves costs for raw materials and components to build the car, such as batteries, electric motors, steel bodies, and tires; labor costs for operating employees; and machine costs, such as electricity and welding rods. Suppose Ajax totals these costs and the variable costs for each car produced equal $3,500. With this information, the analyst can now determine the break-even point, which is the number of units that must be sold to just cover the cost of producing the cars. The break-even point is determined by dividing total fixed costs by the *contribution margin*. The contribution margin is simply the difference between the selling price per unit (SP) and variable costs per unit (VC). Algebraically,

$$BEP_{(in\ units)} = \frac{\text{Total fixed costs}}{\text{Contribution margin}}$$

$$= \frac{FC}{SP - VC}$$

Substituting the Ajax estimates,

$$BEP_{(in\ units)} = \frac{1,500,000}{5,000 - 3,500}$$

$$= \frac{1,500,000}{1,500}$$

$$= 1,000 \text{ units}$$

In other words, the Ajax Company must sell 1,000 cars to just break even (i.e., for total sales revenue to cover total costs).

Alternatively, the analyst may want to know the break-even point in terms of dollar sales volume. Of course, if the preceding analysis has been done, one could simply multiply the $BEP_{\text{(in units)}}$ times the selling price to determine the break-even sales volume (i.e., 1,000 units $\times$ \$5,000/unit = \$5 million). However, the $BEP_{\text{(in dollars)}}$ can be computed directly, using the formula below:

$$BEP_{\text{(in dollars)}} = \frac{FC}{1 - \dfrac{VC}{SP}}$$

$$= \frac{1,500,000}{1 - \dfrac{3,500}{5,000}}$$

$$= \frac{1,500,000}{1 - .7}$$

$$= \$5,000,000$$

Thus, Ajax must produce and sell 1,000 cars, which equals \$5 million sales, to break even. Of course, firms do not want to just break even but want to make a profit. The logic of break-even analysis can easily be extended to include profits (P). Suppose Ajax decided that a 20 percent return on fixed costs would make the project worth the investment. Thus, Ajax would need 20% $\times$ \$1,500,000 = \$300,000 before-tax profit. To calculate how many units Ajax must sell to achieve this level of profits, the profit figure (P) is added to fixed costs in the above formulas. (We will label the break-even point as BEP' to show that we are now computing unit and sales levels to obtain a given profit level.) In the Ajax example:

$$BEP'_{\text{(in units)}} = \frac{FC + P}{SP - VC}$$

$$= \frac{1,500,000 + 300,000}{5,000 - 3,500}$$

$$= \frac{1,800,000}{1,500}$$

$$= 1,200 \text{ units}$$

In terms of dollars,

$$BEP'_{\text{(in dollars)}} = \frac{FC + P}{1 - \dfrac{VC}{SP}}$$

$$= \frac{1,500,000 + 300,000}{1 - \dfrac{3,500}{5,000}}$$

$$= \frac{1,800,000}{1 - .7}$$

$$= \$6,000,000$$

Thus, Ajax must produce and sell 1,200 cars (sales volume of $6 million) to obtain a 20 percent return on fixed costs. Analysis must now be directed at determining whether a given marketing plan can be expected to produce sales of at least this level. If the answer is yes, the project would appear to be worth investing in. If not, Ajax should seek other opportunities.

Net Present Value Analysis

The profit-oriented marketing manager must understand that the capital invested in new products has a cost. It is a basic principle in business that whoever wishes to use capital must pay for its use. Dollars invested in new products could be diverted to other uses—to pay off debts, pay dividends to stockholders, or buy U.S. Treasury bonds that would yield economic benefits to the corporation. If, on the other hand, all of the dollars used to finance a new product have to be borrowed from lenders outside the corporation, interest has to be paid on the loan.

One of the best ways to analyze the financial aspects of a marketing alternative is *net present value* analysis. This method employs a discounted cash flow, which takes into account the time value of money and its price to the borrower. The following example will illustrate this method.

To compute the net present value of an investment proposal, the cost of capital must be estimated. The cost of capital can be defined as the required rate of return on an investment that would leave the owners of the firm as well off as if the project was not undertaken. Thus, it is the minimum percentage return on investment that a project must make to be worth undertaking. There are many methods of estimating the cost of capital. However, because these methods are not the concern of this text, we will simply assume that the cost of capital for the Ajax Corporation has been determined to be 10 percent.[1] Again, it should be noted that once the cost of capital is determined, it becomes the minimum rate of return required for an investment—a type of cutoff point. However, some firms in selecting their new product investments select a minimum rate of return that is above the cost of capital figure to allow for errors in judgment or measurement.

The Ajax Corporation is considering a proposal to market instant-developing movie film. After conducting considerable marketing research, sales were projected to be $1 million per year. In addition, the finance department compiled the following information concerning the projects:

New equipment needed	$700,000
Useful life of equipment	10 years
Depreciation	10% per year
Salvage value	$100,000
Cost of goods and expenses	$700,000 per year
Cost of capital	10%
Tax rate	50%

To compute the net present value of this project, the net cash flow for each year of the project must first be determined. This can be done in four steps:

1. Sales − Cost of goods and expenses = Gross income or

$$\$1,000,000 - 700,000 = \$300,000$$

2. Gross income − Depreciation = Taxable income or

$$\$300,000 - (10\% \times 600,000) = \$240,000$$

3. Taxable income − Tax = Net income or

$240,000 − (50% × 240,000) = $120,000

4. Net income + Depreciation = Net cash flow or

$120,000 + 60,000 = $180,000 per year

Because the cost of capital is 10 percent, this figure is used to discount the net cash flows for each year. To illustrate, the $180,000 received at the end of the first year would be discounted by the factor $1/(1 + 0.10)$, which would be $180,000 \times 0.9091 = $163,638$; the $180,000 received at the end of the second year would be discounted by the factor $1/(1 + 0.10)^2$, which would be $180,000 \times 0.8264 = $148,752$, and so on. (Most finance textbooks have present value tables that can be used to simplify the computations.) The table that follows shows the present value computations for the 10-year project. It should be noted that the net cash flow for year 10 is $280,000 because there is an additional $100,000 inflow from salvage value.

Thus, at a discount rate of 10 percent, the present value of the net cash flow from new product investment is greater than the $700,000 outlay required, and so the decision can be considered profitable by this standard. Here the net present value is $444,560, which is the difference between the $700,000 investment outlay and the $1,144,560 discounted cash

Year	Net Cash Flow	0.10 Discount Factor	Present Value
1	$ 180,000	0.9091	$ 163,638
2	180,000	0.8264	148,752
3	180,000	0.7513	135,234
4	180,000	0.6830	122,940
5	180,000	0.6209	111,762
6	180,000	0.5645	101,610
7	180,000	0.5132	92,376
8	180,000	0.4665	83,970
9	180,000	0.4241	76,338
10	280,000	0.3855	107,940
Total	$1,900,000		$1,144,560

flow. The *present value ratio* is nothing more than the present value of the net cash flow divided by the cash investment. If this ratio is 1 or larger than 1, the project would be profitable for the firm to invest in.

There are many other measures of investment worth, but only one additional method will be discussed. It is the very popular and easily understood payback method. *Payback* refers to the amount of time required to pay back the original outlay from the cash flows. Staying with the example, the project is expected to produce a stream of cash proceeds that is constant from year to year, so the payback period can be determined by dividing the investment outlay by this annual cash flow. Dividing $700,000 by $180,000, the payback period is approximately 3.9 years. Firms often set a maximum payback period before a project will be accepted. For example, many firms refuse to take on a project if the payback period exceeds three years.

This example should illustrate the difficulty in evaluating marketing investments from a profitability or economic worth standpoint. The most challenging problem is that of developing accurate cash flow estimates because there are many possible alternatives, such as price of the product and channels of distribution, and the consequences of each alternative

Years	4%	6%	8%	10%	12%	14%
1	.9615	.9434	.9259	.9091	.8929	.8772
2	.9246	.8900	.8573	.8264	.7972	.7695
3	.8890	.8396	.7938	.7513	.7118	.6750
4	.8548	.7941	.7350	.6830	.6355	.5921
5	.8219	.7473	.6806	.6209	.5674	.5194
6	.7903	.7050	.6302	.5645	.5066	.4556
7	.7599	.6651	.5835	.5132	.4523	.3996
8	.7307	.6274	.5403	.4665	.4039	.3506
9	.7026	.5919	.5002	.4241	.3606	.3075
10	.6756	.5584	.4632	.3855	.3220	.2697

must be forecast in terms of sales volumes, selling costs, and other expenses. In spite of all the problems, management must evaluate the economic worth of new product and other decisions, not only to reduce some of the guesswork and ambiguity surrounding marketing strategy development but also to reinforce the objective of making profits.

Ratio Analysis

Firms' income statements and balance sheets provide a wealth of information that is useful for developing marketing strategies. Frequently, this information is included in marketing cases, yet analysts often have no convenient way of interpreting the financial position of the firm to make sound marketing decisions. Ratio analysis provides the analyst an easy and efficient method for investigating a firm's financial position by comparing the firm's ratios across time or with ratios of similar firms in the industry or with industry averages.

Ratio analysis involves four basic steps:

1. Choose the appropriate ratios.
2. Compute the ratios.
3. Compare the ratios.
4. Check for problems or opportunities.

1. Choose the Appropriate Ratios

The five basic types of financial ratios are (1) liquidity ratios, (2) asset management ratios, (3) profitability ratios, (4) debt management ratios, and (5) market value ratios.[2] While calculating ratios of all five types is useful, liquidity, asset management, and profitability ratios provide information that is most directly relevant for marketing decision making. Although many ratios can be calculated in each of these groups, we have selected two of the most commonly used and readily available ratios in each group to illustrate the process.

Liquidity Ratios   One of the first considerations in analyzing a marketing problem is the liquidity of the firm. *Liquidity* refers to the ability of the firm to pay its short-term obligations. If a firm cannot meet its short-term obligations, there is little that can be done until this problem is resolved. Simply stated, recommendations to increase advertising, to do marketing research, or to develop new products are of little value if the firm is about to go bankrupt.

1. http://finance.yahoo.com/. Input the company symbol to receive financial ratios and other useful information. Under the "Company" heading, "Key statistics," "Competitors," and "Industry" are most useful for comparative ratio analyses.
2. *Annual Statement Studies.* Published by Robert Morris Associates, this work includes 11 financial ratios computed annually for over 150 lines of business. Each line of business is divided into four size categories.
3. *Industry Norms and Key Business Ratios.* Published by Dun & Bradstreet, this work provides a variety of industry ratios.
4. *Almanac of Business and Industrial Financial Ratios.* The almanac, published by Prentice Hall, Inc., lists industry averages for 22 financial ratios. Approximately 170 businesses and industries are listed.
5. *Quarterly Financial Report for Manufacturing Corporations.* This work, published jointly by the Federal Trade Commission and the Securities and Exchange Commission, contains balance-sheet and income-statement information by industry groupings and by asset-size categories.
6. Trade associations and individual companies often compute ratios for their industries and make them available to analysts.

The two most commonly used ratios for investigating liquidity are the *current ratio* and the *quick ratio* (or "acid test"). The current ratio is determined by dividing current assets by current liabilities and is a measure of the overall ability of the firm to meet its current obligations. A common rule of thumb is that current ratio should be about 2:1.

The quick ratio is determined by subtracting inventory from current assets and dividing the remainder by current liabilities. Since inventory is the least liquid current asset, the quick ratio deals with assets that are most readily available for meeting short-term (one-year) obligations. A common rule of thumb is that the quick ratio should be at least 1:1.

Asset Management Ratios   Asset management ratios investigate how well the firm handles its assets. For marketing problems, two of the most useful asset management ratios are concerned with *inventory turnover* and *total asset utilization*. The inventory turnover ratio is determined by dividing sales by inventories.[3] If the firm is not turning its inventory over as rapidly as other firms, it suggests that too much money is being tied up in unproductive or obsolete inventory. In addition, if the firm's turnover ratio is decreasing over time, it suggests that there may be a problem in the marketing plan, because inventory is not being sold as rapidly as it had been in the past. One problem with this ratio is that, since sales usually are recorded at market prices and inventory usually is recorded at cost, the ratio may overstate turnover. Thus, some analysts prefer to use cost of sales rather than sales in computing turnover. We will use cost of sales in our analysis.

A second useful asset management ratio is total asset utilization. It is calculated by dividing sales by total assets and is a measure of how productively the firm's assets have been used to generate sales. If this ratio is well below industry figures, it suggests that the firm's marketing strategies are less effective than those of competitors or that some unproductive assets need to be eliminated.

Profitability Ratios   Profitability is a major goal of marketing and is an important measure of the quality of a firm's marketing strategies. Two key profitability ratios are *profit margin on sales* and *return on total assets.* Profit margin on sales is determined by dividing profit before tax by sales. Serious questions about the firm and marketing plan should be raised if profit margin on sales is declining across time or is well below other firms in the industry.

FIGURE 1   Balance Sheet and Income Statement for Ajax Home Computer Company

Ajax Home Computer Company
Balance Sheet
March 31, 2012
(in thousands)

Assets		Liabilities and Stockholders' Equity	
Cash	$ 30	Trade accounts payable	$ 150
Marketable securities	40	Accrued	.25
Accounts receivable	.200	Notes payable	.100
Inventory	.430	Accrued income tax	.40
Total current assets	.700	Total current liabilities	.315
Plant and equipment	.1,000	Bonds	.500
Land	.500	Debentures	. 85
Other investments	.200	Stockholders' equity	.1,500
Total assets	.$2,400	Total liabilities and stockholders' equity	.$2,400

Ajax Home Computer Company
Income Statement
for the 12-Month Period Ending March 31, 2012
(in thousands)

Sales	.$3,600
Cost of sales	
Labor and materials	.2,000
Depreciation	.200
Selling expenses	.500
General and administrative expenses	.80
Total cost	.2,780
Net operating income	.820
Less interest expense	
Interest on notes	.20
Interest on debentures	.200
Interest on bonds	.300
Total interest	.520
Profit before tax	.300
Federal income tax (@40%)	.120
Net profit after tax	$ 180

Return on total assets is determined by dividing profit before tax by total assets. This ratio is the return on the investment for the entire firm.

2. Compute the Ratios

The next step in ratio analysis is to compute the ratios. Figure 1 presents the balance sheet and income statement for the Ajax Home Computer Company. These six ratios can be calculated from the Ajax balance sheet and income statement as follows:

Liquidity ratios:

$$\text{Current ratio} = \frac{\text{Current assets}}{\text{Current liabilities}} = \frac{700}{315} = 2.2$$

$$\text{Quick ratio} = \frac{\text{Current assets} - \text{Inventory}}{\text{Current liabilities}} = \frac{270}{315} = .86$$

Asset management ratios:

$$\text{Inventory turnover} = \frac{\text{Cost of sales}}{\text{Inventory}} = \frac{2,780}{430} = 6.5$$

$$\text{Total asset utilization} = \frac{\text{Sales}}{\text{Total assets}} = \frac{3,600}{2,400} = 1.5$$

Profitability ratios:

$$\text{Profit margin on sales} = \frac{\text{Profit before tax}}{\text{Sales}} = \frac{300}{3,600} = 8.3\%$$

$$\text{Return on total assests} = \frac{\text{Profit before tax}}{\text{Total assets}} = \frac{300}{2,400} = 12.5\%$$

3. Compare the Ratios

While rules of thumb are useful for analyzing ratios, it cannot be overstated that comparison of ratios is always the preferred approach. The ratios computed for a firm can be compared in at least three ways. First, they can be compared over time to see if there are any favorable or unfavorable trends in the firm's financial position. Second, they can be compared with the ratios of other firms of similar size in the industry. Third, they can be compared with industry averages to get an overall idea of the firm's relative financial position in the industry.

Figure 2 provides a summary of the ratio analysis. The ratios computed for Ajax are presented along with the median ratios for firms of similar size in the industry and the industry median. The median is often reported in financial sources, rather than the mean, to avoid the strong effect of outliers.[4]

4. Check for Problems or Opportunities

The ratio comparison in Figure 2 suggests that Ajax is in reasonably good shape financially. The current ratio is above the industry figures, although the quick ratio is slightly below them. However, the high inventory turnover ratio suggests that the slightly low quick ratio should not be a problem, since inventory turns over relatively quickly. Total asset utilization is slightly below industry averages and should be monitored closely. This, coupled with the slightly lower return on total assets, suggests that some unproductive assets should be eliminated or that the production process needs to be made more efficient. While the problem could be ineffective marketing, the high profit margin on sales suggests that marketing effort is probably not the problem.

FIGURE 2
Ratio Comparison for
Ajax Home Computer
Company

	Ajax	Industry Firms Median ($1–10 Million in Assets)	Overall Industry Median
Liquidity ratios			
Current ratio	2.2	1.8	1.8
Quick ratio	.86	.9	1.0
Asset management ratios			
Inventory turnover	6.5	3.2	2.8
Total assets utilization	1.5	1.7	1.6
Profitability ratios			
Profit margin	8.3%	6.7%	8.2%
Return on total assets	12.5%	15.0%	14.7%

SUMMARY

This section has focused on several aspects of financial analysis that are useful for marketing decision making. The first, break-even analysis, is commonly used in marketing problem and case analysis. The second, net present value analysis, is quite useful for investigating the financial impact of marketing alternatives, such as new product introductions or other long-term strategic changes. The third, ratio analysis, is a useful tool sometimes overlooked in marketing problem solving. Performing a ratio analysis as a regular part of marketing problem and case analysis can increase the understanding of the firm and its problems and opportunities.

Additional Resources

Block, Stanley B., Geoffrey A. Hirt, and Bartley Danielsen. *Foundations of Financial Management.* Burr Ridge, IL: Irwin/McGraw-Hill, 2011.

Brealey, Richard A., Stewart C. Myers, and Alan J. Marcus. *Fundamentals of Corporate Finance.* 6th ed. Burr Ridge, IL: McGraw-Hill, 2009.

Ross, Stephen A.; Randolph W. Westerfield; and Bradford D. Jordan. *Essentials of Corporate Finance.* 7th ed. Burr Ridge, IL: Irwin/McGraw-Hill, 2011.

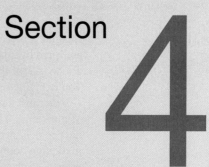

Developing Marketing Plans

Imagine this scenario. After receiving your bachelor's or master's degree in marketing, you are hired by a major consumer goods company. Because you've done well in school, you are confident that you have a lot of marketing knowledge and a lot to offer to the firm. You're highly motivated and are looking forward to a successful career.

After just a few days of work you are called in for a conference with the vice president of marketing. The vice president welcomes you and tells you how glad the firm is that you have joined them. The vice president also says that, because you have done so well in your marketing courses and have had such recent training, he wants you to work on a special project.

He tells you that the company has a new product, which is to be introduced in a few months. He also says, confidentially, that recent new product introductions by the company haven't been too successful. Suggesting that the recent problems are probably because the company has not been doing a very good job of developing marketing plans, the vice president tells you not to look at marketing plans for the company's other products.

Your assignment, then, is to develop a marketing plan for the proposed product in the next six weeks. The vice president explains that a good job here will lead to rapid advancement in the company. You thank the vice president for the assignment and promise that you'll do your best.

How would you feel when you returned to your desk? Surely, you'd be flattered that you had been given this opportunity and be eager to do a good job. However, how confident are you that you could develop a quality marketing plan? Would you even know where to begin?

We suspect that many of you, even those who have an excellent knowledge of marketing principles and are adept at solving marketing cases, may not yet have the skills necessary to develop a marketing plan from scratch. Thus, the purpose of this section is to offer a framework for developing marketing plans. In one sense, this section is no more than a summary of the whole text. In other words, it is an organizational framework based on the text material that can be used to direct the development of marketing plans.

Students should note that we are not presenting this framework and discussion as the only way to develop a marketing plan. While we believe this is a useful framework for logically analyzing the problems involved in developing a marketing plan, other approaches can be used just as successfully.

Often, successful firms prepare much less detailed plans because much of the background material and current conditions are well known to everyone involved. However, our review of plans used in various firms suggests that something like this framework is not uncommon.

We would like to mention one other qualification before beginning our discussion. Students should remember that one important part of the marketing plan involves the development of a sales forecast. While we have discussed several approaches to sales forecasting in the text, we will detail only one specific approach here.

A MARKETING PLAN FRAMEWORK

Marketing plans have three basic purposes. First, they are used as a tangible record of analysis so the logic involved can be checked. This is done to ensure the feasibility and internal consistency of the project and to evaluate the likely consequences of implementing the plan. Second, they are used as roadmaps or guidelines for directing appropriate actions. A marketing plan is designed to be the best available scenario and rationale for directing the firm's efforts for a particular product or brand. Third, they are used as tools to obtain funding for implementation. This funding may come from internal or external sources. For

FIGURE 1
A Marketing Plan
Format

- Title page.
- Executive summary.
- Table of contents.
- Introduction.
- Situational analysis.
- Marketing planning.
- Implementation and control of the marketing plan.
- Summary.
- Appendix: Financial analysis.
- References.

example, a brand manager may have to present a marketing plan to senior executives in a firm to get a budget request filled. This would be an internal source. Similarly, proposals for funding from investors or business loans from banks often require a marketing plan. These would be external sources.

Figure 1 presents a format for preparing marketing plans. Each of the 10 elements will be briefly discussed. We will refer to previous chapters and sections in this text and to other sources where additional information can be obtained when a marketing plan is being prepared. We also will offer additional information for focusing particular sections of the plan as well as for developing financial analysis.

Title Page

The *title page* should contain the following information: (1) the name of the product or brand for which the marketing plan has been prepared—for example, Marketing Plan for Little Friskies Dog Food; (2) the time period for which the plan is designed—for example, 2010–2012; (3) the person(s) and position(s) of those submitting the plan—for example, submitted by Amy Lewis, brand manager; (4) the persons, group, or agency to whom the plan is being submitted—for example, submitted to Lauren Ellis, product group manager; and (5) the date of submission of the plan—for example, June 30, 2012.

While preparing the title page is a simple task, remember that it is the first thing readers see. Thus, a title page that is poorly laid out, is smudged, or contains misspelled words can lead to the inference that the project was developed hurriedly and with little attention to detail. As with the rest of the project, appearances are important and affect what people think about the plan.

Executive Summary

The *executive summary* is a two- to three-page summary of the contents of the report. Its purpose is to provide a quick summary of the marketing plan for executives who need to be informed about the plan but are typically not directly involved in plan approval. For instance, senior executives for firms with a broad product line may not have time to read the entire plan but need an overview to keep informed about operations.

The executive summary should include a brief introduction, the major aspects of the marketing plan, and a budget statement. This is not the place to go into detail about each and every aspect of the marketing plan. Rather, it should focus on the major market opportunity and the key elements of the marketing plan that are designed to capitalize on this opportunity.

It is also useful to state specifically how much money is required to implement the plan. In an ongoing firm, many costs can be estimated from historical data or from discussions with other executives in charge of specific functional areas. However, in many situations (such as a class project), sufficient information is not always available to give exact costs for every aspect of production, promotion, and distribution. In these cases, include a rough estimate of total marketing costs of the plan. In many ongoing firms, marketing cost elements are concentrated in the areas of promotion and marketing research, and these figures are integrated with those from other functional areas as parts of the overall business plan.

Table of Contents

The *table of contents* is a listing of everything contained in the plan and where it is located in the report. Reports that contain a variety of charts and figures may also have a table of exhibits listing their titles and page numbers within the report.

In addition to using the table of contents as a place to find specific information, readers may also review it to see if each section of the report is logically sequenced. For example, situational analysis logically precedes marketing planning as an activity, and this ordering makes sense in presenting the plan.

Introduction

The types of information and amount of detail reported in the *introduction* depend in part on whether the plan is being designed for a new or existing product or brand. If the product is new, the introduction should explain the product concept and the reasons it is expected to be successful. Basically, this part of the report should make the new idea sound attractive to management or investors. In addition, it is useful to offer estimates of expected sales, costs, and return on investment.

If the marketing plan is for an existing brand in an ongoing firm, it is common to begin the report with a brief history of the brand. The major focus here is on the brand's performance in the last three to five years. It is useful to prepare graphs of the brand's performance that show its sales, profits, and market share for previous years and to explain the reasons for any major changes. These exhibits can also be extended to include predicted changes in these variables given the new marketing plan. A brief discussion of the overall strategy followed in previous years also provides understanding of how much change is being proposed in the new marketing plan.

Also useful in the introduction is to offer a precise statement of the purpose of the report as well as a roadmap of the report. In other words, tell readers what this report is, how it is organized, and what will be covered in the following sections.

Situational Analysis

The *situational analysis* is not unlike the analysis discussed in Chapter 1 and Section II of this text. The focus remains on the most critical and relevant environmental conditions (or changes in them) that affect the success or failure of the proposed plan. While any aspect of the economic, social, political, legal, or cooperative environments might deserve considerable attention, there is seldom if ever a marketing plan in which the competitive environment does not require considerable discussion. In fact, the competitive environment may be set off as a separate section called *industry analysis*. The strengths and weaknesses of major competitors, their relative market shares, and the success of various competitive strategies are critical elements of the situation analysis.

Marketing Planning

Marketing planning is, of course, a critical section of the report. As previously noted, it includes three major elements: marketing objectives, target markets, and the marketing mix.

Marketing Objectives

Marketing objectives are often stated in plans in terms of the percentage of particular outcomes that are to be achieved: for example, 80 percent awareness of the brand in particular markets, increase in trial rate by 30 percent, distribution coverage of 60 percent, or increase in total

Understanding an industry and the actions of competitors is critical to developing successful marketing plans. Below is a list of some questions to consider when performing competitive analysis. Thinking about these questions can aid the marketing planner in developing better marketing strategies.

1. Which firms compete in this industry and what is their financial position and marketing capability?
2. What are the relative market shares of various brands?
3. How many brands and models does each firm offer?
4. What marketing strategies have the market leaders employed?
5. Which brands have gained and which have lost market share in recent years, and what factors have led to these changes?
6. Are new competitors likely to enter the market?
7. How quickly do competitive firms react to changes in the market?
8. From which firms or brands might we be able to take market share?
9. What are the particular strengths and weaknesses of competitors in the industry?
10. How do we compare with other firms in the industry in terms of financial strength and marketing skills?

market share by 3 percent over the life of the plan. Similarly, objectives may be stated in terms of sales units or dollars or increases in these. Of course, the reasons for selection of the particular objectives and rationale are important points to explain.

Target Markets

The *target markets* discussion explains the customer base and rationale or justification for it. An approach to developing appropriate target markets is contained in Chapter 5 of this text.

This section also includes relevant discussion of changes or important issues in consumer or organizational buyer behavior: for example, what benefits consumers are seeking in this products class, what benefits does the particular brand offer, or what purchasing trends are shaping the market for this product. Discussions of consumer and organizational buyer behavior are contained in Chapters 3 and 4 of this text.

Marketing Mix

The *marketing mix* discussion explains in detail the selected strategy consisting of product, promotion, distribution and price, and the rationale for it. Also, if marketing research has been done on these elements or is planned, it can be discussed in this section.

Product   The *product* section details a description of the product or brand, its packaging, and its attributes. Product life-cycle considerations should be mentioned if they affect the proposed plan.

Of critical importance in this discussion is the competitive advantage of the product or brand. Here it must be carefully considered whether the brand really does anything better than the competition or is purchased primarily on the basis of brand equity or value. For example, many brands of toothpaste have fluoride, yet Crest has the largest market share primarily through promoting this attribute of its brand. Thus, does Crest do anything more than other toothpastes, or is it Crest's image that accounts for sales?

Discussion of product-related issues is contained in Chapters 6 and 7, and services are discussed in Chapter 12 of this text. For discussion of marketing plans for products marketed globally, see Chapter 13.

Promotion   The *promotion* discussion consists of a description and justification of the planned promotion mix. It is useful to explain the theme of the promotion and to include some examples of potential ads as well as the nature of the sales force if one is to be used. For mass-marketed consumer goods, promotion costs can be large and need to be considered explicitly in the marketing plan.

Discussion of promotion-related issues is contained in Chapters 8 and 9 of this text. Secondary sources, such as *Standard Rate and Data, Simmons Media/Market Service, Starch Advertising Readership Service,* and the *Nielsen Television Index,* provide useful information for selecting, budgeting, and justifying media and other promotional decisions.

Distribution   The *distribution* discussion describes and justifies the appropriate channel or channels for the product. This includes types of intermediaries and specifically who they will be. Other important issues concern the level of market coverage desired, cost, and control considerations. In many cases, the channels of distribution used by the firm, as well as competitive firms, are well established. For example, General Motors and Ford distribute their automobiles through independent dealer networks. Thus, unless there is a compelling reason to change channels, the traditional channel will often be the appropriate alternative. However, serious consideration may have to be given to methods of obtaining channel support, for example, trade deals to obtain sufficient shelf space.

Discussion of distribution-related issues is contained in Chapter 10 of this text. Useful retail distribution information can be found in the *Nielsen Retail Index* and the *Audits and Surveys National Total-Market Index*.

Price   The pricing discussion starts with a specific statement of the price of the product. Depending on what type of channel is used, manufacturer price, wholesale price, and suggested retail price need to be listed and justified. In addition, special deals or trade discounts that are to be employed must be considered in terms of their effect on the firm's selling price.

Discussion of price-related issues is contained in Chapter 11. In addition to a variety of other useful information, the *Nielsen Retail Index* provides information on wholesale and retail prices.

Marketing Research   For any aspect of marketing planning, there may be a need for marketing research. If such research is to be performed, it is important to justify it and explain its costs and benefits. Such costs should also be included in the financial analysis.

If marketing research has already been conducted as part of the marketing plan, it can be reported as needed to justify various decisions that were reached. To illustrate, if research found that two out of three consumers like the taste of a new formula Coke, this information would likely be included in the product portion of the report. However, the details of the research could be placed here in the marketing research section. Discussion of marketing research is contained in Chapter 2.

Implementation and Control of the Marketing Plan

This section contains a discussion and justification of how the marketing plan will be implemented and controlled. It also explains who will be in charge of monitoring and changing the plan should unanticipated events occur and how the success or failure of the plan will be measured. Success or failure of the plan is typically measured by a comparison of the results of implementing the plan with the stated objectives.

For a marketing plan developed within an ongoing firm, this section can be quite explicit, because procedures for implementing plans may be well established. However, for a classroom project, the key issues to be considered are the persons responsible for implementing the plan, a timetable for sequencing the tasks, and a method of measuring and evaluating the success or failure of the plan.

For the direction-setting purpose of objectives to be fulfilled, objectives need to meet five specifications:

1. An objective should relate to a single, specific topic. (It should not be stated in the form of a vague abstraction or a pious platitude—"we want to be a leader in our industry" or "our objective is to be more aggressive marketers.")
2. An objective should relate to a result, not to an activity to be performed. (The objective is the result of the activity, not the performance of the activity.)
3. An objective should be measurable (stated in quantitative terms whenever feasible).
4. An objective should contain a time deadline for its achievement.
5. An objective should be challenging but achievable.

Consider the following examples:

1. Poor: Our objective is to maximize profits.
   Remarks: How much is "maximum"? The statement is not subject to measurement. What criterion or yardstick will management use to determine if and when actual profits are equal to maximum profits? No deadline is specified.
   Better: Our total profit target in 2012 is $1 million.
2. Poor: Our objective is to increase sales revenue and unit volume.
   Remarks: How much? Also, because the statement relates to two topics, it may be inconsistent. Increasing unit volume may require a price cut, and if demand is price inelastic, sales revenue would fall as unit volume rises. No time frame for achievement is indicated.
   Better: Our objective this calendar year is to increase sales revenues from $30 million to $35 million; we expect this to be accomplished by selling 1 million units at an average price of $35.
3. Poor: Our objective in 2012 is to boost advertising expenditures by 15 percent.
   Remarks: Advertising is an activity, not a result. The advertising objective should be stated in terms of what result the extra advertising is intended to produce.
   Better: Our objective is to boost our market share from 8 percent to 10 percent in 2012 with the help of a 15 percent increase in advertising expenditures.
4. Poor: Our objective is to be a pioneer in research and development and to be the technological leader in the industry.
   Remarks: Very sweeping and perhaps overly ambitious; implies trying to march in too many directions at once if the industry is one with a wide range of technological frontiers. More a platitude than an action commitment to a specific result.
   Better: During the 2010–2020 decade, our objective is to continue as a leader in introducing new technologies and new devices that will allow buyers of electrically powered equipment to conserve on electric energy usage.
5. Poor: Our objective is to be the most profitable company in our industry.
   Remarks: Not specific enough by what measures of profit—total dollars, or earnings per share, or unit profit margin, or return on equity investment, or all of these? Also, because the objective concerns how well other companies will perform, the objective, while challenging, may not be achievable.
   Better: We will strive to remain atop the industry in terms of rate of return on equity investment by earning a 25 percent after-tax return on equity investment in 2012.

Knowledge of consumers is paramount to developing successful marketing plans. Below is a list of questions that are useful to consider when analyzing consumers. For some of the questions, secondary sources of information or primary marketing research can be employed to aid in decision making. However, a number of them require the analyst to do some serious thinking about the relationship between brands of the product and various consumer groups to better understand the market.

1. How many people purchase and use this product in general?
2. How many people purchase and use each brand of the product?
3. Is there an opportunity to reach nonusers of the product with a unique marketing strategy?
4. What does the product do for consumers functionally and how does this vary by brand?
5. What does the product do for consumers in a social or psychological sense and how does this vary by brand?
6. Where do consumers currently purchase various brands of the product?
7. How much are consumers willing to pay for specific brands and is price a determining factor for purchase?
8. What is the market profile of the heavy user of this product and what percentage of the total market are heavy users?
9. What media reach these consumers?
10. On average, how often is this product purchased?
11. How important is brand equity for consumers of this product?
12. Why do consumers purchase particular brands?
13. How brand loyal are consumers of this product?

Summary

This *summary* need not be much different than the executive summary stated at the beginning of the document. However, it is usually a bit longer, more detailed, and states more fully the case for financing the plan.

Appendix—Financial Analysis

Financial analysis is a very important part of any marketing plan. While a complete business plan often includes extensive financial analysis, such as a complete cost breakdown and estimated return on investment, marketing planners frequently do not have complete accounting data for computing these figures. For example, decisions concerning how much overhead is to be apportioned to the product are not usually made solely by marketing personnel. However, the marketing plan should contain at least a sales forecast and estimates of relevant marketing costs.

Sales Forecast

As noted, there are a variety of ways to develop sales forecasts. Regardless of the method, however, they all involve trying to predict the future as accurately as possible. It is, of course, necessary to justify the logic for the forecasted figures, rather than offer them with no support.

One basic approach to developing a sales forecast is outlined in Figure 2. This approach begins by estimating the total number of persons in the selected target market. This estimate comes from the market segmentation analysis and may include information from test

FIGURE 2
A Basic Approach to
Sales Forecasting

Total number of people in target markets (*a*)	*a*
Annual number of purchases per person (*b*)	× *b*
Total potential market (*c*)	= *c*
Total potential market (*c*)	*c*
Percent of total market coverage (*d*)	× *d*
Total available market (*e*)	= *e*
Total available market (*e*)	*e*
Expected market share (*f*)	× *f*
Sales forecast (in units) (*g*)	= *g*
Sales forecast (in units) (*g*)	*g*
Price (*h*)	× *h*
Sales forecast (in dollars)(*i*)	= *i*

marketing and from secondary sources, such as *Statistical Abstracts of the United States*. For example, suppose a company is marketing a solar-powered watch that is designed not only to tell time but also to take the pulse of the wearer. The product is targeted at joggers and others interested in aerobic exercise. By reviewing the literature on these activities, the marketing planner, John Murphy, finds that the average estimate of this market on a national level is 60 million persons and is growing by 4 million persons per year. Thus, John might conclude that the total number of people in the target market for next year is 64 million. If he has not further limited the product's target market and has no other information, John might use this number as a basis for starting the forecast analysis.

The second estimate John needs is the annual number of purchases per person in the product's target market. This estimate could be quite large for such products as breakfast cereal or less than one (annual purchase per person) for such products as automobiles. For watches, the estimate is likely to be much less than one since people are likely to buy a new watch only every few years. Thus, John might estimate the annual number of purchases per person in the target market to be .25. Of course, as a careful marketing planner, John would probably carefully research this market to refine this estimate. In any event, multiplying these two numbers gives John an estimate of the *total potential market,* in this case, 64 million times .25 equals 16 million. In other words, if next year alone John's company could sell a watch to every jogger or aerobic exerciser who is buying a watch, the company could expect sales to be 16 million units.

Of course, the firm cannot expect to sell every jogger a watch for several reasons. First, it is unlikely to obtain 100 percent market coverage in the first year, if ever. Even major consumer goods companies selling convenience goods seldom reach the entire market in the first year and many never achieve even 90 percent distribution. Given the nature of the product and depending on the distribution alternative, John's company might be doing quite well to average 50 percent market coverage in the first year. If John's plans call for this kind of coverage, his estimate of the total available market would be 16 million times .5, which equals 8 million.

A second reason John's plans would not call for dominating the market is that his company does not have the only product available or wanted by this target market. Many of the people who will purchase such a watch will purchase a competitive brand. He must, therefore, estimate the product's likely market share. Of all the estimates made in developing a sales forecast, this one is critical because it is a reflection of the entire marketing plan. Important factors to consider in developing this estimate include (1) competitive market shares and likely marketing strategies; (2) competitive retaliation should the product do well; (3) competitive advantage of the product, such as lower price; (4) promotion mix and budget relative to competitors; and (5) market shares obtained by similar products in the introductory year.

Below is a brief list of questions about the marketing planning section of the report. Answering them honestly and recognizing both the strengths and weaknesses of the marketing plan should help to improve it.

1. What key assumptions were made in developing the marketing plan?
2. How badly will the product's market position be hurt if these assumptions turn out to be incorrect?
3. How good is the marketing research?
4. Is the marketing plan consistent? For example, if the plan is to seek a prestige position in the market, is the product priced, promoted, and distributed to create this image?
5. Is the marketing plan feasible? For example, are the financial and other resources (such as a distribution network) available to implement it?
6. How will the marketing plan affect profits and market share, and is it consistent with corporate objectives?
7. Will implementing the marketing plan result in competitive retaliation that will end up hurting the firm?
8. Is the marketing mix designed to reach and attract new customers or increase usage among existing users or both?
9. Will the marketing mix help to develop brand-loyal consumers?
10. Will the marketing plan not only be successful in the short run but also contribute to a profitable long-run position?

Overall, suppose John estimates the product's market share to be 5 percent, because other competitive products have beat his company to the market and because the company's competitive advantage is only a slightly more stylish watch. In this case, the sales forecast for year one would be 8 million times .05, which equals 400,000 units. If the manufacturer's selling price was $50, then the sales forecast in dollars would be 400,000 times $50, which equals $20 million.

This approach can also be used to extend the sales forecast for any number of years. Typically, estimates of most of the figures change from year to year, depending on changes in market size, distribution coverage, and expected market shares. The value of this approach is that it forces an analyst to carefully consider and justify each of the estimates offered, rather than simply pulling numbers out of the air.

Estimates of Marketing Costs

A complete delineation of all costs, apportionment of overhead, and other accounting tasks are usually performed by other departments within a firm. All of this information, including expected return on investment from implementing the marketing plan, is part of the overall business plan.

However, the marketing plan should at least contain estimates of major marketing costs. These include such things as advertising, sales force training and compensation, channel development, and marketing research. Estimates may also be included for product development and package design.

For some marketing costs, reasonable estimates are available from sources such as *Standard Rate and Data*. However, some cost figures, such as marketing research, might be obtained from asking various marketing experts for the estimated price of proposed research. Other

Implementation and control of a marketing plan require careful scheduling and attention to detail. While some firms have standard procedures for dealing with many of the questions raised below, thinking through each of the questions should help improve the efficiency of even these firms in this stage of the process.

1. Who is responsible for implementing and controlling the marketing plan?
2. What tasks must be performed to implement the marketing plan?
3. What are the deadlines for implementing the various tasks and how critical are specific deadlines?
4. Has sufficient time been scheduled to implement the various tasks?
5. How long will it take to get the planned market coverage?
6. How will the success or failure of the plan be determined?
7. How long will it take to get the desired results from the plan?
8. How long will the plan be in effect before changes will be made to improve it based on more current information?
9. If an ad agency or other firms are involved in implementing the plan, how much responsibility and authority will they have?
10. How frequently will the progress of the plan be monitored?

types of marketing costs might be estimated from financial statements of firms in the industry. For example, Morris's *Annual Statement Studies* offers percentage breakdowns of various income statement information by industry. These might be used to estimate the percentage of the sales-forecast figure that would likely be spent in a particular cost category.

References

The *references* section contains the sources of any secondary information that was used in developing the marketing plan. This information might include company reports and memos, statements of company objectives, and articles or books used for information or support of the marketing plan.

References should be listed alphabetically using a consistent format. One way of preparing references is to use the same approach as is used in marketing journals. For example, the format used for references in *Journal of Marketing* articles is usually acceptable.

SUMMARY

Suppose you're now sitting at your desk faced with the task of developing a marketing plan for a new product. Do you believe that you might have the skills to develop a marketing plan? Of course, your ability to develop a quality plan will depend on your learning experiences during your course work and the amount of practice you've had; for example, if you developed a promotion plan in your advertising course, it is likely that you could do a better job on the promotion phase of the marketing plan. Similarly, your experiences in analyzing cases should have sharpened your skills at recognizing problems and developing solutions to them. But inexperience (or experience) aside, hopefully you now feel that you understand the process of developing a marketing plan. You at least know where to start, where to seek information, how to structure the plan, and some of the critical issues that require analysis.

Additional Resources

Cohen, William A. *The Marketing Plan.* 5th ed. New York: John Wiley & Sons, 2006.

Cravens, David W., and Nigel F. Piercy, *Strategic Marketing.* 9th ed. Burr Ridge, IL: McGraw-Hill/Irwin, 2009.

Hiebing, Romon G., and Scott W. Cooper. *The Successful Marketing Plan.* Burr Ridge, IL: McGraw-Hill, 2003.

Hiebing, Roman G., and Scott W. Cooper. *The One-Day Marketing Plan: Organizing and Completing a Plan that Works.* 3rd ed. Burr Ridge, IL: McGraw-Hill, 2004.

Kerin, Roger A., Steven W. Hartley, and William Rudelius. *Marketing.* 10th ed. Burr Ridge, IL: McGraw-Hill /Irwin, 2011.

Lehmann, Donald R., and Russell S. Winer. *Analysis for Marketing Planning.* 7th ed. Burr Ridge, IL: McGraw-Hill/Irwin, 2008.

Walker, Orville C., John Mullins, and Harper W. Boyd, Jr. *Marketing Strategy: A Decision Focused Approach.* 7th ed. Burr Ridge, IL: McGraw-Hill/Irwin, 2011.

Wood, Marian Burk. *Marketing Plan Handbook.* Upper Saddle River, NJ: Prentice Hall, 2011.

Chapter Notes

Chapter 1

1. See Reinhard Angelmar and Christian Pinson, "The Meaning of Marketing," *Philosophy of Science,* June 1975, pp. 208–14.

2. Approved by the American Marketing Association, 2007.

3. Much of this section is based on J. H. Donnelly, Jr., J. L. Gibson, and J. M. Ivancevich, *Fundamentals of Management,* 9th ed. (Burr Ridge, IL: Irwin/ McGraw-Hill, 1998), chap. 7.

4. The process may differ depending on the type of organization or management approach, or both. For certain types of organizations, one strategic plan will be sufficient. Some manufacturers with similar product lines or limited product lines will develop only one strategic plan. However, organizations with widely diversified product lines and widely diversified markets may develop strategic plans for units or divisions. These plans usually are combined into a master strategic plan.

5. For a discussion of this topic, see Gerald E. Ledford, Jr., Jon R. Wendenhof, and James T. Strahely, "Realizing a Corporate Philosophy," *Organizational Dynamics,* Winter 1995, pp. 4–19; and Stephan Cummings and John Davies, "Mission, Vision, Fusion," *Long Range Planning,* December 1994, pp. 147–50.

6. Philip Kotler and Gary Armstrong, *Principles of Marketing,* 6th ed. (Englewood Cliffs, NJ: Prentice Hall, 1994), Chap. 2.

7. Philip Kotler, *Marketing Management: Analysis, Planning, Implementation and Control,* 8th ed. (Englewood Cliffs, NJ: Prentice Hall, 1994), chap. 3.

8. Norton Paley, "A Sign of Intelligence," *Sales & Marketing Management,* March 1995, pp. 30–31.

9. Peter Drucker, *Management: Tasks, Responsibilities, Practices* (New York: Harper & Row, 1974), pp. 77–89; Kotler, *Marketing Management,* chap. 3.

10. Much of the following discussion is based on Drucker, *Management,* pp. 79–87.

11. Noel B. Zabriskie and Alan B. Huellmantel, "Marketing Research as a Strategic Tool," *Long Range Planning,* February 1994, pp. 107–18.

12. Originally discussed in the classic H. Igor Ansoff, *Corporate Strategy* (New York: McGraw-Hill, 1965).

13. For complete coverage of this topic, see Michael E. Porter, *Competitive Advantage: Creating and Sustaining Superior Performance* (New York: The Free Press, 1985). Material in this section is based upon discussions contained in Steven J. Skinner, *Marketing,* 2nd ed. (Boston: Houghton Mifflin Co., 1994), pp. 48–50; and Thomas A. Bateman and Carl P. Zeithaml, *Management Function & Strategy,* 2nd ed. (Burr Ridge, IL: Irwin/McGraw-Hill, 1993), pp. 152–53.

14. For a complete discussion of this topic, see Michael Treacy and Fred Wiersema, *The Discipline of Market Leaders* (Reading, MA: Addison-Wesley, 1995); and Michael Treacy and Fred Wiersema, "How Market Leaders Keep Their Edge," *Fortune,* February 6, 1995, pp. 88–98.

15. Philip Kotler, *Marketing Management,* p. 13.

16. For a discussion of this issue and other mistakes marketers frequently make, see Kevin J. Clancy and Robert S. Shulman, "Breaking the Mold," *Sales & Marketing Management,* January 1994, pp. 82–84.

17. George S. Day and David B. Montgomery, "Diagnosing the Experience Curve," *Journal of Marketing,* Spring 1983, pp. 44–58.

18. P. Rajan Varadarajan, Terry Clark, and William M. Pride, "Controlling the Uncontrollable: Managing Your Market Environment," *Sloan Management Review,* Winter 1992, pp. 39–47.

19. Reed E. Nelson, "Is There Strategy in Brazil?" *Business Horizons,* July–August 1992, pp. 15–23.

20. Peter S. Davis and Patrick L. Schill, "Addressing the Contingent Effects of Business Unit Strategic Orientation on the Relationship between Organizational Context and Business Unit Performance," *Journal of Business Research,* 1993, pp. 183–200.

21. J. Scott Armstrong and Roderick J. Brodie, "Effects of Portfolio Planning Methods on Decision Making: Experimental Results," *International Journal of Research in Marketing,* January 1994, pp. 73–84.

22. Michel Roberts, "Times Change but Do Business Strategies?" *Journal of Business Strategy,* March–April 1993, pp. 12–15.

23. Donald L. McCabe and V. K. Narayanan, "The Life Cycle of the PIMS and BCG Models," *Industrial Marketing Management,* November 1991, pp. 347–52.

Chapter 2

1. Based on Peter D. Bennett, ed., *Dictionary of Marketing Terms,* 2nd ed. (Chicago: American Marketing Association, 1995), p. 77.

2. Gilbert A. Churchill, Jr., and J. Paul Peter, *Marketing: Creating Value for Customers,* 2nd ed. (Burr Ridge, IL: Irwin/McGraw-Hill, 1998), p. 116.

3. For a discussion of some general problems in marketing research, see Alan G. Sawyer and J. Paul Peter, "The Significance of Statistical Significance Testing in Marketing Research," *Journal of Marketing Research,* May 1983, pp. 122–33.

4. This section is based on Churchill and Peter, *Marketing,* pp. 114–16.

Chapter 3

1. Richard P. Coleman, "The Continuing Significance of Social Class to Marketing," *Journal of Consumer Research,* December 1983, pp. 265–80.

2. See William O. Bearden and Michael J. Etzel, "Reference Group Influence on Product and Brand Purchase Decisions," *Journal of Consumer Research,* September 1982, pp. 183–94; and Terry L. Childers and Akshay R. Rao, "The Influence of Familial and Peer-Based Reference Groups on Consumer Decisions," *Journal of Consumer Research,* September 1992, pp. 198–211.

3. See Rosann L. Spiro, "Persuasion in Family Decision Making," *Journal of Consumer Research,* March 1983, pp. 393–402.

4. See Janet Wagner and Sherman Hanna, "The Effectiveness of Family Life Cycle Variables in Consumer Expenditure Research," *Journal of Consumer Research,* December 1983, pp. 281–91. Also see Charles M. Schanninger and William D. Danko, "A Conceptual and Empirical Comparison of Alternative Household Life Cycle Models," *Journal of Consumer Research,* March 1993, pp. 580–94.

5. Russell W. Belk, "Situational Variables and Consumer Behavior," *Journal of Consumer Research,* December 1975, pp. 156–64. Also see Jacob Hornik, "Situational Effects on the Consumption of Time," *Journal of Marketing,* Fall 1982, pp. 44–55; C. Whan Park, Easwer S. Iyer, and Daniel C. Smith, "The Effects of Situational Factors on In-Store Grocery Shopping Behavior: The Role of Store Environment and Time Available for Shopping," *Journal of Consumer Research,* March 1989, pp. 422–33; and Mary Jo Bitner, "Servicescapes: The Impact of Physical Surroundings on Customers and Employees," *Journal of Marketing,* April 1992, pp. 57–71.

6. J. Paul Peter and Jerry C. Olson, *Consumer Behavior and Marketing Strategy*, 7th ed. (Burr Ridge, IL: Irwin/McGraw-Hill, 2005), chap. 4.

7. A. H. Maslow, *Motivation and Personality* (New York: Harper & Row, 1954); also see James F. Engel, Roger D. Blackwell, and Paul W. Miniard, *Consumer Behavior,* 8th ed. (Fort Worth, TX: Dryden Press, 1995), chap. 5, for further discussion of need recognition.

8. For a detailed review of research on external search, see Sharon E. Beatty and Scott M. Smith, "External

Search Effort: An Investigation across Several Product Categories," *Journal of Consumer Research,* June 1987, pp. 83–95. Also see Narasimhan Srinivasan and Brian T. Ratchford, "An Empirical Test of a Model of External Search for Automobiles," *Journal of Consumer Research,* September 1991, pp. 233–42; and Julie L. Ozanne, Merrie Brucks, and Dhruv Grewal, "A Study of Information Search Behavior during the Categorization of New Products," *Journal of Consumer Research,* March 1992, pp. 452–63.

9. For further discussion of information processing, see J. Paul Peter and Jerry C. Olson, *Consumer Behavior and Marketing Strategy,* 8th ed. (Burr Ridge, IL: Irwin/McGraw-Hill, 2008), chap. 3.

10. For a summary of research on attitude modeling, see Blair H. Sheppard, Jon Hartwick, and Paul R. Warshaw, "The Theory of Reasoned Action: A Meta-Analysis of Past Research with Recommendations for Modification and Future Research," *Journal of Consumer Research,* December 1988, pp. 325–43.

11. For further discussion of postpurchase feelings, see Richard L. Oliver, "Cognitive, Affective, and Attribute Bases of the Satisfaction Response," *Journal of Consumer Research,* December 1993, pp. 418–30; and Haim Mano and Richard L. Oliver, "Assessing the Dimensionality and Structure of the Consumption Experience: Evaluation, Feeling, and Satisfaction," *Journal of Consumer Research,* December 1993, pp. 451–66.

Chapter 4

1. This discussion is based on Gilbert A. Churchill, Jr., and J. Paul Peter, *Marketing: Creating Value for Customers,* 2nd ed. (Burr Ridge, IL: Irwin/McGraw-Hill, 1998), pp. 182–84. Also see Michele D. Bunn, "Taxonomy of Buying Decision Approaches," *Journal of Marketing,* January 1993, pp. 38–56.

2. This discussion is based on Eric N. Berkowitz, Roger A. Kerin, Steven W. Hartley, and William Rudelius, *Marketing,* 8th ed. (Burr Ridge, IL: Irwin/McGraw-Hill, 2006), p. 157.

3. For research on influence strategies in organizational buying, see Gary L. Frazier and Raymond Rody, "The Use of Influence Strategies in Interfirm Relationships in Industrial Product Channels," *Journal of Marketing,* January 1991, pp. 52–69; and Julia M. Bristor, "Influence Strategies in Organizational Buying," *Journal of Business-to-Business Marketing,* 1993, pp. 63–98.

4. For research on the role of organizational climate in industrial buying, see William J. Qualls and Christopher P. Puto, "Organizational Climate and Decision Framing: An Integrated Approach to Analyzing Industrial Buying Decisions," *Journal of Marketing Research,* May 1989, pp. 179–92.

Chapter 5

1. Russell I. Haley, "Benefit Segmentation: A Decision-Oriented Research Tool," *Journal of Marketing,* July 1968, pp. 30–35; Russell I. Haley, "Benefit Segmentation—20 Years Later," *Journal of Consumer Marketing,* 1983, pp. 5–13; and Russell I. Haley, "Benefit Segments: Backwards and Forwards," *Journal of Advertising Research,* February–March 1984, pp. 19–25.

2. Roger J. Calantone and Alan G. Sawyer, "The Stability of Benefit Segments," *Journal of Marketing Research,* August 1978, pp. 395–404; also see James R. Merrill and William A. Weeks, "Predicting and Identifying Benefit Segments in the Elderly Market," in *AMA Educator's Proceedings,* eds. Patrick Murphy et al. (Chicago: American Marketing Association, 1983), pp. 399–403; Wagner A. Kamakura, "A Least Squares Procedure for Benefit Segmentation with Conjoint Experiments," *Journal of Marketing Research,* May 1988, pp. 157–67; and Michel Wedel and Jan-Benedict E. M. Steenkamp, "A Clusterwise Regression Method for Simultaneous Fuzzy Market Structuring and Benefit Segmentation," *Journal of Marketing Research,* November 1991, pp. 385–96.

3. John L. Lastovicka, John P. Murry, Jr., and Eric Joachimsthaler, "Evaluating the Measurement Validity of Lifestyle Typologies with Qualitative Measures and Multiplicative Factoring," *Journal of Marketing Research,* February 1990, pp. 11–23.

4. This discussion is taken from J. Paul Peter and Jerry C. Olson, *Consumer Behavior and Marketing Strategy,* 8th ed. (Burr Ridge, IL: Irwin/McGraw-Hill, 2008), pp. 373–75.

5. Ibid, pp. 379–381.

6. See Al Ries and Jack Trout, *Positioning: The Battle for Your Mind* (New York: Warner Books, 1981); and Al Ries and Jack Trout, *Marketing Warfare* (New York: McGraw-Hill, 1986).

Chapter 6

1. Material for this section is based on discussions contained in Louis E. Boone and David L. Kurtz, *Contemporary Marketing,* 8th ed. (Fort Worth, TX: Dryden, 1995), Chap. 2; Gilbert A. Churchill, Jr., and J. Paul Peter, *Marketing: Creating Value for Customers* (Burr Ridge, IL: Irwin/McGraw-Hill, 1995), chap. 1, p. 634; James H. Donnelly, James L. Gibson, and John M. Ivancevich, *Fundamentals of Management,* 9th ed. (Burr Ridge, IL: Irwin/McGraw-Hill 1995), p. 501; Joseph M. Juran, "Made in the U.S.A.: A Renaissance in Quality," *Harvard Business Review,* July–August 1993, pp. 42–47, 50; and Valerie A. Zeithaml, "Consumer Perceptions of Price, Quality, and Value: A Means End Model and Synthesis of Evidence," *Journal of Marketing,* April 1988, pp. 35–48.

2. For a discussion on this topic, see Andrew J. Bergman, "What the Marketing Professional Needs to Know about ISO 9000 Series Registration," *Industrial Marketing Management,* 1994, pp. 367–70.

3. The material for this section comes from Glenn L. Urban and Steven H. Star, *Advanced Marketing Strategy* (Englewood Cliffs, NJ: Prentice Hall, 1991), Chap. 16.

4. For a detailed discussion of this topic, see Anne Perkins, "Product Variety beyond Black," *Harvard Business Review,* November–December 1994, pp. 13–14; and "Perspectives: The Logic of Product-Line Extensions," *Harvard Business Review,* November–December 1994, pp. 53–62.

5. Mats Urde, "Brand Orientation—A Strategy for Survival," *Journal of Consumer Marketing,* 1994, pp. 18–32.

6. James Lowry, "Survey Finds Most Powerful Brands," *Advertising Age,* July 11, 1988, p. 31.

7. Peter H. Farquhar, "Strategic Challenges for Branding," *Marketing Management,* 1994, pp. 8–15.

8. Peter D. Bennett, ed., *Dictionary of Marketing Terms,* 2nd ed. (Chicago: American Marketing Association, 1995), p. 27.

9. Terance Shimp, *Promotion Management and Marketing Communications,* 2nd ed. (Hinsdale, IL: Dryden Press, 1990), p. 67.

10. David A. Aaker and Kevin Lane Keller, "Consumer Evaluations of Brand Extensions," *Journal of Marketing,* January 1990, pp. 27–41.

11. Ibid.

12. For a detailed discussion of brand equity, see David Aaker, *Managing Brand Equity* (New York and London: Free Press, 1991).

13. For a complete discussion of this topic, see Geoffrey L. Gordon, Roger J. Calantone, and C. A. Di Benedetto, "Brand Equity in the Business-to-Business Sector: An Exploratory Study," *Journal of Product & Brand Management,* 1993, pp. 4–16.

14. Jeffrey D. Zbar, "Industry Trends Hold Private-Label Promise," *Advertising Age,* April 3, 1995, p. 31.

15. Karen Benezra, "Frito Bets 'Reduced' Pitch Is in the Chips," *Brandweek,* January 23, 1995, p. 18.

16. Thomas Hine, "Why We Buy," *Worth,* May 1995, pp. 80–83.

17. For a discussion of problems related to this issue, see Geoffrey L. Gordon, Roger J. Calantone, and C. Anthony Di Benedetto, "Mature Markets and Revitalization Strategies: An American Fable," *Business Horizons,* May–June 1991, pp. 39–50.

18. Barry L. Bayus, "Are Product Life Cycles Really Getting Shorter?" *Journal of Product Innovation Management,* September 1994, pp. 300–308.

19. The discussion on benchmarking is based on Stanley Brown, "Don't Innovate—Imitate," *Sales & Marketing Management,* January 1995, pp. 24–25; Charles

Goldwasser, "Benchmarking: People Make the Process," *Management Review,* June 1995, pp. 39–43; and L. S. Pryor and S. J. Katz, "How Benchmarking Goes Wrong (and How to Do It Right)," *Planning Review,* January–February 1993, pp. 6–14.

Chapter 7

1. "Face Value: The Mass Production of Ideas, and Other Impossibilities," *The Economist,* March 18, 1995, p. 72.

2. Greg Erickson, "New Package Makes a New Product Complete," *Marketing News,* May 8, 1995, p. 10.

3. Zina Mouhkheiber, "Oversleeping," *Forbes,* June 15, 1995, pp. 78–79.

4. See C. Merle Crawford and Anthony Di Benedetto, *New Products Management,* 10th ed. (Burr Ridge, IL:McGraw-Hill/Irwin 2011), p. 14.

5. H. Igor Ansoff, *Corporate Strategy* (New York: McGraw-Hill, 1965), pp. 109–10.

6. Richard Stroup, "Growing in a Crowded Market Requires Old and New Strategies," *Brandweek,* August 22, 1994, p. 19.

7. These two examples came from Justin Martin, "Ignore Your Customers," *Fortune,* May 1, 1995, pp. 121–26.

8. "Where Do They Get All Those Ideas?" *Machine Design,* January 26, 1995, p. 40.

9. This section is based on Daryl McKee, "An Organizational Learning Approach to Product Innovation," *Journal of Product Innovation Management,* September 1992, pp. 232–45.

10. The discussion on risk is from Thomas D. Kuczmarski and Arthur G. Middlebrooks, "Innovation Risk and Reward," *Sales & Marketing Management,* February 1993, pp. 44–51.

11. For a more complete discussion on the advantages and disadvantages of strategic alliances, see Richard N. Cardozo, Shannon H. Shipp, and Kenneth J. Roering, "Proactive Strategic Partnerships: A New Business Markets Strategy," *Journal of Business and Industrial Marketing,* Winter 1992, pp. 51–63; and Frank K. Sonnenberg, "Partnering: Entering the Age of Cooperation," *Journal of Business Strategy,* May/June 1992, pp. 49–52.

12. James Quinn, "Managing Innovation: Controlled Chaos," *Harvard Business Review,* May–June 1985, pp. 73–84; and Hirotaka Takeuchi and Ikujiro Nonaka, "The New New Product Development Game," *Harvard Business Review,* January–February 1986, pp. 137–46.

13. For a discussion of this issue, see Eric M. Olson, Orville C. Walker, Jr., and Robert W. Ruekert, "Organizing for Effective New Product Development: The Moderating Role of Product Innovativeness," *Journal of Marketing,* January 1995, pp. 48–62; and Christopher

Meyer, "How the Right Measures Help Teams Excel," *Harvard Business Review,* May–June 1994, pp. 95–97.

14. For a detailed discussion on these stages, see Karl T. Ulrich and Steven D. Eppinger, *Product Design and Development* (New York: McGraw-Hill, 1995); and Glen Rifken, "Product Development: Emphatic Design Helps Understand Users Better," *Harvard Business Review,* March–April 1994, pp. 10–11.

15. Patricia W. Meyers and Gerald A. Athaide, "Strategic Mutual Learning between Producing and Buying Firms during Product Innovation," *Journal of Product Innovation Management,* September 1991, pp. 155–69.

16. For a discussion of this issue, see Christina Brown and James Lattin, "Investigating the Relationship between Time in Market and Pioneering Advantage," *Management Science,* October 1994, pp. 1361–69; Robin Peterson, "Forecasting for New Product Introduction," *Journal of Business Forecasting,* Fall 1994, pp. 21–23; and Tracy Carlson, "The Race Is On," *Brandweek,* May 9, 1994, pp. 22–27.

17. For a discussion of reasons why products fail, see Betsy Spellman, "Big Talk, Little Dollars," *Brandweek,* January 23, 1995, pp. 21–29.

Chapter 8

1. This discussion is adapted from material contained in Gilbert A. Churchill, Jr., and J. Paul Peter, *Marketing: Creating Value for Customers,* 2nd ed. (Burr Ridge, IL: Irwin/McGraw-Hill, 1998), chap. 18.

2. Material for this section is largely based on the discussion of advertising tasks and objectives contained in William Arens and Courtland Bovèe, *Contemporary Advertising,* 5th ed. (Burr Ridge, IL: Irwin/McGraw-Hill, 1994), chap. 7.

3. For more comprehensive coverage of this topic, see George E. Belch and Michael A. Belch, *Advertising and Promotion: An Integrated Marketing Communications Perspective,* 7th ed. (Burr Ridge, IL: Irwin/McGraw-Hill, 2007), chap. 12.

4. For a fuller explanation of the pros and cons associated with push marketing strategies, see Betsy Spellman, "Trade Promotion Redefined," *Brandweek,* March 13, 1995, pp. 25–34; and John McManus, "'Lost' Money Redefined as 'Found' Money Won't Connect the Disconnects," *Brandweek,* March 25, 1995, p. 16.

5. This discussion is based on Donald R. Glover, "Distributor Attitudes toward Manufacturer-Sponsored Promotions," *Industrial Marketing Management,* August 1991, pp. 241–49.

6. For a discussion of this topic, see Murray Raphel, "Frequent Shopper Clubs: Supermarkets' Newest Weapon," *Direct Marketing,* May 1995, pp. 18–20; Richard G. Barlow, "Five Mistakes of Frequency Marketing,"

Direct Marketing, March 1995, pp. 16–17; and Alice Cuneo, "Savvy Frequent-Buyer Plans Build on a Loyal Base," *Advertising Age,* March 20, 1995, pp. S10–11.

Chapter 9

1. Warren Keegan, Sandra Moriarty, and Thomas Duncan, *Marketing,* 2nd ed. (Englewood Cliffs, NJ: Prentice Hall, 1994), p. 654.

2. Material for this discussion came from Ronald B. Marks, *Personal Selling: An Interactive Approach,* 5th ed. (Boston, MA: Allyn and Bacon, 1994), pp. 12–13.

3. Material for the discussion of objectives is adapted from Joel R. Evans and Barry Berman, *Marketing,* 6th ed. (New York: Macmillan, 1994), pp. 640–42.

4. Unless otherwise noted, the discussion on the relationship-building process is based largely on material contained in Barton A. Weitz, Stephen B. Castleberry, and John F. Tanner, Jr., *Selling: Building Partnerships,* 3rd ed. (Burr Ridge, IL: Irwin/McGraw-Hill, 1998); and Rolph Anderson, *Essentials of Personal Selling: The New Professionalism* (Englewood Cliffs, NJ: Prentice Hall, 1995). For an in-depth discussion of this topic, readers should consult these references.

5. The discussion of aftermarketing is based on the work of Terry Vavra, *Aftermarketing: How to Keep Customers for Life through Relationship Marketing* (Burr Ridge, IL: McGraw-Hill, 1995).

6. Ibid.

7. The discussion on national account management is from James S. Boles, Bruce K. Pilling, and George W. Goodwyn, "Revitalizing Your National Account Marketing Program," *Journal of Business & Industrial Marketing,* no. 1 (1994), pp. 24–33.

8. Based on a survey by the National Industrial Conference Board: "Forecasting Sales," *Studies in Business Policy,* no. 106.

9. Much of the discussion in this section is based on material contained in Gilbert A. Churchill, Jr., Neil M. Ford, and Orville C. Walker, Jr., *Sales Force Management,* 4th ed. (Burr Ridge, IL: Irwin/McGraw-Hill, 1993); and William J. Stanton, Richard H. Buskirk, and Rosann L. Spiro, *Management of a Sales Force,* 9th ed. (Burr Ridge, IL: Irwin/McGraw-Hill, 1995), pp. 319–20.

10. For a complete discussion of the skills and policies successful sales leaders use in motivating salespeople, see David W. Cravens, Thomas N. Ingram, Raymond W. LaForge, and Clifford E. Young, "Hallmarks of Effective Sales Organizations," *Marketing Management,* Winter 1992, pp. 57–66; Thomas R. Wortruba, John S. Mactie, and Jerome A. Colletti, "Effective Sales Force Recognition Programs," *Industrial Marketing Management,* February 1991, pp. 9–15; and Ken Blanchard, "Reward Salespeople Creatively," *Personal Selling Power,* March 1992, p. 24.

Chapter 10

1. Peter D. Bennett, *Dictionary of Marketing Terms,* 2nd ed. (Chicago: American Marketing Association, 1995), p. 242.

2. For further discussion of relationship marketing, see Jan B. Heide, "Interorganizational Governance in Marketing Channels," *Journal of Marketing,* January 1994, pp. 71–85; Robert M. Morgan and Shelby D. Hunt, "The Commitment-Trust Theory of Relationship Marketing," *Journal of Marketing,* July 1994, pp. 20–38; and Manohar U. Kalwani and Narakesari Narayandas, "Long-Term Manufacturer-Supplier Relationships: Do They Pay Off for the Supplier Firm?" *Journal of Marketing,* January 1995, pp. 1–16.

3. This section is based on Donald J. Bowersox and M. Bixby Cooper, *Strategic Marketing Channel Management* (New York: McGraw-Hill, 1992), pp. 104–7; Bert Rosenbloom, *Marketing Channels: A Management View,* 4th ed. (Hinsdale, IL: Dryden Press), pp. 440–65; and Roger A. Kerin, Eric N. Berkowitz, Steven W. Hartley, and William Rudelius, *Marketing,* 8th ed. (Burr Ridge, IL: Irwin/McGraw-Hill, 2006), pp. 405–407.

4. This section is based on Gilbert A. Churchill, Jr., and J. Paul Peter, *Marketing: Creating Value for Customers,* 2nd ed. (Burr Ridge, IL: Irwin/McGraw-Hill, 1998), pp. 392–98.

5. This classification is based on Michael Levy and Barton A. Weitz, *Retailing Management,* 8th ed. (Burr Ridge, IL: Irwin/McGraw-Hill, 2012), p. 10.

6. Ibid., Chapter 3.

7. For an excellent discussion of electronic exchange, see David W. Stewart and Qin Zhao, "Internet Marketing, Business Models, and Public Policy," *Journal of Public Policy & Marketing,* Fall 2000, pp. 287–96.

Chapter 11

1. Kent B. Monroe, "Buyers' Subjective Perceptions of Price," *Journal of Marketing Research,* February 1973, pp. 70–80; also see Donald R. Lichtenstein and Scot Burton, "The Relationship between Perceived and Objective Price—Quality," *Journal of Marketing Research,* November 1989, pp. 429–43.

2. For research concerning the effects of price and several other marketing variables on perceived product quality, see Akshay R. Rao and Kent B. Monroe, "The Effect of Price, Brand Name, and Store Name on Buyers' Perceptions of Product Quality: An Integrative Review," *Journal of Marketing Research,* August 1989, pp. 351–57; and William B. Dodds, Kent B. Monroe, and Dhruv Grewal, "Effects of Price, Brand, and Store Evaluations on Buyers' Product Evaluations," *Journal of Marketing Research,* August 1991, pp. 307–19.

3. For further discussion of price elasticity, see Stephen J. Hoch, Byung-Do Kim, Alan L. Montgomery, and Peter Rosi, "Determinants of Store-Level Price Elasticity," *Journal of Marketing Research,* February 1995, pp. 17–29.

4. For further discussion of legal issues involved in pricing, see Louis W. Stern and Thomas L. Eovaldi, *Legal Aspects of Marketing Strategy* (Englewood Cliffs, NJ: Prentice Hall, 1984), chap. 5.

5. For more detailed discussions, see Frederick E. Webster, *Marketing for Managers* (New York: Harper & Row, 1974), pp. 178–79; also see Thomas T. Nagle and Reed K. Holden, *The Strategy and Tactics of Pricing* (Englewood Cliffs, NJ: Prentice Hall, 1995); and Kent B. Monroe, *Pricing: Making Profitable Decisions,* 3rd ed. (Burr Ridge, IL: McGraw-Hill/Irwin, 2003).

Chapter 12

1. Much of the material for this introduction came from Ronald Henkoff, "Service Is Everybody's Business," *Fortune,* June 27, 1994, pp. 48–60; and Tim R. Smith, "The Tenth District's Expanding Service Sector," *Economic Review,* Third Quarter 1994, pp. 55–66.

2. Peter D. Bennett, ed., *Dictionary of Marketing Terms,* 2nd ed. (Chicago: American Marketing Association, 1995), p. 261.

3. The material in this section draws from research performed by Leonard L. Berry, Valerie A. Zeithaml, and A. Parasuraman, "Quality Counts in Services, Too," *Business Horizons,* May–June 1985, pp. 44–52; A. Parasuraman, Valerie A. Zeithaml, and Leonard L. Berry, "A Conceptual Model of Service Quality and Its Implications for Future Research," *Journal of Marketing,* Fall 1985, pp. 41–50; Leonard L. Berry, A. Parasuraman, and Valerie A. Zeithaml, "The Service-Quality Puzzle," *Business Horizons,* September–October 1988, pp. 35–43; Stephen W. Brown and Teresa A. Swartz, "A Gap Analysis of Professional Service Quality," *Journal of Marketing,* April 1989, pp. 92–98; Leonard L. Berry, Valerie A. Zeithaml, and A. Parasuraman, "Five Imperatives for Improving Service Quality," *Sloan Management Review,* Summer 1990, pp. 29–38; A. Parasuraman, Leonard L. Berry, and Valerie A. Zeithaml, "Understanding Customer Expectations of Service," *Sloan Management Review,* Spring 1991, pp. 39–48; and Leonard L. Berry, *On Great Service: A Framework for Action* (New York: Free Press, 1995).

4. Rick Berry, "Define Service Quality So You Can Deliver It," *Best's Review,* March 1995, p. 68.

5. Material for this section is drawn from John T. Mentzer, Carol C. Bienstock, and Kenneth B. Kahn, "Benchmarking Satisfaction," *Marketing Management,* Summer 1995, pp. 41–46; and Alan Dutka, *AMA Handbook for Customer Satisfaction: A Complete Guide to Research, Planning and Implementation* (Lincolnwood,

IL: NTC Books, 1994). For detailed information on this topic, readers are advised to consult these sources.

6. Much of the material for this section was taken from Karl Albrecht and Ron Zemke, *Service America* (Burr Ridge, IL: Irwin/McGraw-Hill, 1985); and Ron Zemke and Dick Schaaf, *The Service Edge 101: Companies That Profit from Customer Care* (New York: New American Library, 1989).

7. Chip R. Bell and Kristen Anderson, "Selecting Super Service People," *HR Magazine,* February 1992, pp. 52–54.

8. James A. Schlesinger and James L. Heskett, "Breaking the Cycle of Failure in Services," *Sloan Management Review,* Spring 1991, pp. 17–28.

9. Leonard L. Berry and A. Parasuraman, "Services Marketing Starts from Within," *Marketing Management,* Winter 1992, pp. 25–34.

10. Ibid.

11. Leonard L. Berry and A. Parasuraman, "Prescriptions for a Service Quality Revolution in America," *Organizational Dynamics,* Spring 1992, pp. 5–15.

12. Bob O'Neal, "World-Class Service," *Executive Excellence,* September 1994, pp. 11–12.

13. This example is from David E. Bowen and Edward E. Lawler III, "The Empowerment of Service Workers: What, Why, How, and When," *Sloan Management Review,* Spring 1992, pp. 31–39.

14. Howard Schlossberg, "Study: U.S. Firms Lag in Using Customer Satisfaction Data," *Marketing News,* June 1992, p. 14.

15. Andrew E. Serwer, "The Competition Heats Up in Online Banking," *Fortune,* June 26, 1995, pp. 18–19.

16. John Labate, "Chronimed," *Fortune,* February 20, 1995, p. 118.

17. Elaine Underwood, "Airlines Continue Flight to E-Ticketing," *Brandweek,* May 8, 1995, p. 3.

18. Peter L. Ostrowski, Terrence V. O'Brien, and Geoffrey L. Gordon, "Determinants of Service Quality in the Commercial Airline Industry: Differences between Business and Leisure Travelers," *Journal of Travel & Tourism Marketing* 3, no. 1 (1994), pp. 19–47.

Chapter 13

1. Jason Vogel, "Chicken Diplomacy," *Financial World,* March 14, 1995, pp. 46–49.

2. For a full explanation on cultural differences, see Rose Knotts, "Cross-Cultural Management: Transformations and Adaptations," *Business Horizons,* January–February 1989, pp. 29–33.

3. Claudia Penteado, "Pepsi's Brazil Blitz," *Advertising Age,* January 16, 1995, p. 12.

4. Karen Benezra, "Fritos 'Round the World,'" *Brandweek,* March 27, 1995, pp. 32, 35.

5. Material for this section is from Craig Mellow, "Russia: Making Cash from Chaos," *Fortune,* April 17, 1995, pp. 145–51; and Peter Galuszka, "And You Think You've Got Tax Problems," *Business Week,* May 29, 1995, p. 50.

6. Mir Magbool Alam Khan, "Enormity Tempts Marketers to Make a Passage to India," *Advertising Age International,* May 15, 1995, p. 112.

7. This section was taken from James F. Bolt, "Global Competitors: Some Criteria for Success," *Business Horizons,* January–February 1988, pp. 34–41.

8. This section is based on George S. Yip, Pierre M. Loewe, and Michael Y. Yoshino, "How to Take Your Company to the Global Market," *Columbia Journal of World Business,* Winter 1988, pp. 37–48.

9. Ibid.

10. The introductory material on foreign research is based on Michael R. Czintoka, "Take a Shortcut to Low-Cost Global Research," *Marketing News,* March 13, 1995, p. 3.

11. Donald B. Pittenger, "Gathering Foreign Demographics Is No Easy Task," *Marketing News,* January 8, 1990, pp. 23, 25.

12. This discussion is based on John Burnett, *Promotion Management* (Boston: Houghton-Mifflin Co., 1993), chap. 19.

13. The material for this section on market entry and growth approaches is based on Philip R. Cateora, *International Marketing,* 8th ed. (Burr Ridge, IL: Irwin/McGraw-Hill, 1993), pp. 325–34; Charles W. L. Hill, *International Business: Competing in the Global Marketplace* (Burr Ridge, IL: Irwin/McGraw-Hill, 1994), pp. 402–8; and William M. Pride and O. C. Ferrell, *Marketing: Concepts and Strategy,* 9th ed. (Boston: Houghton-Mifflin Co., 1995), pp. 111–14.

14. Bruce A. Walters, Steve Peters, and Gregory G. Dess, "Strategic Alliances and Joint Ventures: Making Them Work," *Business Horizons,* July–August 1994, pp. 5–10.

15. Material in this section is based on Subhash C. Jain, "Standardization of International Marketing Strategy: Some Research Hypotheses," *Journal of Marketing,* January 1989, pp. 70–79.

Section II

1. Michael E. Porter, *Competitive Strategy* (New York: Free Press, 1980). Also see Michael E. Porter, *Competitive Advantage: Creating and Sustaining Superior Performance* (New York: Free Press, 1985); and Michael E. Porter, *The Competitive Advantage of Nations* (New York: Free Press, 1990).

Section III

1. For methods of estimating the cost of capital, see Charles P. Jones, *Introduction to Financial Management* (Burr Ridge, IL: Irwin/McGraw-Hill, 1992), chap. 14.

2. See Eugene F. Brigham, *Fundamentals of Financial Management* (Hinsdale, IL: Dryden Press, 1986).

3. It is useful to use average inventory rather than a single end-of-year estimate if monthly data are available.

4. For a discussion of ratio analysis for retailing, see Michael Levy and Barton A. Weitz, *Retailing Management* (Burr Ridge, IL: McGraw-Hill/Irwin, 2007), chap. 5.

Name Index

Subject Index

extended product, 84
extensive decision making, 50
Exxon, 100

F

fabricating parts/materials, 89
facilitating agents, 155
facilitating function, 155
fads, 97
Fairfield Inn, 190
family branding, 90
family life cycle, 46
fashions, 97
federal agencies, 137. *See also individual agencies*
Federal Communications Commission (FCC), 137
Federal Express, 191–192
Federal Trade Commission Act, 176
Federal Trade Commission (FTC), 137, 235
FedStats, 40
financial analysis, 229–238
    asset management ratios, 235, 237
    break-even analysis, 174, 230–232
    current ratio, 235, 236
    inventory turnover, 235, 237
    liquidity ratios, 234–235, 236
    in marketing plan framework, 246
    net present value analysis, 232–234
    profit margin on sales, 235, 237
    profitability ratios, 235–236, 237
    quick ratio, 235, 236
    ratio analysis, 234–237
    return on total assets, 235–236, 237
    sources for financial ratios, 235
    total asset utilization, 235, 237
Firestone Tire & Rubber, 199
fit test, 11
focus groups, 32, 35
Food and Drug Administration (FDA), 92, 137
Ford Motor Co., 99, 161, 183, 200, 244
Forrester Research Reports, 40
forward integration, 161
France, top websites in, 119
franchise extension, 90
franchising, 161, 162, 212
frequency marketing programs, 133
Frito-Lay, 94, 172, 202
Fuji Film, 129
functional relationships, 144–145

G

Gallup Poll, 40, 48
The Gap, 92, 93, 165
Gaskell, 62
gatekeepers, 62
Gateway Computer, 156
General Electric, 4, 14, 27–28, 90, 200, 204
General Electric portfolio model, 14, 27–28
General Foods, 103, 204
General Mills, 87, 124, 133, 212, 219
General Motors, 62, 183, 244
generic product, 84
geodemographic segmentation, 74, 77
geographic-organized sales force, 147
geographic segmentation, 74
Germany, top websites in, 119
Gillette, 12, 48, 90, 93, 95, 103

global companies, 204–206. *See also* global marketing
Global Edge, 40
global marketing, 199–214
    advertising agencies, 211
    advertising strategies, 210–211
    consumers' ability to buy, 206
    consumers' willingness to buy, 207–208
    cultural misunderstanding and, 201–202, 203
    demographics and, 206
    direct ownership, 213
    distribution strategies, 209–210
    economic conditions and, 203–204
    entry/growth strategies, 211–213
    exchange controls and, 202–203
    exporting, 212
    factors favoring global strategy, 204
    franchising, 212
    global branding, 90, 205
    import restrictions and, 202
    joint ventures, 212
    licensing, 212
    market entry problems, 201–204
    marketing research, 206–208
    multinational company organization, 204–206
    national advantage model, 200–201
    organizing for, 201–206
    ownership restrictions and, 202–203
    political uncertainty and, 202
    pricing strategies, 210
    product development, 208
    product strategies, 209
    program development, 206–211
    sales promotions, 211
    strategic alliances, 213
    U.S. companies, global revenues of, 200
gobo (cookie) advertising, 129
going-rate pricing, 176
goods-service continuum, 183
Goodyear, 129
Google, 48, 90, 108, 122
government agencies, 59, 137. *See also individual agencies*
government information sources, 32, 40
GPO Access, 40
Grain Division, 137
Grainger, 59
green zone, 28
grocery receipt advertising, 129
group information sources, 52
growth function methods, 149
growth stage, product life cycle, 96
Grundig, 203
guarantees, 113

H

H. J. Heinz, 219
Hallmark, 104, 122
Harbor View Savings and Loan Assn., 7
Harley-Davidson, 50
Harris Poll, 40
Hartmann Luggage, 12
health care, 194–195
Heileman Brewing Co., 80
Hertz, 172
Hewlett-Packard, 90, 108, 156, 185, 200
hierarchy of needs, 51–52

high/low pricing, 173
Hills Brothers, 103
Holiday Inn, 161, 193
Home Depot, 173
Home Shopping Network, 166
Honda, 13, 90, 122, 178
Honeywell, 7, 204
horizontal marketing, 86
Hormel Meats, 7
H&R Block, 193
Hyundai, 79, 178

I

IBM, 90, 99, 100, 145, 204
idea generation, 106–108, 110
idea screening, 107, 108–109
Ikea, 208
import restrictions, 202
in-flight ads, 129
indirect channels, 156
industry analysis, 217–218, 220, 242, 243
industry attractiveness, 27–28
Industry Norms and Key Business Ratios, 235
inflatables, 129
influencers, 62
Information Resources, 33
information sources, 33, 40, 52, 235
initiators, 61
innovators, 76, 97
inseparability, 184, 185–186
installations, 89
insurance industry, 186, 195
intangibility, 184–185
integrated marketing communications, 118–135
    advertising. *See* advertising
    communication process basics, 126
    consistent voice level, 122
    described, 120–122
    direct marketing. *See* direct marketing
    goals of, 118–119
    good listener level, 122
    levels of, 122
    personal selling. *See* personal selling
    promotion mix, 119–120
    public relations, 120, 121, 123, 133–134
    push *vs.* pull strategies, 130–131
    sales promotion. *See* sales promotion
    unified image level, 122
    world-class citizen level, 122
Intel, 90, 200
intensive distribution, 158
intention to buy, 132
intermediaries, 59. *See also* channels of distribution
internal information sources, 52
internal marketing, 190–192
internal risk, 109
International Dessert Partners, 212
the Internet
    advertising, 127
    commercial Web site development, 167
    direct marketing, 135
    e-services, 185, 193
    multichannel marketing, 166–168
    online sales, 166–168
    top Web sites in France/Germany/Japan, 119
Internet surveys, 35

Quirk's Marketing Research Review, 40
QVC, 166

R

radio advertising, 127
radio-frequency identification (RFID), 37
random lead generation, 142
rate-of-return pricing, 174
ratio analysis, 234–237
raw materials, 85, 89
RCA Corp., 212
reach, 128–130
Reactrix brand play, 129
rebates/refunds, 133
recall tests, 132
receiver, 126
recognition tests, 132
red zone, 28
reference groups, 46, 47
relationship marketing, 160, 189
relay approach, 109
repositioning, 104
research approach, 125
retail cooperative organizations, 161
retailers, 155, 164–168
    catalogs, 165
    convenience stores, 165
    direct mail, 165
    direct sales, 166
    EDLP *vs.* high/low pricing, 173
    mass merchandisers, 164–165
    nonstore retailers, 165–168
    online retailers, 166–168
    specialty stores, 165
    store retailers, 164–165
    television home shopping, 166
    vending machines, 166
    wholesaler benefits, 164
return on total assets, 235–236, 237
risk, 53–54, 109
R.J. Reynolds Tobacco Co., 80
RJR Nabisco, 100
Roadway, 13
Robert Morris Associates, 235, 249
Robinson-Patman Act, 176
Rolex, 12, 175
Roper Center for Public Opinion Research, 40
Roper Reports, 40
routine decision making, 51
Rubbermaid, 13
rugby approach, 109

S

safety needs, 51
salary, 151
sales calls, 143–144
sales expense budget, 150
sales force composite method, 148
sales forecasts, 148–149, 246–248
sales leads, 142
sales management, 146–152
    challenges of, 149
    compensation, 150–152
    customer structure, 147
    effort-oriented measures, 151

evaluation, 151
expense analysis, 150
forecasting sales, 148–149
geographic structure, 147
incentives, 152
major account management, 147–148
motivation, 150–152
product structure, 147
results-oriented measures, 151
sales force control, 148–152
sales force organization, 147–148
sales territories/quotas, 149–150
sales promotion, 120, 130–133
    consumer promotions, 130, 131–132, 133, 134
    ethical/legal issues, 123
    examples of, 130, 133
    global strategy, 210–211
    limitations of, 132–133
    middlemen promotions, 130
    organizational buyer promotions, 61
    purchase decision and, 47, 121
    push *vs.* pull strategies, 130–131
    reseller promotions, 134
    sales force promotions, 130, 134
    trade promotions, 131
sales quotas, 149–150
sales relationship-building process, 140–145
sales trends, 98
sampling, 133
Samsung, 90
Sara Lee, 12
Saturn, 79, 93, 122
Scarborough Research, 33
screening of prospects, 142–143
sealed-bid pricing, 176
Sealtest Dairy, 12
Sears, 112, 161
secondary data, 32
Securities and Exchange Commission (SEC), 137, 235
selected-lead generation, 142
selective distribution, 158
self-actualization needs, 52
sender, 126
service products, 183. *See also* services marketing
services, 182–183. *See also* services marketing
    characteristics of, 184–188
    e-services, 185, 193
    goods *vs.,* 184
services marketing, 4, 182–197
    banking, 194
    challenges for, 186, 194–197
    client relationship and, 184, 186, 191
    customer effort and, 184, 187–188
    customer expectations by industry, 187
    customer satisfaction measurement (CSM), 190
    demand fluctuations and, 186
    determinants of quality, 188
    e-services, 185, 193
    goods-service continuum, 183
    health care, 194–195
    inseparability and, 184, 185–186
    insurance, 195
    intangibility and, 184–185
    internal marketing, importance of, 190–192
    on the Internet, 193

lack of obsolescence and, 193–194
limited competition and, 192–193
limited marketing view and, 192
marketing mix components, 196
noncreative management and, 193
obstacles, overcoming, 192–194
perishability and, 184, 186
professionals, 186
relationship marketing in, 189
service quality, 188–192
services, defined, 182–183
traditional *vs.* relationship marketing, 189
travel industry, 195–196
uniformity and, 184, 188
7-Eleven, 165
Shell Oil, 199
Sherman Antitrust Act, 176
shopping goods, 86, 88
Siemens, 204
Simmons Market Research Bureau (SMRB), 33, 122
Simmons Media/Market Service, 244
simulation models, 149
situation analysis, 14–17, 70, 242
situational influences, 49
skimming pricing policy, 175
skunkworks, 109
slotting allowances, 179
Smith New Court PLC, 193
social environment, 6, 16
social features of situation, 49
social segmentation, 74
sole sourcing, 63
Sony, 104, 203
Southwest Airlines, 12, 13, 196
specialty goods, 86, 88
specialty stores, 165
sponsors, 111
sponsorships, 134
SRI Consulting Business Intelligence, 75
Standard Rate and Data, 244, 248
Starbucks, 13, 50, 93, 103, 145, 200
Starch Advertising Readership Service, 244
Starch Reports, 122
stars, 26
Stat-USA, 40
Statistical Abstracts of the United States, 32, 247
store retailers, 164–165
straight rebuy, 60, 61
strategic alliances (partnerships), 145, 213
strategic business units (SBUs)
    BCG portfolio model, 26–27
    business strength of, 27–28
    cash cows, 26
    characteristics of, 13–14
    dogs, 26
    GE portfolio model, 27–28
    industry attractiveness of, 27–28
    objectives of, 27
    question marks, 26
    stars, 26
strategic plan/planning, 4–19
    choosing organizational strategy, 13
    competitive advantage strategies, 12
    complete strategic plan, 14, 15
    cost leadership strategy, 12
    cross-functional perspective, 19–20
    differentiation, 12